WELLINGTON'S LIGHT DIVISION IN THE PENINSULAR WAR

WELLINGTON'S LIGHT DIVISION IN THE PENINSULAR WAR

THE FORMATION, CAMPAIGNS AND BATTLES OF WELLINGTON'S FAMOUS FIGHTING FORCE, 1810

Robert Burnham

FRONTLINE
BOOKS

First published in Great Britain in 2020 by

FRONTLINE BOOKS
an imprint of Pen & Sword Books Ltd,
47 Church Street, Barnsley, S.Yorkshire, S70 2AS

ISBN: 978 1 52675 890 3

For more information on our books, please visit
www.frontline-books.com, email info@frontline-books.com
or write to us at the above address.

Printed and bound by TJ Books Limited, Padstow, Cornwall
Typeset by Concept, Huddersfield, West Yorkshire
Pen & Sword Books Ltd incorporates the imprints of Pen & Sword
Archaeology, Atlas, Aviation, Battleground, Discovery,
Family History, History, Maritime, Military, Naval, Politics,
Social History, Transport, True Crime, Claymore Press,
Frontline Books, Praetorian Press,
Seaforth Publishing and White Owl

For a complete list of Pen and Sword titles please contact
PEN & SWORD LTD
47 Church Street, Barnsley, South Yorkshire, S70 2AS, England
E-mail: enquiries@pen-and-sword.co.uk

Or

PEN AND SWORD BOOKS
1950 Lawrence Rd, Havertown, PA 19083, USA
E-mail: Uspen-and-sword@casematepublishers.com

Contents

List of Illustrations

Acknowledgements

In May 2018, I had lunch with General Vere Hayes, the Chairman of the Board of Trustees of the Royal Green Jackets Museum. We were discussing my latest book on the British Foot Guards in the Waterloo Campaign,[1] when he suggested I should do one on the Light Division in the Peninsular War. I was noncommittal at the time, but the idea had been planted in my head. This book is the result of his suggestion.

Like all my books, this one is a collaboration with a group of friends who provide encouragement, ideas, information, sources, feedback, proof-reading, etc. I usually put their names in alphabetical order, but this time I will use reverse order. They are: Mark S. Thompson, whose knowledge of the roads and terrain of the area of operations, the Royal Engineers and Fort Concepción is second to none. Then there is my co-author of four other books, Ron McGuigan. His ability to find the most obscure pieces of information, especially in the *London Gazette*, is unrivalled. In twenty-five years of working together, I have never been able to stumped him with a question! AND his proof-reading skills match his research ability.[2] Nicholas Haynes is a new member of the team. He is an expert on the Royal Green Jackets, as well as being a former Green Jacket officer. He provided numerous unpublished sources that I had never heard of before and many photographs of the area of operations. Gareth Glover, whose knowledge of the various archives in Great Britain is phenomenal! He loaned me many diaries and memoirs, that had not seen the light of day in over 175 years! He also spent many hours in the archives finding material for me. Moisés Gaudencio, who provided the archival material on the

---

1. *Wellington's Foot Guards at Waterloo*, which I co-authored with Ron McGuigan. It was published in November 2018.
2. Any typos are my fault and not Ron's.

Portuguese caçadores, most of which has never been published before. Finally there is Steve Brown, who hiked with me over much of the terrain covered in this book. Possibly the most amazing part of my friendship with these six historians is that although I have met Gareth, Mark and Steve, I have never met nor talked with Nick or Moisés. As for Ron, despite having co-authored four books with him, I have only talked with him on the telephone once. I am also indebted to the Napoleon Series History Forum. Numerous individuals answered my questions on a variety of topics, including Tony Broughton, Hans Karl Weiss, Oliver Schmidt, Mick Crumplin, Rod MacArthur, Daniel Lamblat, Rob Griffith, Kevin Kiley and Jack Gill. There are also two individuals who collaborated with me on my first book fifteen years ago: Rory Muir and Howie Muir. Both gave me access to their own research and provided ideas on how to proceed when I reached an impasse.

About the maps. I have corresponded with Mark Thompson for many years, but had never met him until May 2018 when we spent a day hiking Hadrian's Wall. I knew he was an expert on all things related to the Royal Engineers during the Napoleonic Wars, but I had not realized that he was a very talented cartographer. Unless otherwise noted, all maps in this book were drawn by him and used with his permission. The two maps on Busaco are from Willoughby Verner's *History and Campaigns of the Rifle Brigade*. They are from the 1994 Buckland and Brown edition of the book and are used with the permission of Gary Buckland of Naval and Military Press and Richard Brown of Ken Trotman Books.[3]

Finally I have to thank my wife, Denah, who patiently listened to the numerous anecdotes I unearthed. I know she is very happy to get the dining room table back!

---

3. They jointly published the book in 1994 under the Buckland and Brown imprint.

Introduction

Hurrah for the first in the field and the last out of it . . .'[1]
Lieutenant John Kincaid, 95th Rifles

On 22 February 1810, the Adjutant General's Office of the Anglo-Allied Army in Portugal and Spain issued a general order that re-organized the army. Paragraph Three of this order stated:

> The 1st and 2nd battalions of Portuguese Chasseurs[2] are attached to the brigade of General R. Craufurd, which is to be called the light division. These troops will be ordered to join the division to which they belong.[3]

And thus with only thirty-eight words the most famous unit to serve under the Duke of Wellington came into existence. Over the next 50 months the Light Division would fight in nine battles,[4] three sieges,[5] numerous smaller combats and many skirmishes. By the time Napoleon had abdicated in April 1814, the Light Division had become, without a

---

1. Kincaid, John, *Random Shots from a Rifleman*. Philadelphia: E.L. Carey and A. Hart, 1835, p.16. He was actually referring to the 95th Rifles, which was an integral part of the Light Division.
2. These battalions were light battalions and were called caçadores.
3. General Orders dated 22 February 1810.
4. Busaco (27 September 1810), Fuentes d'Onoro (3–5 May 1811), Salamanca (22 July 1812), Vitoria (21 May 1813), the Pyrenees (25–27 July 1813), Nivelle (10 November 1813), the Nive (9–13 December 1813), Orthes (27 February 1814) and Toulouse (10 April 1814).
5. Ciudad Rodrigo (January 1812), Badajoz (April 1812) and San Sebastian (August 1813).

doubt, the most elite unit in Wellington's army, and possibly the most elite unit of any army of the time. Some would say that Napoleon's Old Guard held this honour, but unlike the Light Division, it was rarely committed into battle, being held in reserve most of the time. The Light Division was in the thick of almost every battle Wellington fought from 1810 to 1814.[6]

The Light Division was formed around a core of three British light infantry battalions: the 1st Battalions of the 43rd Foot, the 52nd Foot and the rifle-armed 95th Foot which was also known as the 95th Rifles. Over the next four years the division would be augmented with the 2nd Battalion 52nd Foot and the 2nd and 3rd Battalions 95th Rifles. In 1811 the 2nd Battalion 52nd Foot joined the division but was sent home after 13 months due to casualties. Five companies each from the 2nd and 3rd Battalions 95th Rifles served with them from 1811 to 1814, but only its 1st Battalion was there with most of its companies.

Also part of the core units of the division were the two battalions of Portuguese caçadores. Initially they were the 1st and 2nd Battalions, however within a few months the 2nd Battalion was replaced by the 3rd Battalion, which would serve with the division during the rest of the war. Other than its core battalions, its organization was fluid. In 1812, the 20th Portuguese Line Regiment joined it and in 1813 it was replaced by the 17th Portuguese Line Regiment. Additionally in 1810 and 1811 the Brunswick Oëls were also assigned to it for several months. Furthermore it was one of the first combined-arms units in the British Army. It often had the 1st King's German Legion Hussars,[7] the 14th Light Dragoons, the 16th Light Dragoons and Captain Hew Ross's A Troop of the Royal Horse Artillery attached to it.

The senior leadership also changed over the years. Its first commander was Brigadier General Robert Craufurd, who commanded the Light Brigade before it became the Light Division. A strict disciplinarian who enforced the highest standards, his professionalism and attention to duty was instrumental in instilling in the division a self-confidence that they

---

6. During the Peninsular War, Wellington fought fifteen major battles and sieges. Three of these, Roliça (17 August 1808), Vimeiro (21 August 1808) and Talavera (27–28 July 1809) were fought before the Light Division was formed. The Light Division fought in every one of Wellington's battles after its formation.

7. The official name of the 1st King's German Legion Hussars was the 1st King's German Legion Light Dragoons. On 25 December 1813 they were renamed the 1st King's German Legion Hussars.

could do anything. This belief in themselves and others in the division led them to perform prodigious feats on the battlefield. The death of General Craufurd and the wounding of its senior brigade commander at the siege of Ciudad Rodrigo could have led to the decline in the effectiveness of the division.[8] Yet when one leader fell, another stood up to take his place. Three months after Ciudad Rodrigo, the division fought at the siege of Badajoz. Its temporary divisional commander was Lieutenant Colonel Andrew Barnard of the 95th Rifles. The 1st Brigade was led by Lieutenant Colonel George Elder of the 3rd Caçadores while the 2nd Brigade was commanded by Brevet Lieutenant Colonel Edward Gibbs of the 52nd Foot. Both brigade commanders were seriously wounded in the assault.

Its casualties among its five battalion commanders at Badajoz were also high: Lieutenant Colonel Charles McLeod 43rd Foot and Major Peter O'Hare 1st Battalion 95th Rifles were killed, while Major John Algeo 1st Caçadores was severely wounded. After Lieutenant Colonel McLeod was killed in the assault, the next senior officer in the 43rd Foot, Major Joseph Wells, took command and he too was seriously wounded. By the end of the siege the 1st Brigade was commanded by a brevet major and the 2nd Brigade was commanded by a major, while all five battalions were led by captains. The situation improved somewhat over the next several months, but the division was still short of senior officers. By the end of the year the division had been commanded by a lieutenant colonel, a light cavalry officer[9] and a Hanoverian.[10]

In addition to its superb leadership, one of the intangibles that made the Light Division what it was, was the sense of brotherhood among the regiments, both literally and figuratively. Many British regiments were family regiments, where fathers, brothers, uncles and cousins often served together. This was especially true in the Light Division. In the 43rd Foot there were Edward and William Freer, and Molesworth and William Madden. The 52nd Foot had Charles and Henry Dawson, John and Joseph Dobbs, Charles and William Rowan, John and Kenneth Snodgrass, and George and Thomas Whichcote, among others.

---

8. General Craufurd died of his wound received at Ciudad Rodrigo. The 2nd Brigade commander, General Vandeleur, was seriously wounded during the siege. The 1st Brigade commander was Lieutenant Colonel Andrew Barnard.
9. Major General John Vandeleur.
10. Major General Charles Baron Alten.

The 95th Rifles was no different. There were Charles, Robert and Thomas Sydney Beckwith; Robert and Thomas Cochrane; George and Joseph Simmons; Harry and Thomas Smith who not only served in the same battalion but in the same company; and the Travers Family which had four brothers and two cousins serving in the regiment.

But in many ways, the Light Division was also a family division, for many had brothers and family members serving in the division's other regiments. The most famous was the Napier family: George and his cousin Thomas were in the 52nd Foot. George's brother William[11] was in the 43rd Foot, and their brother Charles, although in the 50th Foot, served as a volunteer staff officer on General Craufurd's staff in 1810. A fifth family member, cousin Captain Charles Napier of the Royal Navy, was with the division two months later at Busaco. There were the Booth brothers, Charles in the 52nd Foot and Henry in the 43rd Foot, who served together in 1810–11. The two Madden brothers in the 43rd Foot, had brothers Edward Marcel in the 95th Rifles and Wyndham Carlyon in the 52nd Foot, as well as their stepbrother, Major Henry Ridewood, in the 52nd Foot.[12] The Freer family had three brothers in the division: Edward and William in the 43rd Foot and Richard in the 95th Rifles.

Having family members serving in the same division increased the chance one or more would become casualties, sometimes in the same battle. Charles Dawson was severely wounded at Badajoz, while his brother Henry was killed in 1812 during the retreat to Portugal. Harry and Thomas Smith of the 95th were both seriously wounded on the Côa in July 1810. All three Freer brothers were wounded at Badajoz in 1812. Seventeen months later 19-year-old Edward was killed at Nivelle, while William was wounded. Both Harvest brothers were killed: Horatio of the 43rd at Badajoz and August of the 52nd at San Sebastian in 1813. The Napier family also paid for their service. Captain Charles Napier, Royal Navy, was shot in the knee at Busaco. His cousin Charles was also wounded at Busaco, where he was shot in the face. George lost his right arm at Ciudad Rodrigo in 1812 and his cousin Thomas lost his left arm at Nive in 1813. William, the historian, was severely wounded twice and slightly wounded once between July 1810 and December 1813.

---

11.   William Napier is best known for writing *History of the War in the Peninsula, and in the South of France, from the Year 1807 to the Year 1814.*
12.   Bromley, Janet and David, *Wellington's Men Remembered.* 2 vols. Barnsley: Praetorian Press, 2015. Vol. 2, p.218.

It was this sharing of mutual hardship, danger, and sacrifice that enhanced the sense of family within the division. Regardless of the regiment, they knew and trusted each other and always had each other's back. Perhaps Lieutenant John Kincaid of the 95th Rifles summed it up best:

> . . . I beg to be understood as identifying our old and gallant associates, the forty-third and fifty-second, as a part of ourselves, for they bore their share in every thing, and I love them as I hope to do my better half, (when I come to be divided,) wherever we were, they were; and although the nature of our arm generally gave us more employment in the way of skirmishing, yet, whenever it came to a pinch, independent of a suitable mixture of them among us, we had only to look behind to see a line, in which we might place a degree of confidence, almost equal to our hopes in heaven; nor were we ever disappointed. There never was a corps of riflemen in the hands of such supporters![13]

Regardless of their regiment or nationality, they were one family.

Before I begin their story, there are several comments I must make about the spelling of place names. This book relies heavily on the diaries, memoirs and letters of the men who served in the Light Division during 1810. Unfortunately at this time spelling was not as standardized as it is today. Many of the place names used were spelled phonetically and were different than the official spelling of the names. Additionally, even if the spelling was correct, often the name of the place has been changed in the past 200 years. This can cause confusion to the reader especially if he wishes to locate the sites on a map. Rather than change the writers' spelling I have kept it and provided a footnote with the modern name of the location. Appendix II is a gazetteer of the names of the locations mentioned in the narrative.

To simplify matters, I have shorten the modern names for consistency. For example Gallegos de Argañán is referred to as Gallegos, while Arruda dos Vinhos is called Arruda. I also have shorten Sobral de Monte Agraço to Sobral, since that is what most contemporary accounts referred to it as.

---

13. Kincaid, John, *Adventures in the Rifle Brigade in the Peninsula, France, and the Netherlands from 1809–1815*. Staplehurst: Spellmount, 1998, pp.16–17.

During the first seven months of 1810, the Light Division served as outposts on the Agueda and Azaba Rivers along the Portuguese–Spanish border. Much of the year these rivers were impassable except at bridges and fords. They were key locations and often fought over by the outposts. Between the creative spelling of the writers and the changing of their names, they can be difficult to find on modern maps. For those readers who are interested in finding a location of a bridge or a ford on either Google Maps or on a 1:50,000 topographical map, I have provided geographic coordinates for them in Appendix III.

Arthur Wellesley is best known as the Duke of Wellington. However, until 26 August 1809, he went by Arthur Wellesley. On that date he was elevated to the peerage as Viscount Wellington. He would not be known as the Duke of Wellington until 3 May 1814. To simplify matters, I will always refer to him as Wellington, regardless of the year.

In most infantry regiments, the subalterns were either ensigns or lieutenants. However, the 95th Rifles had 2nd lieutenants and 1st lieutenants instead of ensigns and lieutenants. It was, and still is, common to refer to a lieutenant as a lieutenant, regardless whether he was a 2nd or 1st lieutenant. To simplify things, I will follow this convention.

Abbreviations and Key to Map Symbols

AAG	Assistant Adjutant General
ACG	Assistant Commissary General
ADC	Aide-de-Camp
AG	Adjutant General
AGC	Army Gold Cross
AGM	Army Gold Medal
AQMG	Assistant Quartermaster General
Bde	Brigade
Bn	Battalion
Bns	Battalions
CB	Companion of the Most Honourable Order of the Bath from 1815
cm	centimetre(s)
CPL	Corporal
CPT	Captain
DAAG	Deputy Assistant Adjutant General
DACG	Deputy Assistant Commissary General
DAG	Deputy Adjutant General
DAQMG	Deputy Assistant Quartermaster General
DoW	Died of Wounds
DQMG	Deputy Quartermaster General
GCB	Knight Grand Cross of the Most Honourable Order of the Bath from 1815

G.O.	General Order
Hon.	Honourable
HQ	Headquarters
KCB	Knight Commander of the Most Honourable Order of the Bath
KCH	Knight Commander of the Royal Hanoverian Guelphic Order
KGA	The King's German Artillery
KGL	The King's German Legion
KIA	Killed in action
km	kilometre(s)
LTC	Lieutenant Colonel(s)
LT	Lieutenant(s)
m	metre(s)
MAJ	Major(s)
MGSM	Military General Service Medal
MIA	Missing in Action
OR	Other Ranks
QMG	Quartermaster General
RA	Royal Artillery
RE	Royal Engineers
RGT	Regiment
RHA	Royal Horse Artillery
RN	Royal Navy
SGT	Sergeant
WIA	Wounded in Action

Key to Map Symbols

HQ ⊠ Light	Light Division HQ
1 ⊠ 43	1st Battalion 43rd Foot
1 ⊠ 52	1st Battalion 52nd Foot
LW ⊠ 52	Left Wing 52nd Foot
RW ⊠ 52	Right Wing 52nd Foot
7 ⊠ 52	No 7 Company 52nd Foot
1 ⊠ 95	1st Battalion 95th Rifles
1 ⊠ 95	No 1 Company 95th Rifles
2 ⊠ 95	No 2 Company 95th Rifles
3 ⊠ 95	No 3 Company 95th Rifles
1 ⊠ Caça	1st Caçadores Battalion
3 ⊠ Caça	3rd Caçadores Battalion
14 ⊿ LD	14th Light Dragoons
16 ⊿ LD	16th Light Dragoons
1 ⊿ KGL	1st KGL Hussars
3 ⊿ Hussars	3rd French Hussars
15 ⊿ Chasseurs	15th French Chasseurs
Simon ⊠ 3	Simon's Brigade French 3rd Division
Ferey ⊠ 3	Ferey's Brigade French 3rd Division

xix

List of Maps

Chapter 1

The Origins of the Light Division

When the British went to war in 1793 against Revolutionary France, its army was still organized and trained to fight the way it had done for the previous 50 years. Although excellent in fighting in line, it was totally unprepared for war against armies that deployed swarms of light infantry fighting in skirmish order, even though they had fought against an enemy who did just that, during the American Revolution from 1775 and 1783. The rebel forces consistently use small units of marksmen who would take every advantage of cover and concealment to fire at British formations. Although not strong enough to stop the advance of the British units, they were quite effective in disrupting a regiment by targeting officers and sergeants. The British army in North America did learn to adapt to this form of warfare, yet after the war ended in 1783 the lessons they learned there were neither remembered nor incorporated into their training.

Major General John Money, who fought in the American War of Independence, wrote 20 years after the war what it was like to encounter the American light troops. 'Seldom were the American's Riflemen seen, the report of his gun you heard, but his ball was felt. My blood ran cold in my veins for years after that unhappy war, when it occurred to my mind the cruel situation my brave countrymen, through ignorance, have been placed in . . .'[1]

During the 1790s the British Army did raise several local light infantry battalions in the West Indies and among German émigrés who were sent there after the 1793 Netherlands Campaign. By 1799 these units were severely reduced and most were incorporated into the new Royal African Corps. The one exception was Hompesch's Chasseurs

---

1. Money, John, *To the Right Honorable William Windham on a Partial Reorganization of the British Army*. London: T. Egerton, 1799, pp.26–27

who formed the 5th Battalion 60th Foot. This battalion would be dressed in green and armed with rifles.[2]

After the two failed expeditions to the Netherlands in the 1790s, reformers in the British Army were afraid that if the French invaded the British Isles, there would be a repeat of the campaigns of the previous years. On 17 January 1800, Lieutenant General Harry Calvert, the Adjutant General of the British Army, sent a letter to the commanders of thirteen infantry regiments ordering each of them to send to Horsham Barracks in West Sussex three officers, two sergeants, two corporals and thirty men. They were to be trained as riflemen and then returned to their regiments. The school was run by Colonel Coote Manningham, but most of the training was done by Lieutenant Colonel William Stewart of the 67th Foot. Among the officers who attended the camp were Captain Thomas Beckwith, 1st Lieutenant Peter O'Hare, and 2nd Lieutenants Loftus Gray, Samuel Mitchell and George Elder, all of whom would be with the Light Division in 1810, as brigade, battalion and company commanders.

After some initial growing pains, they were organized as the Experimental Corps of Riflemen on 1 April 1800. In August 1800 three of its companies went with the expedition to Spain to destroy the shipyard at Ferrol. The Experimental Rifle Corps was redesignated the Rifle Corps on 11 October 1800. The following year two companies participated in the Battle of Copenhagen on 2 April and three other companies were part of the force sent to Egypt.[3]

The political situation in France, which had seen so much turmoil in the 1790s, began to stabilize when Napoleon Bonaparte staged a coup-d'état on 9 November 1799. He was named the First Consul and would rule as such for four years. In a lightning campaign in Italy in 1800, he defeated Austria and by 1801 the only significant power opposing the French was Great Britain. The Treaty of Amiens, signed on 25 March 1802, effectively ended nine years of war between France and much of the rest of Europe. Peace lasted until Great Britain declared war on

---

2. Gates, David, *The British Light Infantry Arm c. 1790 – 1815*. London: B.T. Batsford, 1987, pp.70–1. Verner, Willoughby, *History & Campaigns of the Rifle Brigade: 1800 – 1813*, 2 vols. London: Buckland and Brown, 1995. Vol. 1, p.13

3. Summerfield, Stephen, *Coote Manningham's Shorncliffe Lectures of 1803 and the Origins of the 95th Rifles*. Godmanchester: Ken Trotman, 2001, pp.69–78

France in May 1803. The two countries would be at war, except for a short ten months,[4] until July 1815.

The French Army recognized the need for light infantry and in 1803 had thirty-three numbered light infantry[5] regiments of two battalions each. They also had named infantry battalions, such as the Tirailleurs Corses and the Tirailleurs du Po. By 1812, there were thirty-four numbered light infantry regiments from three to five battalions each, as well as fifteen regiments in the Imperial Guard.[6]

Reformers in the British Army continued to push for the formation of light infantry, among them Major General Sir John Moore, who was the regimental colonel of the 52nd Foot. He volunteered his regiment to be converted to a light infantry regiment and on 18 January 1803, it was redesignated as such. The same day, the Rifle Corps was renamed the 95th Foot. Both regiments were stationed in the Southern District of England, which General Moore commanded. In response to the outbreak of war, a brigade was formed with him as its commander. It consisted of the 4th, 52nd, 59th and 70th Foot, and the 95th Rifles. Among the officers from the 52nd Foot were Captains Henry Ridewood and Charles Rowan, and Lieutenants William Mein, Robert Campbell, George and William Napier, all of whom would play key roles in the early days of the Light Division.[7] On 9 July 1803 the brigade encamped at Shorncliffe and spent the next four months training in light infantry tactics. The 43rd Foot was redesignated as light infantry on 13 July 1803, but did not go to Shorncliffe until January 1804. Despite the efforts of the reformists, the 4th, 59th, and 70th Regiments were not designated as light infantry. After the destruction of the French and Spanish fleet at Trafalgar on 21 October 1805, the threat of a French invasion disappeared and the brigade was disbanded.

In October 1806 Brigadier General Robert Craufurd took command of a small brigade being sent to reinforce the British expedition to Buenos Aires. Within the brigade were five companies of the 1st Battalion

---

4. Napoleon abdicated in April 1814 and peace reigned until March 1815 when he returned to power.

5. They were numbered 1 – 37, however there were no 11th, 19th, 20th and 30th Light Infantry Regiments.

6. Broughton, Tony, 'French Light Infantry Regiments and the Colonels who Led Them: 1791 to 1815'. *The Napoleon Series Online*, 2019.

7. Moorsom, M.S., *History of the 52nd Regiment: 1755 – 1816*. Tyne & Wear: Worley, 1996, p.64.

95th Rifles. This was the first time that he commanded elements of the 95th Rifles. In July 1807, a brigade consisting of the 1st Battalion 43rd Foot, the 2nd Battalion 52nd Foot, 1st Battalion 92nd Foot, five companies from the 1st Battalion 95th Foot and five companies of the 2nd Battalion 95th Foot was stood up. Although similar to the brigade created under General Moore in 1803, it had a new commander. Moore had been promoted to lieutenant general in 1805 and the brigade was now commanded by Brigadier General Richard Stewart, who conducted much of the training at Shorncliffe. The brigade was to deploy as part of the expedition to Copenhagen and was called the Light Brigade.[8] This is the first official reference to a light brigade in the British Army.[9] It was originally commanded by Major General Sir Arthur Wellesley, the future Duke of Wellington, and Stewart was his second in command. When the Reserve Division was created, Wellington was given command of it and General Stewart took command of the Light Brigade.[10] When the force returned to England in November, the brigade was disbanded and the battalions returned to their barracks. The 43rd Foot went to Yarmouth, the 52nd Foot to Deal and the 95th Rifles to Hythe.

By the end of 1807, the British had no presence on the continent of Europe. Napoleon, now an emperor, over the past two years had defeated the Austrians, Prussians and Russians and for all practical purposes he was Europe's master. Unable to defeat Great Britain militarily, he decided to destroy its economy by denying it trade with the rest of Europe. He instituted the Continental System which placed an embargo on all British goods coming into Europe and prohibited all members of the French Empire and any of its allies from trading with Great Britain. It quickly became apparent that Portugal, a country with close ties to Great Britain, would not agree to the Continental System. On 27 October 1807, France and Spain signed the Treaty of Fontainebleau, which called for the ousting of the Portuguese Royal Family and the dismemberment of the Kingdom of Portugal. Part of the agreement was the permission given

---

8. 'Letter from Lord Castlereagh to Lieutenant General William Lord Cathcart dated 27 August 1807' quoted in Muir, Rory, *Wellington*, 2 vols. New Haven: Yale University, 2013. Vol. 1, p.628.

9. Noted historian of the British Army Ron McGuigan has done an extensive search of official correspondence and general orders and this was the first time the term was used.

10. Glover, Gareth, *The Two Battles of Copenhagen 1801 and 1807: Britain & Denmark in the Napoleonic Wars*. Barnsley: Pen & Sword, 2018, p.229

by Spain for a French army under General Jean Junot to cross through Spain to invade Portugal. Thus began the Peninsular War, which would last for seven years.

General Junot's Corps of Observation of the Gironde marched into Spain on 17 October and its advance guard, after marching over 1,000km, entered Lisbon on 30 November. They were too late to capture the Portuguese Royal Family, who had managed to sail for Brazil three days before with the help of the British Royal Navy. Napoleon was not content to just bringing Portugal under his rule. Spain too was ignoring the embargo on British goods. Beginning in November more troops began to pour into Spain and took control of key Spanish fortresses.[11] This was very unpopular with the Spanish people and they rose up in revolt against the Spanish monarchy. King Carlos IV did not want to give up his throne, but reluctantly abdicated on 19 March 1808 in favour of his son, Ferdinand VII. On 20 April 1808, Carlos IV, his wife, and King Ferdinand VII entered France at the invitation of Napoleon to work out a solution. After a few days of negotiations, Napoleon forced Ferdinand VII to abdicate and the Royal Family was held as prisoners in France. Napoleon decided to install his brother Joseph as the new king of Spain and to formally bring Spain into the French Empire.

After hearing the news, the Spanish people rose in revolt on 2 May and soon the whole Peninsula was in flames. The French were forced to withdraw from Madrid and on 21 July a French corps under General Pierre Dupont was surrounded and forced to surrender at Bailén. The British government decided to take advantage of the unrest and sent an expeditionary force under Wellington to Portugal.[12] No light brigade existed in the British Army at the time. For that matter, the British Army did not have a permanent brigade or divisional organization. All infantry and cavalry regiments were assigned to a military district when not on active service. When a need arose to send a force somewhere outside the British Isles, the choice of an overall force commander-in-chief rested with the Secretary of State for War and the Cabinet while the Army's HQ, known as the Horse Guards,[13] would work with him to develop a structure for his force and to provide subordinate general

---

11. By late April over 160,000 French soldiers were in the Iberian Peninsula.
12. He was sent following requests for help from Spain and Portugal. Wellington went to Portugal because the Spanish would not let him land his troops at Corunna.
13. Due to its location in Horse Guards Parade in Whitehall London.

and staff officers. When the expedition or force returned to Great Britain it was disbanded and the regiments went back to their barracks to recruit and train.

Despite the efforts of Moore and other reformers, in 1808 there were only eleven battalions of light infantry in the British Army:

Table 1.1: British Light Infantry Battalions in July 1808

Regiment	Number of Battalions
43rd Foot	2
52nd Foot	2
95th Rifles	2
5th Battalion 60th Foot	1
Chasseurs Britanniques	1
York Light Infantry Volunteers	1
1st King's German Legion Light Battalion	1
2nd King's German Legion Light Battalion	1

Half of Wellington's force sailed from Cork, Ireland on 12 July. With it were four companies of the 2nd Battalion 95th Rifles which were in Brigadier General Henry Fane's brigade.[14] The other half left from Harwich and the Downs on 22 July. Sailing with the second group was Brigadier General Robert Anstruther's brigade consisting of the 2nd Battalions of the 43rd and 52nd Foot, and two companies of the 1st Battalion 95th Rifles, as well as the 97th Foot.[15] Wellington and his force arrived at Mondego Bay, Portugal on 1 August. He did not wait for the transports that sailed from Harwich. He began landing his force and due to the heavy surf, he only finished landing on 6 August. Two days after completing the landing, Major General Brent Spencer came from Gibraltar with four more battalions. This combined force defeated the French at Roliça on 17 August. Three days later the rest of the army landed at Mondego Bay. Now having an army almost twice as strong as it was at Roliça, Wellington was attacked and defeated the French at Vimeiro on 21 August.

---

14. This brigade was designated as the 6th (or Light) Brigade in a General Order dated 7 August 1808.
15. There is no evidence that the brigade was designated a light brigade.

The night before the battle of Vimeiro, a new British commander showed up, Lieutenant General Sir Harry Burrard. He let Wellington command at the battle, but as soon as the French began to retreat, he assumed overall command. On 22 August, another officer assumed command, Lieutenant General Sir Hew Dalrymple. Meanwhile, the French commander, General Junot realized that his position in Portugal was untenable and asked for terms for a ceasefire. On 30 August the Convention of Cintra was signed. The 20,000 French soldiers who occupied Portugal would be allowed to sail back to France on British Royal Navy ships with their weapons and personal baggage. By the end of September the French had evacuated Portugal. The British government was furious when they heard the news and recalled all three generals. A court of inquiry was held in November and although each was cleared, only Wellington would ever have an active command again.

Lieutenant General Moore, the trainer of the light troops at Shorncliffe, arrived in Portugal on the same ship as Burrard. With him were eleven infantry battalions and a regiment of light dragoons. These reinforcements included the 1st Battalion 52nd Foot and three companies of the 1st Battalion 95th Rifles, which were in Major General Edward Paget's 3rd Division,[16] and the 1st and 2nd Battalions of the King's German Legion (KGL) in Brigadier General Baron Charles Alten's brigade. General Moore took command of the army after General Dalrymple was recalled on 6 October and two days later, reorganized it in preparation for operations in Spain. The new organization for the light troops was:

Lieutenant General Alexander Mackenzie Fraser's 2nd Division:

Major General Lord William Bentinck's Brigade:
    1st Battalion 4th Foot
    1st Battalion 28th Foot
    1st Battalion 42nd Foot
    5 companies 5th Battalion 60th Regiment

Major General William Beresford's Brigade
    1st Battalion 9th Foot
    2nd Battalion 43rd Foot
    2nd Battalion 52nd Foot

---

16. Also called the Reserve Division.

Major General Edward Paget's 3rd Division:

> Brigadier General Robert Anstruther's Brigade
> 20th Foot
> 1st Battalion 52nd Foot
> 5 companies 1st Battalion 95th Rifles

> Brigadier General Alten's Brigade
> 1st KGL Light Battalion
> 2nd KGL Light Battalion

Significant reinforcements for the British army in Portugal were also being gathered in England under the command of Lieutenant General Sir David Baird. Among those being sent was

> Colonel Robert Craufurd's Brigade[17]
> 2nd Battalion 14th Foot
> 2nd Battalion 23rd Foot
> 1st Battalion 43rd Foot
> 4 companies 1st Battalion 95th Rifles
> 4 companies 2nd Battalion 95th Rifles

The British reinforcements began arriving at Corunna, Spain in mid-October but did not begin to disembark until 26 October. They had been forced to wait until the local Spanish authorities had received permission from the Spanish Central Junta to allow them to land. Baird had only limited information on what Moore's army was doing, so he delayed moving into Spain. He eventually began sending his troops out by brigades and the first three brigades reached Astorga on 23 November.[18]

While the British were liberating Portugal, Napoleon was marshalling his forces to put down the uprising in Spain. Over 100,000 troops were marched from Central Europe to the borders of Spain in preparation to reinforce the French troops fighting the Spanish. On 4 November,

---

17. Craufurd's rank of brigadier was temporary and only in effect while he was serving with the expedition to Buenos Aires. When he returned to England, he reverted back to colonel.
18. This piecemeal movement of the force was insisted upon by the Spanish to avoid overtaxing the resources of the country.

Napoleon entered Spain with his army and began to advance on Madrid. He captured the city on 3 December.

Moore finished reorganizing his army and started moving into Spain in late October to support the Spanish forces. The mission he received from the British government was to march into Spain and link up with the Spanish armies commanded by Generals Francisco Javier Castaños and Joachim Blake. The goal was to help them defend the Ebro River and prevent Napoleon from re-taking Madrid. The campaign was doomed from the start. Moore split his army into three columns, each taking separate routes. They were to unite at Salamanca. The first elements marched into the city on 13 November. Ten days later, most of his army had assembled. Soon Moore received news of the defeat of the Spanish forces across northern Spain: at Gueñes on 7 November, Espinosa and Gamonal on 10 November, and Tudela on 23 November. General Moore became convinced that the situation was hopeless and ordered the army to retreat to Portugal. Before the orders could be executed, a Spanish delegation from Madrid convinced him that there was still hope to succour the city and on 11 December Moore's army started marching to its relief.

On 13 December, a French dispatch was intercepted. This message announced that Madrid had been captured and laid out the disposition of Napoleon's forces and his plans. Moore realized that he could not hope to free Madrid, but thought if he headed north he could cut the French lines of communication with France. He ordered his army north and on 20 December at Mayorga, he linked up with Baird's reinforcements. Moore re-organized his force and among the changes for the light battalions were:

Major General Beresford's Brigade:
　　1st Battalion 6th Foot
　　1st Battalion 9th Foot
　　2nd Battalion 23rd Foot
　　2nd Battalion 43rd Foot

Brigadier General Anstruther's Brigade:
　　20th Foot
　　1st Battalion 52nd Foot
　　9 companies 1st Battalion 95th Rifles

Colonel Robert Craufurd's Flank Brigade:[19]
　　1st Battalion 43rd Foot

---

19. Some sources call it the 1st Flank Brigade.

2nd Battalion 52nd Foot
8 companies 2nd Battalion 95th Rifles

Brigadier General Alten's Flank Brigade:[20]
1st KGL Light Battalion
2nd KGL Light Battalion

Moore was at Sahagún on 22 December when he received information that Napoleon had changed the focus of his operations. He had responded to the threat to his lines of communications posed by Moore, and was bringing his army north to destroy the British army. Moore knew that there was nothing he could do against the full might of the French army and decided to retreat to Corunna and evacuate his force. This 375km retreat through the most mountainous terrain in Spain in the dead of winter was legendary. Chased by a relentless foe, in freezing snowy weather, over roads that were barely passable in the summer, and alternating between quagmires and frozen ruts, depending on the temperature, saw the light troops come to the fore.

Craufurd's brigade was part of the rearguard for much of the retreat. However, on 31 December Moore ordered Craufurd's and Alten's brigades to leave the army and take a southern route to Vigo.[21] He dispatched them to protect his left flank while the rest of the army marched to Corunna. Craufurd marched from Astorga to Foncebadon to Ponferrada to La Rúa to Ourense, never saw any French, reached Vigo and was evacuated to England on 12 January.[22]

In the main army, General Anstruther's brigade assumed rearguard duties in place of Craufurd's. In this brigade were the 1st Battalions of the 52nd Foot and the 95th Foot. They covered the army's rear for eleven harrowing days until they marched into Corunna. It was during this retreat that their elite reputation was born. Their transports were not there and only appeared on 14 January. The rest of the army made it to Corunna and their ships were beginning to load when the French Army made its appearance. Moore was forced to fight the French on 16 January to give the ships time to finish loading. During the battle Moore, one of strongest supporters of light troops in the British Army,

---

20. Some sources call it the 2nd Flank Brigade.
21. Leach, Jonathan, *Rough Sketches of the Life of an Old Soldier.* Cambridge: Ken Trotman, 1986, p.63
22. Cox, John. 'Extracts from William Cox's Diary'. Hampshire Archives.

was killed. On 18 January, the last unit to be evacuated from Corunna was Beresford's brigade, to which the 2nd Battalion 43rd Foot belonged.

* * *

The fleet carrying Moore's ragged and exhausted army[23] was caught in a storm on its way home, but still made good time and most ships sailed into a harbour along England's southern coast within four or five days. As was the usual practice at that time, upon arriving in England the army was disbanded. The regiments disembarked and returned to their barracks. There they rested and began recruiting back up to strength. Colonel Craufurd went on half pay because he no longer had a staff appointment. Over the past several months he had taken notes of the problems his brigade had on campaign, not in fighting, but in the day-to-day activities, such as marching, setting up camps, and performing their duties. It was during this period that he wrote his *Standing Orders* that sought to correct these deficiencies. They would be the guide that his future command would use.[24] In April Craufurd was appointed a colonel on the staff of the Eastern District, which had its headquarters in Colchester. Because he was only a colonel, he was not authorized an ADC. Captain William Campbell of the 7th Light Dragoons was appointed his brigade major and would serve on his staff for the next three years.

Despite the setback of the Corunna campaign, the British government did not abandon its commitment to Portugal and Spain. In April, Wellington was appointed the commander of the British forces in Portugal and arrived there on 22 April.[25] Prior to leaving England, Wellington had a long discussion with Lord Castlereagh,[26] the Secretary of State for War and the Colonies, about the mission of his force, and what he would need to accomplish it. One of the things he requested was more

---

23. The supply system had broken down during the retreat. Between the horrible weather, little food, and being harried by the French for much of the way, many of the troops were in bad shape. Their clothes were in rags, their equipment falling apart, and on arriving at home, over 3,000 were sent to hospital with fever or dysentery.
24. Craufurd, Alexander, *General Craufurd and His Light Division*. Uckfield: Naval and Military Press, 2004, p.41.
25. Wellington took command on 27 April.
26. Robert Stewart, Viscount Castlereagh.

light troops. Lord Castlereagh agreed with him and wrote to General Sir David Dundas, the Commander-in-Chief of the British Army, on 29 April:

> Permit me to renew the subject of supplying the army in Portugal as early as possible with such a proportion of light troops as our means will admit of. The critical situation of the British army in that country, the importance attached to this species of force by Sir Arthur Wellesley, and the assurances he received before he left England that a corps of this description should follow him without delay, will, I am persuaded, justify me with you for pressing this subject again upon your attention, and with an earnest request that such an arrangement as may be within our power to make with a view to this object may be accelerated.[27]

Shortly after arriving in Lisbon, Wellington wrote to Lord Castlereagh on 24 April to appraise him of the situation in Portugal.[28] He also brought up the subject of a light brigade.

> If the light brigade should not have left England when you receive this letter, I thrust that you will send them off without loss of time; and I request of you to desire the Officer commanding them to endeavour to get intelligence as he shall go along the coast, particularly at Aveiro,[29] and the mouth of the Mondego; and I wish that he should stop at the latter place for orders, if he should find that the British army is engaged in operations to the northward, and that he should not have already received orders at Aveiro.[30]

27. Vane, Charles (ed.), *Correspondence, Despatches, and Other Papers of Viscount Castlereagh, second Marquess of Londonderry*. London: William Shoberl, 1851, Vol. 7, pp.60–1.
28. This was the fourth letter he wrote after arriving in Lisbon.
29. Aveiro is 250km north of Lisbon.
30. Wellington, Duke of, *The Dispatches of Field Marshal the Duke of Wellington, During his Various Campaigns in India, Denmark, Portugal, Spain, the Low Countries, and France, from 1799 to 1818.* Edited by Lt.-Col. John Gurwood. London: John Murray, 1834–9, Vol. 4, p.249. Hereafter referred to as *WD,*

Lord Castlereagh responded to Wellington on 13 May with news that his request had been approved, but it would not be as quick as he wanted it.

> I regret that it has not been in my power sooner to accomplish your wishes with respect to the light brigade. I have pressed the subject almost daily; and, to do the Commander-in-Chief justice, no exertion has been wanting on his part; but the effects of the late campaign in Spain have operated so deeply, that it is only by a selection of men from both the first and second battalions, that we have been enabled to prepare this brigade for service. They are, however, now promised for the 24th. We embark the 1st of the 43rd at Harwich, and the 1st of the 52nd and 95th at Deal. Each of the three battalions will go out 1,000 strong.[31]

Lord Castlereagh might have been overly optimistic promising that the battalions would be 1,000 strong. On 1 March 1809, the 1st Battalion 52nd Foot had 917 sergeants, musicians and other ranks on its rolls. However, only 26 sergeants, 8 buglers, and 269 other ranks were fit for duty.[32] Just as importantly, Lord Castlereagh did not say who would command the brigade. Nine days later, on 22 May, he sent another letter to Wellington to inform him that 'The light brigade, under Brigadier-General Sir R. Craufurd, will embark at Harwich and Deal on the 24th instant. The Brigadier-General will be directed to join you by the shortest route, calling off Oporto, Aveiro, and Mondego, successively, for intelligence of your movements, or any orders you may have despatched to meet him at either of those places.'[33]

On 20 May, the three battalions received orders to march. Included with the orders was the battalion was to have a strength of 1,000 men. This strength was to be their 'effectives' which meant every soldier except for officers, sergeants and musicians. In other words, their other ranks, i.e. their corporals and privates, or in the case of the 95th Rifles, the riflemen. All three battalions had taken heavy casualties in the Corunna campaign, and many of those who had made it back to England were still unfit for active service. They solved this problem

---

31. Vane, Vol. 7, p.64.
32. Moorsom, M.S., *History of the 52nd Regiment: 1755 – 1816*. Tyne & Wear: Worley, 1996, p.110.
33. Vane., Vol. 7, p.69.

by transferring those soldiers fit for duty in their 2nd Battalions to the 1st Battalions. This could be a significant number. For example in the 52nd Foot 349 other ranks were taken from the 2nd Battalion to fill the ranks of the 1st Battalion. The three battalions arrived in Lisbon very close to the required number or exceeding it. The 1st Battalion 43rd Foot had 996 other ranks on 24 June, the 1st Battalion 52nd Foot had 1,004, while the 1st Battalion 95th Rifles had 1,028.[34]

Orders for their deployment on active service were received by each battalion on 20 May. They were told to be ready to march on 24 May. The officers and men spent the next four days preparing to move. Second Lieutenant George Simmons[35] of the 95th Rifles, who had never gone to war before, recorded in his diary on 25 May that

> The order arrived last night, and at two o'clock this morning the Battalion was formed in the Barrack Square, consisting of 1000 as fine young fellows as were ever collected to fight their country's battles. For my part, my heart was as light as a feather when we marched off; and if I may judge from appearances, every person had the same feelings. We entered Dover about six o'clock and marched through it. The windows were crowded with inhabitants; some greeted us, but in general the women seemed sorry to see us depart, knowing well that numbers must never return to their native land again.[36]

They immediately began embarking aboard their transports, the *Fortune*, *Malabar* and *Laurel*.[37] The 52nd Foot marched the 15km from their barracks in Deal to Dover on the same day and also embarked.[38] After all were loaded they sailed to The Downs, an anchorage on the southeast coast of England, and arrived there in the evening. There they met up with the 43rd Foot, which had received their orders to march on

---

34. Bamford, Andrew, 'British Army Individual Unit Strengths: 1808–1815', *The Napoleon Series Online*, 2019.
35. Unlike other British infantry regiments, the 95th Rifles used the rank of 2nd lieutenant instead of ensign.
36. Simmons, George, *A British Rifleman: Journals and Correspondence during the Peninsular War and the Campaign of Wellington*. London: Greenhill, 1986, p.9.
37. Ibid., p.9.
38. Moorsom, p.114.

20 May at 8 p.m. Its commander, Lieutenant Colonel William Gifford, did not issue the movement order until midnight and they marched at 9 a.m.[39] Lieutenant John Brumwell wrote a letter from his transport, the *Sea Nymph*, on 27 May 1809 that they marched 30km to Harwich on 21 May and there they boarded their transports[40] and sailed to The Downs the next day. He complained about how miserable the march was, 'the day being dreadfully hot and the roads full of dust'.[41] This was the first time that the 1st Battalions of the three regiments would serve together under the command of Brigadier General Craufurd. Little did they know that they would be together for the next 60 months.

Foul weather kept the ships from sailing until 3 June, when the winds finally changed. They sailed that day, escorted by the frigate *Nymph* and the sloop *Kangaroo*, but only made it to Saint Helens on the Isle of Wight. The next day, due to poor winds, they only sailed to Cowes Harbour about 25km away. They waited there for six days because of contrary winds and on 11 June sailed for Yarmouth, about 20km away. There they were once again forced to wait for easterly winds. On 18 June the winds shifted and they passed The Needles.[42] While at The Needles, the rocks were swarming with birds, and the Rifles officers broke out their 'rifles and fowling-pieces, with ball, slugs, and swan-shot, were brought into full play on this occasion'.[43] The winds remained good and the convoy arrived off of Lisbon on 29 June.[44]

Craufurd and his staff went ashore to find out his orders and to purchase baggage animals. The troops remained on board until 2 July when they boarded flat-bottomed boats and rowed up the Tagus River. There were not enough boats to take the whole brigade at one time, so it went in two waves. The first wave consisted of the 95th Rifles and the Right Wing of the 43rd Foot.[45] Progress was slow due to

---

39. The 43rd Foot's regimental history says that they did not march until 29 May. Levine, Richard, *Historical Records of the Forty-third Regiment Monmouthshire Light Infantry 1739 to 1867*. Uckfield: Naval & Military, 2014, p.123.
40. Among the other transports was the *Robert Taylor*.
41. Brumwell, John, *The Peninsular War, 1808–1812. Letters of a Weardale Soldier, Lieutenant John Brumwell*. Egglestone, William (ed.). Delhi: Facsimile Publisher, 2019, p.30.
42. Simmons, pp.9–10.
43. Leach, *Rough Sketches* . . ., p. 69.
44. Simmons, pp.9–10.
45. Brumwell, p.34.

having to row against the current, but an incoming tide helped. 'After twenty-four hours spent in this bewitching manner, every man's legs were terribly cramped by being crammed so tight into the boat.'[46]

They landed at Valada at dusk on 3 July after rowing up river for about 70km. Although thankful to be ashore, it was a miserable night for they camped next to the river. Captain Leach, of the 95th Rifles, was convinced that

> . . . all the frogs in the Peninsula had assembled, by common consent on this occasion, to welcome us to Portugal; for such an eternal croaking I never heard before or since. It failed, however, to spoil our night's rest, as sleep the previous night had been quite out of the question, owing to our being constrained to sit upright in the boats.[47]

For Lieutenant Simmons, it was his first bivouac and not a good one. 'Hungry, wet, and cold, and without any covering, we lay down by the side of the river. I put one hand in my pocket and the other in my bosom, and lay shivering and thinking of the glorious life of a soldier until I fell fast asleep.'[48] This half of the brigade stood to at daylight and marched 32km to Santarém. There they waited for four days for the rest of the brigade and its baggage to arrive.

On 8 July, the brigade marched up the Tagus River to Golegã and then to Tancos – a total distance of 40km. The next day they marched another 20km to Abrantes where they crossed the Tagus on a bridge of boats. They bivouacked in woods that night. Many soldiers took the opportunity to cool off by bathing in the river. Before marching, Craufurd assembled his brigade and issued his *Standing Orders*, they were not well received by some. Captain Leach noted in his diary that 'Brigadier General Robert Craufurd (damn him) issued this day to the Light Brigade an immensity of the most tyrannical and oppressive standing orders that were ever compiled by a British officer'.[49] Twenty-two years later, Leach, now a lieutenant colonel and having mellowed a bit, wrote in his memoirs that 'many of them were undoubtedly excellent, and well

---

46. Leach, *Rough Sketches* . . ., p.71.
47. Ibid.
48. Simmons, p.11. Lieutenant Simmons would spend the next four years in similar conditions.
49. Verner; Vol. 2, p.69.

calculated to insure regularity, on the march, in camp, and in quarters; but they were so exceedingly numerous, and some so very minute and tedious, that a man must have been blessed with a better memory than falls to the general lot of mortals to have recollected one half of them'.[50]

After listening to Craufurd they marched for 30km, stopping the night in Gavião. The troops found that the marching on the right bank of the Tagus was not as pleasant as the previous day. The roads were poor, the country was hilly and it was hot.[51] The next day they marched another 30km to Nisa. To alleviate the heat, the brigade started marching 'soon after midnight, and were thereby able, in general to finish the day's work by eight or nine in the morning, and to rest during the heat of the day. In some instances, when we did not commence the march until dawn of day, we had, of course, the full benefit of a southern sun the greater part of the way.'[52]

The officers and men were adjusting to the rigors of the march and sleeping rough. Captain Leach wrote years later that:

I was, unfortunately, one of those restless beings who, after a night spent in marching, could not sleep in the bivouac during the day; and many a time have I envied the happy fellows who lay down like dogs, under a cork-tree, and slept most soundly, until the rations of tough beef (perhaps killed only a few hours before), boiled into an ominium gatherum,[53] with an onion or two, some rice, and a mouldy ship biscuit, were pronounced in a fit state for the table; the said dinner-table being neither more nor less than the turf at the foot of a tree; with a soldier's knapsack by way of camp-chair; a japanned[54] half-pint tin cup stood for wine glass, which, with a pocket-knife, fork, and spoon, and a tin plate, constituted the whole of our dinner service. It being utterly impracticable to have a regimental mess whilst in the field, the officers of each company formed a little mess of their own. Candlesticks not being the fashion of the day, we substituted an empty bottle in their place; and a most bandit-like appearance the interior of our tents presented after dark,

---

50. Leach, *Rough Sketches* . . ., pp.74–5.
51. Simmons, p.13.
52. Leach, *Rough Sketches* . ., p.75.
53. Dog Latin that roughly translates as a solid mess.
54. Covered with a black varnish.

filled generally with such clouds of smoke from our cigars, that I have often since wondered we were not smothered in our sleep from such an atmosphere, in which we reposed rolled up in our cloaks.[55]

Craufurd changed the route and rather than continuing on the left bank of the Tagus, on 13 July ordered his brigade to march 18km northwest and cross the Tagus River via the flying bridge[56] at Vila Velha. It took a while for the 3,500 men to cross and once done they marched 14km to Sarnadas de Ródão where they spent the night. The next day they arrived in Castello Branco, after a short march of 16km and rested there for two days. They left the town on 18 July and spent the night in Ladoeiro, having marched a distance of 25km. The following day they were at Zebreira, close to the Spanish border. They entered Spain on 20 July and spent the night at Zarza la Mayor, having marched 50km in the past two days. The route took them through hilly country and six days later they crossed the Tietar River on a bridge built by Captain Alexander Tod of the Royal Staff Corps on 17 July. The captain had found no suitable material to cross the 22m wide river, so tore the roof off of a nearby tavern and used its rafters to build the bridge.[57]

In Navalmoral they began to hear rumours that Wellington and his army were about to engage the enemy at Talavera. The Light Brigade left the town before sunrise[58] on the next day (28 July) and soon could hear cannon fire in the distance. As was their standing procedure, Craufurd planned to halt his march at La Calzada[59] and rest until the cool of the evening, before resuming the march. They marched the 22km to the village and arrived there about 9 a.m. They were not there long when a courier rode in with a dispatch from Wellington ordering them to march

---

55. Leach, *Rough Sketches . . .*, pp.75–6.
56. A flying bridge was a raft that was connected by ropes to each bank of the river. The men would walk onto the raft and it would be launched into the river, letting the current drag it to the other bank. The raft would be dragged up river and sent back across the river. Muir, Rory and et al. *Inside Wellington's Peninsular Army 1808 – 1814.* Barnsley: Pen & Sword, 2006, pp.236–9.
57. For more information on this and other temporary bridges built by Wellington's Army, see Muir, Rory and et al., pp.226–73.
58. Sunrise on 28 July was at 4:56 a.m.
59. Modern-day Calzada de Oropesa.

Table 1.2: Route of the Light Brigade, 20–27 July 1809

Date	Place	Distance Marched
18 July	Ladoeiro	18km
19 July	Zebreira	25km
20 July	Zarza la Mayor	25km
21 July	Moraleja	30km
22 July	Coria	21km
24 July	Galisteo	27km
25 July	Malpartida	22km
26 July	Venta de Bazagona	17km
27 July	Navalmoral	36km
Total		221km

as quickly as possible to Talavera since a battle was expected shortly. Craufurd immediately ordered the Light Brigade back on the road and they reached Oropesa about noon, having marched another 10km.[60] There Craufurd called a short halt and

> directed the commanding officers of regiments to select and leave at Orapeza [sic] such men as were thought incapable of enduring the forced march which he determined to make, and not to halt until he reached the British army, which was known to be engaged in our front, as the distant but unceasing cannonade plainly announced. Having rested his brigade in this burning plain, where water was not to be procured, General Crawford [sic] put in motion towards Talavera de la Reina. It may well be conceived it was a march productive of the highest degree of feverish anxiety and excitement. The one only feeling was to push forward, to throw our mite [sic] into the scale, and to lend a helping hand to our brothers in arms.
>
> We soon met wounded Spanish soldiers and Spanish soldiers not wounded, bending their course in a direction from the field of battle. I wish I could assert with equal truth that this retrogression was confined our Spanish allies; but the truth must be told; and I regret to say, that stragglers from the ranks of the British army, some without a wound, were also taking a similar direction

---

60. Verner, Vol. 2, p.72.

to the rear. As they passed our column they circulated all sorts and kinds of reports of a most disheartening nature: 'The British army was utterly defeated, and in full retreat;' 'Sir Arthur Wellesley was wounded;' and, by others, 'he was killed.' In short, all was suspense and uncertainty. One thing was, nevertheless, certain – that the cannonade continued without cessation.

We pressed forward until ten o'clock at night, when, having reached a pool of stagnant water near the road, in which cattle had been watered during the summer, and where they had constantly wallowed, a halt was ordered for an hour or two. Those who have never been in similar situations may be inclined to doubt my veracity when I state that the whole brigade, officers and soldiers, rushed into this muddy water, and drank with an eagerness and avidity impossible to describe. The use of such an execrable beverage, except on extreme occasions, like the one in question, where we had been the whole day without water, under a sun as oppressive as can be experienced in Europe, might indeed be deemed extraordinary; but excessive thirst knows no law.[61]

The Light Brigade was spent and Craufurd ordered a halt to rest the men. At 2 a.m. the brigade was back on its feet and started to march again.

After a short repose on the banks of this horsepond, we again got under weigh [sic], and without another halt joined the British army in its position at Talavera . . . to say, that in twenty-four hours it passed over upwards of fifty miles of country; as extraordinary a march, perhaps as is found on record; particularly when it is remembered that each soldier carried from sixty to eighty rounds of ammunition, a musket or rifle, a great coat, (if I recollect rightly) a blanket, a knapsack complete, with shoes, shirts, &c. &c.; a canteen and haversack, bayonet, belts, &c. &c. Such a load carried so great distance, would be considered a hard day's work for a horse. The heat was intense. . . Water was scarcely to be had, and of such quality that the quadrupeds doomed to drink it need not have been envied, much less bipeds. It must also be added, that for some days before we had been very scantily supplied with provisions.[62]

---

61. Leach, *Rough Sketches* . . ., pp.81–3.
62. Ibid., p.83.

This epic march was about 65km long, much of it, according to Lieutenant John Cox of the 95th Rifles, over 'heavy sandy roads'.[63] The Light Brigade arrived at the centre of the position of the British army at Talavera about 6 a.m. on 29 July having completed the forced march in 25 hours.[64] But they were too late to participate in the battle. After two days' fighting the French were unable to defeat the Anglo-Spanish army and pulled back about 7km to the Alberche River. The Light Brigade was sent forward to serve as a screen between the two armies. Captain George Napier of the 52nd Foot wrote later that:

We took up the line of the advanced posts, and were employed burying the dead and saving the unfortunate wounded French from the fury of the Spanish peasants, who murdered them wherever they could find them without mercy. The field of battle was a horrid sight, particularly to us who had not shared either in the danger or the glory, though we did our best to arrive in time. The dry grass had caught fire, and numbers of wounded of all nations were burnt to death, being unable to crawl out of the way of the raging fire; then the dreadful smell from the half-burned carcases [sic] of the horses was appalling. In short, I never saw a field of battle which struck me with such horror as the field of Talavera.[65]

Lieutenant Harry Smith of the 95th Rifles said much the same.

We took up the outposts immediately, and some of us Riflemen sustained some heavy skirmishing. The field was literally covered with dead and dying. The bodies began to putrefy, and the stench was horrible, so that an attempt was made to

---

63. Cox, John, 'Extracts from John Cox's Diary of the Peninsula War'. Hampshire Archives. File # 170A12W/D/0021.
64. Captain William Napier, who was on the march, said in his history that they marched 62 miles (100km) in 26 hours. However, he said they started from Malpartida, which was 39km from Navalmoral. The distance using twenty-first century maps from Google Maps is 65km. Napier, William, *History of the War in the Peninsula and in the South of France*, 6 vols. New York: W. J. Widdleton, 1864, Vol. 2, p.403.
65. Napier, George, *Passages in the Early Military Life of General Sir George T. Napier*. London, John Murray, 1884, pp.109–10.

collect the bodies and burn them. Then, however, came a stench which literally affected many to sickness. The soldiers were not satisfied with this mode of treating the bodies of their dead comrades, and the prosecution of the attempt was relinquished.[66]

Although having beaten the French, Wellington was in a bad position. Prior to agreeing to advance his army into central Spain, he was promised that he would be provided with provisions by the Spanish army. This was an empty promise and shortly after arriving at Talavera, the Light Brigade went on short rations. Captain Leach 'did not believe that more than one day's allowance of bread was issued from the 29th of July to the evening of the 2d [sic] of August, nor were the rations of wine, spirits, and meat forthcoming either'.[67]

On 1 August, the Light Brigade was assigned to the 3rd Division. The division had been commanded by Major General John Randoll Mackenzie, but he was killed at Talavera on 28 July. Craufurd was the senior brigade commander and thus took command of the division. Lieutenant Colonel William Gifford of the 43rd Foot probably took temporary command of the Light Brigade in his place.[68] Wellington soon realized that the longer he waited at Talavera the more untenable his position became. On the night of 1 August, he received intelligence that a French army under Marshal Jean Soult was at Plasencia and threatening his lines of communication with Portugal. The next day, Wellington ordered his army to withdraw back to Portugal beginning on 3 August.

Soon the Light Brigade was marching back along the road to Navalmoral and spent the night of 3 August in Oropesa. The following day the 95th Rifles were detached from the brigade and became part of the rearguard. On 5 August the 3rd Division was detached from the rest of the army and sent west through the mountains to take control of the bridge over the Tagus River at Almaraz.[69] There they stayed until 20 August. Their encampment was miserable. The weather was hot and little food was available. Soon the men were living on 'four ounces

---

66. Smith, Harry, *The Autobiography of Sir Harry Smith: 1787 – 1819*. London: Constable, 1999, p.19.
67. Leach, *Rough Sketches . . .*, pp.87–9.
68. LTC Gifford was never appointed the temporary commander of the brigade, but as the senior lieutenant colonel in it, he would command it in the absence of Craufurd.
69. A sixteenth-century bridge built by Emperor Charles V.

of flour per man served out, which we mixed with water, made it up into small balls and boiled them. As they were less than dumplings, we called them dough-boys and hence we called this encampment "Dough-boy Hill!"'[70] The officers went hungry too. Lieutenant Cox referred to it as the 'valley of starvation'.[71]

On 20 August orders were received for the 3rd Division to withdraw back to Portugal. Their route was:

Table 1.3: Route of the Light Brigade 20 August to 11 September 1809

Date	Place	Distance Marched
20 August	Deleitosa	20km
22 August	Trujillo	40km
23 August	Cáceres	46km
24 August	8km east of Aliseda	32km
25 August	Salorino	28km
26 August	Valencia de Alcantara	33km
28 August	Banks of the Sever River[72]	8km
29 August	Mavão to Castello de Vide	30km
7 September	Portalegre, Portugal	20km
10 September	Arronches	43km
11 September	Campo Maior	24km

Upon arriving in Campo Maior they went into quarters and rested there for three months. Due to being on campaign, the General Orders affecting the Light Brigade were slow in being published. On 21 August, Craufurd was officially appointed a brigadier general on the staff, with a back date of 26 July. The same General Order appointed Captain William Campbell of the 7th Light Dragoons as his ADC and Captain Charles Rowan of the 52nd Foot as his brigade major. Three months later, on 19 November, Captain Campbell was assigned as Deputy Assistant Quartermaster General of the 3rd Division. On 10 December, Lieutenant James Shaw of the 43rd Foot was assigned as Craufurd's

---

70. Green, William, *Where Duty Calls Me: The Experiences of William Green of Lutterworth in the Napoleonic Wars,* John and Dorothea Teague (ed.). West Wickham: Synjon Books, 1975, p.23.
71. Cox, 'Diary entry for 20 August 1809'.
72. The border with Portugal.

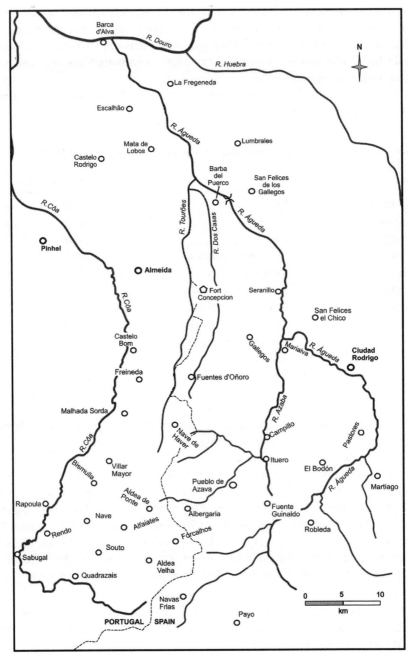

Overview of the Light Division's area of operations, February–July 1810.

ADC, with the appointment backdated to 19 November. All three of these officers would be on Craufurd's staff in the coming year.

On 11 December the Light Brigade received orders to march the next morning. They were moving to what would become their home for the next seven months: the Portuguese–Spanish Border in the vicinity of Almeida and the River Côa. Their march route to the north was:

Table 1.4: Route of the Light Brigade 12 December 1809 – 5 January 1810

Date	Place	Distance Marched
12 December	Arronches	24km
16 December	Portalegre	20km
18 December	Crato	23km
19 December	Ponto do Souro[73]	48km
20 December	Abrantes	35km
21 December	Punhete[74]	16km
22 December	Tomar	21km
24 December	Ourém	20km
25 December	Leiria	35km
27 December	Pombal	28km
28 December	Condeixa[75]	27km
29 December	Coimbra	15km
1 January	Ponte da Mucela	35km
2 January	Galizes	35km
3 January	Pinhanços	30km
4 January	Celorico	34km
5 January	Pinhel	37km

On 7 January the Light Brigade began deploying forward to the area between the Rivers Côa and Agueda. Within ten days, all three regiments were in forward positions. There they would sit for the next six months, observing the French who had moved into the vicinity of Ciudad Rodrigo from Salamanca. It was here that the Light Brigade would become the Light Division and cement its reputation as one of the elite forces of the Napoleonic Wars.

---

73. Modern-day Ponte de Sor.
74. Modern-day Constância.
75. Modern-day Condeixa-a-Nova.

Chapter 2

The Birth of the Light Division, 1 January–18 March 1810

In mid-February the British 3rd Division was located in the vicinity of Pinhel and along the Portuguese-Spanish border just to the east of the fortified city of Almeida. The month also saw Major General Sir Thomas Picton arriving in Portugal. His presence created a problem for Wellington. Picton was senior to Major General Galbraith Cole who commanded the 4th Division and to General Craufurd who was temporarily commanding the 3rd Division. The only position Wellington had for Picton was as the commander of the 3rd Division. If he appointed him commander of the 3rd Division, what was he to do with Craufurd, who had served so ably as the divisional commander for the previous seven months? Compounding the problem was that Craufurd was junior to eight other general officers who were not commanding a division.[1]

Wellington's solution was to re-organize the army. On 22 February 1810, a General Order was issued. In it Picton was appointed the commander of the 3rd Division and Craufurd was given command of the newly-created Light Division. Although this did not solve the issue of Craufurd being junior to eight other brigade commanders, Wellington justified this appointment by keeping the Light Division as the weakest division in the army. It would only have one British brigade and two Portuguese caçadores battalions. Craufurd expressed his concerns about being replaced by a more senior officer to Wellington, who addressed his worries in a letter dated 15 April 1810. In the wording of the last sentence,

---

1. They were, in order of seniority, Major Generals Stafford Lightburne and William Stewart; Brigadier Generals Alexander Campbell, Richard Stewart, Charles Stewart, Sigismund von Low, Alan Cameron and James Catlin Craufurd.

Wellington implies that he may not be able to keep him in command of the division:

> Your feeling respecting your command is exactly what it ought to be, and what might be expected from you. As long as I could make up a division of the proper strength for the service, with your brigade, and Portuguese troops and cavalry, nobody would have had reason to complain; but a Lieutenant General,[2] and the senior Major General[3] of the army, recently arrived, are without commands, and it would not answer to throw more English troops into your division, leaving them unemployed. You may depend upon it, however that whatever may be the arrangement which I shall make, I wish your brigade to be in the advanced guard.[4]

Despite Wellington's overt support of Craufurd, it did not stop the bitterness of those who were not offered the command of the division. As one Rifles officer noted:

> Amongst a certain number (I hope a few only) of malcontents in the army, the very name of the 'Light Division,' or the 'outposts,' was sufficient to turn their ration wine into vinegar, and to spoil their appetite for that day's allowance of ration beef also. In good truth, general officers were to be found, whom I could name, that bore towards us no very good will; perhaps because it was not their lot to hold so prominent a command as that of our more fortunate and favoured brigadier. But, be that as it may, those invidious barkers and growlers, whether in the subaltern or in the higher ranks, in whose mouths was ever uppermost,– 'Ah! The Light Division! what is the Light Division more than any other?'[5]

---

2. Wellington is a bit vague about whom he was referring to. It was likely Lieutenant General Stapleton Cotton, who had no real command as he lost his cavalry brigade upon promotion. In late 1809, his command consisted of General Fane's cavalry brigade and a Royal Horse Artillery troop only. On 20 April 1810, he was appointed commander of the 1st Division.
3. Major General James Leith.
4. *WD*, Vol. 6, p.37.
5. Leach, *Rough Sketches . . .*, p.134.

The creation of the new division was barely noticed by those in it. Lieutenant James Shaw, ADC to Craufurd, noted in his journal on 23 February that 'There is now a new distribution of the army, which was in order as follows.'[6] Despite being called the Light Division in the General Order that created it, that name did not catch on immediately. It would be a month before Shaw even referred to it as the division and not until 26 April did he call it the Light Division. Lieutenant George Simmons of the 95th Rifles wrote in his journal on 30 April that 'The Division is now to be called Light in the future'.[7]

In a letter dated 3 January 1810, Wellington wrote from Coimbra to Craufurd with his specific instructions on what he wanted him to do in regards to serving as the army's outposts.

> On your arrival at your station, I request you will communicate with Brigadier General Cox[8] at Almeida, and obtain from him all the information you can get of the enemy's force, position, etc. upon the frontier.
>
> I request also that you will endeavour, through General Cox, to communicate with Captain Ruman,[9] who is employed to get intelligence on the frontiers of Castille [sic], and desire him to send you all his reports, directed to me, which you will of course peruse. I shall desire Colonel Carroll,[10] who is employed with the Duque del Parque's army,[11] to write to you constantly.

---

6. Shaw-Kennedy, James, 'A Private Journal of General Craufurd's Out-Post Operations on the Coa and Agueda in 1810' in *A Manual of Outpost Duties*. London: Parker, Furnivall and Parker, 1851, p.162.
7. Simmons, p.58.
8. Brigadier General William Cox, the commandant of Almeida.
9. Captain Lewis Ruman 97th Foot was assigned to the Quartermaster General Department and was one of Wellington's exploring officers.
10. William Parker Carroll was a captain in the 88th Foot. He was fluent in Spanish and was attached as a liaison officer to the Spanish army in March 1809. He was a colonel in the Spanish Army and commander of the Spanish Regiment of Hibernia.
11. Lieutenant General Diego Vicente María de Cañas y Portocarrero, duque del Parque, commander of the Spanish Army of the Left, which was located in central Spain.

You will also endeavour to establish for yourself any other sources of intelligence which you think fit, the expense of which I shall defray.

We have a store of provisions in Almeida, from which you will draw what you may require, if it should be necessary; but do not use it unless it is absolutely so. Your Commissary will find Torre de Moncorvo to be very fertile district. I shall desire Mr. Murray[12] to send him a supply of money, which I observe is the best persuasive to the people of the country to give their supplies.

I wish that you would desire Captain Campbell,[13] and any other officers in your division who are capable of it, to examine the course of the Coa, which runs by Almeida, and to report upon it; and likewise the course of the Agueda, if the position of the enemy should allow it. I will defray the expenses of the latter while employed on this service.

I shall be here for some days, in order that I may arrange every thing relating to our supplies; and hereafter I shall fix my headquarters at Viseu, and shall go forward to pay you a visit.

P.S. Do not work the hussars[14] at Pinhel by sending them with letters. I should prefer to pay a messenger. General Sherbrooke's division[15] is at Viseu, and towards Celorico and Trancoso. The 4th division[16] will be at Celorico, Guarda and Pinhel.[17]

With this letter, it became clear that Craufurd had the mission of serving as the army's outposts along the Spanish border in the northeast. Yet this was more of a precaution than any anticipation of a French move on the Spanish fortress city of Ciudad Rodrigo and then into Portugal. They were really deployed there because it was a good place for winter quarters for his troops.[18] Craufurd was proactive and on 17 January moved the Light Brigade forward. The 95th Rifles occupied Figueira de Castelo Rodrigo,

---

12. John Murray, the Commissary General of Wellington's army.
13. Captain William Campbell, 23rd Regiment, was the DAQMG assigned to the 3rd Division at the time. When the Light Division was formed, he became its Assistant Quartermaster General.
14. 1st King's German Legion Hussars.
15. Lieutenant General John Sherbrooke commanded the 1st Division.
16. Commanded by Major General Galbraith Lowry Cole.
17. *WD*, Vol. 5, pp.395–6.
18. Ibid., Vol. 5, pp.533–5.

Mata de Lobos, and Escalhão which were about 6–10km from the River Douro, while the 43rd and 52nd Foot were deployed to their right and further south. Lieutenant Simmons noted in his journal that 'The banks of the Douro are extremely rocky, wild, and romantic – in short, the country all round, with few exceptions is wild and stony. We have had a very heavy fall of snow, in which I observed innumerable prints of wolves.'[19]

Craufurd complied with his instructions and sent officers out to conduct a reconnaissance of the two rivers. Lieutenant Shaw, his ADC, was one of those who went. He left on 30 January and spent the next six days travelling along the Côa River from the bridge below Almeida to the where it flowed into the Douro River in the northwest. Shaw wrote in his journal on 4 March:

> The principal results of my reconnoissance [sic] of the Coa, were to discover that below the Bridge of Pinhel there are sixteen places at which it is possible to cross the river. From the bridge to where the Coa joins the Douro is between six and seven leagues. The banks of the river, from the bridge to Azeva[20] are very rugged and difficult; from thence, to where it is joined by the Masueme,[21] its banks are singularly high, rugged, rocky, and perpendicular; from that to the Douro they are high, but not so rocky. Upon the whole, that part of the river may be defended by a very few men. Villa Novo[22] and Torre de Moncorvo are two very good towns; the former is close to where the Coa joins the Douro.[23]

Wellington planned to return to Lisbon in early February, a distance of about 400km. He would be out of touch with his army for several days and he needed to ensure that the lead elements knew what to do should the French attack. On 31 January 1810, Wellington wrote Craufurd a letter in which he laid out his intentions.

---

19. Simmons, p.46.
20. Modern-day Azevo.
21. I have not been able to find a river with the name Masueme. It is probably the stream that flows into the Côa River at 40°58'17.7'N 7°06'06.8'W
22. Vila Nova de Foz Côa.
23. Shaw, p.158.

I don't think the enemy is likely to molest us at present; but I am desirous of maintaining the Coa unless he should collect a very large force, and obviously intend to set seriously to work on the invasion of Portugal. If that should be the case, I do not propose to maintain the Coa, or that you should risk any thing for that purpose; and I beg you to retire gradually to Celorico, where you will be joined by General Cole's division. From Celorico I propose that you should retire gradually along the valley of the Mondego, upon Sir John Sherbrooke's division, and other troops which will be there. If you quit the Coa bring the Hussars with you. I mention this in writing in case of accidents during my absence, which, however, I do not think likely to occur. If you should withdraw from the Coa, bring with you the 12th Portuguese regiment, which is in the villages on your right, having been sent out of the garrison of Almeida.[24]

In the meantime, the French began making preparations to capture Ciudad Rodrigo. On 8 February troops of Marshal Michel Ney's 6th Corps marched southwest from Salamanca towards Ciudad Rodrigo and three days later were spreading out around the city. A summons to surrender was made to the city's governor, Lieutenant General Don Andrés Péres de Herrasti, who refused. Marshal Ney had hoped to take the city without having to conduct a formal siege. He had not brought a siege battery nor sufficient supplies to feed a large enough force that could effectively besiege the city. The next morning, he withdrew back to Salamanca, but left his 1st Division, commanded by Général de Division Jean-Gabriel Marchand, in the vicinity of Vitigudino, to keep an eye on Ciudad Rodrigo.[25]

Craufurd was not aware of the movement of the French until they reached Ciudad Rodrigo on 11 February.[26] In accordance with his instructions, by 14 February, he redeployed the Light Brigade from the vicinity of the Douro River and had it and Captain Hew Dalrymple Ross's troop of Royal Horse Artillery, in the following locations:

---

24. *WD*, Vol. 5, pp.459–60.
25. Horward, Donald, *Napoleon and Iberia: the Twin Sieges of Ciudad Rodrigo and Almeida, 1810*. London: Greenhill, 1994, pp.10–12
26. Shaw, p.159. Simmons, p.47.

Table 2.1: Location of the Light Brigade 19 February 1810[27]

Unit	Location
Division Headquarters	Pinhel
43rd Foot	Battalion HQ: Azinhal; Companies also at: Valverde, Peva, Chavelhas, Treixe,[28] Aldeia Nova
52nd Foot	Pinhel
95th Rifles	Battalion HQ: Vilar Torpim; Companies also at Reigada, Cinco Vilas,[29] Escarigo
Royal Horse Artillery	Pinhel

All units were west of the Côa River, except for the 95th Rifles which was in three villages about 20km north of Almeida and 30km from Pinhel. The 43rd Foot was in five villages near Valverde, about 15km from Pinhel and 6km west of the bridge over the Côa River near Almeida. Although not attached to the Light Division, the 1st King's German Legion Hussars had one troop, under the command of Captain Wilhelm Aly, also at Escarigo.[30]

On 15 February word reached General Craufurd that a party of French foragers had crossed the Agueda River and occupied Barba del Puerco.[31] They did not remain there long. On 27 February, No. 1 Company of the 1st Battalion 95th Rifles, commanded by Captain Jasper Creagh, was sent on a reconnaissance patrol from Escargio towards to Barba del Puerco. Their route took them via the village of La Bouza, then over the Dos Casas River, and into Barba del Puerco. There they found French cavalry and infantry. After a short skirmish, Captain Creagh, in obedience to his orders, withdrew to Escarigo. He was joined there by Captain Leach and his rifle company. Lieutenant Colonel Beckwith, the commander of the 95th Rifles, sent Captain Peter O'Hare's company to Escarigo to support Creagh and Leach.

---

27. Shaw, p.160.
28. I have not been able to find the location of this village. It is possibly Escarigio which is near La Bouza.
29. Most contemporary sources called the village Cinqua Villas.
30. Shaw, p.160. Beamish, N. Ludlow. *History of the King's German Legion.* London: Buckland & Brown, 1993, Vol. 1, p.269.
31. Modern-day Puerto Seguro.

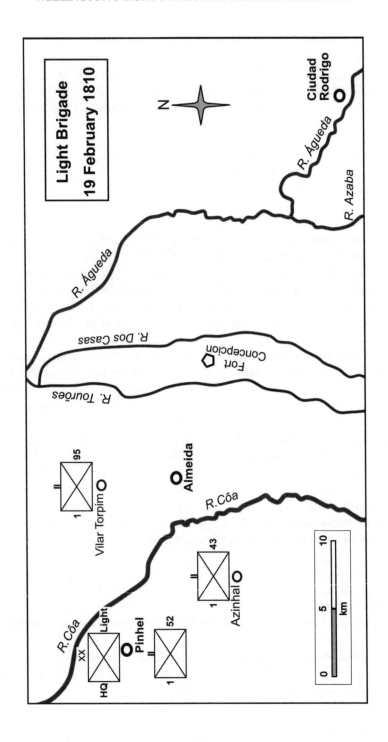

Early the next day, the three companies were sent to the village and found it had been abandoned by the French. Their approach caused the French to hastily retreat down the hill and across the bridge, leaving the bread that they were baking. Once the village was secured, the riflemen dined on hot bread for breakfast.[32] Captain Leach sent a small patrol down the steep ridge to a masonry bridge which crossed the River Agueda. On the far side of the bridge was a French infantry and cavalry picquet. Leach also talked with the village's priest who informed him that the French force at San Felices de los Gallegos consisted of 3,000 infantry, and cavalry commanded by Général de Brigade Claude-François Ferey. After withdrawing to Escarigo, Captain O'Hare sent a report, which was forwarded to the division headquarters in Pinhel. This information was confirmed by Captain Aly of the 1st KGL Hussars who reported the same information.[33]

On 4 March the 95th Rifles were ordered to move closer to the Agueda River. Four companies were located at Villar de Ciervo, four companies in Barba del Puerco, a company in Almofala, and the last company to the north in Escalhão at the junction of the Agueda and Douro Rivers. The battalion was spread out over 50km, with the company in Escalhão being almost 20km from its closest support. The four companies at Barba del Puerco had the Dos Casas River to their rear. Before long heavy rains began and caused the river to flood. If the enemy attacked Barba del Puerco in force, the four companies would be unable to retreat. Craufurd eventually ordered the position to be evacuated until the rains subsided. Another concern of the general was that if the officers did not know the terrain behind their positions, in event of a fighting withdrawal, there would be chaos. To prevent this, the companies often were switched from one village to the other. This allowed the officers to learn the roads, river crossings and the lay of the land between the Agueda and Côa Rivers.[34]

Lieutenant Shaw noted in his journal on 4 March that 'This is a wet, blowy day, and appears the commencement of bad weather. The people still expect rain and unsettled weather at this season of the year.'[35] The local weather forecast was accurate. It rained frequently which caused the rivers to rise and become fast moving.

---

32. Simmons, p.60.
33. Shaw, p.162. Leach, *Rough Sketches . . .*, pp.124–5.
34. Leach, *Rough Sketches . . .*, p.125. Simmons, p.52.
35. Shaw, p.164.

Living conditions for the soldiers varied from village to village. Lieutenant Simmons wrote to his parents on 28 February that he would be

> . . . sometimes sleeping and living in the grandest houses in the country, and at others in the most wretched hovels not as good as an English pig-sty. Our present quarters are truly miserable; on all sides stupendous mountains. . . houses are built of rough stone, generally 7 or 8 feet high (some exceptions to this rule), with no outlet for smoke; the fire is made by the wall side, and consists generally of mountain heather or broom, which produces a most intolerable smoke, and gives a person who is not well seasoned a copious flow of tears. . . the house is entirely enveloped in smoke, and every side of the wall is like a chimney, which they never take pains to sweep clean.[36]

Despite having relatively dry billets, life on the outposts was not easy. Rifleman William Green of Captain O'Hare's company, wrote that:

> If in the winter we were in our cantonments we could not take off our clothes; and when off duty, and retired in the houses, we were allowed to take off our stocks and jackets only; to be ready at a few minutes notice, or to turn out at the first sound of the bugle. Our practice was often to get under arms an hour before daylight; and to stand under arms until broad day, when the enemy were near.[37]

Outpost duty was occasionally exciting, but usually boring. In addition to the companies from the 95th Rifles being deployed, General Craufurd had their officers posted with the advance outposts of the 1st KGL Hussars. Each of these outposts had beacons and the officers 'had orders to watch the enemy with their telescopes, and, in case of any movement, to report or fire the beacon'.[38] Captain Leach wrote later that when beacons were not available

> . . . on a body of the enemy's cavalry being perceived moving towards their posts, the following signal might be made, – one of

---

36. Simmons, p.50.
37. Green, pp.25–6.
38. Smith, pp.25–6.

the videttes [sic] to hoist his chako [sic] on the point of a sword, and elevate it as much as possible above his head. If a combined force of cavalry and infantry should be seen approaching, one of the videttes could continue to canter his horse round in a circle on the summit of the hill. Should artillery accompany the other two arms, both the videttes [sic] might canter round in that manner.[39]

Lieutenant Harry Smith wrote of one of his experiences as being with the advance vedettes of the 1st Hussars on the Agueda River:

I was on this duty in rather a remote spot on the extreme left of our posts. The vedette was from the 1st Hussar picquet. These men would often observe a patrol or body of the enemy with the naked eye which was barely discernible through a telescope, so practised were they and watchful. Towards the evening my servant ought to have arrived with my dinner (for we officers of the look-out could take nothing with us but our horse and our telescope), but he must have missed his way, and as my appetite was sharpened by a day's look-out, I began to look back, contrary to the vedette's idea of due vigilance. He asks 'What for Mynheer so much look to de rear?' I, sad at the fast, 'hussar, you are relieved every two hours. I have been here since daylight. I am confounded hungry, and am looking out for my servant and my dinner.' 'poor Yonge man! But 'tis notings.' 'Not to you" said I, 'but much to me.' 'You shall see, sir. I shall come off my horse, you shall up climb, or de French shall come if he see not de vedette all right.' I suspected what he was about. Off he got; up get I en vedette. With greatest celerity, he unbuckled his valise from behind his saddle and took out a piece of bacon (I had kept up a little fire from the sticks and bushes around me), from a cloth some ground coffee and sugar, from his haversack some biscuit, and spread on the ground a clean towel with a knife, fork, and a little tin cup. He had water in his canteen – his cooking-tin. He made me a cup of coffee, sliced some bacon, broiled it in the embers, and in ten minutes coffee, bacon, biscuit were ready and

39. Leach, Jonathan, *Recollections and Reflections Relative to the Duties of Troops Composing the Advanced Corps of an Army*. London: T. and W. Boone, 1835, pp.35–6.

looked as clean as if in a London tavern. . . . I was highly amused to observe the momentary glances the Hussar cast on me and my meal, for no rat-catcher's dog at a sink-hole kept a sharper look-out to his front than did this vedette. In the course of my service I never was more amused, and nothing could be more disinterested than the Hussar's conduct, which I never forgot.[40]

Lieutenant Smith's servant eventually showed up and he gave his dinner to the hussar.

Captain Leach and his company were on duty in Almofala about 2km from the Agueda River when he

. . . witnessed a disgusting and cruel sight. Having gone with another officer to the mountainous bank which overhangs the river not far from the village, to visit the picket, we perceived a French soldier, unarmed, running down the mountain on the opposite side of the river, no doubt with the intention of trying to cross over and desert to us. Three Spanish shepherds who were tending their sheep on the same side of the river, intercepted him, and beat him to death with their clubs in less time than it has taken me to write an account of the sickening sight. We called out, and made signals to them to desist, and to spare him, but in vain. We fired several shots over their heads to intimidate them, but it had no effect, and the butchery went on without our being able to interfere, or to interrupt those savages in what they considered no doubt, a most patriotic and meritorious exploit. A deluge of rain had so swollen the river, which roared at the foot of the mountain, that to pass it was impossible; and, indeed, could we have effected it, the blood-thirsty shepherds would have escaped, before we could by possibility have reached them. To have inflicted the summary punishment on them with a rifle ball, which we all felt well inclined to do, would have been only an act of justice; but it was a step, nevertheless, which the higher authorities would have visited with a heavy punishment.[41]

It rained for most the first week in March. On 4 March, Captain Georg von Müller and his troop of 1st KGL Hussars reinforced Captain Aly at

---

40. Smith, pp.26–7.
41. Leach, *Rough Sketches* . . ., pp.125–6.

Escarigo.[42] Three days later word reached the Division HQ that about 200 French had crossed the bridge and moved into Barba del Puerco. The message stated that they only remained there for two hours and then withdrew. Whether this was accurate is unknown. However, the next day 1,500 French were in the village and moved west, taking Escarigo and Villar de Ciervo. The German hussars in the villages were driven back to Val de Cuelha. Casualties were light, only one man who was wounded and a horse killed. The French plundered the village, stripping it of provisions, and then retreated back across the Agueda River. Upon receipt of the news, Lieutenant Shaw rode the 32km to Val de Cuelha to assess the situation. He spent the next day there and then rode another 32km to Barba del Puerco via Aldea del Obispo and Villar de Ciervo. He found General Craufurd and Captain Campbell at Barba del Puerco. While there they saw that the French had a sentry on the far side of the bridge and an outpost on the hill behind it. Word had also reached the governor of Ciudad Rodrigo of the French incursion at Barba del Puerco and he sent a detachment of Spanish soldiers to garrison the village.[43]

Craufurd had had enough of the French crossing the Agueda River at Barba del Puerco and sent Lieutenant Shaw with orders for the 95th Rifles to send two companies to the village and one to La Bouza. He rode the 40km back to Pinhel via La Bouza, Escarigo, and Vilar Torpim. While he was in Escarigo he found Lieutenant Colonel Beckwith and passed Craufurd's orders to him. The next morning Captain Peter O'Hare's company and one other[44] were sent to Barba del Puerco and Captain Francis Glass's company occupied La Bouza. Captain Creagh's company was at Almofala.[45]

Although Wellington had given Craufurd a general idea on what he wanted him to do in the letter dated 31 January, his instructions were a bit vague. Craufurd was unhappy that he had received no specific orders, especially in regards of the role of Generals Picton and Cole in the event the French attacked. Furthermore the two divisions were at Guarda and Celorico, which were 50km and 75km away from his division, and in no position to provide immediate support. In early March he met with Picton '. . . to consider the best measures to be taken, and did not altogether agree in their opinions as to the distribution of

---

42. Shaw, p.164.
43. Ibid., pp.164–5.
44. I have not been able to identify whose company it was.
45. Shaw, p.155.

the out-post'.[46] On 6 March, Craufurd wrote to Wellington about his concerns. On 8 March, Wellington wrote a lengthy letter to Craufurd that laid out the scope of what he wanted the Light Division to do:

> I am very much obliged to you for your letter of the 6th, which I received last night. The fact is, that the line of cantonments which we took up, principally with a view to the accommodation of the troops during the winter, and to their subsistence on a point on which it was likely that it might be desirable to assemble the army, will not answer our purpose of assembling upon the Coa, if eventually that should be deemed an object. Neither does our position, as at present occupied, suit the existing organization of the army. For these reasons I have long intended to alter our disposition, as soon as the season would permit the troops to occupy the smaller villages on the Coa, and as I should be able to bring up the Portuguese light troops of your division to the front.
>
> Since we took up the position which we now occupy, our outposts have come in contact with those of the French, and although there is some distance between the two, still the arrangement of our outposts must be made on a better principle, and the whole of them must be in the hands of one person, who must be yourself. I propose, therefore, as soon as the weather shall allow of an alteration of the disposition of the advanced corps, that your division, with the hussars, which will be put under your orders, should occupy the whole line of outposts; and with this view, the Portuguese corps shall be brought up to the front, as soon as the state of the weather will allow them to march.
>
> I am desirous of being able to assemble the army upon the Coa if it should be necessary; at the same time that I am perfectly aware that, if the enemy should collect in any large numbers in Estremadura, we should be too forward for our communication with General Hill even here, much more so upon the Coa. But till they shall collect in Estremadura, and till we shall see more clearly, than I can at present, what reinforcements they have received, and what military object they have in view, and particularly in the existing disposition of their army, I am averse

---

46. Shaw., p.166.

to withdrawing from a position so favourable as the Coa affords, to enable me to effect that object. The left should probably be Castel Rodrigo,[47] and I believe you must have a post as far as Alfayates[48] on the right. However, you must be a better judge of the detail of this question than I can be; and I wish you to consider it, in order to be able immediately to carry the plan into execution, when I shall send to you. In the mean time, the state of the weather, which, from all I can learn, is as bad everywhere as it is here, and the consequence of which must to fill all the rivers, is no bad security against the effects which might result from the continuance of the existing system of outposts for a few days longer.

I intend that the divisions of General Cole and General Picton should support you on the Coa, without waiting for orders from me, if it should be necessary; and they shall be directed accordingly.[49]

Wellington's letter made five things very clear:

1. General Craufurd had the responsibility for the forward outposts.
2. The mission of Generals Picton and Cole was to support him.
3. The 1st KGL Hussars would be placed under Craufurd's command.
4. The Light Division was to move forward and defend the villages along the Côa River.
5. The two Portuguese caçadores battalions that were assigned to the Light Division would be sent to him as soon as the weather permitted. They were located in Coimbra about 250km away and it would be several weeks before they arrived.

Wellington was a bit vague when he said he wanted to assemble the army upon the Côa. However he expected the Light Division to man outposts from Castello Rodrigo to Alfaiates, a distance of 65km. This meant moving all of his battalions to the east side of the Côa. The real decision for Craufurd was how to deploy his division as dictated by

---

47. Modern-day Castelo Rodrigo.
48. Modern-day Alfaiates.
49. *WD*, Vol. 5, pp.533–5.

Wellington's instructions. He had less than 3,400 men[50] and four artillery pieces[51] to cover an area that was essentially a two-day march from one end of the line to the other. Ciudad Rodrigo was held by a strong Spanish garrison, and the Spanish Fort Concepción was also along the main road from Ciudad Rodrigo and Almeida.

Craufurd's staff had conducted a reconnaissance of the Agueda River and knew that although long, the river itself served as a natural barrier that would be easy to defend.

> From where this river falls into the Douro, which it does about two leagues and a half North-East of Castello Rodrigo, to within half a league of Ciudad Rodrigo, its banks are very high, rugged, and difficult to pass, with the exception of three or four of the fords. From Ciudad Rodrigo upwards, its banks do not form any serious obstacle, also for half a league below it, they are quite low and flat. After heavy rain, it is impossible to ford the river from the Bridge of Navas Frias[52] (which is about two leagues South-East of Alayates)[53] to its mouth, and from thence to the Douro there are only three bridges,[54] viz., that of Villar,[55] which is about a league below Navas Frias, and that of Ciudad Rodrigo, which is under the guns of the place, and that of San Felices,[56] which is so exceedingly difficult to pass, from the banks of the

---

50. For the effective strength of the Light Division in mid-March 1810, see Appendix I.
51. Captain Ross's Royal Horse Artillery troop had only four of its six guns. Two guns under the command of Lieutenant William Elgee were at Santiago as part of the army's artillery reserve. Santiago is a village near Seia and about 120km southwest of Almeida. The British referred to the village as St. Jago.
52. Navasfrias, Spain. The village is about 50km south of Ciudad Rodrigo.
53. Modern-day Alfaiates
54. There were actually four bridges, the fourth being the bridge at Navasfrias.
55. The bridge at Villar is a medieval bridge built on the remains of an old Roman one. Its modern name is Puente Arrellanos. It is located 5km north of El Payo on CV-199 and 13.5km south of Fuenteguinaldo on the same road.
56. This is the bridge that in the gorge below Barba del Puerco.

river being uncommonly high and inaccessible, so that a small number of men may defend it against a large force.[57]

In March, the main threat was the French force that was 40km to the north of Ciudad Rodrigo in the vicinity of San Felicies de los Gallegos. Craufurd could not ignore this force and he reasoned that should the French move to threaten Ciudad Rodrigo from Salamanca he would have ample time to redeploy his forces. Thus he had the 95th Rifles to continue to cover the Agueda River in the north. Its headquarters was at Villa de Ciervo. A company was sent to Barba del Puerco to reinforce the three there, while there were also companies at La Bouza, Escarigo, and Almofala. The 43rd Foot was send forward to the Tourões River about 5km east of Almeida. The battalion headquarters was at Malpartida[58] and its companies were billeted in three villages: Malpartida in the north, Vale de Coelha in the centre and Vale da Mula in the south. They were responsible for a 12km stretch of the river. The 52nd Foot was kept as the division reserve and occupied the villages that the 95th Rifles vacated: Vilar Torpim, Reigada, Cinco Vilas. Captain Ross and four light 6-pounder guns were also brought forward. Their exact location is unknown, but they were probably co-located with the 43rd Foot in Vale da Mula.[59]

On 18 March 1810, the 1st KGL Hussars were formally attached to the Light Division.[60] This was the beginning of a long and close association between the Light Division and the KGL Hussars. The regiment was commanded by 55-year-old Lieutenant Colonel Friedrich von Arentschildt, an Hanoverian officer who joined the British Army in 1804 after Hanover was invaded by the French. He led the regiment from the time of their creation in January 1805. Von Arentschildt led them in the expedition to Hanover in 1805, the Baltic Expedition of 1806, and to the Peninsula in 1809. He was instrumental in honing them into the premier light cavalry regiment in the British Army. One of the things he did was

---

57. Shaw, pp.173–4.
58. Modern-day Malpartida de Plasencia.
59. Lieutenant Shaw has them at Aldea Bispo. I have not been able to find any town with that name. The closest is Aldea del Obispo, Spain, which is 3km east of Vale da Mula on the far side of Fort Concepción. Although possible, it puts the artillery forward of the supporting infantry. Shaw, p.168.
60. Beamish, Vol. 1, p.270.

write a manual for how his regiment would conduct outpost duties.[61] Lieutenant John Kincaid of the 95th Rifles later wrote that Arentschildt '. . . was a perfect soldier and worthy of being of such a band, for he was to them what the gallant Beckwith was to us – a father, as well as a leader!'[62] High praise from someone who was in a different regiment.

The 1st Hussars were given the responsibility of screening the division's right flank along a 70km stretch of the Agueda River from Villar de Ciervo to El Payo, Spain. The regimental headquarters and one squadron were located at Villa de Ciervo with a troop at Barba del Puerco and another at Villar de la Yegua. South of them was a squadron in reserve at Barquilla, while a third was 6km east of Barquilla at Serranillo along the river. The last squadron, under the command of Captain Georg Krauchenberg, showed up on the same day the regiment was attached to the Light Division and was sent to Gallegos. It was responsible for a 50km stretch south to El Payo. Krauchenberg kept his troop in Gallegos and sent another troop 20km south to Ituero de Azaba. The commander there was responsible for watching 27km of the river. To do this, he sent two out detachments, each commanded by an officer. One was at Fuenteguinaldo, about 10km from Ituero and another was sent to El Payo, which was 10km east of Navasfrias and 20km south of Fuenteguinaldo. In addition to these, a sergeant and eight hussars were also sent to Escalhão at the junction of the Agueda and Douro Rivers.[63]

To ease the passing of orders to the Hussars, Cornet Ernst Cordeman was unofficially assigned to Craufurd's staff.[64]

---

61. The booklet was called *Instructions for Officers and Non-Commissioned Officers of Cavalry on Outpost Duty* and was first published in 1809. It was re-published many times after that.
62. Kincaid, *Random Shots* . . ., p.96.
63. Shaw, p.177.
64. Ibid., p.170.

Chapter 3

Barba del Puerco,
19–31 March 1810

The Light Division was generally deployed along the Agueda River, which served as the border between Spain and Portugal in the region. Its headwaters are in the Serra das Mesas, a mountainous region south of Ciudad Rodrigo. It runs for about 130km in a northerly direction and flows into the Douro River close to Barca de Alva, Portugal. Except in the winter and early spring, when the weather can be very rainy, the river is not much of a military obstacle. Its banks are generally low and its width is less than 20m in most places. It can be forded by infantry and cavalry without too much difficulty, although it would be impassable for artillery.

About 10km north of Ciudad Rodrigo, the river begins to flow through 40km of a deep canyon until it reaches the plains around the Douro River. This gorge has high steep walls on both sides and during the rainy season the river is a torrent. From December through March, the only way it can be crossed by infantry is over the bridge between Barba del Puerco and San Felices de los Gallegos. This bridge was built circa 1250 AD.[1] Two kilometres to the west is the small village of Barba del Puerco, while the town of San Felices de los Gallegos is 8km to the east.

The bridge is about 50m long, 5m wide and 20m high. It would have been a major crossing point for any force moving into Portugal except there were no roads to it. Access from either side of the canyon is down a narrow, winding road that by 1810 was little more than a goat

---

1. The exact date is unknown. It was not the first bridge built there. The Romans built one a thousand years before.

path. The steep sides of the canyon fall over 250m in less than 600m.[2] The slopes were covered with rocky outcrops and very little vegetation.

Barba del Puerco[3] was a small farming village of about 100 buildings.[4] Most of these buildings were single storey. There was a small two-storey tavern in the centre of the town and a small chapel at the southern end of the village close to the path that led down to the bridge. Including the small farms in the immediate area, its population was about 600.[5]

General Craufurd recognized that Barba del Puerco was the closest point along the Agueda River to the nearest enemy forces. The French had demonstrated several times in the past month a willingness to send foragers across the bridge and into territory that the Light Division had responsibility for. Craufurd realized that if the French attacked in force he did not have the men to prevent them from taking the village. However, he could not just abandon it to the enemy. Instead he decided that it would serve as his most forward outpost. He ordered the 95th Rifles to send four rifle companies, about 350 officers and men, to the village. These included Captains Peter O'Hare's, Samuel Mitchell's and Francis Glass's companies.[6] They were to defend the village long enough to delay the enemy, but to retreat should the enemy be too strong.

---

2. About 25 degrees of slope or 44 per cent of slope. Degree of slope is measured by taking the height of a hill and dividing it by the horizontal distance from its bottom to its top.

3. The village changed its name to Puerto Seguro in the early twentieth century.

4. Burnham, Robert, 'Estimated Population of Spain and Portugal in 1808', *The Napoleon Series Online*, February 2019.

5. The last national census was conducted in 1797 and gave its population as 609. de Miñano y Bedoya, Sebastián, *Diccionario geografico-estadistico de España y Portugal*, 11 vols. Madrid, 1826–9, Vol. XI, p.93.

6. I have not been able to identify the fourth company. Nor have I found any primary source that definitively states that Captains Mitchell's and Glass's companies were present. However, the quarterly Battalion Pay Rolls lists every soldier's company number and whether he was a casualty. I then took the list of casualties and cross referenced them against the list of company commanders and their company number that can be found on p.272 of Volume 2 of George Caldwell's and Robert Cooper's *Rifle Green in the Peninsula* 4 vols. Leicester: Bugle Horn, 1998. The unidentified company took no casualties.

The general had very specific ideas on how his division should perform its outpost duties. These ideas were the basis for his *Standing Orders* to the division. They included preparing to march, what to do on the march, how to march over difficult terrain and through defiles, how to prevent straggling, baggage, assigning billets and duties in the camp. The *Standing Orders* provided very detailed instructions for the officers and non-commissioned officers. They were updated as the situation required.[7] The *Standing Orders* were expected to be followed and the wrath of General Craufurd would come down upon the officer who was caught disobeying them.

Although the *Standing Orders* were very specific when it came to outpost duty, Craufurd did allow the commanders some latitude in how they set up an outpost. Articles I, II, III, and IV of Section IV 'Duties in Camp or Quarters' covered picquets and outposts. Lieutenant Simmons of the 95th Rifles, left a detailed account of life at Barba del Puerco, especially how the four rifle companies set up and ran the outpost there. They closely followed the *Standing Orders* including the ones below.

Article I. Number of Officers on Duty[8]

2. When there are not a sufficient number of Field Officers to do this duty without material inconvenience, the senior Captain of one or more regiments of the brigade will take the duty of Field Officer of the inlying piquet [*sic*], and will of course be exempted from the regimental duty as Captain of the day, or of the inlying piquet; but he will take his tour of outlying piquets.

5. The number of Officers on duty, or in waiting in each battalion (exclusive of those on outlying piquets) will, at all times, as long as the brigade remains abroad, and whether in camp or cantonments, consist of one Captain, and two Subalterns of each wing, who must constantly remain in camp, or quarters. Lieutenants commanding companies may be ranked as Captains for this duty, but the roster must be so regulated, that there shall not be less than one effective Captain.

---

7.   Campbell, William and James Shaw, *Standing Orders as Given Out and Enforced by the Late Major-Gen. Rob Craufurd for the Use of the Light Division during the Years 1809, 10, and 11.* Godmanchester: Ken Trotman, 2006, pp.v–vii.

8.   Campbell, pp.36–7.

6. The Officers on duty, or in waiting in the lines, as directed in the preceding paragraph, will have charge of the inlying picquet by day, when there is one, and will besides do all the orderly and other internal regimental duties, including the quarter guards.

7. They will always leave word at the quarter, or barrack guard, and at their own tent, or quarters, where they are to be found.

Article II. Piquets[9]
1. The outlying piquets will, in general, consist of one company per battalion; when more are required, or less are sufficient, it will be notified in orders.

3. When inlying piquets are required by day, they will consist of one-fourth of the Non-commissioned Officers and privates of each company who are not upon duty, and will be commanded by the Officer on duty, or in waiting as mentioned in paragraph No. 5 of the first Article of this Section.

4. The company's piquet will be allowed to leave off duty, a sufficient number of men to draw provisions, and cook; and the Brigade-Major will therefore, from time to time, give out in brigade orders, the number of rank and file, which the companies of the several regiments are to produce under arms on piquet.

5. The inlying piquet will be inspected after the evening parade of the brigade, by the Field Officer of the day, and will remain accoutered, and in constant readiness to turn out, during the night.

Article IV Orders to Guards[10]
1. The Officer on Guard, or piquet, is to write down all orders which he receives, whether these orders come to him verbally or in writing, and deliver over these orders in writing, to the Officer who relieves him.

2. In order to simplify the duties of the sentries, each individual man is to retain the same post during the whole of the guard, or piquet; that is to say, that each time a man goes on duty as a sentry, he must have the same post that he had the first time; the most intelligent, trusty, and experienced soldiers being chosen for the most difficult and important post.

---

9.   Campbell, pp.38–9.
10. Ibid., pp.40–1.

3. The Officers will most particularly examine each sentry upon his post, respecting the orders that he has received, immediately after he is placed there the first time; and before he is marched off, to take the same post a second time, the Officer will question him for the purpose of ascertaining whether he recollects his orders.

4. It is the duty of the Officers to ascertain that every individual is instructed in what he has to do, and it is to them, therefore, that the responsibility attaches, if any accident or irregularity shall occur in consequence of orders not being accurately given.

Although only four of the battalion's ten companies were sent to Barba del Puerco, Lieutenant Colonel Beckwith decided to accompany them. Legend has it that he and his staff set up their headquarters in the tavern.[11] The village chapel would serve as the staging post for the company on picquet duty. Each company was given their own section of the town, and generally eight soldiers would be billeted together in one building. The officers were billeted in the same area as their company. After the company was dismissed to their billets, the NCOs were brought together and the officers' billets were shown to them.[12]

For medical support, the 1st Battalion 95th Foot had Surgeon Joseph Burke and Assistant Surgeon William Jones assigned to it.[13] Because there more likely to be casualties with the four companies at Barba del Puerco than with the six companies in the rear, Surgeon Burke also went there. Assistant Surgeon Jones remained with the rest of the battalion.

Unlike other areas, as long as the heavy rains continued the Agueda River was impassable, so setting up picquets was fairly simple to do

---

11. I was told this by my guide during a visit to the village in 2018. I found no contemporary source that verifies it. However, the tavern was one of the largest buildings in the village, so it would make sense.
12. Campbell, pp.31–5.
13. Assistant Surgeon Joseph Abbell was also assigned to the battalion but not present with it. The March 1810 *Army List* has him assigned to the 1st Battalion. Lionel Challis's 'The Peninsular Roll Call' also has him assigned to the battalion and in the Peninsula. The theatre returns for February also has him with the battalion, however the returns for March and April do not. He may have been on detached duty at a hospital in the rear.

at Barba del Puerco. The only approach the French could make was across the bridge. The rushing river deep in the canyon, combined with intermittent rain, masked the sounds of approaching troops, so the picquets had to be posted as far forward as possible to prevent surprise. The outlying picquet's job was to sound the alarm should the enemy come and then retreat back up the hill. This warning would alert the duty company that something was amiss and they in turn would notify the troops in Barba del Puerco to stand to and be ready for the enemy.

The Rifles' plan was fairly simple. Picquet duty was rotated between the companies with each taking a 24-hour shift before being relieved by the next company on the roster. The outlying picquet would consist of a two-man outpost on the near side of the bridge. About 50m up the trail a corporal and six men were placed to provide support to those on the bridge. Near the top of the ridge was the inlying picquet of a sergeant and ten men. The picquets would be changed every four hours. The rest of the duty company stayed in the chapel on the top of the hill. A tent was pitched near the chapel for the duty officers. These officers and men had to be ready to respond at a moment's notice. They were allowed to sleep, but were not permitted to remove their clothes or accoutrements. The exact locations of the outlying picquets varied depending on which company had the duty. To keep the French from knowing the locations of the picquets, they were posted at night and then withdrawn before first light. During the day, a watch was kept at the top of the ravine to ensure the French made no sudden movements across the bridge.[14]

The Rifles shared the picquet duties with a company of Spanish infantry.[15] They would picquet a trail that broke off from the main path and came up the hill further south of the village. The duty company was responsible for sending a corporal and several men there to serve as liaison with them.[16]

On the far side of the river were the French picquets. They were set up in a similar way to the British. On the French side of the river was a small stone building that they used to shelter the small outpost they kept at the bridge. Further up the hill were another seventy men. Depending on the source, relations between the two opposing picquets were either

---

14. Green, p.26. Costello, Edward, *The Peninsular and Waterloo Campaigns.* Hamden: Archon Books, 1968, p.25. Simmons, pp.61–2.
15. I have not been able to find which regiment this company belonged to.
16. Simmons, p.55.

very hostile or very friendly. Twenty-four-year-old Lieutenant Simmons wrote that 'we for some time were in the habit of looking at each other with only about half a mile in a direct line between us. They now and then tried to pick some of our men off, but their shots never took effect.'[17] Twenty-one-year-old Rifleman Edward Costello supported this, claiming that

> we were greatly harassed; our picquets and the French were constantly in the habit of firing at each other, and scarce a day passed without some of the men being brought in, either killed or wounded. We had not yet established that understanding with the enemy, which avoided unnecessary bloodshed at the outposts which afterwards tended much to humanize the war.[18]

Twenty-six-year-old Rifleman Green, however, had a different experience. He wrote that

> In the day time we had orders not to fire unless they came over the bridge. We used to hold up our canteens of wine and ask them to come over and drink with us. They would answer in the Spanish language, 'They would come that night.' We little thought that they would make the attempt but they did.[19]

Although the enlisted men manned the outposts, the officers still had to check up on them throughout the night. The weather tended to be overcast and quite dark, even though within a week there would be a full moon.[20] This could cause problems for the officers checking the outposts. One night about midnight, Lieutenant Simmons went down the hill to visit the sentries when he got lost and spent the rest of the night wandering the hillside.[21]

Captain Peter O'Hare's company had outpost duty on 19 March. According to Lieutenant Simmons, the company disembarked in Portugal the previous July with 100 officers and men. But eight months of active campaigning had taken a toll on it and the company could now only

---

17. Simmons, p.61.
18. Costello, p.29.
19. Green, p.26.
20. The full moon was on 21 March at 02.39 hours.
21. Simmons, p.61.

muster four officers and forty-three men.[22] The accuracy of this number cannot be determined. Three weeks previously, the battalion had reported in its monthly returns that it had 872 sergeants, buglers and other ranks fit for duty for an average of 87 per company. It is highly unlikely that the company would be short 50 per cent of its effective strength without engaging in any combat.

O'Hare was the senior captain in the regiment and was one of the original officers assigned to the Experimental Corps of Riflemen in 1800. He had commanded his company since its formation in August 1803. He was noted for his ferociousness in battle and a contemporary called him a 'truly gallant soldier'.[23] One soldier in his company described him as '. . . a man whose eccentric habits were equalled only by his extremely ugly countenance. . . as brave as a lion. . .'.[24] Despite this open familiarity with the ranks he was a strict disciplinarian and would not tolerate thieves or drunkenness. The previous December, his boots were stolen. The culprit was caught, tried and sentenced to be flogged. O'Hare 'had command of the detachment when the sentence of the court-martial was put into execution. He gave the man every lash, and recommended the buglers to lay it on lustily and save the fellow from the gallows.'[25] He was also known to break up any of the soldiers' stills whenever he came across one.[26]

Yet O'Hare truly cared for his men and they loved him for it. They referred to him as Peter, although it is doubtful they ever called him that to his face.[27] He took the time to get to know his men and was known to give them impromptu words of encouragement. In 1811, the company had just received several new recruits who were about to go into battle for the first time, he

> . . . thought proper to say a few words by way of advice to them, on so momentous an occasion; accordingly, he gave the command, 'Recruits to the front'. Some ten or twelve immediately stepped forward, wondering, no doubt, what they were wanted for.

22. Simmons, pp.63–4.
23. Leach, *Rough Sketches*. . ., p.258.
24. Costello, p.6.
25. Simmons, p.41.
26. Costello, p.43.
27. Ibid., p.6.

'Do you see those men on that plain?' Asked the Major,[28] as he pointed to the French camp. On several of the men answering 'Ees Zur!' Major O'Hare, with a dry laugh continued, 'Well then, those are the French, and our enemies. You must kill those fellows, and not allow them to kill you. You must learn and do as those old birds here do,' pointing to us, 'and get cover where you can. Recollect, recruits, you come here to kill, and not be killed. Bear this in mind: if you don't kill the French they'll kill you.' – 'Ees, Zur!' Said they again. The Major's logic, although it elicited roars of laughter from the old soldiers, I believe had more effect with the recruit than if Demosthenes had risen for the purpose.[29]

Sunset was at 6:21 p.m. and nautical twilight[30] was at 7:20 p.m. In two days it would be a full moon and the moon began to rise about 6 p.m. and would reach peak about 2:30 a.m. Dawn would begin with nautical twilight at 5:17 a.m. and sunrise at 6:16 a.m. The moon would not set until 7:30. It was slightly overcast, but an occasional wind kept the clouds from obscuring the moon.[31]

In addition to being responsible for the outposts, Captain O'Hare's company was also responsible for the manning the interior guard posts. They would be manned throughout the night and the sentries were relieved every two hours. At 9 p.m. Rifleman Green was the sentry at Lieutenant Colonel Beckwith's and Adjutant Stewart's[32] quarters in the tavern. 'The adjutant came out and asked me the time of night? I said, "It is about 10, sir." He said, "The colonel and me sleep in this lower room; if any alarm is made you will tap this window." When I was relieved I gave this additional order to the man who took my post.'[33] After he was relieved, Rifleman Green returned 'to the picquet-house,[34]

---

28. This incident happened on 14 March 1811 at Casal Novo. Captain O'Hare would not be promoted to major until the following month.
29. Costello, p.58.
30. The time when the sun is below the horizon but some sunlight and stars can be seen.
31. Costello, p.25.
32. 1st Lieutenant James Stewart.
33. Green, p.26.
34. The chapel at the south end of the village.

put my rifle in a certain place, lay down with the men, and dropped asleep; it was still and quiet.'[35]

About 8 p.m. Captain O'Hare and Lieutenant Simmons went forward to post the sentries. They walked down the hill and stopped about 50m from the bridge, where Sergeant Tuttle Betts and twelve men would serve as the main outlying post. Their orders in the event of the enemy attacking they were to try to hold their ground until the duty company came to their assistance. The two officers and Riflemen Thomas Maher and John M'Cann crept further down the hill and stopped at a large rock about 15m from the bridge. This would be the forward outpost. The two riflemen were to stay alert and if the French approached they were fire their rifles to alert the other outposts and then retreat back to where the sergeant and the sentries were. After placing the two sentries, Lieutenant Simmons was ordered to cross the bridge to retrieve a paper that was in the building on the far side. He crawled across the bridge 'to the French side to see if I could see their sentries or observe if any of them were coming near the bridge, but saw nothing'.[36] He and O'Hare climbed back up the hill to the picquet house. O'Hare was not feeling well, so he turned over command of the outposts to Lieutenant James Mercer. In addition to Lieutenants Mercer and Simmons, the company also had Lieutenant Alexander Coane[37] with it. The outposts would be changed at midnight. No one expected anything but a quiet night or should there be action, it would be a firefight between the outposts that would quickly die down. They could not have been more wrong.

The French were preparing to invade Portugal and needed to take Ciudad Rodrigo first. They knew that the forward elements of the British army were along the border with Portugal but were not sure of the British intentions. Would they stay forward and try to prevent the capture of Ciudad Rodrigo, or would they move back to the Tagus and Guadiana Rivers? to Général de Division Louis Henri Loison, commander of the 3rd Division of Marshal Ney's 6th Corps, was ordered to find out. He sent orders to General Ferey to take his brigade, which was occupying San Felices de los Gallegos, to probe the British lines. He was to 'disperse the enemy's advance posts on the Agueda and push on as far as possible

---

35. Green, p.26.
36. Lieutenant Simmons never revealed what the paper was or why he was sent to retrieve it. Simmons, pp.52 and 62.
37. Lieutenant Simmons misspells his name as Cowan. Ibid., p.54.

to Almeida'.[38] His brigade consisted of three battalions of the 66th Line Regiment, two battalions from the 82nd Line Regiment, one battalion of the 32nd Light Regiment, and the two-battalion Hanoverian Legion, a total of about 3,500 men. How many men actually were part of the operation is not known. Since it was a reconnaissance in force and he had no intention of occupying ground west of his cantonments in San Felices, Ferey had to leave part of his brigade to guard his rear. It is likely that only troops from the 82nd Line and 32nd Light Regiments took part. The number of men was probably not more than 1,500.

Ferey formed a combined battalion from the two grenadier companies of the 82nd Line and the carabinier company of the 32nd Light. They would quietly march down the steep path to the bridge and assault across it. They hoped they would be able to take the British by surprise and be on top of the far side of the canyon before they could react. Rumour had it that Ferey had promised '. . . them there was only one company of the British in the village, and he would give each man a Spanish dollar, with a double allowance of bread and wine, if they would storm the hill!'[39] He also admonished them to 'to bring all the English wounded and take care of them, and not use the prisoners ill'.[40] Once the combined battalion was across the river, the rest of the brigade would descend into the canyon and line the river bank to provide fire support.

About 11 p.m. Ferey moved his brigade for several kilometres along a trail that was little more than a muddy goat path down the steep canyon side. In order to prevent the British outposts from learning of their approach no lights could be used to mark the path. The general hoped that the rushing river would mask the sounds of the moving troops, but there was a chance that an accidental discharge of a musket or a soldier cursing as he stumbled and fell was likely to alert the sentries on the other side of the river. In what had to be one of the greatest feats of sound and light discipline in the history of Napoleonic warfare, the French troops made it to the river undetected.

The French grenadiers and carabiniers rushed across the bridge and were finally spotted by the two British riflemen at the base of the hill. One of them was able to get a shot off before they were overpowered and

---

38. Letter from Marshal Ney to General Junot, dated 23 March 1810. Quoted in Horward, pp.19–20.
39. Green, p.27.
40. Simmons, p.64.

taken prisoner. This shot alerted Sergeant Betts and the twelve men who were 50m up the hill. The French quickly pushed on and were brought under fire by the picquet. Betts realized that his small detachment could not slow the down the French and ordered his men to fall back as fast as possible. His orders did not come too soon, as he was shot in the jaw. Despite his grievous wound, his men did not abandon him and helped him up the hill.[41]

All surprise was lost and the French commander ordered their drummers to beat the 'Pas-de-Charge', a tune played when French troops were attacking.[42] The sound of so many shots and the beating of the French drums quickly alerted the duty officers that it was not just random shots by the picquets. First Lieutenant James Mercer, a near-sighted 26-year-old Scot from Catterline, Kincardineshire who wore glasses,[43] was the senior officer present. He immediately sent Lieutenant Coane to find Captain O'Hare and let him know what was going on. Lieutenant Simmons was sent to rouse the riflemen in the chapel who were off-duty and get them ready to fight. Rifleman Green '. . . was awoke by the voice of the officers with the words "Be quick men, and load as you go to the brow of the hill!" I jumped up, got my rifle, and overtook them.'[44]

As the men rushed out of the chapel into the dark, they were met by Mercer who formed them into a column to march them the 300m to the crest of the ridge.[45] For some of the men, it was the first time they were under fire. Among them was Rifleman Costello:

> I was now, as it were, but a young sleepy-headed boy, and as yet had been scarcely around to a true sense of the profession I had embraced. I had never been under the fire of a French musket, and I felt an indescribable thrill on this occasion. The chilly hour of the night and peculiar inclination to sleep, at the time, had sunk my senses below zero. But I was speedily startled out of my lethargy by the whizzing of the enemies' bullets, as they greeted my astonished hearing. My surprise soon, however, gave place to perfect recollection, and in less than a minute we were all under

---

41. Simmons, p.55.
42. The British soldiers nicknamed this tune 'Old Trousers'.
43. Simmons, p.63.
44. Green, p.26.
45. Simmons, p.62.

arms, the balls of the French whistling about us as a column came rushing over the bridge to force our position.[46]

As the Rifle company moved forward they were met by the outposts who had moved rapidly up the steep slope. They were closely followed by a mass of men. There was some confusion on who they were. They challenged the men in front of them and received the response that they were Spanish. Mercer yelled '"Don't fire, men, they are not French." The words were scarcely out of his mouth, when a musket-ball struck him on the head, and he was a corpse in a minute.'[47]

Lieutenant Simmons gives a different version of the incident.

We soon met a man coming with information that the French were passing the bridge in great force. We marched forward and found them forming in line, with drums beating and yelling furiously. They fired to the amount of five hundred rounds, the balls whistling over our heads.

Our gallant Commander ordered us not to let the men fire until we came within fifteen yards of them. The French fired another volley. We still moved on as silent as possible, fired, and gave them an English huzza. The men opposed to us were a little staggered. We again loaded and came breast to breast. Lieutenant Mercer called, 'Simmons,' and rushed on towards a stone several had got behind, while he drove others in front. Our men were shooting them in every direction . . . [48]

Mercer realized that he had not put on his glasses and paused to do so. He turned to Simmons and 'an unlucky ball passed through poor Mercer's head just as he was saying, "Our brave fellows fight like Britons." At this moment three or four fell wounded near him.'[49]

After Mercer was killed, Simmons took command. For the next 15 minutes Captain O'Hare's company stood and fought the French onslaught.

In a moment, after the arrival of the main body of the piquet, the French were literally scrambling up the rocky ground within ten

---

46. Costello, pp.25–6.
47. Green, p.27.
48. Simmons, pp.62–3.
49. Ibid., p.62.

yards of us. We commenced firing at each other very spiritedly. Their drums beat a charge, and the French attempted to dislodge us without effect. . . Several were now falling, and the moon for a few minutes shone brightly, then disappeared, and again at intervals let us see each other. We profited by this circumstance, as their belts were white and over their greatcoats, so that where they crossed upon the breast, combined with the glare of the breast-plate, gave a grand mark for our rifles. Our men being in dark dresses, and, from their small number, obliged to keep close together, the ground also being exceedingly rugged, were all favourable circumstances.[50]

Rifleman Green saw

about 500 big grenadiers, half drunk, had made a rush over, and extending themselves, were climbing the rocks, and out-flanked our little company, both right and left . . . The moon shone very bright, so that we could see them; they were spent out climbing up the rocks. Three of these big ugly fellows came within ten yards of me and my front-rank man; I had got my ball in my rifle, but had not time to return the ramrod, so both ball and ramrod went through one of them. My comrade fired, and the ball struck another in the breast. I threw my rifle down, as it was no use to me without a ramrod, and retired about 20 yards. A sergeant of ours lay on his back, a musket ball having passed through his belly, I said 'Sergeant Bradley,[51] are you wounded?' He was groaning, poor fellow; and I said 'Lend me your rifle I have fired my ramrod away with the ball! I had not time to return it, as the Frenchman had his firelock at his shoulder, and probably in another moment I might have been killed or wounded!' The sergeant bid me take his rifle, and said 'It is of no use to me, they have done me, I am dying!' I left him; and running to join my comrade, I saw our officer stretched on his back, his sword in one hand, and his spy-glass in the other. I said 'Mr. Mercer, are you wounded?' but his spirit had fled.[52]

---

50. Simmons, p.54.
51. Rifleman Green is slightly mistaken. The man was Private James Brady of Captain Glass's company. He had been a sergeant but had been reduced to private earlier in the month.
52. Green, p.26.

While the initial fighting continued, Lieutenant Coane was able to find Captain O'Hare who rushed to the scene of the fight. '. . . .with his characteristic coolness, immediately gave us the word to "seek cover", and we threw ourselves forward among the rocky and broken ground, from whence we kept up a galling fire upon those who had commenced storming our heights'.[53] Lieutenant Simmons' description of the initial stages of the fight was different than Riflemen Costello's and Green's. He wrote home a few weeks later

> Our gallant Commander [Lieutenant Mercer] ordered us not to let the men fire until we came within fifteen yards of them. The French fired another volley. We still moved on as silent as possible, fired, and gave them an English huzza. The men opposed to us were a little staggered. We again loaded and came breast to breast. . . A French officer I had the satisfaction to see fall also. A fine young fellow put his rifle to the officer's throat and shot him dead, crying out, 'Revenge the death of Mr. Mercer'. He instantly received seven shots in his body. At this time the enemy were surrounding us in every direction. Captain O'Hare called out, 'We will never retire. Here we will stand. They shall not pass but over my body.' The shots flew round us as thick as hailstones, and they were advancing upon us, but we kept up a terrible fire. The moon showed sufficiently to let us see their numbers. I saw French officers beating their men with their swords to make them try to drive us from the rocks we occupied, and several letting their muskets fall and clapping their hands upon their sides or arms when they had received a wound and scampering.[54]

It is likely that Captain O'Hare sent Lieutenant Coane to the tavern to inform the battalion commander of the situation with the outposts. Lieutenant Colonel Beckwith immediately alerted the other three companies. One company was sent to the right where a path led up from the bridge, while Captain Glass's and Mitchell's companies were sent to reinforce O'Hare.[55] They were a welcome sight.

---

53. Costello, p.26.
54. Simmons, p.63.
55. Lieutenant Simmons stated it was half an hour. Simmons, p.54.

I saw the three companies[56] coming to our assistance – the pleasantest sight I ever beheld. We set up a most furious shout. The French soon knew the reason. Our companies fixed swords and came on like lions, the Colonel at their head, the French scampering off in the greatest dismay, throwing down their arms and running down the precipices and carrying off their killed and wounded, as they generally endeavour to do, in order that the number they lose should not be well ascertained by their enemies. . . The French, luckily for us, fired very high, or, from their great superiority, they must have destroyed every man of our company before the other three came to our assistance.[57]

Despite the much-needed reinforcements, the fight continued for some time. Lieutenant Colonel Beckwith was in the thick of the fighting.

We were exceedingly hard pressed when three companies of our regiment, under Colonel Beckwith, came up to our relief, and the contest for a while was both doubtful and bloody. But, after about an half an hour's hard fighting, the enemy were obliged to retreat with much precipitation, and under a close and murderous fire from us. During this brief conflict some incidents occurred that, perhaps, are worth mentioning. Colonel Beckwith actually employed himself, at one time, in heaving large fragments of stone upon the French as they attempted to ascend the acclivity on which we were placed . . . Another officer of ours, the adjutant, Lieutenant Stewart, a fine tall fellow, was engaged in a personal contest with two or three grenadiers, a number of whom had managed to ascend the hill on our right; at this critical moment one of our men, named Ballard,[58] fortunately came to his aid, and shot one of his assailants, at which the other instantly surrendered.[59]

---

56. Most sources states that all three companies were sent. However, Lieutenant Colonel Beckwith was worried that the French might outflank his position by taking the path up the ridge that was guarded by the Spanish on his right. Leach, Jonathan, *Sketch of the Services of the Rifle Brigade*. London: T. & W. Boone, 1836, p.12.
57. Simmons, p.63.
58. Rifleman George Ballard.
59. Costello, p.26.

Lieutenant Colonel Beckwith was almost killed in the fight.

A young Frenchman that was taken, fired into Colonel Beckwith's face. A Rifle Man was just going to blow his brains out, when the Colonel stopped him, saying, 'Let him alone; I daresay the boy has a mother. Knock the thing out of his hand, that he may do no more mischief with it, and give a kick on the bottom and send him to the rear.' The next morning the boy was given a hearty breakfast at the Colonel's house. On being questioned about firing so wantonly, he said he was in such agitation that he was not aware his finger was upon the trigger of his gun. The ball through the Colonel's cap peak, which, being turned up, made it take a slanting direction; it passed through and grazed the top of his head.[60]

Eventually the French had had enough and retreated back down the hill. The British remained on high alert and the companies were posted in a chain along the top of the hill.[61]

While the fighting was going on, the corporal and several riflemen who were on the far right with the Spanish company heard the firing. The Spanish commander was considering withdrawing from the unknown force and suggested the corporal do so also. The corporal refused to abandon his post and saying he '. . . was determined to wait until the enemy over-powered him . . .'. The Spanish captain lost control of his company and all but him and four of his men fled. This outpost was eventually relieved by other riflemen.[62]

The following morning search parties were sent out to find their missing friends and any French who had not made it across the river. Rifleman Green was in one of the parties.

We were ordered to climb the rocks to see if there were any wounded. Me and my comrade found a young Frenchman with his head in the hole of a rock, and his legs and part of his body were visible. I said 'Here's a wounded Frenchman.' I laid hold of his legs and pulled him out. He had received no wound, and appeared to be about eighteen years of age. He most likely was

---

60. Simmons, pp.54–5.
61. Green, p.27.
62. Horward, pp.20–1. Simmons, p.55.

frightened, as it might have been the first time he had been in action. We took him to the top of the hill where the rest of the prisoners stood with a guard around them.[63]

Casualties among the British were heavy. Captain O'Hare's company lost one officer, a sergeant, and ten riflemen. They were all buried in a common grave. Among the wounded were Sergeant Betts, who had been shot in the jaw and Rifleman 'William David, who had his skull blown off and his dura mater exposed'.[64] Despite the severity of his wound, Rifleman David lived for another 24 hours before dying. Rifleman Green claims that they had 'killed, one officer, one sergeant, ten rank and file; wounded, one sergeant, one corporal, and six rank and file. The wounded all died afterwards, save one. We buried the officer, sergeant, and ten men in one grave.'[65] Lieutenant Simmons wrote later that 'In the morning we found our loss to be one officer and five men killed, seven men badly wounded. The other three companies lost two killed and eight wounded.'[66]

There is some doubt about the accuracy these figures. For example Lieutenant Simmons wrote in his journal that Rifleman Robert Fairfoot was taken prisoner but there is no record of him being so. He also lists Rifleman Cornelius Gallegher[67] as being killed, which he was not.[68] A check of the monthly pay roll states only one officer and two riflemen killed, five riflemen wounded of whom three died from their wounds, and two riflemen captured and wounded. How they determined the two captured men were wounded is not said.

Rifleman William Green said Rifleman Cornelius Gallagher who was in his company died of his wounds. According to the Pay Rolls Rifleman Gallagher was not a casualty.

It is difficult to determine the extent of the French casualties. Lieutenant Simmons initially claimed that the search parties had found

Two French officers, a Light Infantry captain and a subaltern, and seventeen men lay stretched upon the rough ground.

63. Green, p.27.
64. Simmons, p.55.
65. Green, p.27.
66. Simmons, p.64.
67. Cornelius Gollougher.
68. Simmons, p.55.

Table 3.1: 1st Battalion 95th Rifles Casualties at Barba del Puerco 19–20 March 1810

Company	Casualty
Captain O'Hare's	Lieutenant James Mercer killed
	Rifleman John Whitney killed
	Rifleman Patrick Bachan died of wounds on 16 April 1810
	Rifleman William David died of wounds on 21 March 1810
	Sergeant Tuttle Betts wounded in the jaw
	Rifleman Thomas Maher captured and wounded
	Rifleman John M'Cann captured and wounded
Captain Mitchell's	Rifleman John Rouse wounded
Captain Glass's	Rifleman William Matthews killed
	Rifleman Thomas Blythe died of wounds on 20 March
	Rifleman James Brady died of wounds on 20 March

We afterwards heard from a deserter that the colonel who led the attack was shot through the mouth and his jaw broken. He was making a great noise before, but this circumstance made him so quiet that a child might have played with him. Several other officers were wounded and a number of men were carried off during the affray.[69]

Six weeks later, in letter to his father he said that they '. . . found twelve Frenchmen and two officers killed. Some of them had six or seven wounds. We also picked up five poor fellows most desperately wounded and caught three prisoners.'[70]

However, French sources list only two officer casualties: Sous-Lieutenant Périé of the 32nd Light Regiment as being killed and Captain Capdevielle of the 82nd Line Regiment as being wounded. There is no record of a French colonel being wounded.[71] At least one French sergeant was wounded in the knee and had been captured. Surgeon Burke, with

---

69. Simmons, p.55.
70. Ibid., p.64.
71. Martinien, Aristide, *Tableaux par Corps et par Batailles des Officiers Tués et Blessés pendant les Guerres de l'Empire (1805 – 1815)*. Paris: Éditions Militaires, ND, pp.202 & 461.

the assistance of Lieutenant Simmons, was unable to save his leg and was forced to amputate it.[72]

For many of the riflemen, this was their first time in combat. For Lieutenant Simmons it gave him a huge boost in his confidence.

> This night gave me a good opinion of myself. I fought alone for some time with fearful odds, my friend dead at my feet. It had been often joked and told, 'Would you not like to be at home again?' After this night I was considered a soldier fit to face the devil in any shape. . . I consider myself very lucky in not receiving a scratch, being exposed so long to the enemy's fire. I now know what it is to meet the enemy in the field, and am confident I shall always do my duty when opposed to the foes of my country. My captain was pleased to say my conduct had given him the greatest satisfaction.[73]

General Craufurd and his staff were many kilometres away undertaking a reconnaissance of the southern sector of the division's area of responsibility. They spent the night of the attack and the following day in the vicinity of Fuenteguinaldo. The village was over 50km from Barba del Puerco and it was not until 9 p.m. on 20 March was he notified of the attack by a dispatch from Captain Campbell, the division's DAQMG. They left the village at 10 p.m. and rode 28km to Gallegos, arriving there at 1 a.m. After resting for several hours, Craufurd and Campbell rode 25km to Barba del Puerco to assess the situation. Lieutenant Shaw was sent to Almeida to inform General Cox, the city's governor.[74] It is possible that Cox already knew about the attack. It is unclear if he rode the 28km from Almeida to Barba del Puerco, but he did write a letter to Marshal William Beresford, the commander of the Portuguese Army, on 21 March:

> The bodies of two officers and seven men have been found dead, a sergeant and five men wounded have been taken prisoner, and three have been taken who were not wounded of the French . . . [a detachment of 50 Spanish soldiers] behaved shamefully: they all ran away except the captain and four men without

---

72. Simmons, pp.55–6.
73. Ibid., pp.56–7, 64–5.
74. Shaw, pp.173–4.

firing a shot, but as soon as the French retired they were all present to pillage the wounded, and would have gloriously put them to death if they had not been prevented by our soldiers.[75]

After seeing the situation at Barba del Puerco, Craufurd decided to reinforce the four rifle companies there. He ordered two more companies from the 95th Rifles, one company from the 43rd Foot and two companies from the 52nd Foot to the village. Lieutenant John Brumwell of the 43rd Foot was in the company that was sent there. It was a full moon the night they arrived and several officers decided to explore the site of the skirmish. They soon found the French were more alert than they had bargained for.

> It was nearly as light as day, therefore at early morning two officers and myself went down to see what was going on. Our curiosity tempted us to go to the bottom of the bank, and then to cross the bridge. Immediately we returned they commenced firing upon us. We were not more than three hundred yards from their sentries. Their balls came very near but they did no damage.[76]

After reviewing the events of the skirmish, Craufurd issued a division order recognizing the efforts of the 95th Rifles:

> Brigadier-General Craufurd has it in command from the Commander-in-Chief to assure Lieutenant-Colonel Beckwith and the officers of the 95th Regiment who were engaged at Barba del Puerco that their conduct in this affair has augmented the confidence he has in the troops when opposed to the enemy in any situation. Brigadier-General Craufurd feels peculiar pleasure in noting the first affair in which any part of the Light Brigade were engaged during the present campaign. That British troops should defeat a superior number of the enemy is nothing new, but the action reflects honour on Lieutenant-Colonel Beckwith and the Regiment, inasmuch that it was of a sort that Rifle Men of other Armies would shun. In other Armies the Rifle is considered ill calculated for close action with an

---

75. Horward, pp.20–1.
76. Brumwell, pp.42–3.

enemy armed with Musket and Bayonet, but the 95th Regiment has proved that the Rifle in the hands of a British soldier is a fully efficient weapon to enable him to defeat the French in the closest fight in whatever manner they may be armed. (Signed) T. Graham, D.A.G.[77]

On 23 March, Wellington wrote from Viseu to Craufurd about the fight, the situation in Spain and other matters affecting the Light Division.

I received this morning your letter of the 20th, informing me of the attack on the post at Barba de Puesco [sic], which I imagine ought to have been dated the 21st, and that the attack was made on the night of the 19th.

I beg that you will assure Colonel Beckwith, and the officers and soldiers under his command, that their conduct in this affair has augmented the confidence which I have in the troops, when opposed to the enemy in any situation.

If the wounded should be unable to march, you had better send them back to the hospital in Coimbra.

I think that the enemy are not likely to disturb you again at present. They have withdrawn Mortier's Corps[78] from its position at Zafra to Monasterio, at the entrance of the Sierra Morena, and it is probable that the corps at Merida will not stay long where it is.

I hope that you will find Mr. Downie,[79] whom I propose to send to you, as useful as you expected to find Mr. Ogilvie.[80] The latter has charge of a most important department, which cannot well be made over to another; and nothing but the urgency of the case could have induced the Commissary General

---

77. Simmons, p.56. Lieutenant Simmons was incorrect about who signed the order. It was signed by the Light Division's DAAG, Captain Henry Graham of the 26th Foot, not T. Graham.

78. Marshal Édouard Mortier, 1st Duc de Trévise, commanded the French 5th Corps.

79. Assistant Commissary General (ACG) John Downie served with the Light Division until May and then left the Peninsula.

80. ACG Ogilvie served in the Peninsula for most of the war, but was never assigned to the Light Division.

to allow him to go to you. You will find Mr. Downie, however, very active and intelligent.

I wish that I could send you some money, but we are in the greatest distress, and, what is worse, have no hopes of relief. The late gales have prevented the import of specie into Lisbon from Gibraltar and Cadiz, and the delay of the arrival of the packet as usual prevents the negotiation of bills at Lisbon. To this add, that Government leave me to my own inventions in this, as well as in other respects. If the money were now at Lisbon, a fortnight would elapse before it could possibly reach the army. But I fear there is no chance.

Is it true, as the Governor of Ciudad Rodrigo informs General Cox, that the enemy have withdrawn from that neighbourhood towards Salamanca again?

The 800 pairs of shoes are gone to Celorico for your division. The Caçadores[81] will be at Celorico, I think, tomorrow. Ten mules are gone to Almeida, to enable you to mount hussars for the communication duty.[82]

---

81. The 1st and 2nd Caçadores Battalions.
82. *WD*, Vol. 5, pp.568–9.

Chapter 4

23 March–30 April 1810

By late March, Napoleon's troops had occupied most of Spain except for Cadiz in the south and areas along the Portuguese border. There the fortress cities of Ciudad Rodrigo and Badajoz were still held by Spanish troops. Wellington knew that the French would eventually move into Portugal, but he did not know when. The most likely threat was from Marshal Ney's 6th Corps which was in the vicinity of Salamanca. Ney had the mission of taking Ciudad Rodrigo but had not been given the resources to do so. His command was scattered, with one division garrisoning Salamanca and another conducting operations 130km south in the vicinity of Plasencia. His third division was about 70km west centred around the town of Vitigudino. Furthermore, Ney had no heavy guns to subdue the defenders of the city. A small siege train, that had been sent from France for his use, was at Burgos in early March, about 250km away. It moved very slowly due to its heavy guns and it was unlikely that it would make it to Salamanca before the end of the month at the earliest. Compounding his problems, his siege engineers had arrived without their equipment and had no way of digging entrenchments. Despite the pressure from his superiors, Ney was not about to undertake the siege with Wellington and his army so close.[1]

The immediate threat to Ciudad Rodrigo and to the Light Division was General Loison's 3rd Division. General Craufurd had received intelligence on 24 March that estimated their strength at 6,000–7,000 men and four guns. Attached to Loison's division were the 3rd Hussars. The French division was too large to billet in one town so the troops were split between several towns and villages. Their cantonments were in Vitigudino, Yecla de Yeltes, Bañobárez and along the Agueda River at San Felices de los Gallegos. Each of the cantonment areas was about

---

1. Horward, pp.21–3.

10km from the other and in an emergency, could be reached in about two hours of hard marching.[2]

Craufurd was faced with a dilemma. The Agueda River was a natural barrier to set up his chain of outposts, but he had less than 5,000 troops to cover 130km of frontage. In the vicinity of Ciudad Rodrigo, for about 15km north and south, the river meanders through open countryside and during the dry season was passable to both infantry and cavalry. Further south, the course of the river runs through increasingly higher hills as it approaches its headwaters in the Sierra de Gata. As noted before, there are two bridges south of Ciudad Rodrigo at Navasfrias[3] and Casería Villar de Flores.[4] As the river flows north past Ciudad Rodrigo, where there is also a bridge, it travels through a steep canyon for about 50km.[5] The only bridge across the river north of Ciudad Rodrigo is at Barba del Puerco. About 20km north of Ciudad Rodrigo, in the vicinity of Serranillo, are three fords: one that crosses the river 600m to the southeast and connects the village of Castillejo de Martin Viejo, and the fords at Copera and Valldespino 1.5km and 2.5km north of Serranillo respectively.[6] During the winter months when there are heavy rains, the river is impassable except at the bridges.

The 130km of river front was a huge area of responsibility and Craufurd recognized that he could not effectively screen all of it. He also knew that Ciudad Rodrigo sat across the most likely French avenue of approach and thus the city protected the southern half of his sector. The Spanish troops would provide him with enough notice of any enemy force coming along the main road from Salamanca that he could deploy his division to counter them. Furthermore, he had been informed that a Spanish infantry division of about 2,000 men under the command of Major General Martin Carrera was located in Coria about 100km south of Ciudad Rodrigo. and thus would give him warning of any enemy troops advancing from that direction.

---

2. Shaw, p.176.
3. Navasfrias, Spain. The village is about 50km south of Ciudad Rodrigo.
4. The bridge is located where CV-199 crosses the Agueda. About 15km downstream of Navasfrias.
5. The river and the canyon are part of the Arribes del Douro y Águeda National Park.
6. A bridge now spans the river at the ford southeast of Serranillo. On modern maps the two fords north of the village are near Molino de Copera and Molino de Valdespino.

On 30 March, Wellington wrote to Craufurd with news and a warning about placing too much trust in General Carrera.

> I enclose a letter for General Carrera, in which I have requested him to communicate with you. I beg you to observe, however, that very little reliance can be placed on the report made to you by any Spanish General Officer at the head of a body of troops. They generally exaggerate on one side or the other, and make no scruple of communicating supposed intelligence, in order to induce those to whom they communicate it to adopt a certain line of conduct.
>
> The movement of the French through the Puerto de Baños[7] has been probably occasioned by their desire to oblige Carrera to fall back, and a wish to confine Ciudad Rodrigo on that side. They will find it difficult to cross the Alagon,[8] or to make any impression on that side.[9]

The only real threat Craufurd faced was from General Loison's troops located to the north of Ciudad Rodrigo. The majority of the division was within a day's march of the Agueda. Although the French had twice the number of men as he did, Craufurd decided to use the river to his advantage. As long as it rained, he knew that Loison could only cross it at Barba del Puerco. Yet Craufurd also could not ignore Wellington's warning about a possible threat coming from the south, despite Carrera's Spanish troops guarding the approach. Since he could not guard every place, his plan would be to use the 1st KGL Hussars to picquet the likely Agueda River crossing sites as well as the main approach from the south and to keep his infantry in reserve. Once he received word of where the French were advancing, he could move his troops to counter them.

The 1st KGL Hussars deployed accordingly. Lieutenant Colonel Arentschildt had one squadron based in Gallegos and it had the responsibility of covering the 70km stretch south to Navafrias. Its primary mission was to watch the southern approach from Coria. Another squadron would cover the fords in the vicinity of Serranillo. A third squadron was stationed

---

7. Puerto de Baños's modern name is Baños de Montemayor. It is about 80km northeast of Coria.
8. The 200km-long Alagón River is the main tributary of the Tagus River.
9. *WD*, Vol. 5, p.586.

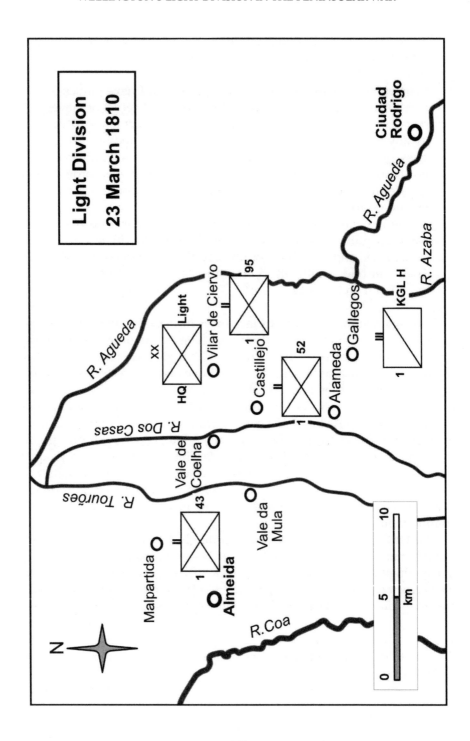

in Villar de Ciervo and it had the northern approaches, including Barba del Puerco. The fourth squadron was at Villar de la Yequa, which was halfway between Villar de Ciervo and Serranillo. The 95th Rifles would be placed so they could respond to any force approaching from either Barba del Puerco or Serranillo within 2–3 hours. The 43rd and 52nd Foot were located about a four or five-hour march from Barba del Puerco or Serranillo.

The 1st KGL Hussars manned their outposts 24 hours a day. The picquets were placed on high ground so that they could see any enemy movement at a distance. These individual outposts were visible to those on their left and right. Each position had a pile of wood that could be lit in the event the enemy advanced at night, which in theory would create a chain of beacons.[10] The practice of having a Rifles officer attached to the Hussars's picquets continued. Lieutenant Harry Smith was on one such picquet duty at the ford just east of Villar de Ciervo when one night:

Two of my vedettes (two Poles elegantly mounted) deserted to the enemy. The old sergeant, a noble soldier, came to me in great distress. 'O mein Gott, upstand and jump up your horse; she will surely be here directly!' I was half asleep, with my horse's reins in my hand, and roared out, 'Who the devil is she?' 'The Franzsen, mein Herr. Two d----d schelms have deserted.' So we fell back to the rear of the village, sitting on our horses the remainder of the night, every moment expecting the weakness of our party would cause an attempt to cut us off. At daylight we saw fifty French dragoons wending their way on the opposite bank to the ford. I immediately got hold of the padre and alcalde (priest and magistrate), and made them collect a hundred villagers and make them shoulder the long sticks with which the drive their bullock-carts and ploughs, which of course at a distance would resemble bayonets. These villagers I stationed in two parties behind two hills, so that the 'bayonets' alone could be seen by the enemy. Then with my sergeant and ten Hussars (two having deserted) I proceeded to meet the enemy, first riding backwards and forwards behind a hill to deceive him as to my numbers. The French sent over the river about half their number. I immediately galloped up to them in the boldest manner, and

10. Shaw, p.177.

skirmished advancing. The enemy were deceived and rapidly retired, and I saved the village from an unmerciful ransacking, to the joy of all the poor people.[11]

The weather turned rainy and as expected the Agueda River became flooded. On 23 March, Craufurd decided that there was not much chance of the French attacking and ordered all the infantry in Barba del Puerco to be withdrawn. They were replaced with a troop of 1st KGL Hussars.[12] The Light Division was re-deployed in the following locations

Division HQ:	Villar de Ciervo, Spain
1st Battalion 43rd Foot	HQ: Malpartida, Vale de Coelha, and Vale da Mula, Portugal
1st Battalion 52nd Foot	Castillejo, Spain[13] and Almeida, Portugal
1st Battalion 95th Rifles	HQ: Villar de Ciervo, Spain
Captain Ross's RHA Troop	Barquilla, Spain
1st KGL Hussars HQ	Gallegos, Spain
1st KGL Hussars sergeant and eight Hussars	Escalhão, Portugal[14]
1st KGL Hussars Troop	Barba del Puerco, Spain
1st KGL Hussars Squadron	Villar de Ciervo, Spain
1st KGL Hussars Troop	Villar de la Yequa, Spain
1st KGL Hussars Squadron	Barquilla, Spain
1st KGL Hussars Squadron	Serranillo, Spain
1st KGL Hussars Squadron	Gallegos, Spain
1st KGL Hussars Troops	Ituero de Azaba, Fuenteguinaldo, and El Payo, Spain

In an effort to appease his superiors in Madrid, Ney ordered Colonel Louis-Marie Levesque de la Ferrière, of the 3rd Hussars, to conduct a reconnaissance in force to the walls of Ciudad Rodrigo. He left San Felices de los Gallegos with 150 of his hussars and two infantry battalions on 24 March. He pushed back the Spanish outposts and was soon on the outskirts of the city. He took a handful of prisoners and then

---

11. Smith, pp.24–5.
12. Simmons, p.57. Brumwell, p.43. Shaw, p.177.
13. Modern-day Castillejo de dos Casas.
14. At the confluence of the Agueda and Douro Rivers.

retreated to San Felices unmolested by the British troops. He reported to Ney that there were no new defensive works.[15]

The order creating the Light Division gave it the Portuguese 1st and 2nd Caçadores Battalions as part of its establishment. Craufurd also asked for the 3rd Caçadores Battalion to be assigned to him. Wellington considered this, but on 21 March wrote back stating 'It impossible to get Elder's[16] corps for you, otherwise you may depend upon it that I should have been happy to make your division so much stronger.'[17] Wellington had some reservations about the quality of the two battalions and wrote to Craufurd on 26 March that:

> By this time you will have been joined by the 2 battalions of the caçadores, and will be the best judge what to do with them. I believe that Beresford[18] had attached to them Baron Eben,[19] whom you will find a useful officer; but I am not quite certain whether it was to them or to 2 other battalions. You will find the officer who commands the first battalion a very respectable one.[20] The 2d battalion is not so well commanded at present, but Beresford proposes to attach to it Major Nixon,[21] of the 28th regt., who has served in the light infantry, and who has been placed under his orders.[22]

The caçadores were raised in October 1808 and trained as light infantry. Each was organized into five caçadores companies of musket-armed troops, and a tiradore (sharpshooters) company armed with Baker rifles. They were authorized 683 officers and men.[23] In March 1809, an

---

15. Horward, p.21.
16. Lieutenant Colonel George Elder commanded the 3rd Caçadore Battalion.
17. *WD*, Vol. 5, p.559.
18. Marshal William Beresford, a British general who was appointed the commander of the Portuguese Army in March 1809.
19. Colonel Frederick Eben was a former Prussian officer. He was a major in the British De Roll's Regiment, when he joined the Loyal Lusitanian Legion in 1808.
20. Lieutenant Colonel Jorge de Avilez.
21. Major Robert Nixon.
22. *WD*, Vol. 5, p.575.
23. *Compilação das Ordens do Dia, Quartel General do Exercito Portuguez Concenentes a Organização, Disciplina, e Economia Miitares na Campanha de 1810*, pp.33–4.

effort to modernize its army, the Portuguese government authorized the recruitment of British officers.[24] The British government agreed to this plan and allowed any officer who joined the Portuguese service to retain their commissions in the British Army. As an inducement for joining the Portuguese Army, the British officers would be promoted to the next higher rank, i.e. a major in the British Army would be brought into the Portuguese Army as a lieutenant colonel. The plan was to have every infantry battalion or cavalry regiment commanded by a British officer or if the unit was commanded by a Portuguese officer, then the next senior officer would be British. The initial intake was 20 officers, but within 15 months, 158 British officers had joined the Portuguese Army.[25] Neither the 1st Caçadores nor the 2nd Caçadores had any British officers assigned to them in March 1810.

On 28 March word reached the division the two battalions were at Pinhel. From there they marched to Villar Torpim and were inspected by Craufurd on 5 April. The two battalions had a combined strength of about 700 men.[26] The general was not impressed with what he saw and wrote that night to Wellington about his concerns. Wellington replied on 9 April:

. . . regarding the Portuguese battalions of caçadores, which it is obvious are not in the state in which I expected that you would find them, from what I saw of them in December last. Bad troops in the rear of the army may do well enough; but it will not answer, obviously, to put those in the front who are likely to do more harm than good. . . the state of these corps disappoints me much. . . Elder's corps, which is better than the others, was kept in the rear to be an example to others, and to assist in their formation; for in the happy situation in which I am placed, I am obliged to be ready to meet the enemy in front, at the same time that the formation and organization of the young troops, and all the elementary arrangements, are to be provided for in the rear. I have ordered forward Elder's battalion, and when that arrives, the 2 others must return. But still Elder's battalion does not add sufficiently to your strength; and I doubt whether its

---

24. British non-commissioned officers were also recruited and given commissions.
25. de Brito, Pedro, *British Officers in the Portuguese Service 1809–1820*. Academia.edu. Accessed 7 March 2019.
26. Shaw, pp.177 & 179.

services in front will compensate for the disadvantages of its advance from the rear, and the want of its example in the formation of the others.[27]

Craufurd chose to ignore the orders for him to send the 1st and 2nd Caçadores to the rear, correctly thinking Wellington would not notice it for a while. On 30 April, Wellington wrote to him again about the caçadores, but this time to tell him that he could keep all three battalions.[28]

Wellington and Craufurd were not the only one with a less-than-favourable opinion of the caçadores. Lieutenant Colonel Benjamin D'Urban, the Quartermaster-General of the Portuguese Army, wrote in his journal on 10 April that 'The Brigade of Chasseurs (1st and 2nd) which were sent to General Craufurd, are returned unfit for service; this does not at all astonish me. Why they were sent I wonder – certainly the worst in the army.'[29] Lieutenant William Freer of the 43rd Foot wrote in a letter home that they were 'such miserable starved wretches I've seldom seen'.[30] Rifleman Costello was even more damning. He noted that:

They were the dirtiest and noisiest brutes I ever came across. . . I never knew them to perform one gallant act. On the line of march they often reminded me of a band of strollers. They were very fond of gambling, and every halt we made was sure to find them squatted, and with cards in their hands.[31]

It was quiet along the front during late March and early April. It had finally stopped raining on 25 March and the fords over the Agueda had become passable by 28 March. The weather continued to be cold and windy. The companies of the 52nd Foot, which were billeted in Almeida, were hit by an unknown fever and they were moved to Castillejo, where the rest of the battalion was. On 6 April at 10:00 a.m. Lieutenant Colonel Arentschildt came to the Division HQ in Villar de

27. *WD*, Vol. 6, pp.26–7.
28. Ibid., Vol. 6, p.69.
29. D'Urban, Benjamin, *The Peninsular War Journal: 1808–1817*. London: Greenhill Napoleonic Library, 1988, p.97.
30. Freer Family Letters. Unpublished letter from William Freer to his brother John dated 4 April 1810.
31. Costello, p.28.

Ciervo with news that a large body of French dragoons and infantry were along the river. The 95th Rifles, who were billeted in Villar de Ciervo, were alerted, as well as all of the 1st KGL Hussars. Craufurd and his staff rode the 8km to Serranillo and learned that about 200 dragoons and 300 infantry had been seen along the river. The French infantry were deployed at the Castillejo de Martin Viejo, Molino de Copera, and Molino de Valldespino Fords to prevent the British from crossing the river. Once the crossings were secured, the dragoons moved south to Saelices el Chico, where they gathered provisions, and then pulled back. As they withdrew and passed by each ford, the infantry abandoned their positions and marched back to San Felices. The dragoons served as the rearguard as the column returned to San Felices. Craufurd ordered Lieutenant Colonel Arentschildt to send a squadron[32] to cross the river at the Molino de Copera ford and chase them back to San Felices. The German hussars followed the retreating French north for about 10km until they reached the Granja River and then turned back. By the end of the day it began to rain with a mixture of snow.[33]

Rain continued for most of the next week, causing the fords to be impassable. On 8 April Craufurd took the opportunity to rotate his battalions. The 95th Rifles were replaced by the 52nd Foot and the 43rd Foot also moved locations. The new billets for the infantry were:

1st Battalion 43rd Foot	Vilar Formoso and São Pedro do Rio Seco, Portugal[34]
1st Battalion 52nd Foot	Villar de Ciervo, Spain
1st Battalion 95th Rifles	HQ: Malpartida, Vale de Coelha, and Vale da Mula, Portugal

On 11 April the 95th Rifles received word to consolidate the men from two companies and send the officers and some non-commissioned officers home. The battalion had arrived in Portugal on 2 July 1809 with 1,023 riflemen. By 25 March, they had lost 12 per cent of their effectives: 119 men dead and another 2 captured.[35] And that was not counting the

---

32. About 100 men.
33. Shaw, pp.177–80. Simmons, p.57.
34. About 30km west of Ciudad Rodrigo. Simmons, p.57, states they were at San Pedro and Valermosa.
35. Almost all the dead died from disease. Three died at Barba del Puerco and the other two were captured.

sick. In the 25 March 1810 return, they had 10 sergeants, 2 buglers, and 80 riflemen sick. The battalion was reporting only 809 riflemen fit for duty. They had loss 20 per cent of their effectives in eight months and had been in only one skirmish. Captains Francis Glass' No. 9 Company and William Balvaird's No. 10 Company were selected for consolidation. Two captains and six subalterns[36] were soon on their way home for recruiting duty. Surprisingly, Captain Balvaird was not one of those who went home. Instead Captain Loftus Gray, the commander of No. 8 Company, went in his place. Nor were all the lieutenants from No. 9 and 10 Companies. Lieutenant James Percival was in No. 2 Company. Among the sergeants who returned to England, was Tuttle Betts, who had been shot in the jaw at Barba del Puerco.

By this consolidation, the remaining companies were brought up to an effective strength of 100 riflemen. Every company was commanded by a captain except for Captain James Stewart's company. He was absent and his company had a lieutenant as its temporary commander.[37]

The rainy weather finally broke on 15 April and for the next ten days it was sunny.[38] A few days later Craufurd ordered the three British infantry battalions to Fort Concepción and he held a review of them on 21 April.[39] There is no mention of the Portuguese caçadores taking part. After the review, the general ordered the battalions to rotate again: this time the 43rd Foot was to be in the most forward position. Their new cantonments were:

1st Battalion 43rd Foot	HQ and 7 companies: Villar de Ciervo, Spain; 3 companies at Castillejo, Portugal[40]
1st Battalion 52nd Foot	Malpartida, Vale de Coelha, and Vale da Mula, Portugal
1st Battalion 95th Rifles	Vilar Formoso and São Pedro do Rio Seco, Portugal[41]

---

36. Lieutenants Thomas Diggle, Bartholomew Keappock, William Cox, James Percival, John Malloy and Francis Bennett.
37. Captain Stewart was serving as the brigade major to his brother Major General William Stewart.
38. Shaw, pp.180–1.
39. Simmons, p.58.
40. Levine, p.131.
41. Simmons, p.58.

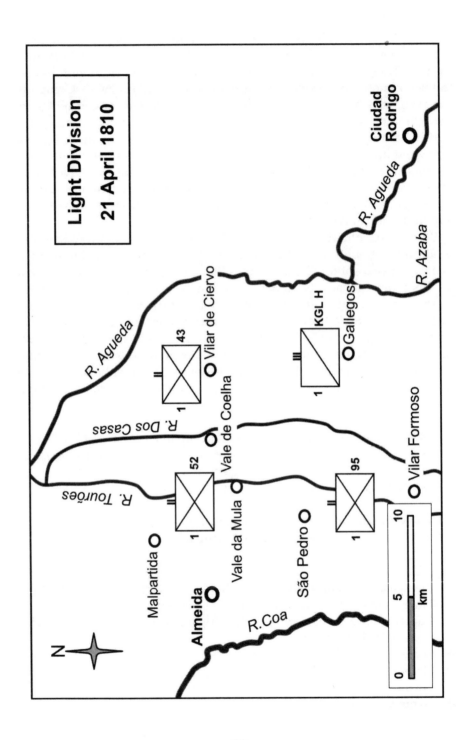

It began to rain again on 25 April and with the rain the first reports of French movement were received at the Division HQ. The initial reports had French troops in Zamarra which was 15km southeast of Ciudad Rodrigo. That night an officer came from Ciudad Rodrigo with a message that a French force, consisting of 4,000 men and 6 light guns could be seen from the walls. Craufurd sent Captain Campbell to Ciudad Rodrigo the next day to find out what they knew. He returned that evening with more accurate news. The French force was only 2,000 men.[42]

Over the next couple of days more information slowly filtered in. General Loison also stepped up his activity and sightings of French patrols were seen along both banks of the Agueda. A large number of wagons were seen on the road to Salamanca but no siege artillery was spotted. General Carrera had fallen back to San Martín de Trevejo, about 60km south of Ciudad Rodrigo, but with French forces in Zamarra, he was in danger of being cut off. He agreed to meet with Craufurd and arrived in Gallegos on 29 April.[43]

In response to the French movements, Craufurd began moving his infantry forward. By 30 April their new positions were along the Azaba River,[44] which was about 15km further east and about 12km away from Ciudad Rodrigo. The 1st KGL Hussars now covered a line along the Agueda River from Barba del Puerco in the north to Serranillo, the junction of the Azaba River near Marialba, then south to Carpio de Azaba where they occupied a height from which they could see Ciudad Rodrigo and then south along the Azaba River to Campillo de Azaba, a distance of about 45km. On 29 April the 95th Rifles were sent to occupy Gallegos and Espeja with four companies each, but the next day two companies were sent to Marialba and the other two joined the rest of the battalion at Espeja. The 1st and 3rd Caçadores occupied Gallegos. The 43rd Foot was split between Almeida and Sao Pedro do Rio Seco, while the 52nd Foot remained in Malpartida, Vale de Coelha, and Vale da Mula.[45]

---

42. Shaw, p.182.
43. Simmons, p.58. Shaw, p.182.
44. Most contemporary sources call it the Azava River. It flows into the Agueda about 10km north of Ciudad Rodrigo.
45. Simmons, p.58. Shaw, p.183.

On 30 April, the men of the Rifles officially heard that, two months after it was formed, they now belonged to the Light Division.[46] Why it took so long for the information to filter down to them is unknown, because Lieutenant William Freer of the 43rd Foot wrote home on 25 February 'We who at present form the 3rd Division of it are to have that number taken from us & the Name of a Light Division given in its stead . . .'[47]

---

46. Simmons, p.58. Cox, John, *Unpublished Diary of Lieutenant John Cox 95th Rifles*. Surprisingly both officers recorded the announcement in their diaries on the same date.
47. Freer Family Letters. Unpublished letter from William Freer to his brother John dated 25 February 1810.

Chapter 5

May 1810

Although there was some French movement towards Ciudad Rodrigo by the end of April, Wellington had no firm idea of when or even if a French invasion was imminent. But they were not alone. Marshal Ney did not know either. Although Napoleon intended to invade Portugal and eject the British, it was not a high priority for him in the early spring of 1810. He was distracted by his pending nuptials. As part of the Treaty of Schönbrunn, which ended the 1809 war between the French and Austrian Empires, Princess Marie Louise, the 18-year-old daughter of the Austrian Emperor, was to marry Napoleon. She arrived in Paris in late March and on 3 April they were married in a religious ceremony at the Louvre.[1]

Not until 16 April did Napoleon finalize his plans and appoint a commander of the invasion force. The man chosen to lead the invasion was 51-year-old Marshal André Masséna, the Prince of Essling. This came as a surprise to the marshal, who tried to turn the post down, citing wounds he had received the previous year. Napoleon was sympathetic but refused to rescind the appointment. The next day, on 17 April, Napoleon created the Army of Portugal and it was composed of General Jean Reynier's 2nd Corps, Ney's 6th Corps and Junot's 8th Corps, a force of about 75,000 men.[2]

On 18 April, Masséna received Napoleon's guidance for the campaign. The marshal was 'to put himself in a position to hold in check 25,000 English commanded by General Wellington, and to follow the army to

---

1. This was the couple's third wedding ceremony. They were officially married in Vienna, by proxy, on 11 March and then in a civil ceremony at Saint-Cloud on 1 April.
2. Horward, p.50. Oman, Charles, *A History of the Peninsular War*, 7 vols. Oxford: AMS, 1980, Vol. 3, pp.532–7.

attack and destroy it. . .' After he captured Ciudad Rodrigo and Almeida, he was to advance into Portugal and '. . . constantly threaten to advance on Lisbon, and from there, force the English to cross to the left bank of the Tagus. . .' and eventually force the British to evacuate Portugal. In a very optimistic and totally unrealistic estimate of the challenges involved, Napoleon expected the invasion to begin in May.[3]

The Advance of the French

The first obstacle that faced Marshal Masséna was distance. Ciudad Rodrigo was almost 1,400km from Paris. He left Paris on 26 April and arrived in Valladolid, Spain on 11 May, travelling 1,100km in 15 days.[4] About the time Masséna started his long journey, Ney finally began half-heartedly to move his troops towards Ciudad Rodrigo. Due to a lack of siege artillery he planned to blockade the city instead of trying to reduce the walls. He ordered General Jean-Gabriel Marchand, the commander of the 1st Division, to advance on the city. The first troops to arrive were General Antoine-Louis Maucune's brigade, who had with them the 3rd Hussars and three guns. They occupied Pedro Toro, a village 6km east of Ciudad Rodrigo. Maucune also sent troops southwest and they occupied the Monastery of La Caridad, which was about 100m from the Agueda River and a kilometre north of Sanjuanejo. These were the troops reported to General Craufurd on 26 April.

In early May, General Pierre-Louis Marcognet left Salamanca and occupied the village of Tenebrón, which was located about 10km to the east of General Maucune's area of operations. Ten kilometres further east, about 20km east of Ciudad Rodrigo, at the gorge of Sancti Spiritus, were the 4,000 men of General Mathieu Labasée's brigade.[5] Covering their lines of communication back to Salamanca was General Louis-Joseph Cavrois's cavalry brigade.[6] By the end of the first week in May, Ney had all the approaches to Salamanca covered, except towards the west, where the Light Division was deployed.

Numerous reports began to filter in to Craufurd's headquarters and on 4 May they estimated that Maucune had 2,500 troops in

---

3. Horward, p.53.
4. An average of 75km per day.
5. They were part of General Julian-Augustin Mermet's 2nd Division.
6. The 10th and 11th Dragoons. Horward, p.54. Oman, Vol. 3, pp.532–7.

Zamarra.[7] They also received word that the French had occupied Martiago about 25km south of Ciudad Rodrigo. These troops were probably a foraging party from Maucune's brigade.[8]

General Craufurd's Response

The movement of the French towards Ciudad Rodrigo caused General Carrera and his Spanish division to move north to help with its defence. By 4 May his division was deployed along the Agueda River. Its headquarters was at Puebla de Azaba, which was 30km southwest of Ciudad Rodrigo. Two infantry battalions were in Fuenteguinaldo, while his cavalry was screening along the Azaba and Agueda Rivers, including Robledo, Campillo de Azaba and Ituero de Azaba. During their meeting the previous week, Craufurd and Carrera came up with a plan of action. Neither expected the French to attack Carrera's troops since they were not deployed along the main road to Almeida. However, should they attack the Light Division they would 'assemble in the wood behind Espeja: and if the enemy's force was superior to that of the Light Division, that it was to fall back and join that of General Carrera at Nave de Aver,[9] where the two divisions would wait the attack, if the enemy was not very superior . . .'[10] Their plan would allow them take up the same defensive positions that Wellington would a year later during the Battle of Fuentes de Oñoro.[11] Should the enemy be too strong, they would avoid a fight and withdraw to Vilar Maior.[12]

Craufurd was spoiling for a fight and had contacted Wellington the previous month with a plan that would allow him to probe the enemy to keep them off balance. Wellington, however, would not give him permission to do so. In a letter dated 20 April he wrote back:

---

7.   This figure seriously underestimates the strength of Maucune's brigade. Although no figures are available for its strength in May 1810, four months later, at the Battle of Busaco, his strength was 3,200 officers and men. Oman, Vol. 3, p.535.

8.   Shaw, p.184.

9.   Modern-day Nave de Haver.

10. Shaw, p.184.

11. Wellington would fight and beat Masséna there on 3–5 May 1811.

12. Vilar Mayor, which is about 25km west of Puebla da Azaba. Shaw, pp.184–5.

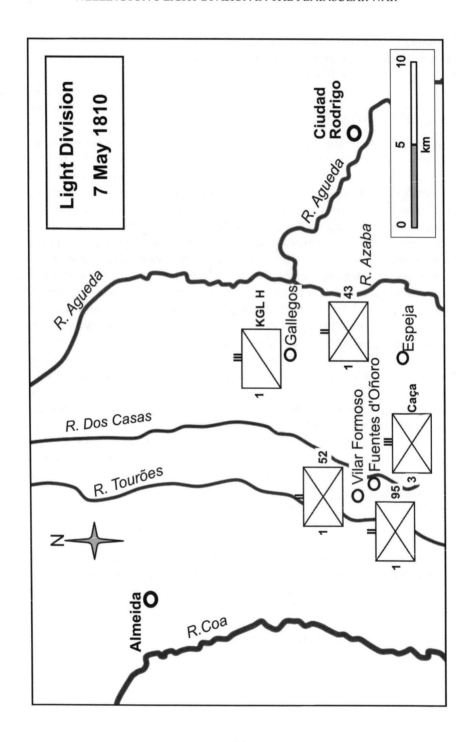

I received yesterday your letter of the 18th, which I would not answer immediately, that I might give to your proposition all the attention it deserves

The consequence of the attack which you propose would be to commence a description of warfare upon our outposts, in which we should certainly sustain some loss of men, and I should be obliged to bring up the army to the front, than which nothing could be more inconvenient and eventually injurious to us. I don't know whether the state of tranquillity in which affairs have been for some time is advantageous to the French, but I know that it is highly so to us.[13]

So the Light Division had to sit and observe, not that there was much to see. It rained virtually every day in May causing the Agueda River to flood and be unfordable most of the time. Upon the arrival and deployment of the French, Craufurd knew his main threat would come from south of Ciudad Rodrigo and not from San Felices. He could now redeploy his infantry from guarding the approaches from the north and have them cover the southern routes. On 7 May he assembled the division for an inspection on the road between Almeida and Espeja. Two days later, the battalions went to their new cantonments, which sat across the main road into Portugal from Ciudad Rodrigo. The 43rd Foot relieved the 95th Rifles and moved into Espeja and Gallegos, the 52nd Foot were at Villar Formoso, while the 95th Rifles and the 3rd Caçadores pulled back to Fuentes de Oñoro. The 1st KGL Hussars would continue screening forward along the Azaba River.[14]

Logistical Problems

The tactical problems Craufurd had were minor compared to logistical issues. Finding enough food and grain to feed his men and the hundreds of horses and pack animals was a constant worry. Wellington forbade taking supplies from the local population without paying for them. But his army was chronically short of money and had no way of paying cash for any supplies they procured locally. The solution was that they issued receipts for what they took. Once money did become available they were very scrupulous about paying the farmers when they presented

---

13. *WD*, Vol. 4, p.24.
14. Simmons, p.68. Shaw, p.184.

the receipts. However, there were several problems with this system. The first was the farmer was usually not given a choice. He was often forced to hand over what he had and given a receipt with a promise to pay in the future. This could lead to the farmer and his family starving. In a way, this method was little more than bureaucratic robbery. Although the receipts were given with every intention of re-paying the farmer sometime in the future, the problem was these receipts were only redeemable far in the rear. This required the farmer to travel for weeks to get his money. Not only was this impractical, but once the French invasion reached deep into Portugal it became almost impossible.

As big an issue as finding food was the lack of transportation to move it when it was available. The most common way to do so was by ox carts, which were requisitioned from the local peasants. Wellington recognized this and often used mules in place of the carts, but the number needed was staggering. He estimated he required between 100–150 mules per infantry brigade, cavalry regiment and artillery brigade to keep them supplied for three days.[15] The Light Division needed about 500 mules. Ox carts could carry more, but they were very slow moving, averaging less than 15km a day. With a cart you needed two oxen, which would be requisitioned at the same time the cart was. And of course someone had to drive it and this individual had to be paid. Not surprisingly, the local peasants were reluctant to give up their crops and their ox carts. If he gave up his crops his family would go hungry. If he gave up his cart, unless he went with it, he would most likely never see it again. If he went with the cart his family would be left to fend for themselves.

Once requisitioned, the carts and mules hauling food were assigned to the Army's Commissary Department. In an effort to find more carts, units that used them instead of wagons, especially within the artillery, were told to return them to the commissary and were given mules instead. In March, Captain Ross's horse artillery troop was forced to give up six of its ox carts and was given a 'brigade of twelve mules, with a capitross[16] and muleteers' as replacements. It was also given a 'mule cart, for the conveyance of spare wheels, instead of their being carried on one drawn by bullocks'.[17]

In most cases, the commissary officers did not make direct requisitions, but went through the local magistrate with their requirements.

---

15. Tennant, Richard, 'Wellington's Mules', *Napoleon Series Online*. 2019, p.8.
16. A leader.
17. Ross, p.9.

The magistrates tried to do their best but there were limits to what they could provide. It was springtime and it would be months before the harvest would be brought in. The little grain or corn that was left would be what the farmer needed to feed his own family or seeds for planting. The Light Division had been in the area of Almeida for several months and any excess from the previous harvest had been taken long before.

Few soldiers left accounts of how their food was procured, but Lieutenant William Freer of the 43rd Foot did write home how difficult it was to get wine for their regiment. He and Lieutenant Henry Booth were sent with ten soldiers to escort a convoy of ox carts from São João da Pesqueira back to Almeida, a distance of about 115km. The wine had been contracted from a local merchant at a price fixed by the Oporto Wine Company. When they came to the village near the Douro, they found that the merchant had taken a 20-dollar commission for each pipe of wine supplied and had not paid the local farmers. The farmers were of course angry about this and refused to give up their wine. The two lieutenants refused to take no for an answer and had their men break down doors to get their wine. This was only the beginning of their problems. They also had to requisition carts and forty yokes of oxen to be used to bring the wine back to Almeida. The drivers were reluctant to go with them to Almeida for they had heard that the wine was destined for Barba del Puerco and were afraid they would be taken by the French. Freer overheard them talking about escaping with their animals that night. To prevent this he placed guards on the carts and the oxen. The next morning he found that despite these precautions, two of the yokes of oxen had disappeared. Freer posted several of his men as guards every night during the seven-day return trip to prevent any further losses.[18]

Unfortunately Freer did not mention how many pipes of wine he procured but the problem he had was an oxcart could hold a weight of about 270kg. Each pipe held about 477 litres (126 gallons or 1,008 pints) and weighed about 500kg (1,100lbs). This would have exceeded the cart's carrying capacity in both weight and space. Port wine barrels came in 225 or 500 litres capacity. It is likely that the wine was stored in smaller casks that weighed no more than 225kg (225 litres).[19] The forty

18. Freer Family Letters. Unpublished letter from William Freer to his brother John dated 4 April 1810.
19. 'Used Port Wine Barrels', *Luso Barrel: Specialty Wooden Barrels from Portugal*. Online. 2019.

barrels would have provided about 9,000 litres or 18,000 of pints of wine. Each soldier was authorized half a litre[20] of wine per day.[21] Therefore Freer's wine run was enough to provide his regiment with wine for 15 to 20 days.

Craufurd had a reputation for doing whatever it took to feed his troops and soon rumours began to spread about some his methods. Private Thomas Garretty of the 43rd Foot wrote later that 'Craufurd, notwithstanding his prodigious activity, being unable to procure food for the division, gave the reins to his fiery temper, and seized some church plate, with a view to the purchase of corn'.[22] This might only had been an old soldier's tale except there was some element of truth in it. The situation became so bad that General Cox, the British commander of Almeida, wrote to Marshal Beresford about these abuses. He gave specifics in his letter but did not name names. His accusations included the 'dragging of the capitão mor[23] of Castelo Bom from his home and imprisoning him at Gallegos, as well as inflicting corporal punishment upon a civil magistrate of the same district because he did not furnish a quantity of corn, which. . . did not exist in the whole territory under his jurisdiction'.[24] Lieutenant Shaw also said that other prisoners were also taken, including some local clergy. He wrote in his journal on 5 May that he 'went this morning to Val de Mula,[25] from whence the Priests of Toras were marched prisoners to Gallegos'.[26] Gallegos was where the Light Division HQ was at the time.

In the same letter to Beresford, Cox wrote that the requisitions were 'the adoption of an unnecessary system of vexation and terror amongst a willing and obedient people'.[27] Beresford forwarded the letter on to Wellington who was not pleased with it. He wrote directly to Cox on

---

20. One pint.
21. Glover, Michael, *Wellington's Army in the Peninsula 1808–1814*. New York: Hippocrene, 1977, p.102.
22. Garretty, Thomas, *Memoirs of a Sergeant Late in the Forty-third Light Infantry Regiment previous to and during the Peninsular War*. Cambridge: Ken Trotman, 1998, p.86.
23. The capitão mor was the commander of the local militia called the Ordenança.
24. Horward, p.67.
25. Modern-day Vale da Mula.
26. Shaw, p.184.
27. *WD*, Vol. 6, p.110.

14 May rebuking him for making slanderous charges against unnamed individuals. In the same letter, Wellington justified the requisitions.

> I can have no objection to an officer in our situation forwarding any complaint which comes into his hands; but I think if he takes any view of the subject particularly in an official paper which may become a public document, it ought to be liberal towards others . . . War is a terrible evil, particularly to those who reside in those parts of the country which are the seat of the operations of hostile armies; but I believe it will be found upon inquiry, and will be acknowledged by the people of Portugal, that it is inflicted in a less degree by the British troops than by others, and that eventually all they get from the country is paid for, and that they require only what is necessary.
>
> In our present situation it is necessary that the people of Portugal should furnish the troops with carriages to move our magazines, or that they should feed the troops in advanced stations, or the troops must be withdrawn.[28]

Wellington wrote to Craufurd on the same day about the matter.

> I enclose you a letter to Brigadier General Cox from the magistrates of Castello [sic] Bom, &c., &c., and I request that if you should have reason to believe that the complaints are well founded, and the people cannot supply Mr. Downie's[29] requisitions, you will refrain from enforcing them, and rather draw from Almeida.[30]

Cox wrote back to Wellington on 16 May naming the individuals involved. Wellington responded the next day with a semi-apology.

> I have received your letter of yesterday's date. The statement of a fact is very different, and has an effect more powerful than a general reflection. Neither I, nor any other officer in the British service, has the power of confining and punishing

---

28. *WD*, Vol. 6, p.110.
29. John Downie, the Assistant Commissary General assigned to the Light Division.
30. *WD*, Vol. 6, p.111.

a magistrate, whatever may be the nature of his crime; and I certainly shall not permit such a practice. I beg to know the office of the civil magistrate of Castello Bom, who received corporal punishment.[31]

Wellington also wrote a letter the same day to Craufurd telling him to refrain from such practices.

I wish to mention to you, that neither I, nor any other officer of the British army, have the power of confining or punishing the magistrates or others in authority in Portugal. All that can be done, in case they do not exert themselves to comply with your requisitions, is to report them to me, stating specifically their offence, which is, I imagine generally one of omission of duty; and I shall order them to head quarters, and thence to Lisbon, to be punished by the government.[32]

Craufurd responded with a proposal for how the Commissary Department would act when assigned to the Light Division. Wellington reviewed it and provided a very lengthy reason why it would not work. Basically it came down to the fact that the Commissary Department was controlled by the Treasury and not by the Army.[33]

One positive affect of General Cox's letters was that the complaints of abuse against the British Army by the local government officials did decrease.

Impact of the Supply Problems on the Light Division

The irregular supply system was beginning to affect the men and horses. The 1st KGL Hussars had been manning the forward outpost for almost two months with no relief. They had a reputation for being superb cavalry troopers who always put the welfare of their horses first. One officer wrote that:

The Germans certainly treat their horses the best, and keep them in much better condition than the English do. It is said

---

31. *WD*, Vol. 6, p.119
32. Ibid., p.120.
33. Ibid., pp.124–34.

they feed and water them when they please, but if a horse that is known to be of a good constitution falls off in condition, they punish the man. These people are great plunderers, but with respect to their horses, they steal for them, and not from them, and take great pains to provide them with some sort of litter to lie down in – a thing of consequence to the English horses.[34]

Yet the constant patrolling in abysmal weather conditions began to take a toll on both the men and the horses. The same officer who noted how good care they took of their horses wrote on 6 May while he was in Celorico, 75km west of the Azaba River, 'A number of horses belonging to the hussars passed through, and went out towards Barraçal,[35] half of them led and with sore backs . . .'[36] Over the past three months, in addition to the horses that were sick or injured, another fifteen had died and in May alone fifty were in such bad condition that they were no longer fit for service and were disposed of. An auction was held at Almeida on 29 May to sell those horses considered unserviceable. To offset these loses the KGL Hussars received 145 replacement horses in May.[37]

Captain Ross's Royal Horse Artillery troop was also beginning to show the strain of a long campaign with little rest. In the past ten months he had lost so many men and horses he could only field four guns. On 7 April he received a letter from Captain John May, the Brigade Major for the Royal Artillery in the Peninsula, that his troop was being replaced by Captain George Lefebvre's RHA troop. He would turn over his men and horses that were still fit to Captain Lefebvre and return to England. On 18 May he was notified by Lieutenant Colonel Hoylet Framingham, the acting Commander of the Royal Artillery with Wellington, that the situation had changed and Lefebvre's men and horses would be used to bring his troop back up to strength. Ross broke the news to his wife Mary in a letter dated 20 March:

---

34. Burgoyne, John, *Life and Correspondence of Field Marshal Sir John Burgoyne*, 2 vols. Wrottesley, George. (ed.) London: Richard Bentley, 1873. Vol. 1, p.72.
35. Modern-day Baraçal.
36. Burgoyne, Vol. 1, p.71.
37. Shaw, p.189. The numbers are taken from the Monthly Returns for March, April and May 1810.

Fortune seems to have been willing to make up to us for past disappointments in the ill luck of Captain Lefebvre's troop, which was coming out to take my place; for by the mishap of one of his transports (which for a time supposed to be lost) losing her masts in the Bay of Biscay, she was driven into a port in Ireland in the utmost distress, having been on fire in this helpless state, and very narrowly escaping shipwreck. The consequence is that mine being found more effective than his troop, it is ordered to be completed from his. He is also to give Captain Bull[38] whatever he may require, and with the little that will then remain of his troop, Lefebvre instead of Ross will proceed to England to make a new troop.[39]

Increased French Activity

Upon arriving in the vicinity of Ciudad Rodrigo, the French first found secure cantonments for their troops and then began preparing for the siege. Marshal Ney did not go with his troops, choosing instead to remain in Salamanca. His main concern was how isolated his corps was along the Portuguese border in case Wellington decided to attack. He hoped that Junot would move in support of him. On 10 May, Ney, trusting that someone higher up would order Junot to move, wrote to Marshal Soult, King Joseph's chief-of-staff, in Madrid:

Half of my army corps is camped beneath the walls of Ciudad Rodrigo to open the trenches, and I only await the decision of the Duc d'Abrantes [General Junot] to furnish a garrison for Zamora, to relieve my communication posts, and to know that he intends to support me in case of necessity.[40]

General Julien Mermet, the commander of the French 2nd Division, had the initial responsibility of conducting the siege. On 12 May he sent a staff officer who approached the city under a flag of truce with a summons

---

38. Captain Robert Bull, RHA.

39. Ross, Hew D., *Memoir of Field-Marshal Sir Hew Dalrymple Ross, G.C.B., Royal Field Artillery with a New Introduction by Howie Muir*. Godmanchester: Ken Trotman, 2008, p.9.

40. Ibid., p.55.

to surrender.[41] If the Spanish Governor, General Herrasti, agreed to surrender, the garrison would be allowed to return to their homes unharmed or to join the forces of King Joseph. Furthermore the civilians in the city would be protected. The staff officer ended with

> ... if you refuse all accommodation, His Excellency [Ney], whose arms have always been crowned with success. . . will act with all the force at his disposal, and in a few days he will reduce the fortress that you will be unable to defend and the garrison that you will be unable to save . . . As far as I am concerned, I will regret having to shed innocent blood, and you . . . will have cause the loss of an important and unfortunate town . . . The critical moment has arrived and there is no other path for you to take . . . A valiant man has more right to public esteem, when he complies with conditions compatible with honour and the necessity of circumstances than when, through willing stubbornness, he shows himself insensible to conciliation and the voice of reason.[42]

Herrasti's response was quite succinct and left no doubt in anyone's mind his resolve. 'Since the answer I have given previously is final, it should be understood that no more representatives will be admitted in the future under a flag of truce. Now we have to talk only with guns.'[43]

On 10 May, Masséna rode into Valladolid where he rested and met with Junot. Five days later, he and Junot travelled the 120km to Salamanca and he consulted with Ney, who proposed uniting the army and attacking Wellington prior to undertaking the siege of Ciudad Rodrigo. It is likely that he also pushed for more support from Junot. The next morning Masséna returned to Valladolid and began to plan the invasion of Portugal.[44] It was not until 21 May that Masséna ordered Junot to support the siege of Ciudad Rodrigo. He also ordered the siege train at Astorga to join the siege train in Salamanca that was to be used against Ciudad Rodrigo.[45]

---

41. Pérez de Herrasti, Andrés, *Relacion historica y circunstanciada de los sucesos del sitio de la plaza de Ciudad-Rodrigo en el año de 1810*. Madrid, 1814, p.78.
42. Horward, p.55.
43. Ibid.
44. Pelet, Jean, *The French Campaign in Portugal, 1810 – 1811*. Minneapolis: University of Minnesota, 1973, p.33.
45. Horward, p.60.

Ney was finally convinced he had the resources to successfully undertake the siege. He ordered the siege train already in Salamanca to move to Ciudad Rodrigo, because he did not want to wait for the siege train coming from Astorga to arrive due to how long it would take.[46] On 29 May the siege train left Salamanca.[47] Ney also departed the same day and arrived at the Monastery of La Caridad the next day. On 31 May he made a reconnaissance of Ciudad Rodrigo and decided to attack the northwest corner of the city.[48]

Most noticeable for the Light Division was the increase in the aggressiveness of the French outposts and reconnaissance patrols. Through early May, it was relatively quiet, but by the middle of the month, the French began patrolling in force. On 19 May, an attempt was made to cross the Azaba River via the ford at Vado de Flores[49] to see how deep it was. The German hussars were alert and would not let them near the water. The following day Lieutenant Shaw went to the ford and found a group of French infantry on the far bank. He spoke briefly to the French officers there and they did not attempt a crossing.[50] Until this time, British staff officers would cross the Agueda and ride into Ciudad Rodrigo, but soon found that the French had caught on to them doing this and it became dangerous. Whenever an officer was spotted by the French sneaking into the city '. . . some of their dragoons ford the river near the convent[51] about a mile and a half above the town and endeavour to intercept him'.[52]

Deserters and Intelligence

The large number of French troops in the vicinity of Ciudad Rodrigo saw an increase in the number of deserters that made it to the British lines. They were of all nationalities serving with the Army of Portugal,

---

46. Because of the poor roads and inclement weather, 20km a day would be exceptionally fast.
47. Pelet, p.48.
48. Horward, pp.83 & 96.
49. Vado de Flores is a ford across the Agueda River near where the Azaba River flows into it, about 4km east of Gallegos. It was called Molinos de los Flores in the nineteenth century.
50. Shaw, p.53
51. The Monastery of La Caridid.
52. Burgoyne, Vol. 1, p.76.

including French, many Germans from the Hanoverian Legion[53] and Italians from the Legion du Midi.[54] An officer[55] was put in charge of interrogating them and once he was done with them they were escorted to the rear.[56]

On 17 May an officer from the 6th Light Regiment of General Maucune's brigade of the 1st Division of the 6th Corps deserted to the Spanish in Ciudad Rodrigo. He had wounded his company commander in a duel and was afraid he would be court-martialled and executed. The Spanish sent him on to the Light Division.[57] He turned out to be a treasure trove of information and provided a detailed order-of-battle of the Army of Portugal. His report was recorded by Lieutenant Shaw in his journal and is one of the few surviving intelligence documents from this period. The unnamed French officer said:

> Marshal Massena, the Prince D'Essling, has been announced in orders of the French army as Commander of what is called the Army of Portugal. This army consists of the second, sixth, and eighth corps of the army of Spain. Massena arrived at Salamanca on the 15th instant. The French army is divided into corps, the corps into divisions, and the division into brigades.
>
> The brigades consist of two regiments each; and the regiments, some of two, and some of three battalions. Each battalion has six companies, and he averages the battalions at between 500 and 600 men each. Of the second corps he knows nothing. The sixth is commanded by Marshal Ney, and the eighth by Junot. The sixth corps consists of three divisions, and the eighth of two. The following is the detail of the divisions, brigades, and regiments of the sixth or Ney's corps.
>
> First division, Commander, Marchand, and 6th and 69th regiments of foot. Brigadier-General, Mauchule[58] [sic]. 39th and 50th regiments of foot, Brigadier not known.

---

53. The Hanoverian Legion was raised in 1804 and wore red jackets. It was disbanded in 1811.
54. The Legion du Midi was a light infantry regiment raised in the Piedmont Region of Italy. It was disbanded in 1811.
55. I have not been able to identify this officer.
56. Shaw, pp.146 & 184. Burgoyne, Vol. 1, p.72. Simmons, p.68.
57. Shaw, p.186.
58. General Maucune.

Second division, Commander, Mermet, 25th and 27th regiments of foot, Brigadier-General, Feré.[59] 59th and 76th regiments of foot, Brigadier not known.

Third division, Commander, Loison, 66th and 82nd regiments of infantry, Brigadier not known; 32nd and another not known, nor the Brigadier, but supposed the 26th.

There are before Ciudad Rodrigo three hut camps; and in each camp there is one brigade and one regiment of cavalry, amounting to about 3,000 men in each, and making the whole encampment 9000 men.

The following is the detail he gives of the regiments in the camp: first, in their right camp, which is on the Val de Carros[60] road, there are the 66th and 82nd regiments of foot, and 15th chasseurs–à-cheval; he thinks that the proper Commander of this brigade, is General Larcha,[61] but that he is absent, and it is now commanded by a Colonel.

Second, in their centre camp are, the 25th and 27th foot, the 10th and 24th chasseurs–à-cheval, and two four-pounders, commanded by Feré.

Third, their left camp, which is at Pedro de Toro, consists of the 6th and 69th foot, and 3rd hussars, two four-pounders and a howitzer. He says that Mermet commands the camp. He is not certain of what artillery was in each camp, but believes there are three in each; in all nine. Junot's corps consist of only two divisions.

The following is the establishment of a regiment of two battalions complete:

1 Colonel, Gros Major,
2 Chefs de Battalion,
2 Adjutant Majors
36 officers.

In each battalion there are six companies, and to each company, one serjeant-major, four serjeants, and eight corporals. The company is 120 rank and file when complete. Regiments of the

---

59. General Ferey.
60. Valdecarros, which is a town southeast of Salamanca.
61. General Labasée.

ligne have four companies du centre, one du grandiers [*sic*], and one du voltigeurs. The light infantry battalions have

4 companies du centre,
1 company du carbinier [*sic*],
1 du voltigeurs

Besides the regiments mentioned above as forming Loison's division he has also the Légion du Midi, or first légère infantry, and the fifteenth légère infantry.[62]

When this information is compared to the orders-of-battle in Charles Oman's *History of the Peninsular War*,[63] there are a few discrepancies but they are not significant. The information provided by the French junior officer was accurate for his own brigade and he was able to name all but two of the infantry regiments assigned to the corps, those being the Hanoverian Legion and the Legion du Midi, which were in the 3rd Division. He also correctly identified each brigade the regiments were assigned to except for the 50th and 76th Regiments. He had the 50th Regiment in the other brigade of his division, and the 76th Regiment in the 2nd Division. It should have been the other way around. One of the most important things that the deserter did from an intelligence standpoint was that he told what he knew and did not make up information when he did not know an answer. His only misidentification of brigade commanders was when he said that General Feré (Ferey) was in the 2nd Division instead of the 3rd Division.

Possibly the most critical piece of intelligence came from another deserter, whom Lieutenant Shaw provides no details about. He said '. . . that a portable bridge had arrived at St. Espirituo[64] from Salamanca. Massena remained only a very short time at Salamanca, and was understood to have returned to Valladolid, accompanied by Junot.'[65]

This intelligence was extremely important for several reasons. Up until now, the Agueda River could only be crossed at the several fords and bridges. Knowing this, Craufurd could screen most of the river with a minimum of troops and use the majority of his force to

---

62. Shaw, pp.183–7.
63. Oman, Vol. 3, pp.532–43.
64. Sancti Spiritus, where General Labasée's brigade was.
65. Shaw, pp.188–9.

cover the likely crossing sites. A portable bridge was a game changer, for it would allow the French to cross the river almost anywhere. The information about Masséna was also correct. He had arrived in Salamanca on 15 May but as the deserter said, had returned to Valladolid after consulting with Ney the following day.[66] What is the most surprising part of this information was that the deserter knew about this meeting within four days of it happening.

66. Horward, p.59.

Chapter 6

The War of the Infantry Outposts, June 1810

'It is sufficient to observe, that from the beginning of March until the 24th of July, we were stationed so close to the outposts of the French, as to render it necessary for the soldiers to sleep fully accoutered, and the officers, with their clothes on, ready to get under arms in an instant; and we were, as a matter of course, always under arms one hour before the break of day.'[1]

Captain Jonathan Leach, No. 2 Company
1st Battalion 95th Rifles

'Seven minutes sufficed for the Division to get under arms in the middle of the night; and a quarter of an hour, night or day, to bring it in order of battle to the alarm-posts, with the baggage loaded and assembled at a convenient distance in the rear. And this not upon a concerted signal, or as a trial, but at all times and certain.'[2]

Captain William Napier, 43rd Foot

'The rule which those who were mounted, and had to be with the Outposts fell into, was that of not sleeping in our clothes, which was found unrefreshing, but to be able to dress and have a small bed packed up and placed upon the mule in time that another man was bridling merely the riding horse.'[3]

Lieutenant James Shaw, ADC to General Craufurd

---

1. Leach, *Rough Sketches*. . ., p.134.
2. Napier, William, *History*, Vol. 2, p.169.
3. Shaw, p.147.

'This Division was in the highest state of Discipline and although close to a numerous and formidable Enemy kept its ground & avoided all surprises. A few Minutes during Day or Night was sufficient to get it under Arms and assembled at its alarm Posts. The Baggage sent to the Rear. No wheel Carriage of any description accompanied us. Mules & Horses were alone employ'd & could travel with expedition in the worst of Roads.'[4]

Captain James Fergusson, 43rd Foot

Wellington's Concept of Operations

Wellington knew that he could not prevent the French from invading Portugal. He estimated that the French invasion force would be about 100,000 men, almost twice as many as he could muster.[5] Although the combined British-Portuguese Army could number over 50,000 men, half were Portuguese who were poorly equipped and just beginning to be trained to British standards. If he risked a fight at the border and lost it, the consequences would be catastrophic. Not only would Portugal likely fall, Britain would likely lose its only field army. Wellington explained this again to General Craufurd in a letter dated 12 June.

> With an army of one-fourth inferior in numbers, a part of it being of a doubtful description, and at all events but just made, and not more than one-third of the numbers of the enemy's cavalry, it would be an operation of some risk to leave our mountains, and bring on a general action in the plains, and would, most probably, accelerate the period of our evacuation of the Peninsula.[6]

Wellington's strategy was to delay the French along the border with Spain as long as possible. Within 50km of each other were three border fortresses that sat astride the main invasion route into Portugal: Ciudad Rodrigo and Fort Concepción in Spain, and Almeida in Portugal. The French would have to take them in order to secure their lines of communications back into Spain. Once they fell, Wellington would pull

---

4. Fergusson, James. 'Memoirs 1803 – 1818'. Typed transcription by Eileen Hathaway, 1999. Soldiers of Oxfordshire Museum. File # sofo2135, p.9.
5. Oman, Vol. 3, p.220.
6. *WD*, Vol. 6, p.182.

his army back to Lisbon, where he was building the massive defensive Lines of Torres Vedras. As they retreated the Allied army would evacuate the civilians and conduct a scorched-earth campaign to deprive the French of any means to support their army from local sources. Once behind the defensive positions around Lisbon, the Allied army would wait, because the French had very few options, none of them good. They would be constrained by a logistics situation that would worsen the further they advanced into Portugal. By the time they reached Lisbon, their supply lines would stretch 500km through hostile territory back to Salamanca. Compounding their supply problems, the countryside would be stripped of almost all food and forage, limiting their ability to live off the land. Masséna would be left with only two choices. He could attack the defensive positions or he could wait. If he chose not to attack he would have only a few months before his army began to starve and he would be forced to retreat into Spain.[7]

This strategy hinged on the three fortresses. Wellington had no illusions that they were impregnable, so he made the hard decision to sacrifice them in the hope that they would delay the French long enough for the Lines of Torres Vedras to be built. He was willing to help by sending food and ammunition into them, but at no point would he reinforce them with his troops or to continue to supply them if it placed his troops at risk. The exception was Fort Concepción. He initially intended to abandon it because it was in a state of disrepair.[8] However, on 26 May he sent Captain John Burgoyne of the Royal Engineers to repair it.[9] About the same time General Picton, the commander of the 3rd Division, was ordered to send troops to the fort as its garrison. He chose the 9th Portuguese Regiment, which was commanded by Lieutenant Colonel Charles Sutton.[10] He also sent four companies of the British 45th Foot, under the command of Major William Smith.[11] They would occupy

---

7. Wellington did not expect the French army to last as long as they did and was amazed by their resilience.
8. It had been garrisoned by French soldiers until the autumn of 1808. When they withdrew, they blew a breach in one of the walls.
9. Burgoyne, John, Vol. 1, p.79.
10. Charles Sutton was a major in the British 23rd Foot, but had volunteered for service in the Portuguese Army in August 1809.
11. Brown, Steve, *Wellington's Red Jackets: The 45th (Nottinghamshire) Regiment on Campaign in South America and the Peninsula, 1805–14.* Barnsley: Frontline, 2015, p.110.

Aldea del Obispo and Vale da Mula, two villages within a kilometre of the fort. On 27 May, General Cox, the commandant of Almeida, was ordered to send

> Four Portuguese 6 pounders ready to go from Almeida immediately. Four Spanish 8 pounders, eight Spanish 4 pounders: carriages to be prepared immediately. Two Howitzers, ready to go from Almeida immediately. All to have 100 rounds per gun.[12]

On 28 May, Wellington wrote to Lieutenant Colonel Sutton with instructions about what to do while at the fort. He informed him about the guns and ammunition that was supposed to come from Almeida and that:

> The Commissary General of the British army has orders to place in store at La Conception, [sic] 12000 rations of bread, meat, rum, and wood, for the use of the troops under your command, in case they should remove into the fort; and the Commissary of the Ordnance at Almeida has orders to lodge in the fort 100,000 rounds of musket ammunition.
>   In case you should be attacked, you will defend the place to the last extremity, and you may be certain that you will be relieved.[13]

Four days later, Wellington sent a memorandum to Generals Thomas Picton, Galbraith Cole[14] and Craufurd. Picton and Cole commanded the two divisions which were the nearest to the Light Division. This memorandum laid out how Wellington envisioned the operations would go and how Picton and Cole would support the Light Division.

> Brigadier General Craufurd is requested to direct his posts of hussars at Barba del Puerco, Villa de Ciervo, Villa de Yegua,[15] and any others he may have on the lower parts of the Agueda, to communicate with the officer in command of the troops belonging to the 3rd division at Aldea del Obispo and Val de la

---

12. *WD*, Vol. 6, p.143.
13. Ibid., p.145.
14. The commander of the 4th Division.
15. Villar de la Yequa.

Mula,[16] destined for the occupation of the fort of La Conception, and he will communicate with that officer himself.

In case the enemy should cross the Agueda in force, Major General Picton's division, with the exception of the troops at La Conception, are to be collected at Pinhel; and Major General Picton will observe the ford of Puerto de Vide,[17] as well as the bridge over the Coa, under Pinhel; and Major General Cole will move his division forward from Guarda, and occupy the villages behind the Coa, towards Ponte de Sequeiros,[18] Castello Mendo,[19] and Castello Bom,[20] so as to be able to observe and guard those passages over the river.

If the enemy should cross the Agueda in superior force, it will be necessary that Brigadier General Craufurd should retire, and I wish that he should retire upon La Conception and Almeida, if it should be possible. This must, however, depend in a great measure upon the strength and disposition of the enemy, and if he should retire upon any of the upper passages of the Coa, he will apprise Major General Cole of his doing so, who will in that case detach a brigade from the left of his division to Almeida.[21]

This memorandum gave Craufurd much latitude on how he was to man the outposts. Wellington was willing to let him keep the Light Division as close as possible to Ciudad Rodrigo, but only until the French crossed the Agueda River in force. At that point, he was to bring his men back to the Azaba River. If the French advanced across the Azaba, the Light Division was to withdraw to the vicinity of Fort Concepción.

---

16. Vale da Mula.
17. I have not been able to identify the location of this ford. It is probably in the vicinity of Vale de Madeira.
18. A medieval bridge over the Côa River about 40km south of Almeida.
19. A village about 30km south of Almeida and 1km west of the Côa River.
20. A village 15km south of Almeida and 1km east of the Côa River.
21. WD, Vol. 6, p.144.

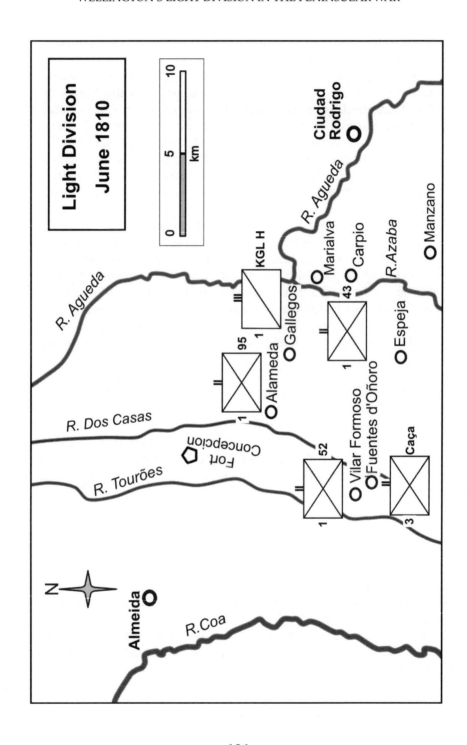

How the Outposts Operated

In previous chapters I covered the location of the outposts, but I did not explain how they worked. It varied depending on whether it was manned by cavalry or infantry, but in general they acted upon the same principles. The manning of the outposts were based on

> . . . confidence arising from the enemy's cautious and systematic proceedings, and to the admirable conduct of the 1st Hussars; for we began to think that nothing could go wrong when they were in front. The operation in general, however, was founded upon a calculation of time and distance, that is, that the cavalry out-posts, were so arranged, that the information given by them should give time for withdrawing the infantry to the Coa before it could be over taken, and obliged to come to action with a superior force of infantry.[22]

The confidence Craufurd had in the 1st KGL Hussars was key, but he did not take them for granted. He knew how he wanted them to perform their duties and took great care to ensure they did. His ADC, Lieutenant James Shaw, wrote that:

> Another peculiarity of this case was the great knowledge of Out-post Duties possessed by the 1st Hussars of the German Legion. General Craufurd in fact worked out the most difficult parts of the long line he had to guard, by his personal communications with the Captains chiefly of that admirable corps, men who were all masters themselves of the subject. They knew his plan for each space that they covered, but not his general plan, and each worked out his part most admirably. The General communicated with them direct. He had the advantage of possessing, with great abilities, and activity, and energy, uncommon bodily strength, so that he could be on horseback almost any length of time.[23]

Where and how far in advance of the infantry were the cavalry picquets deployed depended on the terrain and how far they could

---

22. Shaw, pp.142–3.
23. Ibid., p.140.

see. Lieutenant Shaw said that it varied from one to six miles.[24] The real question was what kind of information were they to send and how did they communicate the information they saw in a timely matter? Craufurd was quite specific about what he was looking for.

> Reports in general terms as to the enemy's movements were objected to by General Craufurd; when reports were made of the enemy's being in motion, his supposed force in actual numbers were desired to be stated, and of what arm or arms that force was composed. Reports in general terms of the enemy being in motion caused unnecessary alarm when the numbers were small.[25]

How information was transmitted depending on whether it was night or day. Captain William Napier of the 43rd Foot wrote that during daylight 'The horsemen mounted, and riding once round a beacon indicated a movement; for example, – twice round, large bodies of cavalry; three times round, advancing; vidette on foot moving round, indicated infantry; and so on.'[26] At night beacons were used. Upon arriving at its location, the picquet would gather firewood that would be used to alert those in the rear. Rifleman Costello wrote that often an outpost would consist of both a German hussar and a single rifleman, who 'were placed near the beacon in case of the picquets being attacked, to give alarm by discharging his piece into the combustibles, and so setting it on fire. . .'[27]

Yet lighting the beacons was only part of the answer. The inlying picquet duty officer in the rear of the outposts had to know which beacon had been lit, not something as easy as it may seem. Captain Leach, of the 95th Rifles, wrote of the problem and the solution they came up with.

> In various elevated spots near the fords and bridges; and as the eye is at that time very apt to be deceived in the precise direction of objects, and as shepherds and others frequently

---

24. Shaw, p.143.
25. Ibid., p.149.
26. Fitzclarence, Frederick, *A Manual of Outpost Duties*. London: Parker, Furnivall, and Parker, 1851, p.13.
27. Costello, p.28.

kindle fires at night, the most certain plan of avoiding mistake is the following: – Let a high pole be driven into the ground close by each beacon, and then lash to it firmly with cords two other poles, pointing them horizontally, and in the exact direction of the beacons on its right and left. If a fire is perceived at night, the party on duty at the beacon can, by ranging the eye along the horizontal poles in the same manner as on the barrel of a musket, ascertain, almost to a certainty, whether the fire is from a beacon or not; and by igniting that over which they have charge, the alarm can be given along a very extensive line of the country in the shortest possible time.[28]

Darkness was also a problem for the picquets for they were often dependent on sound and light to determine the location of the enemy and his activity. Like the duty officer in the rear, the picquets would set up two forked sticks with 'another stick laid horizontally across them, so as to point out, by looking along it, the situation of the enemy's posts'.[29]

At times the first notice that the inlying picquet had of approaching enemy was the picquet retreating quickly. Lieutenant Kincaid, who would not arrive in the Peninsula for another three months, wrote that:

The first regiment of hussars were associated with our division throughout the war and were deserved favourites. In starting from a swampy couch and bowling along the road long ere dawn of day, it was one of the romances of a soldier's life to hear them chanting their national war songs – some three or four voices leading and the whole squadron joining in the chorus. As I have already said, they were no less daring in the field than they were surpassingly good on out-post duty. The hussar was at all times identified with his horse, he shared his bed and his board, and their movements were always regulated by the importance of their mission. If we saw a British dragoon at any time approaching in full speed, it excited no great curiosity among us, but whenever we saw one of the first

28. Leach, *Recollections and Reflections. . .*, pp.30–1.
29. Sinnott, John, *A Manual of Light Infantry and Other Duties*. London: Parker, Furnivall, and Parker, 1849, p.91. Shaw, p.149.

hussars coming on at a gallop it was high time to gird on our swords and bundle up.[30]

Although this shows the trust the Light Division officers had in the German hussars, this was not what they were trained to do. The commander of the 1st KGL Hussars wrote in his manual that:

On the march to the spot where the Picquet is to be placed, the Officer must pay great attention in examining the country, and particularly observe the places where he would make a stand in case the Picquet should be attacked by the Enemy; for instance, behind a bridge, a ravine, between bogs, &c., in order to keep off the enemy as long as possible. This is of the utmost importance to give the Corps time to turn out. The Commander of a Picquet who retires with his men at full speed, and the enemy at his heels, deserves the severest punishment, he must retire as slow as possible, and constantly skirmish.[31]

Major Charles Napier[32] was not impressed with this tactic after he observed one such skirmish.

---

30. Kincaid, *Random Shots. . .*, p.162.
31. Arentschildt, Friedrich von, *Instructions for Officers and Non-Commissioned Officers of Cavalry on Outpost Duty*. London: Parker, Furnivall, and Parker, 1844, p.4 .
32. Major Napier was in the 50th Foot, which was not in the Peninsula at this time. He was wounded at the Battle of Corunna on 16 January 1809 and captured by the French. He was paroled by Marshal Ney to recover from his wounds in England. A condition of his parole was that he could not be on active service until he was exchanged for a French officer of equivalent rank who was a British prisoner. This exchange did not take place until January 1810. Major Napier's regiment was still recovering from the effects of the disastrous Walcheren Expedition. He did not want to sit in England while his brothers, George and William, were serving in the Peninsula, so he took a leave of absence and went to Portugal. He travelled to Celorica where he met with Wellington on 15 June who signed his certificate of exchange. On 21 June he arrived at the Light Division headquarters and volunteered his services as an ADC to General Craufurd.

The enemy drove back our picquet from Marialva and Carpio, beyond the bridge and fords of the Azava. Soon afterwards a troop of our German hussars crossed the bridge and skirmished, but using only carbines and pistols, only one man and two horses were killed: the spectacle was as pretty as it was ridiculous. Such trifling work serves no purpose whatever, it risks brave men and teaches them to trifle with service; we should fight or let it alone; the latter is most to my taste. Everything convinces me that light cavalry has no business with carbines. The Germans understand outpost work better than our cavalry, but if the English err they will fight themselves through; and though Germans are brave enough, they certainly have not the fire of our men; wherefore, taking all risks from drinking and ignorance, I would rather have two British of regiments infantry or cavalry than three German regiments, and that is saying a great deal.[33]

The Latest Intelligence

French troops continued to arrive in the vicinity of Ciudad Rodrigo and by the end of May the headquarters of the Light Division was getting a more detailed picture of the size of the force that was facing them. Lieutenant Shaw wrote on 30 May that:

Positive intelligence was received this evening by the Governor of Ciudad Rodrigo, that the enemy's battering cannon left Salamanca on the 28th instant. Captain Ally,[34] the officer of hussars at Martillan,[35] reported that he saw a column of 3,000 infantry and 400 horse, pass through San Felices Chico this afternoon, and take the road towards Ciudad Rodrigo. Lights were seen this night on a hill, called Biban Rey,[36] and the enemy established a camp there, which appeared to be a brigade of infantry, with cavalry and two field pieces. The enemy established himself also

---

33. Napier, Charles, *Life and Opinions of General Sir Charles James Napier*, 4 vols. London: John Murray, 1857, Vol. 1, p.129.
34. Captain Wilhelm Aly.
35. Martillan is 8km north of Gallegos and 2km west of the Agueda River.
36. I have not been able to identify this hill. It is likely a few kilometres northwest of Ciudad Rodrigo.

on the right of the town by a camp, the left of which was at the Convent of La Caridad, and fronting the town.[37]

Although Craufurd had a fairly good idea about the composition and strength of Ney's corps, he was missing two key pieces of intelligence that would have major impact on operations. The first was where was the French siege train and when could they expect it to be at Ciudad Rodrigo. The second was when would Masséna arrive. They would soon find out about Masséna, but where the siege train was, was a mystery. The first part of it left Salamanca on 29 May and made it to San Muñoz on 4 June, a journey of 50km in 7 days. Over the next two or three days the rest of the train arrived. Here the Army of Portugal's artillery park was established. When it would show up in the vicinity of Ciudad Rodrigo was anyone's guess, because San Muñoz was 50km from Ciudad Rodrigo.[38]

On 1 June Craufurd decided to take a ride along the outposts to see what the French were up to. He left Almeida by late morning and rode 30km to Gallegos. After finishing some business there he rode towards Ciudad Rodrigo. With him was Lieutenant Shaw and an escort of hussars under the command of Captain Georg Krauchenberg. As they left Gallegos, they received a report that Spanish guerrillas were skirmishing with a party of French soldiers near a ford across the Agueda River at Molino Carbonero Craufurd decided to continue on to see for himself, but by the time he and his party had ridden the 8km to the ford, the French had departed. This ford was only 4km from Ciudad Rodrigo so he decided to visit the town. While there he had dinner with its governor, General Herrasti.

After dinner, Craufurd and Lieutenant Shaw climbed the bell tower of the Romanesque Santa Maria Cathedral to observe the French positions. Nothing appeared out of the ordinary until they looked south towards La Caridad where they saw a large number of men along the banks of the river. This was unexpected and the general decided to ride the 5km south to see what was going on. Don Julián Sánchez,[39] the leader of the guerrillas in the area, offered to ride with him, and provided an escort of 20–30 men. Much to their surprise they soon found French cavalry on the west bank of the river. They were there to provide

37. These were General Maucune's troops. Shaw, p.190.
38. Pelet, p.48.
39. Julián Sánchez García led a guerrilla force of 200 lancers during the siege.

security to the French engineers who were building a trestle bridge. They had been working on the bridge for a while. Lieutenant Shaw did not mention it in his journal, but Craufurd must have been furious with what they saw. Neither Carrera, who was responsible for screening that stretch of the river, nor the Spanish troops in Ciudad Rodrigo, had reported this critical information. Craufurd rode the 50km back to Almeida and arrived at midnight, having rode over 100km that day.[40]

Masséna inspected the bridge on 3 June. His ADC, Chef-de-Bataillon Jean Jacques Pelet, who was a topographical engineer, described the bridge as follows:

> This bridge, not yet finished, was on trestles and all the wood needed for its construction had to be carried from Salamanca. The water was then five feet deep, and there was danger it would rise at any moment. The bridge, already protected by the heights of the right bank which butted against the cove, was later covered by a lunette for one hundred and twenty-men. It seemed appropriate to occupy the entire plateau in front as well as the flanks of the small area separating it from the Agueda in order to facilitate the retreat of a detachment placed on the left bank.[41]

It was not long before a French deserter was brought to the Light Division's headquarters. He reported that the French had six regiments of dragoons near the bridge: the 3rd, 6th, 10th, 11th, 15th, and 25th Regiments totalling about 2,500–3,000 cavalry. He also stated that Marshal Masséna was at Ciudad Rodrigo and had reviewed the troops on 3 June. This was the first word the British had that he was there.[42] The deserter's information was very accurate. The six dragoon regiments were Masséna's 2nd Dragoon Division, commanded by General Anne Trelliard. The division had three brigades each of two dragoon regiments.[43]

Craufurd was faced with a difficult decision. The French had success-fully crossed the Agueda River in force south of Ciudad Rodrigo. The

40. Shaw, pp.190–1.
41. Pelet, pp.51–2.
42. Shaw, p.191.
43. Burnham, Robert, *Charging against Wellington: Napoleon's Cavalry in the Peninsular War 1807 – 1814*. Barnsley: Frontline, 2011, p.40.

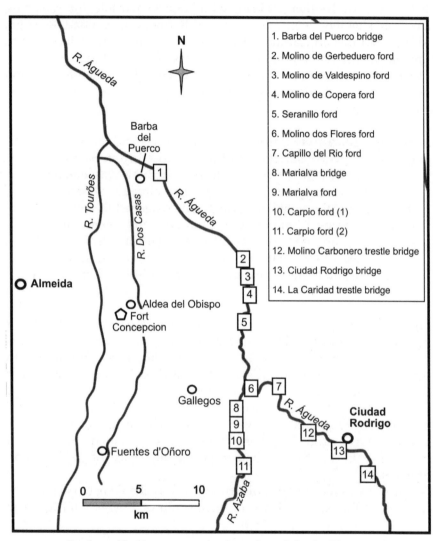

Fords and bridges across the Agueda and Azaba Rivers.

longer he kept his outposts in the vicinity of the city along the river, the greater the chance they would be trapped there by the French, but if he pulled them back to the Azaba River 10km to the west he would lose his ability to communicate with and resupply the city. It rained all day on 3 June and the waters of the Agueda River began to flood again. The next day, Craufurd met with General Carrera at Carpio de Azaba and while there word was received that French troops were at the Molino Carbonero Ford. Upon their arrival they spotted troops carrying material to construct another trestle bridge.[44] The French chose this site for the bridge because it was originally only 33m wide and had a small island in its middle. What they did not do was to take into account all the rain and by the time they began to build it the river had flooded to 110–130m wide. Redoubts were also being planned to protect the builders.[45]

When he returned to his headquarters, Craufurd ordered the KGL Hussars and Captain Ross's horse artillery to move to the hill above the ford that night so they could harass the French engineers the following morning. The heavy rains through the night prevented the guns from moving forward but they made it to the hill later in the day. By the time they got to the top of the hill they discovered that the French had brought up artillery to protect the bridge. Furthermore the hill was within musket-shot of the French on the east bank. The British withdrew without doing any damage to the bridge.[46]

Wellington was concerned with both the bridges at La Caridad and Molino Carbonero. He suggested in a letter to General Craufurd that:

> If the rain is as heavy in your quarter as it is with us, the Agueda must have swelled again. Could not Carrera, by floating large trees down the river, destroy the bridge above the town; and the people of the town do something of the same kind by the lower bridge? A bridge upon chevalets cannot be very strong.[47]

The Spanish tried that a few days later, but the winding nature of the course of the river and its rocky banks prevented any trees that avoided

---

44. Shaw, p.193.
45. Pelet, p.52.
46. Shaw, p.194.
47. *WD*, Vol. 6, p.171.

grounding themselves from building up enough speed to damage the bridges.[48]

The bridge at Molino Carbonero was completed on 7 June and the next day French infantry and cavalry were seen on the west side of the Agueda River. Craufurd could wait no longer and ordered his outposts to withdraw 10km west and form a new line along the Azaba River. The Agueda would only be picqueted from the confluence of it and the Azaba north to Barba del Puerco. The division would man three company size outposts east of the Azaba. They were at the villages of Marialba, Carpio de Azaba, and el Manzano. The line along the Azaba was contracted to about 10km long. The southern flank would be covered by Carrera's Spanish troops.

The small village of Marialba was the line's northern anchor. It was about a kilometre east of the only bridge across the Azaba. Its company was reinforced with twenty-four riflemen. The company responsible for Marialba was also tasked to provide a picquet to watch the Vado de Flores ford across the Agueda, which was about 3km north of the village. Two kilometres south of Marialba was the much larger village of Carpio de Azaba. Directly to its east was the Manzanillo Heights which provided a good view all the way to Ciudad Rodrigo, but also of the bridge at Molino Carbonero. Five kilometres southeast of Carpio de Azaba was el Manzano, a small collection of huts. Directly to its east was Manzano Heights which also provided a good view of Ciudad Rodrigo. At night, the areas between the villages were covered by the KGL Hussars vedettes. The countryside east of the outposts was no man's land and would be heavily patrolled by the cavalry.

On the west side of the Azaba River were the duty battalions, one located at Gallegos and the other 8km south in Espeja. They would be the ones that would respond to any French movement. About an hour west of them was the rest of the division. The forward battalions would be rotated with the battalions in reserve so that all would remain fresh.

Forty years later, Captain William Napier of the 43rd Foot described the situation in a letter:

> When Craufurd occupied Gallegos and Espeja . . . he had Picquets of Cavalry at Carpio, and a chain of cavalry forts from Carpio along the woody heights lining the Azava, connecting it with an Infantry Picquet at Marialva. The woods were there a

---

48. D'Urban, p.111.

prize and from Carpio to Marialva we could see over an open plain to Ciudad Rodrigo, then besieged by Massena. The French often menaced us, and the affair was very critical; but Craufurd had beacons and vedettes at openings in the woods, so that no movement could be made, except at night, without a signal being given to the brigades in Gallegos and Espeja.[49]

The War of the Infantry Outposts Begins

Captain William Napier commanded the company that initially occupied Marialba. It was not pleasant duty. Years later he wrote:

> The ford you see on the left over the Agueda below the junction of the Azava, we watched, but only with sentries hidden at some distance, because at first we did not know if the French were aware of it, and we did not wish to point it out. There was a house at Marialva, and a very little hillock on the left of it, and the Bridge of Marialva was behind. One day I had just taken the Picquet of two Companies, a Rifle Company and the 43rd Company, when a very large body of cavalry were descried coming towards us, followed by some infantry. The orders were at that time to fight with the Picquet until the Brigade got under arms, as the General designed to defend the Bridge of Marialva. I did not like the appearance of a great body of cavalry who could ride round me and get at the bridge, so I sent off the Rifles to the ford below on the left, placed some men in the windows of the Picquet's house, and with the rest in a very short time threw up with our bayonets, and hands, and bill-hooks, a tambour round the hillock, of about two feet high, and I made the men lie down and only show their heads and muskets above, as if we were behind a high rampart. The thing took, the French cavalry stopped, looked at us, and went back.[50]

On 12 June Craufurd inspected the outposts at Marialba, Carpio de Azaba, and el Manzano. After listening to what happened to Captain Napier at Marialba he ordered that it and Carpio be fortified.[51]

---

49. Fitzclarence, pp.12–13.
50. Ibid., p.12.
51. Shaw, p.197.

Over the next week he also ordered Captain Ross to construct a one-gun battery to cover the ford across the Azaba 2km southwest of Carpio de Azaba and a two-gun battery at the Aldehuela de Don Clemente Arjona ford 2km west of Carpio. Captain George Jenkinson was tasked to build the battery to the southwest, while Lieutenant George Smyth was given the mission of building the one at Aldehuela. Captain Duffy's company of the 43rd Foot provided the labour. To protect the bridge at Marialva, Craufurd also ordered a two-gun battery built at on the hill above Puentecilla. These batteries were built, but were not intended to be manned until needed. Although a battery was not built there, Captain Ross was told to ensure the road that led to the hill above the Vado des Flores Ford was capable of moving artillery along it.[52]

During Craufurd's inspection of the outpost at Carpio de Azaba, a party of French 3rd Hussars approached carrying a white flag. The company commander of the outpost drew up his company at the entrance of the village. An officer, possibly Lieutenant Shaw, rode out to meet the French. He halted the hussars at a distance that was close enough for them to see that the village was occupied in force but not close enough to inspect the defences. The French hussars were an escort for their commander, Colonel Levesque de la Ferrière, who was carrying a letter for Wellington from Marshal Ney. The colonel also passed on a personal message for Captain Krauchenberg of the KGL Hussars. Apparently a local dog had adopted Captain Krauchenberg and followed him wherever he went, including on patrol. A few days before, during a skirmish between his patrol and one from the 3rd Hussars, the dog became confused and followed the French back to their lines. Levesque de la Ferrière asked that they let Krauchenberg know that his dog was safe and would be returned at the first opportunity.[53]

While Craufurd was on his inspection tour of the outposts, the French were also active. A large number of infantry crossed the bridge at Molino Carbonero and occupied the Palacios and Pizarral Heights. This placed them within 2km of Marialva. Behind both of these hills were the Capilla del Rio and the Pizarral Fords. By occupying these heights, it gave them control of two more places to cross the Agueda. General Craufurd responded to this threat by ordering the 52nd Foot to

---

52. Ross, p.10. Duffy, John, 'Diary'. National Army Museum File # MS 9204-182-2.
53. Shaw, p.197. 'Letter from Captain Hew Ross dated 12 June 1810' in Burgoyne, Vol. 1, p.80.

move to the Puentecilla Hill to the east of Gallegos before daylight the next morning, while the 43rd Foot, the 95th Rifles, and the 1st Caçadores were placed behind the village by 5 a.m. Perhaps these precautionary movements showed the French that they would not catch the Light Division by surprise, because two days later, the French withdrew their troops from Palacios and moved back across the Agueda River.

Despite having the city being completely surrounded by the French, the governor of Ciudad Rodrigo was able to get messages out to the British. He never asked for troops, but he did request more ammunition and food. An attempt was made on 10 June to smuggle in some ammunition but the French had a tight cordon around the city for the waggons to make it into it.[54] Wellington was notified of this and the resupply attempt. He wrote to Craufurd on 12 June telling him not to try it again.

> The state of the musket ammunition in Ciudad Rodrigo is not so bad as to render it necessary that you should incur the risk of any loss, in order to throw in an additional quantity. It is what they are most deficient in, and it would have been better if their wants had been fully supplied in time. But they are not in such want to induce me to recommend that you should incur the risk of losing part of your cavalry to supply them, or to make a larger arrangement to cover a communication with the place. I am apprehensive that I shall not be able to do more for them than oblige the enemy to keep a large force collected in this quarter for the purpose of the enterprise.[55]

Two days later, on 14 June, Wellington wrote to Craufurd again to encourage him to keep his outposts as far forward as possible, but at the same time warning him to be ready to withdraw them should the French advance in force.

> It is very desirable that we should keep our advanced posts and the picquets from them, in a forward situation, as long as possible; at the same time I am convinced that when the rivers shall fall, the enemy will pass the Agueda upon your left with the right of his army, as soon as he shall have brought

---

54. Shaw, p.196.
55. *WD*, Vol. 6, p.182.

up the ordnance and materials for the siege. The reasons which induce us to wish to maintain our advanced posts in a forward situation, would induce them to desire to force us in, and with their strength they can have no difficulty in effecting their object. I beg you to advert to this circumstance, and be in readiness to withdraw, when you shall find that the enemy pass the Agueda in strength.[56]

Most contact with the French at this time was between the cavalry patrols. The KGL Hussars quickly became respected by their foes. Lieutenant Ernst Cordemann wrote in his journal of an incident, where one of his troopers were singled out by the French.

The many rencontres[57] which took place at the outposts during this period, led to frequent exhibitions of individual bravery, and among the most conspicuous on the side of the British, was a private in the German hussars named Schroeder. Schroeder was an excellent horseman and swordsman, and gifted with a degree of daring seldom equalled. He was regularly the first in the attack, and the last in retreat, and so often distinguished himself on these occasions, that he became at length known by name to the French. Ah! Vous voila monsieur Schroeder! Was often heard from their ranks, as the German was described in advance, ready to signalize himself by some new exploit. A French officer, who, one day, came over to the British posts with a flag of truce, begged that he might be presented to the famous monsieur Schroeder, of whom he had heard so much, and having been formally introduced, paid him some him compliments on his gallantry. It has been ascertained that between 1810 and 1812, this man individually cut down twelve different persons, wounded many, and took twenty-seven prisoners.[58]

General Craufurd was determined to keep his soldiers in the highest state of readiness. In addition to frequent inspections of the outposts,

---

56. *WD*, Vol. 6, p.187.
57. Meetings.
58. Beamish, Vol. 1, p.274.

he also questioned the duty officers to ensure they were following procedures set down in his *Standing Orders*. He had no patience for the officer who did not know the specifics of his duty and would harshly discipline him as necessary. On 14 June, he was dining at Alameda with the field officer of the day from the 52nd Foot, as well as Captains Ross and Jenkinson of the Royal Horse Artillery. After dinner, General Craufurd questioned the sentry who was posted at the door of quarters to see if he had been briefed on his duties. The sentry was unable to respond in a satisfactory manner.

> The Officer who was on guard was sent for by the General, and upon the General's asking him whether or not he had received any particular knowledge of the orders which the sentries had. The Officer who had been relieved this evening was next called for, and gave much a similar answer. Both were put under arrest, and the General declared he would bring them both to a court-martial. . . The General's reason for putting these two Officers under arrest was, their not having received and not knowing the particular orders of the sentries of their guard.[59]

The lieutenant did not help his case when he was further questioned by the general and admitted that he had not inspected his sentries since coming on duty at sunset, about 90 minutes before. The two unnamed lieutenants were released from arrest the following morning.[60]

Despite being censured by Wellington for mistreating the local officials, by mid-June Craufurd had had enough of excuses. Captain Burgoyne, who was repairing Fort Concepción, had reported that they were slow to respond to his request for assistance, especially in providing ox carts. To remedy the situation, the general

> made a requisition for 200 bullock cars from the villages round him, which not having been complied with, he has sent to imprison the alcaldes [magistrates] of these villages, and ordered a party of cavalry to collect the cars, as well as all the tools they can find fit for entrenching or hutting.[61]

---

59. Shaw, pp.200–01.
60. Ibid., pp.201–02.
61. Burgoyne, Vol. 1, p.84.

More Intelligence Comes In

One positive side of the forward movement by the French and the daily skirmishes by the patrols was the increase in the number of prisoners who were captured and the number of deserters making their way to British lines. By mid-June the British were getting a better picture about the number of troops they were facing. Wellington wrote to Craufurd on 19 June with the first solid numbers they had on the strength of Ney's 6th Corps, but even then the information was six weeks out of date:

> I have received this morning the substance of some dispatches and returns of the 1st May, from Ney, intercepted in Biscay which make his infantry, in effectives, 23,105; cavalry effectives, 4856, 4993 horses; field artillery, 1229; siege artillery 1415; miners, &c. 1006: total 31,611. Besides these there are 5023 men of this corps in the hospital.[62]

They also suspected that Junot's 8th Corps had arrived in the area. Lieutenant Shaw noted in his journal that Captain Jeremiah Crampton of the 95th Rifles, who was picqueting the Vado de Flores ford, had reported 'seeing 1000 men and 80 waggons seen entering Felices Chico[63] and another column marched towards Castelligo.[64] We supposed this to be the arrival of the advance of Junot's corps.' The identification of Junot's corps was later confirmed by deserters who crossed the bridge at Barba del Puerco.[65]

The biggest unknown was the location of the French siege artillery. On a clear day, the outposts could see activity near Ciudad Rodrigo, and as late as 13 June, no siege guns had been spotted. They did receive a report from a Spanish spy that said that in San Muñoz, where the French army's artillery park was located, there were twenty-eight heavy artillery pieces. Additionally, a convoy with three large and one small mortars, as well as eleven howitzers and ammunition had left San Muñoz on 10 June. Considering it was 50km to Ciudad Rodrigo, they probably did not arrive prior to 15 June.[66] The next day five French

---

62. *WD*, Vol. 6, p.194.
63. Modern-day Saelices el Chico.
64. Modern-day Castillejo de Martín Viejo.
65. Shaw, pp.203 & 208.
66. Ibid., pp.199–200.

artillerymen deserted and upon being questioned, they confirmed that that there was no siege artillery with the forces around the city.[67]

On 15 June, more French deserters were brought in and they said that the troops had been ordered to start digging trenches on the heights of San Francisco that night. These heights were about 500m from the northern walls of the city. Craufurd and Lieutenant Shaw rode to the heights near Marialba on 17 June to see for themselves. Shaw recorded that:

> The enemy's first parallel was to-day distinctly observed from the height above Marialva, it could not be seen yesterday owing to the haziness of the day. This parallel of the enemy ran along the crest of the height of San Francisco, and extended from thence to the river, on which its right rested. No other parallel was necessary, for, from this one, they were not more than 500 yards from the wall of town, and saw nearly to the bottom of it . . . A battery, capable of holding about ten guns was observed in front of the enemy's parallel . . .[68]

Life on the Outposts

Despite being far in advance of the rest of the army, the officers and men of the Light Division appeared to enjoy it. Rifleman Costello wrote that it was mostly

> from the novelty, however, of the picquet duty, the men preferred it always to any other: as we amused ourselves generally at night watching the shells exchanged between the besieged and the assailants, the sight was very beautiful, sometimes as many as seven or eight-and-twenty crossing each other, like so many comets.[69]

As the month went on, sometimes the two foes would meet and fraternize. Captain George Napier of the 52nd Foot had picquet duty at the Aldehuela de Don Clemente Arjona ford to the west of Carpio,[70]

---

67. Burgoyne, Vol. 1, p.84.
68. Shaw, pp.200–02.
69. Costello, p.29.
70. Also known as the Carpio ford.

where opposite to us the enemy had now also a picket, some of the French soldiers asked my leave to come across and get tobacco from our men, as they had none, and could not get any, in consequence of the siege. I allowed two of them to come, who immediately stripped off their clothes and swam across (for I would not let them try the ford), got the tobacco, told us all the news from France, and returned quite happy.[71]

However, some thought that the French went out of their way to make their lives miserable. Captain Fergusson of the 43rd Foot felt that the French would deliberately wait until the British started cooking before they began their advance and then would retire after ruining their counterpart's meal.

They watchd [sic] our Cooking & at the Moment our Kettles were prepared they advanced, which obliged us to empty the contents of them, pack up & be off. When they accomplished this object they retired, but we in general had fresh Rations served out & in the end accomplish'd our object & satisfied our empty Stomachs.[72]

Rifleman Costello would have agreed with Captain Fergusson, because:

The weather was intensely hot, and we delighted in bathing in a small river that flowed between the beacon-hill and the village. Many of us, while so amusing ourselves, would take these opportunities to wash our shirts in the running stream, laying them out to dry on the sand. Frequently, however, when thus employed, the alarm gun would be fired, and it a moment we might be observed, like so many water sprites, jumping out of the stream and hurrying on the wet shirts, actually wringing, and throwing them over our shoulders, while we fell in with our comrades.[73]

For Lieutenant Simmons of the Rifles it was more personal. He and his fellow officers would meet in the local taverns at night and the

---

71. Napier, George, pp.114–15.
72. Fergusson, p.9.
73. Costello, p.29.

Spanish would insult them for their lack of effort to take the fight to the French.

> The Spaniards are astonished at us remaining idle, as they term it, and allowing the French to invest their town, consequently they have no high opinion of our valour. The young women, with whom we joke and talk, make no scruple in calling us cowards, and say if we fought as well as we eat and drink wine, we should be fine fellows indeed. These observations are very galling, and people who are not conversant with military movements might easily imagine we do not attack the enemy from fear. We know that it would be impossible to give the least assistance to the besieged only being in advance of our army as a Corps of Observation. I often feel distressed that we cannot do the place any service.[74]

Even those who knew the reasons why they did not try to go to the aid of Ciudad Rodrigo were not happy about being idle. Lieutenant Colonel Benjamin D'Urban, a British officer serving as the Quartermaster General of the Portuguese Army, was upset. He wrote in his diary: 'This unfortunate Ciudad Rodrigo! 'Tis lamentable that it should fall before our very eyes without an effort. We had better have kept at a distance. I'm afraid it won't tell in favour of our National Honour.'[75]

Fort Concepción

On 18 June Captain Burgoyne wrote to Wellington 'that the breaches in the flanks of Fort Concepción were closed up, and their parapets nearly finished; that the body of the fort was therefore perfectly out of danger of assault, and that mines were preparing to ruin this front worse than ever, should it be necessary'.[76] The next day Wellington responded to his letter, with instructions to prepare

> to destroy all the bastions and the detached work at Concepcion [sic], and I shall be very much obliged to you if you will suggest arrangements accordingly. We see from what we have ourselves

---

74. Simmons, p.69.
75. D'Urban, p.119.
76. Burgoyne, Vol. 1, pp.84–5.

done, that the destruction of the works before destroyed is not of much consequence, and it is desirable that if there is time to make the preparations, the remainder of the works should be destroyed also.[77]

On the same day Wellington wrote to Craufurd about his plans for the fort:

I have occupied Concepcion with a view to be enabled to relieve Ciudad Rodrigo, and to cover your retreat upon Almeida, if you should be obliged to withdraw. At the same time that we are prepared for the evacuation and effectual destruction of that fort, if we should be obliged to withdraw entirely from the frontier.

From the enemy's strength in our front, of which we have now a positive knowledge, it is almost certain that if you are obliged to withdraw from your position at Gallegos, it will be useless to hold Concepcion. All the preparations are made for destroying the fort; and I write to General Cox to have in readiness the means for drawing off the guns and stores from that place at a short notice.[78]

In the same letter, Wellington reiterated his instructions that the Light Division was not to attempt to relieve the city or to make an attempt to re-supply it.

There is certainly no want of food at Ciudad Rodrigo. I fear there is much more food than the garrison and inhabitants can consume. They had provisions for forty days for the whole population when invested. To the last moment the markets of the place were well supplied. Under these circumstances, and at this period of the operations, I do not think it would be proper to make an attempt to give them relief.

From the numbers which it is now evident we have in our front, we may find it impossible to make the attempt at any period of the siege; but I do not think that any peculiar advantage would result from making the attempt at present; and not only

---

77. Burgoyne, Vol. 1, p.85.
78. *WD*, Vol. 6, p.196.

would any relief given hereafter have much more effect, but it would be much more justifiable to incur a risk to make the attempt, after the garrison shall have shown their determination to resist, by standing a serious attack. We must, however, look to what, I fear is the more probable event, that the place will be lost, and that we shall not be able to make any attempt to relieve it.[79]

Relief of the 1st KGL Hussars

Although the 1st KGL Hussars received 145 replacement horses in May, the regiment had been in the front lines for over three months and it was beginning to take a toll. Surprisingly their effective strength fell by only one trooper, but this was probably due to a lower number of men reported as sick than the previous month. However, although only one man had been killed in the daily skirmishes, thirty-one troopers and one trumpeter had been taken prisoner. This was 7 per cent of their effective strength. Wellington recognized this and wrote to Craufurd on 20 June:

> As the Hussars want refitting a little, and it will give Colonel Arentschildt an opportunity of bringing the foreigners to the rear, I propose to send you two squadrons of the 16th Light Dragoons, to relieve two of the Hussars. The 16th are very strong; when I saw them the other day they were 59 file [sic] a squadron.[80]

The news reached the 16th Light Dragoons on the same day and Lieutenant William Tomkinson wrote in his diary that:

> General [George] Anson arrived from England, and as it was necessary to relieve part of the Hussars with General Crawford [sic], two squadrons of the 16th were ordered up. This I heard on the dining at headquarters on the 20th, and that the whole brigade would have gone up, had General Anson been junior to Crawford.[81]

---

79. *WD*, Vol. 6, pp.195–6.
80. Ibid., p.200.
81. Tomkinson, William, *The Diary of a Cavalry Officer in the Peninsular War and Waterloo: 1809–181.* London: Frederick Muller, 1971, p.24.

The lieutenant touched on something that would cause problems for Wellington throughout his time in the Peninsula. It would make sense to reinforce the Light Division with General Anson's cavalry brigade. Half of the brigade, the 1st KGL Hussars, were already attached to the Light Division. So sending the rest of the brigade would not only give Craufurd more cavalry, but also provide a cavalry general to oversee the cavalry operations. However, Anson was senior to Craufurd. Wellington could not attach Anson to the Light Division without placing him in command of both formations and Wellington would not do this. He trusted Craufurd and did not trust Anson, whose performance during the Talavera Campaign left a lot to be desired.[82]

Wellington's initial solution was to replace the hussars with the 16th Light Dragoons. General Craufurd protested vehemently about this, for he had great confidence in the Germans and did not want to lose them at a time when French probing of his outposts was a daily occurrence. As a compromise Wellington ordered the 16th Light Dragoons to send two squadrons to the Light Division, while the regimental headquarters and two other squadrons would remain with the brigade. They would replace two squadrons of the 1st KGL Hussars. Thus military protocol would be maintained. The Light Division would get fresh cavalry, while Anson would have, at least on paper, two regiments under his direct control.[83] Wellington would later acknowledge the correctness of Craufurd's position by writing to him and telling 'I have said nothing about the relief of your posts of hussars on the lower Agueda; because I think the duty of them will be much better done by the hussars, than by any other of the troops.'[84]

The Portuguese Caçadores

Through all of May and early June, Craufurd ignored Wellington's suggestions that he relinquish control of the 2nd Caçadores and return

---

82. General Anson lost control of his brigade on the second day of the Battle of Talavera (28 July 1809) and the 23rd Light Dragoons were effectively destroyed during a charge. For more information on this incident see pp.14–15 of McGuigan, Ron and Robert Burnham, *Wellington's Brigade Commanders: Peninsula & Waterloo*. Barnsley: Pen & Sword, 2017.
83. Beamish, Vol 1, p.273. Tomkinson, p.24.
84. *WD*, Vol. 6, p.225.

them to the Portuguese Army. Although he was able bring the 1st and 3rd Caçadores up to Light Division standards, the 2nd Caçadores had too many problems, and by mid-June he released them. This came as a surprise to Marshal Beresford and he ordered:

> The 2nd Bat. of Chasseurs arrive on the 24th at Reteiro [Ratoeiro] on the Mondego. They halt there till the Marshal shall have inspected them, which he proposes to do on the 25th and then they will proceed to Coimbra. This Corps has been sent back in consequence of General Craufurd's Report of their being unfit for service, and he has also reported the 1st Chasseurs to be so, because of the bad and weak physical qualities of the Men; – as (whatever their discipline may be, which certainly might have been improved by this time, as they have been at the Out Post with Genl. Craufurd for those three months) they have never appeared to the Marshal inefficient for want of strength, or deficient in point of stature, considering the Standard height of the country; indeed he has long used every exertion to get rid of every old, feeble, and infirm Soldier from this as well as the other Corps; – as Men therefore he has always judged them fit for Service, and his Returns have so stated them to Lord Wellington and to the Government. The decisive way in which General Craufurd has stated this Corps to be unserviceable, must of course wear an odd aspect, and it is necessary that it should be inspected, and reported upon in its present state; – in sending me to the Out Posts therefore (which several circumstances have induced the Marshal to direct me to visit) he has ordered me to inspect the 1st Chasseurs most minutely and carefully, and to make a Report upon them as to the points of inefficiency above mentioned.[85]

The Affair of 21 June

The rainy weather finally broke and 20 June was a hot day. The French continued to build their entrenchments and for the first time the British outposts reported that three guns had been moved into them. The next day, French foraging parties were spotted on the west side of the Azaba River early in the morning. The Light Division went on the alert and by 10 a.m. its five infantry battalions formed up behind

---

85. D'Urban, p.118.

the hill to the east of Gallegos along the road to Ciudad Rodrigo. Captain Ross's guns fired seven rounds at the French, who promptly retreated. The French responded in force and about noon brought forward four cavalry and two infantry regiments. Major Charles Napier, a volunteer on General Craufurd's staff, was visiting the outposts with Captain Henry Mellish,[86] who had just been appointed as the Division's Deputy Assistant Adjutant General. They were there when the French cavalry came forward. Despite being senior and more experienced than Captain Mellish, Major Napier could only observe and advise the captain if requested. He made some scathing remarks in his diary about how Captain Mellish handled the incident.

> This morning we fired five shots at a foraging party. At noon Marshal Ney reconnoitred us with some squadrons, driving our posts within the line of the Azava river. Captain Mellish – the celebrated sporting Mellish, a brave fellow, he was on the staff – and myself were at the outposts; he made a fool of himself and I laughed at him. He made our people give up two posts without a shot, and the lieutenant of the 43rd asked my advice, so did Mellish, and I was to occupy the ground again; this was done easily, as the enemy had made his observations, which he should not have done if I had commanded the post.[87]

Captain John Duffy of the 43rd Foot was in command of the company outpost that overlooked the ford that was 2km southwest of Carpio. His day began quite early and they left their cantonments at 4 a.m. and marched to Gallegos. Once there he was informed that he would command the picquet at the southern ford. He wrote that:

> About 10 o'clock an alarm was given of the enemy being in motion. At 2 p.m. beacons were set fire to. The Enemy's Cavalry soon after made their appearance on the hills near Carpio skirmishing with our Hussars who were obliged to retired across the Azava. The Enemy's skirmishers approached the Ford. Several dismounted and commenced firing upon the advanced Party of my Company after a short time finding them at a good distance & to prevent them reconnoitring the Ford

---

86. Captain Henry Francis Mellish 87th Foot.
87. Napier, Charles, pp.128–9.

their fire was returned which in a few minutes drove them back.
. . About 5 o'clock the Enemy's Cavalry marched up to the Hill
near Carpio to the amount of a thousand – in the Evening they
retired & our Hussars occupied their former Positions.[88]

Not willing to risk his outposts, Craufurd quickly ordered those
at Carpio and Marialba to abandon their positions and to pull back
across the Azaba River. Lieutenant Georg Bergmann kept his troop of
about thirty hussars on the east side of the river and skirmished with a
force twice as strong as his for about four hours. The Germans took no
casualties and claimed to have inflicted about a dozen on the French,
who withdrew in the evening. The British re-occupied Carpio and
Marialba the next morning.[89]

Preparing for the Capitulation of Ciudad Rodrigo

With reports coming in that the French siege artillery had made it to
Ciudad Rodrigo, Wellington knew that once the guns opened up, it
would be only a matter of time before the city fell. To ensure that the
commanders of the two divisions closest to the enemy knew what he
wanted them to do, he wrote to Craufurd and Picton on 22 June:

> In the event of the surrender of Ciudad Rodrigo, I am desirous
> that Brig. General Craufurd should retire with his advanced
> guard upon La Conception. On his arrival there, that fort is to
> be evacuated by the troops of the 3rd division who are to march
> to stations Major General Picton will allot for them, in the
> cantonments of the 3rd division; and the guns, ordnance, and
> provision store in Fort Conception are to be sent back to Almeida,
> according to arrangements already made for that purpose.
>
> The Portuguese six pounder brigade, now in Almeida, is then
> to join the 3rd division.
>
> The officer commanding at Fort Conception is to point out to
> Brig. General Craufurd all the arrangements which he shall have
> made for the destruction of Fort Conception.
>
> Brigadier General Craufurd will keep his advanced guard
> in front of Almeida, till threatened by an attack by a superior

---

88. Duffy, Diary entry dated 21 June 1810.
89. Shaw, p.204. Beamish, Vol. 1, p.272

force, and when he retires from Fort Conception, he will blow up that fort.[90]

The French Open Fire on Ciudad Rodrigo

The next couple of days were relatively quiet. However, late in the night on 24 June the French began to bombard Ciudad Rodrigo. Lieutenant Shaw recorded in his diary that:

A heavy fire was heard all this night from Ciudad Rodrigo, and at day-break the enemy opened their batteries against the place. The fire from the place during the night must of course have been in consequence of the enemy's [sic] bringing their battering guns into the trenches. The enemy's fire from the trenches was extremely heavy, but returned by the garrison with great spirit. During the middle of the day the firing was not brisk, but again became heavy in the evening . . . I rode out with the General to see the place from the hill above Marialva, and to examine the enemy's batteries, etc. I soon returned, but while the General remained there (till about half-past 7 o'clock,) the enemy advanced with a considerable body of cavalry, and took possession of Marialva and Carpeo, [sic] from which places our picquets retired behind the Azava. We lost two horses and no men. . . The French showed no disposition to leave Carpeo and Marialva, and continued there with a considerable force of cavalry.[91]

Picquet duty once again fell on Captain Duffy and his company from the 43rd Foot. This time he was given the bridge at Marialva. They relieved the outpost at 4:30 a.m. It was not just his company that was there. He was augmented by forty riflemen and the 1st KGL Hussars maintained a vedette in Marialva a kilometre to the east. At 9 a.m. the French cavalry advanced towards Carpio and drove the German hussars back across the bridge. 'Their skirmishers come down to the Azava fired repeatedly at our Piquets but we did not return it. The Brigade moved out to support us but the Enemy did not attempt to cross the River. About

---

90. WD, Vol. 6, p.212
91. Shaw, pp.206–07.

11 they retired.'[92] The advance of the cavalry caused the division to form up in front of Gallegos in response. Rumours began to fly about why the French had come forward. Lieutenant Simmons thought it was because some previous movement was spotted by the French outposts and the French thought the British were moving to raise the siege.[93] Regardless of why the French had advanced, General Craufurd had decided that it was too dangerous to keep the infantry picquets so far forward and ordered them to stay on the west side of the Azaba River.

Craufurd had written to Wellington for further clarification of his instructions that were laid out in the letter of 22 June and received a response from him.

> I received your letter of the 23rd instant. The instruction which I sent you on the 22nd was to provide for a particular event, viz., the surrender of Ciudad Rodrigo. As soon as this should happen, it was obvious that the enemy would have his whole force disposable, and I should find it difficult, if not impossible, to cover the evacuation of Fort Conception, excepting in the manner stated in that instruction.
>
> The instruction of the 28th May goes to provide for a different event, viz., the passage of the Agueda by the enemy in superior force to you, during the continuance of the siege of Ciudad Rodrigo. In that case I should have no difficulty in keeping up the communication with Fort Conception as long as I might think proper, and at last I should be able to evacuate the fort.
>
> According to this interpretation of the instructions, you will see that, if attacked during the siege of Ciudad Rodrigo, I wish that you should retire upon Fort Conception and Almeida if possible; but of course that must depend upon the enemy's movements upon your left; but that as soon as Ciudad Rodrigo surrenders, you should withdraw upon Fort Conception, for which I conclude you will have time.
>
> My object is to be able to continue in our present situation as long as possible, both to encourage a continued resistance at Ciudad Rodrigo, and to be able to relieve the place, if it should be advisable to attempt it, in consequence of any alteration in

---

92. Duffy, Diary entry dated 25 June 1810.
93. Simmons, p.70. He had mistaken the date of this incident as happening on 24 June.

the enemy's force. This does not appear to be a very probable event at present, and ought not to be provided for according to the common rules of prudence at any risk; and there is a case not provided for in either of the memorandums of instruction, viz., the surrender of Ciudad Rodrigo, and the passage of the lower Agueda by the enemy in force at the same moment.

In that case I should wish you to retire as directed by the memorandum of the 28th May; and I should wish you to send directions to the commanding officer at Conception to evacuate that fort, and blow it up, and retire upon Almeida.

In order to be nearer the scene of action at this critical movement, and not to throw upon others more responsibility than belongs to them, I propose to move the military branch of head quarters to Almeida to-morrow. I think it may be expedient immediately to diminish our equipment at Fort Conception, so as to render the evacuation of that fort more easy, upon which I shall decide to-morrow morning when I shall at Almeida.[94]

Wellington was true to his word. He reached Almeida about 2 p.m. the next day after riding 65km from Celorico. He sent a short message to Craufurd about his intentions for Fort Concepción and his expectations of him:

I have directed the officer commanding at Fort Conception to evacuate that fort when you shall desire him to do so, removing those equipments [sic] which he has the means of moving, and blowing up the rest with the works. If you should retire upon Fort Conception, and the blowing up should devolve upon you under that memorandum of the 22nd, I beg you to remove all that there will be means to remove, which I believe is every thing, excepting some musket ammunition and provisions.[95]

Wellington also wrote to Lieutenant Colonel Sutton[96] 'that the fort is to be evacuated and destroyed, on notice from General Crawfurd [sic] that he is retiring; if he cannot retire upon Concepcion [sic], he is

---

94. *WD*, Vol. 6, pp.214–15.
95. Ibid., p.217.
96. Lieutenant Colonel Charles Sutton, 23rd Foot, was commander of the 9th Portuguese Regiment.

to send word to evacuate; and accordingly, thinking matters might be pressing, a working party was employed all night, getting the mines forward.'[97]

Wellington rode forward the next morning to do his own reconnaissance. With him was General Brent Spencer, the commander of the 1st Division. They stopped in Gallegos and then rode to the Vado de Flores ford. The outpost was manned by rifleman, one of whom was Edward Costello. Wellington approached the rifleman who wrote many years later about 'his Grace placing his telescope on my shoulders to take a view of the enemy's position'.[98]

That night Wellington wrote to Craufurd about the arrangements he had made for Fort Concepción:

> I have told Colonel Sutton that you should arrange a signal with him to let him know when he should evacuate Fort Conception, upon your retiring by the other road. There is certainly a very long tract of open country from your piquets to Gallegos, and from Gallegos to Alameda, to the River Dos Casa, and I wish it could be arranged to hold the ground on which your piquets are, and to have your infantry, or at least the main body, in the wood in front of Alameda, with your cavalry, and one battalion in Gallegos. I wish you would turn this disposition over in your mind, and see whether, by means of it, the piquets of infantry in front, which, after all, must be supported in their march across the plain to Gallegos by the cavalry, would not be as well supported as they are by the existing disposition.[99]

French General Officer Reconnaissance

Throughout June, French senior officers were spotted checking the fords. Their reception by the outposts varied from friendly to hostile, depending on which unit was observing the ford. On 14 June, the KGL Hussar outpost that was observing the ford across the Agueda at Molino de Valdespino,[100] reported seeing General Loison there.

---

97. Burgoyne, Vol. 1, p.87.
98. Costello, pp.29–30. Napier, Charles, pp.129–30.
99. *WD*, Vol. 6, p.218.
100. This ford is about 2km from Villar de la Yegua.

The reason why they knew who it was, was because they had engaged him in conversation.[101] Yet Marshal Ney did not receive such a friendly reception when he inspected the ford near Gallegos.[102] Captain George Napier's company of the 52nd Foot was manning the outpost.

> One day I was on picket at a ford in front of the village of Gallejos [sic], when I observed a general officer and his staff coming down the road on the opposite bank towards the ford. I called out across the river, which was narrow, to desire them to go back, and at the same time drew up my men and told the French general that I would fire at him if he persisted in coming down to the ford. They seemed to hold my threat in perfect contempt and still moved down; upon which I fired, and shot one of their horses. This had the desired effect, and they wheeled about and went back at a trot. The general, who was your uncle Charles' old Marshal Ney, rode a white horse; and I was not aware at the time that it was he, I made my men do all they could to shoot him, as it is always a good thing to shoot your enemy's general, as it must make a great confusion in his army.[103]

Interestingly his cousin Charles disagreed with his actions and wrote in his diary on 26 June:

> Marshal Ney supposed to have passed the ford where my brother's picquet was, and the men fired at him without George's orders, wounding one person of his suite. Had Ney been hit it would not have been creditable; it is not right to fire at people without necessity, like Indian savages. The marshal, or whoever it was, had rode up the river and crossed safely, so no end was answered by pelting him as he was going home.[104]

Charles Napier's objections may be based on a recent incident he had at a ford when he was shot at.

---

101. Shaw, p.201.
102. The Aldehuela de Don Clemente Arjona ford.
103. Napier, George, pp.114–15.
104. Napier, Charles, Vol. 1, pp.129–30.

Brigadier-General McKinnon,[105] Colonel Pakenham,[106] and myself, with others, had ridden a few hours before close to their picquets, at the very same place, and instead of firing on us they only joked, and good-humouredly asked us to come across the river; when our men fired they returned the compliment, but our firing was stopped by George immediately.[107]

The Arrival of the 16th Light Dragoons

On 26 June the 16th Light Dragoons marched to Gallegos and immediately went on outpost duty with the 1st KGL Hussars. Lieutenant Tomkinson wrote that they:

> marched from La Alameda [La Alameda de Gardón] so as to arrive at Gallegos by daybreak,[108] and when the piquets were relieved, occupied the quarters which the two squadrons of Hussars had left in the village of Gallegos . . . Picquets of infantry and cavalry occupied the line of the Azava from the right as far as Carpio, to its junction with the Agueda, and on that river at the ford of Molleno de Floris.[109] General Crawford's [sic] headquarters with his infantry were in Gallegos; the Cacadores [sic] encamped on the hill on the right of Gallegos, opposite Carpio. Two squadrons of the 16th, with one of the Hussars, in Gallegos; the other detached to Villa de Puerca [Villar de Argañán],[110] a league to the left, watching the passes of Barba de Puerca,[111] and the others up to our chain of posts . . . The enemy have about 8,000 men over the Agueda, which makes us particularly on the alert. We never unsaddle excepting in the evening, merely to clean the horses;

---

105. Charles Napier is mistaken about his rank. Henry Mackinnon was only a colonel in 1810. He was not appointed a brigadier general until July 1811. He was the commander of the 1st Brigade of the 3rd Division in June 1810.
106. The Honourable Edward Michael Pakenham was a Deputy Adjutant General on the Army Staff.
107. Napier, Charles, Vol. 1, p.130.
108. A distance of 6km.
109. Vado de Flores ford.
110. Villar de Puerco changed its name in 1953 to Villar de Argañán.
111. Barba del Puerco.

and at night the men sleep in their appointments, with their bridle reins in their hands, ready to turn out in an instant. At two in the morning, the whole turn out and remain on their alarm ground until the piquets relieved, come in, and all is quiet.[112]

Two squadrons of the German hussars were sent to the rear. One squadron left on the same day they were relieved and went to Minneal. The other squadron left the next day and marched to Maçal do Chão. Three days later, Wellington ordered the 14th Light Dragoons to Fort Concepción and gave its commander, Lieutenant Colonel Neil Talbot, the following instructions:

> The object in placing the 14th light dragoons at Val de la Mula, &c., is to keep open the communication between Fort Concepcion [sic] and Almeida, and to assist and protect the retreat of the garrison to Almeida, under the orders which Col. Sutton had received. The officer commanding the 14th light will communicate with Col. Sutton on this point. When the garrison shall have retired to Almeida, the 14th light dragoons are to cross the Coa by the bridge of Almeida, and to march upon Freixedas. If Gen. Craufurd should move the advanced guard to Fort Concepcion, the officer commanding the 14th light dragoons is to put himself under his command.[113]

Needless to say, Craufurd would take full advantage of the 14th Light Dragoons at the first opportunity. With them, he would have three cavalry regiments attached to his division, but no general to command them. Fortunately, the senior cavalry commander was Lieutenant Colonel Arentschildt, in whom he had the most trust. Wellington also trusted the German colonel. When he learned that Craufurd had creatively interpreted his instructions about withdrawing the German hussars his response was 'I have said nothing about the relief of your posts of hussars on the lower Agueda; because I think the duty of them will be much better done by the hussars, than by any other of the troops.'[114]

---

112. Tomkinson, pp.24–5.
113. WD, Vol. 6, p.143.
114. Ibid.

Barba del Puerco: view of the Agueda River from the British position. (Author's collection)

Barba del Puerco Bridge from the British position. (Nicholas Haynes collection)

Barba del Puerco Bridge. (Nicholas Haynes collection)

Barba del Puerco: view of the French side of the river. (Author's collection)

Barba del Puerco: British position at the top of the ridge overlooking the Barba del Puerco Bridge. It was here Lieutenant Simmons and his men fought the French coming up the ridge. (Author's collection)

Barba del Puerco: British position at the top of the ridge overlooking the Barba del Puerco Bridge. It was here the 95th Rifles stopped the French advance. (Author's collection)

The chapel at Barba del Puerco where the British picquets were based. (Author's collection)

Interior of the chapel at Barba del Puerco. (Author's collection)

Agueda River about 20km downstream of Ciudad Rodrigo. (Nicholas Haynes collection)

Azaba River near the Carpio Ford. (Nicholas Haynes collection)

The Marialba Bridge over the Azaba River. (Nicholas Haynes collection)

The Dos Casas River near Castillejo de Dos Casas. (Nicholas Haynes collection)

Terrain near Villar de Puerco. The French square was in left centre between the wall and the horizon. (Nicholas Haynes collection)

Terrain south of Barquilla looking towards Villar de Puerco. (Nicholas Haynes collection)

Fort Concepción: breach in wall. (Author's collection)

The rolling terrain to the east of Fort Concepción. (Author's collection)

This increase in the cavalry was just in time, for the French also began to aggressively patrol up to the Azaba River. Captain Ernst von Linsingen, a KGL Hussars troop commander, was one of those who were not sent to the rear. He wrote several letters which were paraphrased in *The History of the King's German Legion*:

> Within the last few days the enemy had occupied the stream with strong detachments of infantry, and to a corporal's picquet of hussars, consisting of five or six horses, full a hundred of the enemy were often opposed; but the vigilance of the small British posts amply compensated for their deficiency in number, and so much was the enemy's jealousy excited on this occasion by the alertness of the German cavalry, that a hundred doubloons are stated to have been offered by the general who commanded their outposts, to any party that would cut down one of the small British piquets.[115]

Lieutenant Tomkinson wrote in his diary on 27 June how the outposts were set up.

> The 16th, this day, took their share of the duty. The three squadrons found four officers' piquets along the chain of posts. Right piquet at Carpio Ford, an officer, sergeant, and two corporals, and eighteen men supported by infantry at night. The Mill Ford,[116] an officer and eighteen, sergeant and corporal. Marialva Bridge; the same with infantry. Molleno de Floris (on the Agueda), an officer and twelve of cavalry, with an officer and twenty of infantry. There was a captain of the cavalry piquets who remained at night at the Mill Ford, with a field officer of the day, who visited the chain of posts without remaining out at night. Two guns were out night and day, ready to support the piquets.[117]

The Light Division Withdraws

By 27 June the situation in Ciudad Rodrigo was grim. A letter received the previous day from the governor of the city put a positive spin

---

115. Beamish, Vol. 1, pp.273–4.
116. The ford 2km southwest of Carpio.
117. Tomkinson, p.26.

on the situation, but it was only a matter of time before it would fall and the French turned their attention to the British. General Craufurd had a contingency plan for the withdrawal of the Light Division back to the vicinity of Gallegos and sent it to Wellington, who responded the next day.

> Your situation gives me a great deal of uneasiness; and it appears that, if the enemy should make their preparations to attack you before the daylight in the morning, and should make the attack at daylight, you would find it very difficult to withdraw your corps. It is certainly very desirable, but we must not risk such a loss as your corps would be. I have no apprehensions for the day or the night, but I am uneasy respecting the time which intervenes between the night and broad daylight. I think that if your division was halted in the woods between Gallegos and Alameda, having one battalion and the cavalry and three pieces of artillery at Gallegos, and the picquets in their present situation, all would be safe. The piquets of infantry should withdraw to Gallegos at night, two or three hours after dark, and resume their situation after daylight in the morning.
>
> I have just received your letter of this morning. You propose exactly what I recommend in the beginning of this letter, viz., to show the infantry piquets on the heights in front of Gallegos, or in their present situation, and withdraw them at night. If you put them out, you must keep a battalion in Gallegos in the day time to support them. Indeed, in the day time, I do not think there is any danger for any thing. At night the battalion and picquets might go back to the woods, or remain at Gallegos, as you might think best. I conceive, however, that at present it would be in no danger at Gallegos, and to leave it there would be less harassing to the troops. I beg you to make your arrangements accordingly for to-morrow morning.[118]

On 29 June Craufurd rode to the outpost at Vado de Flores and could see a sizable breach in the walls of the city. The time had come to withdraw his troops.[119] The plan involved a bit of deception. The

---

118. *WD*, Vol. 6, p.222.
119. Shaw, p.210.

infantry were withdrawn first and marched about 5km to La Alameda, where they halted in the woods near the town. Craufurd wanted to make the French think they were still manning the outposts as the withdrawal began so half the 95th Rifles were sent back to Gallegos in the evening. Lieutenant Simmons recorded that 'The Division marched into camp into a wood near Alameda.[120] In the evening before dark we formed sections, and opening out very considerably so as to make it appear at a distance that a very large body of men were upon the march, we returned to Gallegos.'[121] Lieutenant Colonel Arentschildt, with his two squadrons and a squadron of the 16th Light Dragoons, was left in Gallegos to maintain the ruse. To ensure that they could withdraw as quickly as possible, all baggage was sent to the rear with the infantry.[122]

---

120. La Alameda de Gardón.
121. Simmons, p.71. Shaw, p.211.
122. Tomkinson, p.27.

Chapter 7

The War of the Cavalry Outposts, July 1810

'The duty at Gallegos was very severe. Every morning before 3 a.m. on the alarm ground, and the subalterns were nearly every night on piquet. When off duty in the daytime, we had so many alerts that little rest could be had. The evenings from the heat of the weather, were the pleasantest part of the day, and at first we did not lie down so soon as we ought, considering the early hour we turned out. We soon learnt to sleep in the day or at any time – never undressed – and at night all the horses were bridled up, the men sleeping at their heads, and the officers of each troop close to their horses altogether.'[1]

Lieutenant William Tomkinson, 16th Light Dragoons

'. . . we were in a state of continual alarm, we were sometimes turned out two or three times through the course of the day. We were always under arms at day-break which is a thing of course with the advance of the army as we were and have been, ever since we came to this part of the country, with some cavalry and some flying artillery. Our own pickets were very frequently having little skirmishes with the enemy but of no great consequence.'[2]

Lieutenant John Brumwell, 43rd Foot

With the withdrawal of the infantry from the Azaba River, the cavalry had the sole responsibility for picqueting the river. For the first week, four cavalry squadrons covered a distance

---

1. Tomkinson, p.30.
2. Brumwell, p.46.

of about 35km. The 1st KGL Hussars and the 16th Light Dragoons each provided two squadrons.

Regiment	Squadron	Commander
1st KGL Hussars	1st	Captain Philip von Gruben
	3rd	Captain Georg Krauchenberg
16th Light Dragoons	1st	Captain Robert Ashworth
	3rd	Captain John Belli

The four squadrons had a total strength of about 500 officers and men to screen the front.

	LTC	Maj	CPT	Subalterns	SGT	Trumpeters	Other Ranks	Total
1st KGL	1	–	3	10	18	4	214	250
16th LD	–	1	4	10	18	4	243	280

The one shortage that was really felt was among junior officers, especially in the 1st KGL Hussars. The regiment had only thirteen subalterns (lieutenants and ensigns) of twenty-four authorized (a 45 per cent shortage) and theoretically they should have been spread evenly among the eight troops. Prior to sending half the regiment to the rear in late June, Lieutenant Colonel Arentschildt reorganized his junior officers and kept ten of them with the two squadrons who would remain on outpost duty. The 16th Light Dragoons had seventeen subalterns with the regiment, and its commander kept ten with the two forward squadrons. This was not a war of formed cavalry regiments facing each other, but of small-unit actions, where the junior officers had far greater responsibilities. Captain Edward Cocks of the 16th Light Dragoons noted in a letter to Lieutenant General Stapleton Cotton, the commander of the British cavalry, that the picquets always had an officer in command of them. Each of the squadrons were responsible for two picquets, which meant that eight out of twenty subalterns were on duty at all times. This meant that in a five-day period, a subaltern would be on picquet duty for 48 hours.[3]

3.　Combermere, Mary W., *Memoirs and correspondence of Field-Marshal Viscount Combermere*, 2 vols. London: Hurst and Blackett, 1866, Vol. 1, pp.137–40.

The senior cavalry commander, Lieutenant Colonel Arentschildt of the 1st KGL Hussars, was responsible for controlling these picquets and deciding which squadron was responsible for each sector. The main threat was thought likely to come from an avenue of approach along the Azaba River, but the enemy could still approach from the Agueda River, so the outposts had to cover from Barba del Puerco in the north to Espeja in the south, a distance of about 35km. The 1st Squadron 1st KGL Hussars was billeted in Villa de Puerco[4] and were responsible for watching a 20km stretch of the Agueda River north to Barba del Puerco. The 3rd Squadron 1st KGL Hussars and the two squadrons from the 16th Light Dragoons occupied Gallegos and covered the Azaba River from its junction with the Agueda River in the north and to Espeja in the south, a distance of about 15km.

Each squadron provided four 10–20-man picquets, which were commanded by a subaltern with a sergeant in support. The officer and his sergeant would find a central location and then send their outposts to spots overlooking the fords and bridges across the Azaba and Agueda Rivers. These observation points would change daily in order to prevent creating a pattern that the enemy could detect and thus surprise them. However, since the number of crossing points were limited, there were only so many suitable places for an outpost. The outpost was usually two troopers during the day and at night they would be doubled. Thus a chain of twelve outposts watched for enemy activity along the Azaba River 24 hours a day. Since there were so few crossing points across the Agueda River, Captain Gruben and the 1st Squadron 1st KGL was able to maintain a similar chain of outposts with the same number of men. Behind these chains was a captain, who was responsible for all the outposts. It is likely that for the outposts along the Azaba River this duty rotated between the troop commanders in the three squadrons at Gallegos. For those watching the Agueda River, the duty fell to the two captains in Captain Gruben's Squadron.

The picquets were kept busy watching the area. Their primary mission was to spot any French movement that would indicate an advance in force towards the British lines. French patrols to gather intelligence or to forage for food were spotted daily. After an unspoken agreement was reached with the French, Captain Cocks noted in his journal that:

---

4.   Modern-day Villar de Argañán.

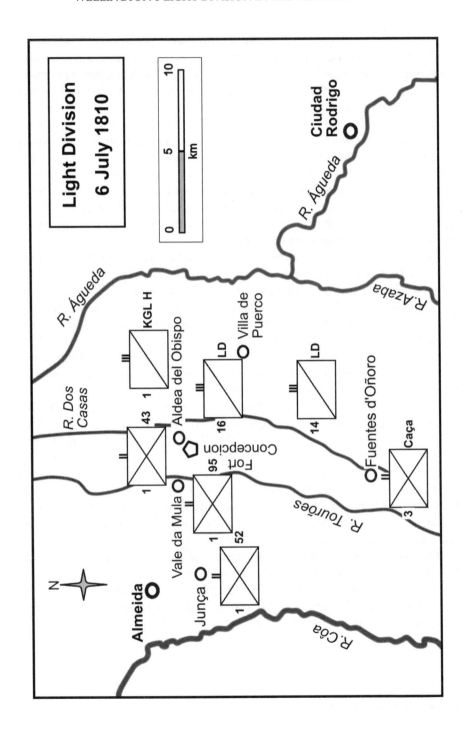

We are on very good terms with the French. The night before they attacked us at Gallegos I had a long conversation with a French officer, a little brook only divided us. Both parties made a point of never firing on single officers in this way without calling to them first.[5]

Yet this was not always the case. Captain Burgoyne wrote in his diary that:

. . . we have had vedettes [sic] on the commanding heights above Barquilla during the day, but withdrawn to near Castillejo, a mile in front of the fort, during the night. This morning, this picket of one subaltern and twenty dragoons, went out as usual, and the non-commissioned officer went forward to plant the vedettes on the summit of the height, where are three stone crosses on the road, when he saw a Frenchman rise up in the corn a little in front of him; he snapped off his carbine, which missed fire, and about two companies of infantry rose up and fired; the vedettes galloped back to the picket, but the French infantry returning, the vedettes were placed as usual at the crosses. A large body of the enemy's cavalry were then seen, who foraged, and a man of the infantry, who had purposely hid himself in the corn, gave himself up as a deserter; he says their intention was to surprise the picket, and drive us farther back . . .[6]

The French were not the only aggressive ones. Lieutenant Colonel Arentschildt recalled the initiative shown by one his corporals on picquet duty.

Corporal Heuer. In the year 1810, Heuer was on picquet with serjeant [sic] Schumacher. The inhabitants of a neighbouring village begged assistance against French infantry, who had marched in there to levy supplies. As the number of the enemy was given at eighty men, and the serjeant had only six under his command, he at first declined complying with the request, but, on the pressing entreaties of Heuer, finally consented, and the

---

5. Cocks, p.63.
6. Burgoyne, Vol. 1, p.93.

picquet advanced in double files upon the village. Heuer and his coverer chose for themselves the most difficult part of the attack, being that upon the two vedettes on the high road; however when Heuer dashed towards one of these his comrade rode off, and he was left quite alone.

The Frenchman shot, but missed, and was taken; without losing a moment, Heuer attacked the other, who met with the same fate. He now heard infantry in his rear; – made a signal for his comrades to advance, and as soon as they appeared upon the height, the French fled through the village leaving behind them a large quantity of provisions which they had collected.[7]

Although the 1st KGL Hussars were veterans at outpost duties, all did not go well with the 16th Light Dragoons initially. Lieutenant William Alexander had the picquet overlooking the Vado de Flores ford on the Agueda River. His picquet consisted of twelve troopers, plus a sergeant. Because of the distance from the top of the hill to the ford, the outpost at the ford consisted of six men. The relief party, led by a corporal, went down the hill and got lost. They eventually found the outpost, but the corporal, instead of returning to the top of the hill immediately, chose to stay there for a while. Lieutenant Alexander began to worry when the corporal and his party had not returned. Instead of going forward to see what happened to them, he decided that they had been surprised by the enemy and captured. The lieutenant raced back to Gallegos with the news that the French had crossed the Agueda. Captain Cocks was the duty officer that night and went forward to find out what was going on. While he rode the 4km to the outpost, the news that the outpost had been in contact with a French force of an unknown size was passed to General Craufurd. Upon arriving at the hill overlooking the river, Cocks found the corporal and his men. The corporal explained to the captain that he had gotten lost. Furthermore, when questioned, he admitted that he had not gone down with Lieutenant Alexander to see where the outpost was prior to going down with the relief. Once Craufurd heard what had really happened, he ordered the lieutenant to be placed under arrest for not following the division's *Standing Orders*.[8]

---

7. Beamish, Vol. 2, p.502.
8. Tomkinson, p.27. Shaw, pp.212–13.

Wellington's Concept of Operations

By this stage Wellington did not believe that Ciudad Rodrigo would hold out much longer. He wanted to ensure that all his subordinate commanders knew exactly what he wanted them to do after the city fell and the French pushed into Portugal. On 1 July he wrote a detailed letter explaining his intentions to Generals Picton, Cole, Slade, Campbell, and Craufurd.

> Upon the surrender of Ciudad Rodrigo, the royal dragoons under Major General Slade, and the troops composing the 3rd and 4th divisions of infantry, and General Craufurd's advanced guard including with the latter, the 14th light dragoons, two squadrons of the 16th, and two of hussars will be situated as follows.
>
> Brigadier Craufurd's advanced guard at Fort Conception, or in front of Almeida; the 3rd division of infantry at Pinhel, Porto de Vide, and one regiment of Portuguese infantry at Fraxedas[9] [sic]; the 4th division of infantry, General Campbell's brigade, at Castanheira, &c., observing the passages of the Coa at Castello Bom and Castello Mendo,[10] and the remainder of the division at Guarda, the royal dragoons observing the upper passages of the Côa as far as Sabugal.
>
> The officers are requested to communicate with each other, and with head quarters.
>
> In case the enemy should attack General Craufurd with a superior force, I wish him to retire upon Almeida, and eventually, should he find it necessary, across the Coa, holding the high grounds on the left of the river and Valverde, and keeping open the communication with the fort as long as may be practicable.
>
> If the enemy should pass the Coa at Castello Bom or Castello Mendo in force, General Campbell is to collect his brigade at Jurumelha, and is to retire gradually upon Guarda, taking care to give intelligence to General Craufurd at La Conception of his movement, as well as to General Slade. In this case General Slade with the Royals is likewise to retire upon Guarda.

---

9.   Freixedas.
10. Modern-day Castelo Mendo.

If the enemy should cross the Coa at any of the upper passages of the river, General Slade and General Campbell are to retire upon Guarda.

It is desirable that, if it should be practicable, General Slade with the Royals should join General Campbell's brigade in these movements, and General Cole will be in readiness to protect their retreat upon Guarda with the remainder of the division.

When General Craufurd shall receive the account of the retreat of General Campbell, he will retire upon Fraxedas.

When General Picton shall receive the account of the retreat of General Campbell, he will collect his division at Pinhel, and as soon as General Craufurd shall have arrived at Valverde, he will retire by Souropires [Souro Pires] upon Alverca,

If the enemy should attempt the lower fords and passages of the Coa in force, instead of the upper, or at the same time with the upper, or at the same time with an attack upon General Craufurd, General Picton is to give notice of this attempt to General Craufurd, who is to fall back upon Valverde, if not already there. As soon as General Craufurd shall have arrived at Valverde, General Picton will retire by the road of Trancoso till he shall pass Povoa del Rey, and will come to the heights on which are situated Villa Franca, Foidal, and Povoa de Concilio, &c, and General Craufurd will retire upon Alverca, and General Campbell and General Slade upon Guarda.

The regiment of Portuguese infantry of the 3rd division at Fraxedas will receive orders from head quarters.[11]

What is important about this letter is that it lays out what every division commander was to do in the event the French advanced in force. Craufurd was told he should retire towards Almeida and only cross the Côa River if necessary. Furthermore he should keep in contact with the fortress as long as possible. How he was to do this if he did pull back to the western bank of the Côa was not explained.

French Activity in the First Days of July

Until the end of June, the French appeared to be content to stay east of the Agueda River. There were daily patrols into the countryside

---

11. *WD*, Vol. 6, pp.230–1.

between the Agueda and Azaba Rivers, however it was a no man's land for all practical purposes. Neither side had troops billeted there. On 1 July, the French moved to start occupying it. Until this time the patrols were usually cavalry, however late in the day British outposts began to see infantry outposts along the Azaba River.[12] Early the next morning General Craufurd was on the top of the hill in front of Gallegos, when he saw the French 1st Provisional Dragoon Regiment[13] and six to eight artillery pieces move into Marialba. Craufurd immediately ordered the infantry at La Alameda to march to the high ground to the west of Gallegos.[14]

Lieutenant Tomkinson had command of the picquet overlooking the Marialba Bridge that night and the next morning found:

> The enemy approached close to the bridge, and by passing some light infantry down the opposite banks attempted to remove the cars from off the bridge. At the same time their cavalry mounted for foraging, and their infantry got under arms; through this, I reported that the enemy had an intention of passing, and the troops in Gallegos turned out.[15]

This report caused Craufurd to advance all the infantry to the hill behind Gallegos where they formed into line. When Lieutenant Tomkinson made his report, he assumed that the French were moving the carts that had been placed on the bridge to block it in order to advance across the river. Unfortunately he did not follow up his initial report. Lieutenant Shaw rode forward to see what was going on and found 'upon getting to the Bridge of Marialva, we found that this report was occasioned by a small party of the enemy having carried off one of the cars which were laid across the bridge, so as to obstruct the passage'.[16]

The massing of the Light Division on the hill west of Gallegos had an unforeseen consequence. It was reported to Masséna, who thought that they might be the advance guard of a relief force for Ciudad Rodrigo. He ordered Junot to find out. 'Send . . . General Sainte-Croix or such others

---

12. Shaw, p.212.
13. The 1st Provisional Dragoon Regiment consisted of the 3rd and 4th Squadrons of the 1st and 2nd Dragoons.
14. Tomkinson, pp.27–8. Shaw, p.213.
15. Tomkinson, p.28.
16. Shaw, p.214. Simmons, p.71.

as you judge advisable with 600 or 800 cavalry and artillery, if you believe necessary, with orders to overthrow all the principal posts in order to know the exact location of the British army and the line they hold.'[17]

Général-de-Brigade Charles d'Escorches de Sainte-Croix was 27 years old and had been in command of the 1st Provisional Brigade since its formation in December 1809. It consisted of the 1st, 2nd, and 3rd Provisional Dragoon Regiments, which were formed by taking the 3rd and 4th Squadrons from six other dragoon regiments. The provisional regiments were a temporary arrangement that allowed Napoleon to expand the number of cavalry regiments without incurring the cost of adding a new permanent regiment to the army. The organization of the three regiments were:[18]

1st Provisional Regiment	3rd and 4th Squadrons from the 1st and 2nd Dragoons
2nd Provisional Regiment	3rd and 4th Squadrons from the 4th and 9th Dragoons
3rd Provisional Regiment	3rd and 4th Squadrons from the 14th and 26th Dragoons

Each regiment was authorized 660 officers and men, but by July 1810 they were probably down to a strength of 500.[19] The brigade had about 1,500 men on 4 July 1810. The 3rd Hussars, who had been in the area for several months, were attached to the command because of their familiarity with the terrain. In addition to the cavalry, the reconnaissance force had five battalions of infantry and an artillery battery.[20]

The Affair of 4 July

Four outposts were being manned on the night of 3/4 July. The 16th Light Dragoons had three of the picquets which were led by Lieutenants William Hay, Henry Van Hagan and William Tomkinson. A fourth picquet was manned by the KGL Hussars. Captain John Belli was the

---

17. Horward, p.159.
18. Burnham, *Charging against Wellington*, pp.38, 40–1.
19. Lemaitre, Louis, *Historique du 4ᵉ Régiment de Dragons*. Paris: Henri Charles-Lavauzelle, 1894, p.212.
20. I have not been able to identify the infantry or artillery units. Horward, p.159.

duty officer.[21] Lieutenant Tomkinson had 2 July off, but was back on duty 36 hours later on a hill that overlooked a ford that was about a kilometre southeast of the Marialba Bridge. In addition to watching the ford, one of his other duties was to light the beacon that would warn the troops in the rear the French were advancing. The sun had set at 6:45 p.m. and what little moonlight they had would be gone within the hour.[22] The troops were tired, having been on outpost duty almost every other day, and the night was dark. The day had been hot and the night was warm. Staying awake was a problem. Sergeant Robert Liddle sang most of the night to keep his men alert. About 4:30 a.m. Lieutenant Tomkinson heard some noise on the other side of the ford and saw

> a light go down their line as if they were counting men in their ranks on the opposite side of the river. I mounted my men (which was fortunate), as they came on at a gallop, and I had some difficulty in getting all away . . . the enemy passed the ford . . . with two hundred cavalry as an advance, driving in my piquet at a gallop; they were close at our heels for two miles, we firing as much as we could to give the other piquets notice, and cutting at them as they came up to us.[23]

The amount of firing coming from Lieutenant Tomkinson's picquet was enough to alert Captain Belli that something was amiss. Fortunately for the British the three squadrons in Gallegos were already standing to, which was their normal practice, and they immediately mounted.[24] Lieutenant Shaw had spent the night in La Alameda and was woken with the news that the beacon had been lit. He raced the 6km to Gallegos to find out what was going on. Upon arrival there:

> Columns of the enemy's cavalry having now passed the Azava, they advanced in three bodies, and a line of skirmishers in their

---

21. Letter from Captain Edward Cocks of the 16th Light Dragoons to Lieutenant General Stapleton Cotton dated 6 July 1810. Combermere, Vol. 1, p.138.
22. Moonset was 7:39 p.m.
23. Tomkinson, p.28.
24. Letter from Captain Edward Cocks, of the 16th Light Dragoons to Lieutenant General Stapleton Cotton dated 6 July 1810. Combermere, Vol. 1, p.138.

front. One of the enemy's columns entered Gallegos, while two others turned it upon either flank. Our cavalry and guns withdrew gradually, and kept up a constant skirmish with the enemy. Behind Gallegos, there is a small stream, with a stone bridge over it; the enclosures here obliged the enemy's centre column to pass by the bridge. Our skirmishers had got over, and Captain Krauchenberg, of the 1st hussars, had about half his troop formed behind the bridge.[25]

While Lieutenant Shaw went forward, General Craufurd ordered the infantry and two guns from Captain Ross's Royal Horse Artillery troop to march towards Gallegos. As the infantry and artillery started moving, Lieutenant Shaw left a vivid description of what happened next.

Between Gallegos and Alameda the road crosses a small stream by a stone bridge,[26] the enclosures above and below which prevented the cavalry from passing easily other than by the bridge. At half cannon shot from the Bridge, on the Alameda side, is a height commanding it on which were two guns of Ross's Troop commanded by MacDonald. Our cavalry having passed Krauchberg's [sic] Troop of the 1st Hussars, and a troop of the 16th Light Dragoons near to the Bridge below Vallele to the left of the heights where the guns were, a body of French cavalry advanced in column, at a charging pace, upon the Bridge, diminishing their front as they approached the Bridge, and preserving the most perfect order notwithstanding some well-directed shots which they received from MacDonald. Just as the French Cavalry got upon the Bridge, Krauchenberg charged them with a part of his troop, sabred the French officers and men who were at the head of the column and repulsed it. General Craufurd exclaimed that whatever officer had led the charge must be a fine fellow; although looking at the charge, he did not know that this just compliment was paid to Krauchenberg.[27]

---

25. Shaw, pp.214–15.
26. The bridge no longer exists. Although it is described as a stream, Captain Cocks described it as a 'bog with a narrow causeway across it'. Combermere, Vol. 1, p.138.
27. Unpublished letter from James Shaw to William Napier, dated 18 February 1830. Napier Collection, Bodlean Library, Oxford. (f.228 d242).

During the fighting between Captain Krauchenberg's hussar squadron and the French dragoons, two hussars were noted for their actions. Captain Krauchenberg and Lieutenant Ernst Cordemann provided testimonials about their actions. Sergeant Major Louis Engle '. . . distinguished himself, cutting a French officer from his horse and taking another prisoner',[28] while

Corporal Almstedt . . . opposed the superior numbers of the enemy with such preserving bravery, corporal Almstedt distinguished himself. He was always one of the foremost in repelling the attacks, and saved the life of serjeant Bergmann, who, surrounded and wounded, was rescued by his cutting down several of those who were taking the sergeant away a prisoner, and putting the rest to flight, In general, upon all occasions when volunteers were required, Almstedt was the first to offer himself.[29]

Lieutenant Simmons of the 95th Rifles saw individual duels among the cavalry, including

a Light Dragoon attack a French Horse Grenadier[30] and trounce him handsomely. The man's helmet was nearly all brass, with large bards across in various ways; he had literally cut through this and also the man's head most severely and brought him in a prisoner. Our General sent the cap home as a present to some of his friends to show with what strength the Englishman had dealt his blows upon the Frenchman's head.[31]

Lieutenant Tomkinson, whose picquet was the first to encounter the French that morning, wrote that after conducting a fighting withdrawal through a hot sun-drenched plain covered with wheat to the bridge

Here the enemy, perceiving it our intention to withdraw over the brook, and that the greater part was already over, made

---

28. Beamish, Vol. 2, p.499. Based on the testimony of Captain Krauchenberg.
29. Ibid., pp.501–02. Based on the testimony of Captain Krauchenberg and Lieutenant Cordemann.
30. Lieutenant Simmons mistook the bearskin-wearing elite companies of the dragoon regiments for horse grenadiers.
31. Simmons, p.72.

a dash at our rear skirmishers, who were withdrawn in good order by Captain Krauchenburgh [sic] of the Hussars; and we having allowed a certain number to pass the bridge charged them back with great success. Two French officers, leading their men, behaved most gallantly, and were killed on the bridge. This success did not retard their advance one moment, for on our right they kept advancing with two regiments, and we remained rather long. For the last half-mile we were obliged to gallop, with the French dragoons close at our heels, and formed in rear of the infantry, which was drawn in line in front of the village of La Alameda.[32]

As Lieutenant Tomkinson pointed out, Captain Krauchenburg's counter-attack only temporarily halted the French cavalry. Although the regiment that charged across the bridge was stopped, the two other regiments crossed the stream a little further south and threatened the flank of his squadron. He ordered it to retreat. The cavalry began a fighting retreat back up the road to La Alameda with the French in hot pursuit. Lieutenant Shaw, who was still with the retreating cavalry found that as they approached the village,

> . . . we were much disappointed to find that the infantry, in place of being formed, were advancing upon the road in columns; the 43rd and 52nd were halted, and the 95th formed in line in front and extended a little. The Caçadores were formed in line on the left of the 95th. Our squadrons of cavalry formed in line with the infantry, also two pieces of artillery. A squadron of the enemy came very close to our left, and received the fire of the 3rd Caçadores, upon which the squadron retired.[33]

Captain Cocks of the 16th Light Dragoons, who commanded one of the troops in the fight, wrote two days later that:

> We could have stopped them here longer in front had not their numbers enabled them to encircle our right. It is understood they had about 2000 cavalry. Our artillery was served very well, and with considerable effect. I saw several shrapnels [sic] burst

---

32. Tomkinson, p.29.
33. Shaw, p.217.

in the middle of the enemy's squadron. About a mile from the bridge the enemy were pressing us hard, when we met our infantry. We drew the enemy close to them, and Elder's caçadores poured a volley into them. This checked them completely, and we were no more annoyed. The enemy's artillery hardly ever got into action.[34]

Major William Warre, the ADC to Marshal Beresford, had gone to Gallegos that morning to visit the outposts and was caught up in the fighting. He saw

two French Officers were severely wounded and some men, and one prisoner was taken, though, poor devil, he was covered with wounds, 6 in the head, and his arm nearly cut off, also run through the body, and wonderful to say, he is expected to recover. The French seemed much irritated by this check, and kept up a very brisk fire up the road we retreated by, within about 50 yards from us. Nor were they sparing in abuse, confident of still cutting us off, when we arrived at our Infantry which checked them, and a Squadron of their 3rd Hussars coming unexpectedly on the 3rd Portuguese Caçadores (an excellent Corps commanded by Lt. Col. Elder) received a very warm salutation which dispersed them. The Battalion behaved very steadily and well, and gives us hope of the Portuguese troops on whose conduct the issue of this Campaign must in great measure depend.[35]

This skirmish was the baptism of fire for the 3rd Caçadores. Until then no one was sure how they would perform.

After stopping the French advance, Craufurd decided to not risk a general engagement and ordered his infantry to retreat across the Dos Casas River. The 43rd was the first to withdraw, followed by the 52nd, and the 3rd Caçadores. They stopped on the high ground on the far side of the river overlooking the bridge. The 95th Rifles were the last of the infantry to withdraw, followed by the horse artillery and the cavalry. The Rifles stayed by the bridge while the rest of the division withdrew.

---

34. Combermere, Vol. 1, p.138.
35. Warre, William, *Letters from the Peninsula: 1808 – 1812*. Staplehurst: Spellmount, 1999, p.88.

They were soon brought under fire by the French dragoons. The professionalism of the dismounted dragoons impressed the riflemen.

> I am amused by the dexterity displayed by a body of French Dragoons (Grenadiers a Cheval) who passed through Alameda and dismounted, leaving their horse in line under the charge of some of their men. They then trotted off in their big jack boots and large hairy caps as Light Infantry to skirmish with us. As we had got the high ground across the river, and they could neither check nor impede our progress, they returned to their horses and became Dragoons again. A body of men of this description at the end of a hard day's march would be unpleasant neighbours.[36]

Once the British were across the Dos Casas River, the French commander had found the information he was looking for. No significant number of troops had been brought up to relieve Ciudad Rodrigo. He ordered his men back and proceeded to occupy Gallegos with picquets and his new line of vedettes was along the Dos Casas. The Light Division withdrew its infantry 10km northwest to the vicinity of Fort Concepción.[37]

Casualties were one-sided. Lieutenant Shaw reported the division had five men wounded. Lieutenant Tomkinson reported that '. . . our loss, Hussars one man killed, three wounded – two horses wounded. The 16th lost one man, two horses wounded; had they brought guns, we should probably have suffered equally.'[38] No casualties were reported for the infantry.

The French took many casualties, although the exact number of soldiers killed and wounded is unknown. The number among officers was quite high. Lieutenant De Gelorès of the 3rd Hussars was wounded in the left arm by a sabre.[39] In the 1st Provisional Dragoons Sous-Lieutenants Courtrez (of the 1st Dragoons), Jacques Mimin, Libault and Coutrez (all of the 2nd Dragoons) were wounded. In the 2nd Provisional Dragoons Sous-Lieutenant Leleu (of the 4th Dragoons) was wounded.[40]

---

36. Simmons, p.72.
37. Shaw, pp.218–19.
38. Shaw, p.219. Tomkinson, p.29.
39. Dupuy, Raoul, *Historique du 3e Régiment de Hussards de 1764 à 1887*. Paris: Librairie Française, 1887, p.132.
40. Martinien, pp.538, 539, 541 & 618.

Sous-Lieutenant J. Mimin died of his wounds in Salamanca on 15 July. General Sainte-Croix reported to General Junot that:

> The 2nd Dragoons continues to work wonders. Sous-Lieutenant Jacques Mimin distinguished himself in a reconnaissance carried out under the cannon of the fort. He cut his right arm with a cannonball and died of this wound at Salamanca Hospital on July 15th. This officer is one of the bravest soldiers counted in the 2nd Dragoons; He was known as a dragoon at Heilsberg and Friedland, and he was still distinguished on the day he fell gloriously before the enemy. His brother Jean had died in Portugal on May 8 previous. Lieutenant Libault, injured, is cited in the same case.[41]

Withdrawal into Portugal

General Craufurd knew that the Azaba River line was indefensible and his only option was to keep his infantry far enough back from the river so that they could respond to any French advance. Before receiving word of the French attack Wellington wrote to Craufurd at 1 p.m. that 'It would be desirable that if in your power you should occupy a height between Castillejo dos Caras [Castillejo de Dos Casas], and Val de Puerco, from whence you will have nearly as good a view of the plain and of Ciudad Rodrigo, as you had on the Azava.'[42] Craufurd chose to ignore this suggestion and moved all of his infantry back across the Tourões River, which was the border between Portugal and Spain. The division headquarters was in Vale da Mula, while the infantry was bivouacked in the vicinity of the village. The cavalry was kept behind the Dos Casas River, except for a picquet at Castillejo de Dos Casas, which was less than 200m on the other side of the river. The four squadrons of the 16th Light Dragoons and the 1st KGL Hussars formed a line of outposts along the Dos Casas River from Aldea del Obispo in the north to Fuentes de Oñoro in the south, a distance of about 20km. Don Julian Sanchez's cavalry and General Carrera's Spanish division

---

41. Bruyère, Paul, *Historique du 2ᵉ Régiment de Dragons*. Chartres: Garnier, 1885, p.17.
42. *WD*, Vol. 6, p.233.

covered the right flank from Fuentes de Oñoro south.[43] Much of the area that they were picqueting was covered with rye. It grew so high it 'reached nearly to our knees as we rode through it, and the grain flew out at every step'.[44]

The 9th Portuguese Line Regiment and the four companies of the 45th Foot, which were occupying Fort Concepción, were ordered to evacuate the fort and by the evening they were marching to Pinhel to rejoin their division in Pinhel.[45] The eighteen artillery pieces were sent to Almeida. In order to provide a guard for the mines that had been set by Captain Burgoyne, two companies of the 95th Rifles, including Captain O'Hare's, were ordered into the fort. Lieutenant Simmons was happy to be in a sheltered place and took the time to explore it. He was in luck for he found 'in a corner of a large place that had on some occasion been made a depot for provisions a cask of brandy and three casks of fine biscuit'.[46]

The next day, 5 July, Wellington again wrote to Craufurd with suggestions on how to conduct his operations:

> I have received your letter, dated two p.m. the 4th, and I am highly gratified by the conduct of Captain Krauchenberg, and Cornet Cordeman and his squadron of Hussars.
>
> I beg that you will tell Colonel Arentschildt that I will take an opportunity of reporting to his Majesty my sense of the conduct of the excellent regiment under his command, during the long and trying period that they have been at the outposts with you.
>
> If the enemy have drawn in again from Gallegos, I think it would be desirable that you should resume your position at Alameda, and place your picquets of cavalry on the Agueda, so as at all events to have a view of the place, encourage its continued resistance, and know what is going on. In that case I would throw the troops of General Picton's division again into La Conception, and the 14th Dragoons should continue there.
>
> If you think you are better on this side of the Dos Casas, you might either keep the 14th Dragoons with you, or send a

---

43. Shaw, pp.218–19. Tomkinson, p.29.
44. Tomkinson, p.30.
45. Burgoyne, Vol. 1, p.90.
46. Simmons, p.73.

part, or the whole of them, to the rear, as you may think proper. If you want to keep only four squadrons with you, they had probably better be two of Hussars, and two of the 14th, sending the 16th back. If you wish to have six squadrons, keep two of each regiment; and if eight squadrons, keep the whole.[47]

Craufurd decided that it was too risky to move back to the Azaba River, no less moving another 8km forward to the Agueda River. Instead he chose the last option of keeping his outposts on the west side of the Dos Casas River. He of course, decided he would take Wellington up on his offer of allowing him to keep the 14th Light Dragoons. He now had about 1,000 cavalry organized into eight squadrons to cover 20km of outposts. These were:

Regiment	Squadron	Commander
1st KGL Hussars	1st	Captain Philip von Gruben
	3rd	Captain Georg Krauchenberg
14th Light Dragoons	1st	Major Felton Hervey
	2nd	Major Charles Butler
	3rd	Captain Charles Baker
	4th	Captain Thomas Brotherton
16th Light Dragoons	1st	Captain Robert Ashworth
	3rd	Captain John Belli

Table 7.1: Strength of Cavalry Attached to the Light Division in July 1810

	LTC	Maj	CPT	LT	Cornet	SGT	Trumpet	Other Ranks	Total
1st KGL	1	–	3	3	4	18	4	214	247
14th LD	1	2	8	11	1	39	7	499	568
16th LD	–	1	4	8	2	18	4	243	280

The 1st KGL Hussars and the 16th Light Dragoons bivouacked in a wood just south of Vale da Mula and about 4km west of their picquets

---

47. *WD*, Vol. 6, pp.235–6.

along the Dos Casas River. The 14th Light Dragoons were the furthest forward with three troops in Aldea del Obispo, three in Vale da Mula and two troops in Castillejo de Casas.[48] The land between the Dos Casas and the Azaba Rivers became the new no man's land. Both sides patrolled the area, but neither occupied it in force. Along the Dos Casas River a squadron of the 1st KGL Hussars and one from the 14th Light Dragoons were responsible for picqueting the area to the north of Aldea del Obispo, while one squadron each of the 14th Light Dragoons and two squadrons of the 16th Light Dragoons were responsible for the sector south to Fuentes de Oñoro.[49]

The doubling of the amount of cavalry under his control allowed Craufurd to be more aggressive. Three outposts were manned 24 hours a day 'one near Fuentes de Oñoro, one at the bridge near La Alameda, and the third on the main road in the wood leading from that village to Fort Concepcion [sic], of the same strength as on the Azava'.[50] Patrols were sent across the Dos Casas and Lieutenant Shaw went on one patrol with Colonel Pakenham,[51] Colonel Hardinge[52] and Major Warre to Barquilla and Villa de Ciervo. There they saw the results of the French foraging.

> The inhabitants had fled from all these villages. The enemy occupy Gallegos with a picquet only, but had entered it at noon-day with a considerable body, probably to forage. A small party of the enemy was in Valla de Yequa last night, also in Serranilla and Martillan, but they did not remain in these villages. The appearances were sufficiently melancholy during our ride today. We met the unfortunate inhabitants flying from their homes, and the whole of the people of some of the villages encamped in the fields, having with them all their property which they could carry off upon their cars.[53]

---

48. Hanley, William, 'Letter to William Napier dated 25 January 1856', *United Services Magazine*, 1856, Part I, p.346.
49. Letter from Captain Edward Cocks, of the 16th Light Dragoons to Lieutenant General Stapleton Cotton dated 6 July 1810. Combermere, Vol. 1, p.139.
50. Tomkinson, p.30.
51. Colonel Edward Pakenham, the Deputy Adjutant General of the Army.
52. Lieutenant Colonel Henry Hardinge, Deputy Quartermaster-General of the Portuguese Army.
53. Shaw, p.220.

Even Craufurd himself occasionally joined the patrols. On 6 July, he rode almost 10km deep into the contested area to

Barquilla, and from thence to a hill, from which we could see Gallegos, at which place it appears by the account of the natives, that the enemy has only a picquet. A small part of the enemy's cavalry entered Villa de Puerco [Villar de Puerco] and Cismeiro [Sexmiro] this morning, and plundered them; they had also completely destroyed and plundered everything in Alameda, when they entered it on the 4th . . . Our patrols go into Villa de Puerco, and to Gallegos. As our force of cavalry amounts to upwards of 800 men mounted, we are now in a state to take more liberties on the flat open country in our front.[54]

Although many of the men were bivouacking in the woods, rations for the cavalry were plentiful for both the men and horses. However, the evacuation of Gallegos caused the 16th Light Dragoons to abandon their wine.

We have been very well foraged since we have been here. We have generally had more than our allowance; sometimes wheat, sometimes, Indian corn, sometimes rye, with plenty of green forage. The men have been well off except for wine. A pipe, which we had just procured at Gallegos, we could not bring away, and were obliged to stave it. Some supplies of biscuit were also left behind. The horses have not fallen off, though they have been almost constantly saddled at Gallegos.[55]

On 7 July, Wellington changed his mind again about how far forward he wanted the Light Division. This time he was very specific. 'I am not desirous that you should move across the Dos Casas, unless it should be perfectly convenient, or if you are to be exposed to an attack, and retire again.'[56]

---

54. Shaw, pp.221–2.
55. Combermere; Vol. 1, p.139.
56. *WD*; Vol. 6, p.240.

Latest Intelligence

By 8 July General Craufurd was getting a better picture of what forces he was facing. It was not good news. A sergeant had deserted from the Irish Regiment and gave the first detailed account of General Junot's corps.

> 22nd regiment, 4 battalions, 600 per battalion
> > 2nd, 7th, and 15th dragoons
> > 4th, and 10th hussars
> > 17th Chasseurs

The deserters generally state, that there are 8 regiments of cavalry with Junot's corps. The 22nd forms a brigade commanded by Godarvo. A regimental provisor and a regiment of the line, formed the other brigade, and these two brigades a division.

Another account of the 8th Corps, was given as follows by a deserter, who appeared to be very intelligent.

1st Division
> 38th regiment, one battalion, 600 strong
> 46th regiment, one battalion, 600 strong
> 50th regiment, one battalion, 600 strong
> 75th regiment, one battalion, 600 strong

This is the 2nd brigade, and is commanded by General Lopem.
> 19th regiment, one battalion, 600 strong
> 25th regiment, one battalion, 600 strong
> 38th regiment, one battalion, 600 strong
> 34th regiment, one battalion, 600 strong

This is the 1st brigade and is commanded by General ****
2nd Division
> 1st brigade, 22nd regiment, 4 battalions, 2000 strong
> 2nd brigade, 65th regiment 4 battalions, 2000 strong
3rd Division
> 1st brigade: 70th regiment, 4 battalions, 2000 strong
> 2nd brigade:
Irish Brigade, 2 battalions, 700 strong

Polish Brigade, 1 battalion, 500 strong[57]
Bavarian regiment, 600 strong[58]
Total 3800[59]

Lieutenant Shaw did an analysis of the information provided by the Irish sergeant and concluded that

> ...it is evident that many regiments which belong to Junot's corps, are altogether omitted in the above statements of it. Three men of the 1st Prussian regiment stated that their regiments belongs to the 2nd division of the 8th corps, of which division they gave the following account:

	Strength
1st Prussian regiment,	1300
Irish brigade	600
52nd regiment of line,	1800
58th regiment of line,	1800
	5500

And state that the division is commanded by General Sallina. By the accounts most to be depended upon, it appeared that the cavalry of the Provisional, which amounted in all to about 5000 men.

Ney's corps. The sixth.

The corps is certainly underrated [as reported in 30 May]... by averaging the battalions (of which there are 37) at 500 per battalion, as the whole corps, when before Ciudad Rodrigo, did certainly not amount to less than 22,000 infantry. The following statement of the 6th corps . . .

1st Division, (Marchand)
Manenule

---

57. This was incorrect. There were no Polish troops serving in the Army of Portugal.
58. This too was incorrect. There were no Bavarian troops serving in Spain.
59. Shaw, pp.213–16.

6th légèrc, 2 battalions
69th line, 3 battalion
Marconnier
    39th line, 3 battalions
    76th line, 3 battalions
2nd Division (Mermet)
La Passet
    25th légère, 2 battalions
    27th line, 3 battalions
Bertè
    50th line, 3 battalions
    59th line, 3 battalions
3rd Division (Loison)
Simon
    26th line, 3 battalions
    82nd line, 4 battalions
    Légion du Midi, 1 battalion
Ferre
    32nd line, 2 battalions
    66th line, 3 battalions
    Hanovarion legion, 2 battalions

Also the 15th légère, 1 battalion, is in one of General Loison's brigades. The statement of the cavalry attached to this corps, [report of. . .] is confirmed by the accounts of deserters, and that it appears that Lancé commands one of the cavalry divisions.

The two above stated corps (6th and 8th) together with the 2nd, which is commanded by Marshal Regnier,[60] were avowedly those intended for the conquest of Portugal, and were called the Army of Portugal, of which Massena was Commander. Of this last (the 2nd corps) we had but little information, but it was supposed to consist of from 15,000, to 17,000 men in cavalry and infantry . . .[61]

Craufurd forwarded this intelligence to Wellington, who replied by sending him his own assessment.

---

60. General Jean Reynier.
61. Shaw, pp.216–19.

I believe I told you that I had the return of Junot's corps in detail. The account of the deserter is perfectly correct, but he has not stated all the troops of any division. The total effective infantry of this corps is 19,899; the cavalry, divided into eight, instead of three provisional regiments, is 4716. The total effectives of the corps, including the artillery, is 25,956.[62]

The Affair of 11 July

French patrols continued into the territory west of the Azaba River, mostly to forage for food and fodder. In an effort to stop them, on 8 July Lieutenant Shaw rode to the cavalry encampment at 10 a.m. and accompanied a large force to try to intercept a patrol which had hit Villa de Puerco that morning. It took a while to organize the cavalry and they did not depart until 1 p.m. They rode to La Alameda and through the woods at Villa de Puerco and then on to Sexmiro, but were too late to intercept the foragers. Two days later, word reached the division headquarters that the French had pillaged the villages of Barquilla and Villar de Ciervo.[63]

This was becoming a regular occurrence and Craufurd decided to do something about it. He wrote to Wellington:

The enemy had, during the last three or four days, been in the habit of coming with detachments of infantry and cavalry into Barquilla, and with infantry into Cesmiro and Villa de Puerco, and I was desirous of cutting them off. But considering the vicinity of the enemy's position, and his strength in cavalry, I did not think it prudent to send a small detachment, and I therefore ordered all that were off duty of six squadrons to assemble behind the Dos Casas at twelve at night, on the road which leads from La Conception to Alameda.[64]

The operation was to be a combined-arms affair. Its mission was to capture the enemy foragers that were expected to return to Barquilla, Sexmiro and Villa de Puerco. The six cavalry squadrons were: Captain Krauchenberg's 3rd Squadron of the 1st KGL Hussars; Major Hervey's

---

62. *WD*, Vol. 6, p.242.
63. Shaw, pp.223–4.
64. *WD*, Vol. 6, p.252.

1st Squadron, Major Butler's 2nd Squadron, and Captain Brotherton's 4th Squadron of the 14th Light Dragoons; and Captain Ashworth's 1st Squadron and Captain Belli's 3rd Squadron of the 16th Light Dragoons. There were seven companies of the 95th Rifles and two companies from the 52nd Foot, one of which was Captain Robert Campbell's company, as well as two guns from Captain Ross's RHA troop. Among the Rifle companies were Captain Leach's No. 2 Company and Captain O'Hare's No. 3 Company. The 3rd Caçadores would provide the reserve.

In order to surprise the French, sound and light discipline was strictly enforced. Lieutenant Colonel Neil Talbot ordered the 14th Light Dragoons to 'to draw swords to prevent jingling in the scabbards'.[65] Rifleman Costello recalled:

> A few days after our arrival at Val de Mula, a part of the division formed a night expedition to surprise and cut off one or two French regiments that nightly occupied an advanced position on our right, retiring every morning about daylight . . . We soon guessed that some secret enterprise was about to be undertaken, as strict orders were issued to keep the men from talking, and to make them refrain from lighting their pipes, lest our approach should be noticed by the enemy. Even the wheels of two of Captain Ross's guns that accompanied us were muffled round with haybands to prevent their creaking.[66]

The infantry was formed up at Fort Concepción and the whole force moved out at midnight. Five squadrons of cavalry, the 52nd Foot and the 3rd Caçadores marched south for about 2km before crossing the Tourões River by a ford. It continued southeast using the ridgeline to the east of the river to mask its movement. It crossed the Dos Casas River by the bridge that was about 2km west of La Alameda. The 3rd Caçadores were left to guard the bridge where the force crossed and also the ford along the road from Alameida to Fort Concepción about 2km north of the bridge. After departing La Alameda the force marched the 5km to Villa de Puerco. There they stopped a wooded low lying area about a kilometre south of the village, near a large farmhouse called Hurtada.[67]

---

65. Hanley, p.346.
66. Costello, pp.30–1.
67. Shaw, pp.224–5. Unpublished Letter from James Shaw to William Napier, dated 18 February 1830. Napier Collection, Bodlean Library, Oxford.

Major Butler's squadron of the 14th Light Dragoons, the four companies of riflemen and two guns were not part of the main group. The cavalry was cantoned in Castillejo de Dos Casas which was 4km west of Barquilla. They only needed to link up with the infantry and guns before moving out. They might have been impatient to get going because one source[68] said they began their march before the 95th Rifles and the two guns had made it to Castillejo de Dos Casas. However, by sunrise the cavalry, infantrymen and guns were hidden behind a hill with three crosses[69] on the north side of Barquilla.

The main force of cavalry was in position well before sunrise, which was at 4:49 a.m. The troopers were allowed to dismount, but at least in the 14th Light Dragoons, 'The colonel forbade any man to leave his horse's head, and the strictest silence enjoined on all.'[70] About 6 a.m. Craufurd rode forward and saw French cavalry entering both Barquilla and Villa de Puerco. He hurried back and gave the order to spring the trap. The cavalry moved in an open column of divisions with the left in front, led by Krauchenberg's Squadron, which was followed by the 16th Light Dragoons, and then the 14th Light Dragoons. Lieutenant Colonel Talbot ordered his 'squadrons to wheel, threes right, and, standing in stirrups, said, "Fourteenth, the enemy – honour and glory are before you. Keep your horses well in hand, and follow me. Advance by threes from the right, leading rank – left, wheel, at a canter – march!"'[71]

They marched to the south of Villa de Puerco. The terrain was hilly, and their approach was delayed by having to cross a defile that funnelled the cavalry into a narrow approach. As the 14th Light Dragoons'

> . . . squadrons crossed the summit, leaving the village Villa de Puerco about 400 yards on the left, and crossed the Gallegos road, passing through a gateway formed by two rough pieces of quarried stone, entered the wheat field then growing saddle

---

(f.228 d242). Leach; *Rough Sketches. . .*, p.141. Dawson, Henry and Charles, *'Every Implement of Destruction Was Used against Us': The Lives of Henry and Charles Dawson, 52nd Regiment of Light Infantry Based on their Peninsular War Letters.* Philip Abbott (ed.). Privately published, 2015, p.27.

68. Hanley, p.346.
69. These crosses no longer exist, however the hill is known as 'Los Cruces' (The Crosses).
70. Hanley, p.346.
71. Ibid., pp.346–7.

high. In passing the gateway, rear rank had to double on the front; meanwhile the pace, 'at a canter,' continued, without reforming ranks of threes, division, troop, or squadron.[72]

By the time the British cavalry made it to the other side of the village, across the hilly terrain and through the gateway, the French had been alerted to the British presence and had pulled back towards Sexmiro.[73]

On the far side of Villa de Puerco was a low ridge, which combined with the fields of wheat, significantly reduced visibility. Before the lead squadron of the cavalry passed through the defile, the French had disappeared. Lieutenant Shaw volunteered to ride forward with Captain William Campbell, the division's DAQMG. As they rode towards the hill they 'saw upon the hill some of the enemy's cavalry; two or three hussars. And Campbell and myself galloped on. Upon my arrival nearly at the summit I came within about seventy yards of a body of infantry, which were formed.'[74] The French infantry was the Grenadier Company 3rd Battalion, 22nd Line Infantry Regiment commanded by 35-year-old Captain Pierre Gouache.[75] He had about 100 men with him and formed them into a square, with a half-section of 25 men on each side. This gave them a frontage of about twelve men on each face of the square.

They rode back to General Craufurd, who upon hearing this, ordered Captain Krauchenberg and his squadron to charge. Captain Ernst von Linsingen, the other troop commander in the 3rd Squadron, described what happened.

The hussars made straight for the enemy's cavalry, but before they had yet come within charging distance, Krauchenberg, perceiving the glimmer of bayonets in the corn, through which he rode, immediately apprized General Craufurd that they had infantry to contend with. The general briefly replied 'charge them,' and hurried on with the squadron, whose progress was much impeded by a stony road over which it had to pass, and the files became consequently extended; Krauchenberg, however, formed them up in as good order as the general's impatience

---

72. Hanley, p.347.
73. Tomkinson, p.31.
74. Shaw, pp.25–6.
75. Lievyns, A. et al. *Fastes de la Légion-d'honneur: biographie de tous les décorés*, 5 vols. Paris: 1847. Vol. 5, p.381. Horward, pp.188–9.

would permit, and led his men towards the bayonets, which quickly disappeared, the infantry lying down as the hussars approached. When, however, the squadron had arrived within about fifty paces of the French, they jumped up, shewing a square of about two hundred men, and fired. Two horses were killed, and eleven men and eight horses were wounded.[76]

About this time some French cavalry was noticed in the distance near the village of Barquilla. Behind them came another large body of cavalry. According to Captain von Linsingen,

But only one wing of the squadron having received the fire of the square, the rest remained effective, and Krauchenberg was about to charge with these while the French were yet reloading, when general Craufurd ordered him to leave the infantry to the other squadrons and attack the cavalry; he therefore, galloped on.[77]

What happened next caused so much controversy over the next few weeks that Wellington himself had to intervene. Next in line was the 16th Light Dragoons. According to Lieutenant Tomkinson the '16th were ordered to form line to the left, and pursue some cavalry near Barquilla'.[78] Yet Captain Cocks, a troop commander in the 16th Light Dragoons, said that Captain Ashworth's 1st Squadron charged the square with the KGL Hussars.

Had Ashworth been allowed to remain in the rear of the hussars, where he had formed, he would have had an opportunity of making an effectual charge when the hussars opened out, in consequence of the fire; but he was ordered by some staff officer to form in line with the hussars, and as the latter outflanked the infantry on both flanks, Ashworth's squadron, which was to the left, of course, completely cleared the infantry, and was protected from their fire by the hussars filling round the flank of the enemy. After the charge, therefore, they again formed. An order was given to form to the left and attack the cavalry. It appears

---

76. Beamish, Vol. 1, pp.280–1.
77. Ibid., Vol. 1, p.281.
78. Tomkinson, p.31.

perfectly natural, for the cavalry were dispersing and preparing to escape, à la débandade, and it was necessary to secure them instantly, particularly as we did not know whether Gruben's and Butler's squadrons were friend or foe.

When the two leading squadrons began to go off to the left, the next squadron (Bellis') had not cleared the crest of the hill. It was more broken in the defile than the others, in consequence of having more ground to make up. It could not have seen the infantry, even had the dust cleared up, and as it followed Ashworth's squadron it was not opposite to them. The fire was independent, and no one of this squadron could tell whether it proceeded from infantry or cavalry. When, therefore, the order was passed down to move on the cavalry, it was obeyed with alacrity and without surprise, as they were the only enemy to be discerned.[79]

Lieutenant Tomkinson confirms the lack of visibility during the charge.

We followed the Hussars in their charge. I heard the fire from the enemy's infantry; but such was the haste with which the attack was conducted, that had it not been for the whizzing of the shot, I should not have known we were under fire, not seeing where the enemy stood.[80]

The French dragoons were a detachment of the 1st Dragoons, part of the 1st Provisional Dragoons. The officer commanding it knew they were in trouble. To their immediate rear, coming out of Barquilla, was Major Butler's squadron. To the northeast, along the road to Villar de la Yegua came Captain von Gruben's squadron, which had been sent to the northeast the night before to cut off any possible French retreat to the north. To their south, were the three squadrons of the 1st KGL Hussars and 16th Light Dragoons. The French were outnumbered 20 to 1. The first to appear was Major Butler's squadron and the French commander decided to fight rather than surrender. It was a very one-sided affair. Many of them 'were a good deal hacked and cut about the head'.[81] Two

---

79. Combermere, Vol. 1, pp.149–50.
80. Tomkinson, p.32
81. Simmons, p.73.

officers and twenty-nine men became prisoners. Among the wounded captives was Sous-Lieutenant Bonbrain.[82]

While these clashes were going on the riflemen in Barquilla were becoming impatient. Rifleman Costello wrote later that:

> We had all loaded before marching, and were anxiously looking forward to the result, when a whispering order was given to enter a large field of standing corn and to throw ourselves on the ground. There we anxiously waited the first dawn of day for the expected engagement. At length the cold grey of the morning appeared faintly in the east, when the commands were given with scare a pause between to 'fall in', 'double', and 'extend'. This was accomplished in a moment, and forward we ran through the corn-field up to an eminence, looking down from which we beheld a gallant skirmish on the plain below . . .[83]

General Craufurd was furious at what happened and he made a mistake that would shake his confidence and tarnish his reputation. Instead of waiting for the two guns to come forward to bring the French square under fire, he ordered the 14th Light Dragoons to charge. At the time they were about to follow the rest of the cavalry and this order took them by surprise. Captain Brotherton's 4th Squadron was given the order. According to Brotherton, Craufurd,

> came up to the officer commanding the leading half-squadron of the 14th, and in a hasty, and as far as regarded the object to attack, rather indistinct manner, gave a peremptory order to charge, merely pointing to the supposed direction in which the enemy were, without any farther instructions. Though the enemy afterwards proved to be so very close, yet at the moment they were invisible, being hidden in standing corn. The officer who had received Gen. Craufurd's order, immediately changed his direction towards the spot pointed to by the General. At this instant Colonel Talbot came up, and on inquiring the reason of this change of direction, formed half squadrons, and had proceeded but a very few yards, when the gallant little square

---

82. Beamish, Vol. 1, p.281. *WD*, Vol. 6, p.253. Martinien, p.538.
83. Costello, pp.30–1.

started up from their hiding-place, when we were almost on the points of their bayonets, and poured in a destructive volley.[84]

Lieutenant Colonel Talbot led the charge and Captain Campbell, the Light Division's DAQMG joined them. Captain Brotherton later wrote that:

My squadron came within pistol-shot of it, and was beautifully steady. We charged it most gallantly, but they fired a deadly volley into us, and half my men fell killed or wounded. Colonel Talbot, who commanded the Regiment, had put himself at the head of the squadron along with me. Poor fellow, he fell pierced by eight balls, literally on the enemy's bayonets. The moment the square fired into and so badly crippled us, it moved off to join its support close by, and we were so shattered as not to be able to follow.[85]

Trooper Hanley, of the 3rd Troop, was part of the charge.

A light breeze was blowing in our rear, which carried a cloud of dust before our horses, and, at the same time, concealed the enemy from view. Having reached the lower end of the field, our leading ranks of threes, received a salutation from one face of the square. I am of opinion the square consisted of from 250 to 300 bayonets. Several dragoons were wounded as they entered the field; and Lieut.-Colonel Talbot, Quartermaster M'Cormack [Angus McCormick], eight dragoons, and two horses, lay killed on the bayonet point.[86]

Major Hervey's 1st Squadron 14th Light Dragoons was about to make the fourth charge but were ordered back at the last moment.

Meanwhile, the second squadron, having passed the defile, gateway, formed troops, advancing at a trot over the wounded

---

84. *United Services Journal*, 1832, Part 1, p.529.
85. Brotherton, Thomas, *A Hawk at War: The Peninsular War Reminiscences of General Sir Thomas Brotherton*. Bryan Perrett (ed.). Chippenham: Picton Publishing, 1986, p.22.
86. Hanley, p.347.

men and horses that had fallen, until it reached the shattered first squadron, accompanied by several riderless horses. The enemy, taking advantage of the disorder into which the first squadron was thrown, retired in square across a broke, rugged cart-track, on a rising ground, and halted, and most courteously declined to fire a second round at us.[87]

The casualties among the cavalry, especially in the 14th Light Dragoons were very high. Initial reports were: Lieutenant Colonel Talbot, Troop Quartermaster Angus McCormick,[88] six troopers and thirteen horses killed. The 16th Light Dragoons had one trooper and two horses killed, and one man wounded. The 1st KGL Hussars had thirteen men wounded and thirteen horses killed.[89]

Major Charles Napier later wrote:

Certainly both they and their opponents were noble soldiers! And so was William Campbell, the brigade major, known then and afterwards throughout the army for every generous quality. He was sententious of speck, quixotic of look, but handsome and strong, and his sentiments of honour were worthy of the Spanish don, his courage as high, yet purged of folly: he was indeed a gallant English gentleman in thought, look, word and deed. In this combat he charged so home that his horse was killed close to the French bayonets, but being himself unhurt he arose, and though alone, slowly stalked away, disdaining haste as he disdained danger. The gallant French captain, Guace [sic], would not let his men slay the proud soldier; thus all was noble on both sides, and William Campbell escaped death.[90]

---

87. Hanley, p.347.
88. Up until 1808, the cavalry regiments did not have a regimental quarter-master. This function was at the troop level and each troop had a troop quartermaster, who was a noncommissioned officer. In 1809 this position was abolished and each regiment was assigned a regimental quartermaster, who was an officer. In place of the troop quartermasters, each troop was authorized a troop sergeant major, who was the senior NCO in the troop. For some reason, as late as March 1813, the 14th Light Dragoons still had troop quartermasters.
89. Tomkinson, pp.31–2.
90. Napier, Charles, pp.132–3.

After the French infantry retreated,

the squadrons dismounted, the wounded were assisted, and several remounted. The killed remained on the ground where they so nobly fell, with the exception of Lieut.-Colonel Talbot and Quartermaster M'Cormack [sic], whose bodies were conveyed to Aldea del Bispo [sic], and placed in the chancel of the chapel previous to interment. Some days after they were buried both, side by side (as they fell on the bayonet point), on the glacis of Fort Conception.

When the squadrons dismounted Trumpeter M'Enerny,[91] the colonel's field trumpeter, Sergeant Alfred P___y,[92] Private Thos. Atwell,[93] and the writer, lifted the colonel's body, placing it across the saddle of his charger, bleeding from some three or four bayonet wounds in the chest, during which some pieces of silver fell from the waistcoat pocket of the corpse, which the sergeant picked off the ground and secreted. Woodford, the colonel's valet, having heard of the dishonest act, reported him to Colonel S. Hawker. He was placed in confinement, and tried by a regimental court-martial. The colonel left Aldea del Bispo on urgent affairs without confirming the decision of the court, and the enemy having advanced in force from Ciudad Rodrigo, driving our advanced posts before them, the sergeant, then a prisoner in Captain Baker's troop at Villa del Mula [Vale da Mula] was released. It would be unpardonable to forget not to observe that shortly after the regiment's return to England he was discharged, although a young active man, and fit for duty.

Before I conclude I beg to observe that the brave Lieut.-Colonel Talbot, on the day alluded, was dressed in nankeen[94] trowsers, wore a buff waistcoat under his dress jacket, and rode on a plain hunting saddle.[95]

---

91. Trumpeter John McEnerny.
92. Sergeant Alfred Percy.
93. Hanley is mistaken. It was John Atwell.
94. A pale yellowish cloth.
95. Hanley, pp.247– 8.

However, Captain Brotherton claimed he returned the next day to retrieve Lieutenant Colonel Talbot's body.

> I went out with a flag of truce to fetch his body. When I arrived at the fatal spot where the murderous charge of my squadron had taken place, I saw lying on the ground only three French soldiers, one of whom was dead and the other two much mutilated by our sabres, but this was all the execution we had done in return for our severe loss. I brought poor Talbot's body back, and we buried him on the glacis of Fort Conception [sic].[96]

In his after-action report, Craufurd put the total casualties for his force as:[97]

	Officers	Sergeants	Rank & File	Horses	Total loss of Officers, NCOs, & R&F
Killed	2[98]	–	7	15	9
Wounded	–	2	20	16	22
Missing	–	–	1	1	1

A copy of his after-action report can be found in Appendix IV.

Many of those who witnessed the action commented on the courage of the French soldiers. Captain Brotherton, whose squadron was the one that charged, praised them immensely.

> The French infantry behaved beautifully on this occasion. It was the 61st of the Line.[99] Marshal Massena immediately bestowed the Cross of the Legion of Honour on the commanding officer and several of the non-commissioned officers and men. So steady and cool was this little square, that though my horse fell, with the wounded, within two yards of their ranks, not a man moved

---

96. Brotherton, p.23.
97. *WD*, Vol. 6, p.253.
98. This is incorrect. General Craufurd includes Troop Quartermaster McCormack as an officer.
99. Captain Brotherton misidentifies the regiment. The 61st Line never served in Spain.

out to bayonet me, but the square retired in admirable order. We were repulsed, suffered great loss, and left our commanding officer amongst others, dead on the field.[100]

While Captain Leach of the 95th Rifles, who watched it from Barquilla, said,

> . . . this invincible little body of Frenchmen, who steadily resisted their charges, and, without leaving in our hands one of their brave band, succeeded in making good their retreat over the plain. Some hundreds of the finest cavalry of which the British army could boast continued hovering about, ready to pounce on and to break them, if the least disorder should be detected. It was impossible not to respect and admire the exemplary conduct of the French infantry; and this affair may probably tend to open the eyes of many men who talk with great composure of riding down and sabring infantry on a plain with cavalry, as if it was the most simple and feasible operation imaginable.[101]

The captured French dragoon officers were questioned and they revealed that Ciudad Rodrigo had capitulated the previous evening at 5 p.m. and the French had marched into the city at 6 p.m. General Craufurd suspected this had happened since they had not heard any firing from the city all day. He decided that he had accomplished his goal of stopping the French foragers and ordered his troops to withdraw back to their lines via Barquilla and Castillejo de dos Casas.[102]

There is some question about what happened to Captain Gouache and his 3rd Company of Grenadiers. Lieutenant Harry Smith claimed that as soon as the cavalry began to withdraw the '. . . gallant fellow in command gave the word, "Sauve qui peut".[103] In a moment all disperse, ran through the standing corn down to the banks of the river and were saved without the loss of a man.'[104] This, however, probably did not happen,

---

100. Brotherton, p.23.
101. Leach, *Rough Sketches*. . ., p.142.
102. Shaw, pp.226–7.
103. 'Sauve qui peut' meant every man for himself and was yelled when the situation was hopeless and the unit disintegrated.
104. Smith, p.29.

since the infantry was about 4km from the river and enemy cavalry was still around. Their only chance of surviving was to march away in a column while being prepared to form a square should the cavalry return. Captain Gouache and his men made it back across the Azaba River and when they marched into their cantonments, one observer saw that many of their muskets were '. . . were slashed by the English swords'.[105] For his superb handling of his company in such a dangerous situation, Gouache was promoted to chef-de-bataillon on 28 July. His senior NCO, Sergeant François Potait,[106] was awarded the Legion d'Honneur.

Masséna wrote to Marshal Berthier, Napoleon's Chief-of-Staff, the next day about the action.

To Marshal Berthier from Marshal Masséna
At the bivouac near Ciudad Rodrigo, on July 12, 1810.
The beautiful conduct of the 3rd Company of Grenadiers of the 22nd Line, against an English party, cannot be passed over in silence. This company, sent to Villar de Puerco [sic] in the morning to support a reconnaissance of dragoons, had passed beyond the village, when an English cavalry party of more than 400 horses left the woods on the left of the road and charged the grenadiers. The captain of this company immediately formed a square by half-sections; he waited firmly for the enemy; a well-fed fire made at 30 paces, stopped the enemy cavalry, which was already slashing the ranks, and the blows were hitting only the muskets and bayonets. A 2nd charge was the same; 12 bayonets testify that they were sunk into the horses' chest. The enemy would attempt a third charge; but he changed his mind, and recapitulating the losses he had just made, he resolved to retire. The first two charges have left around 24 cavalrymen dead, including the leader of the troop and 20 horses. We did not have on our side neither wounded nor killed. Captain Gouache's presence of mind and firmness and Sergeant Patois' courage served as an example to the brave grenadiers of the 3rd Company of the 22nd Line. This example deserves our encouragement and a reward. I beg your Highness to propose the first for the rank

---

105. Hulot, Jacques-Louis, *Souvenirs Militaires du baron Hulot*. Paris: Spectateur Militaire, 1886, p.308.
106. Some sources spell his name as Potais, however the Legion d'Honneur rolls spell it Potait.

of battalion commander, which has been asked several times for him; and for the second the decoration of Legionnaire.[107]

Impact of the 11 July Affair

Although the skirmish at Villa de Puerco was relatively minor, it did have effects on the morale of officers and men of the Light Division and how they viewed their commander. Captain Cocks of the 16th Light Dragoons perhaps summed it up the best from the cavalry perspective.

It is probable that General Craufurd was hurried by the idea of Ciudad Rodrigo having surrendered, those officers to whom he spoke say his manner was that of a man who had lost his presence of mind. It is certain that had we only surrounded and watched the infantry and sent for the guns – which were in the neighbourhood and could have come up in twenty minutes – we should have annihilated them had they not first surrendered. But this I feel convinced they would have done but they had no opportunity, they were charged the instant our cavalry appeared and had not time to throw down their arms. Other things were ill-managed. General Craufurd appeared to have forgot his own arrangements and our own squadrons were repeatedly pointed out to us as enemies. On the whole it was a very mortifying that an affair, ably planned and favourably carried on to the moment of action should, in the end, turn out so ill through a too great precipitancy in the execution.[108]

Captain James Fergusson of the 43rd Foot had a different viewpoint, stating that 'Good infantry are not to be defeated by Cavalry & Crawford [sic] ought to have known better. There was no occasion for his rashness having both Artillery & Infantry with him.'[109]

Captain Ross of the Royal Horse Artillery also had words about General Craufurd's performance.

The scene of action was a plain, where Horse Artillery could haven used to the greatest advantage, and were not called upon;

---

107. *WSD*, Vol. 13, p.421.
108. Cocks, pp.64–5.
109. Fergusson, p.9.

and that the officers posted in command at the different places were left ignorant of the points from whence they were to look for support.[110]

Craufurd knew he performed badly and it affected his mood. Rifleman Costello was at Lieutenant Colonel Talbot's funeral and thought the general '. . . wore a troubled look, as though he took our failure to heart'.[111] On the evening 12 June, Craufurd sent for Captain Ross to purportedly find out if he had been resupplied with ammunition 'and after some time spoke of the affair of yesterday; said it was unfortunate, and appeared desirous of drawing from me my opinion respecting the use that artillery might have been made of, and hinted that he thought they would not. In answer, I remarked, in such open country we could move with great facility; upon which he dropt [sic] the conversation, and desired me to dine with him tomorrow.'[112]

Craufurd compounded his problems when he forwarded his after-action report to Wellington and blamed the 16th Light Dragoons for the failure to capture the infantry.

The hussars received the fire of the square; but being unable to penetrate it, they passed on, leaving it to their left. Had the 16th come straight upon it, the square being then without fire, it would probably have been broken; but they were too much to their left and passed it on the other flank. At this moment a most unfortunate mistake took place, to which alone is to be attributed the escape of the infantry.[113]

This report caused quite a stir at Army HQ and rumours of cowardice by the 16th Light Dragoons spread like wildfire through the army. Part of the gossip also said that this should not have been surprising considering their failure to support Captain Krauchenberg in his counter-attack of the French cavalry on 4 July.[114] It was not long before the rumours reached Lieutenant General Stapleton

---

110. Ross, p.10.
111. Costello, p.31.
112. Ross, p.10.
113. *WD*, Vol. 6, p.253.
114. The accusation about their performance on 4 July was spread by those who were not there.

Cotton. As the commander of the British cavalry as well as a supernumerary[115] colonel of the 16th Light Dragoons, he took the gossip personally and wrote to Wellington enclosing a letter from Captain Cocks about the action. Wellington responded on 14 July that he was

> much obliged to you from the perusal of Cocks' letter, which contains a very clear account of the events of the 11th. I can show you Craufurd's letter to me, which does not throw any blame whatever upon the 16th, and indeed I never heard a doubt upon the subject.
>
> The cause of the failure to take the infantry as well as the cavalry is, as Craufurd states to be, that a body of our cavalry, which I conclude were Gruben's Hussars, were seen coming out of Barquilla, and were taken by mistake for the enemy, which stopped the attack of the rear squadrons. The 16th had nothing to do with this mistake, nor probably is any body to blame for it. The French infantry appear to have behaved remarkably well, and probably were so posted that no efforts of cavalry could have forced them.
>
> It would really not be fair to the 16th, to have any inquiry into their conduct in this affair. I have no doubt how it would turn out, but the very fact of inquiry supposes some grounds, which to suppose even would be injurious to them.[116]

This did not stop the gossips and it was not long that word of it reached the 16th Light Dragoons and they were not happy. On 16 July, Cocks sent a long letter to Cotton in which he expressed his feelings about the matter.

> I felt as much surprised as hurt when I received your letter mentioning the reports, which idle or ignorant men have presumed to spread in the rear. I had not heard one word of them here, nor do I believe that anything of that nature has been said at the outposts in any way whatever.

---

115. Although he was a general officer in the army, he still held regimental rank in the 16th Light Dragoons as a lieutenant colonel.
116. *WD*, Vol. 6, p.257.

There are two circumstances which, if not fairly spoken of, might be supposed to give some colour to these injurious misrepresentations, namely, our having suffered so little, our being the only regiment which was not actually engaged with the infantry, and the idea that the squadrons here were about to be relieved so soon.[117]

In the meanwhile, Cotton decided to take matters into his own hands. In addition to sending out copies of Wellington's letter of 14 July, he wrote to Major General Cole, the commander of the 4th Division, that

I thought it my duty, from commanding the division to which that regiment belongs, to have the matter investigated, in order to bring those to whom blame or suspicion is attached to trial, or that, if there were no grounds for these evil reports, their unfavourable effect should be done away with. I therefore made known to Lord Wellington that such were in circulation, and I received the following very satisfactory letter in return. But it is not sufficient that the corps and I should be satisfied, it is necessary that the actual conduct of the regiment should be generally known, and that the persons circulating these reports should be called to account for them.[118]

Cotton concluded his investigation and brought the results to Wellington. On 23 July Wellington wrote to Craufurd that

I have been much annoyed by the foolish conversations and reports and private letters, about the 16th Light Dragoons. General Cotton wrote to me shortly after the affair of the 11th, to request that the conduct of that regiment might be inquired into; to which I replied, that in your report you had not made any charge against the 16th, and that it would not be just towards that regiment to make their conduct the object of inquiry, for a failure which appeared to me to have been produced by various unfortunate accidents, which could not be prevented.

Two or three days afterwards General Cotton came here and told me that he had traced some of those reports and

---

117. Combermere, Vol. 1, pp.148–9.
118. Ibid., p.145

conversations to General Stewart, the A.G.[119] Upon which I had General Stewart and him before me: after having pointed out to the former the inconvenience and impropriety of a person in his situation circulating any reports about the troops, I declared my determination, if I heard any more of it, to oblige him to come forward with a charge against the 16th. So the matter stands here . . .

All this would not much signify, if our Staff and other officers would mind their business, instead of writing news and keeping coffee houses. But as soon as an accident happens, every man who can write, and who has a friend who can read, sits down to write his account of what he does not know, and his comments on what he does not understand, and these are diligently circulated and exaggerated by the idle and malicious, of whom there are plenty in all armies. The consequence is that officers and whole regiments lose their reputation, a spirit of party, which is the bane of all armies, is engendered and fomented, a want of confidence ensues; and there is no character, however meritorious, and no action, however glorious, which can have justice done to it. I have hitherto been so fortunate as keep down this spirit in this army, and I am determined to persevere.[120]

General Stewart at this point shut up and the matter was put to rest.

On 11 July, unaware that the combat at Villa de Puerco was going on, Wellington had sent a letter to Craufurd informing him that General Cotton requested that the 16th Light Dragoons be relieved of their duties and returned to their brigade by 16 July.[121] Wellington's timing could not have been worse, because this only reinforced the rumours about the regiment's performance at Villa de Puerco and that they were being relieved for some cause. By late afternoon, Wellington had received word from Craufurd about the capitulation of Ciudad Rodrigo and Villa de Puerco. He wrote to Craufurd at 7:30 p.m. about what he wished the Light Division should do when the French advanced in force.

---

119. Major General Charles Stewart was Wellington's Adjutant General and had the reputation for being a notorious gossip.
120. *WD*, Vol. 6, pp.275–7. General Stewart's name was not included in *Wellington's Dispatches*, but it is in Alexander Craufurd's *General Craufurd and His Light Division*, p.118.
121. *WD*, Vol. 6, p.245.

The fall of Ciudad Rodrigo was to be expected, and the defence has been greater than we had a right to expect. I regret poor Talbot, he is a great loss.

I have looked over my instructions to you,[122] and I see nothing to add excepting the word 'threaten' in the fourth paragraph. That is to say, it will run, 'In case the enemy should threaten to attack General Craufurd.' In short, I do not wish to risk any thing beyond the Côa, and indeed, when Carrera is clearly off, I do not see why you should remain any longer at such a distance in front of Almeida.

It is desirable that the communication with Almeida should be kept open as long as possible, in order that we may throw into that place as much provisions as possible, and therefore I would not wish you tall back beyond that place, unless it should be necessary. But it does not appear necessary that you should be so far, and it will be safer than you should be nearer, at least with your infantry.

If you should retire towards Almeida, and should break off your communication with the posts in front of Castello Bom, and Castello Mendo, it would be desirable that you should leave a small body of cavalry in that quarter, to communicate with, and fall back upon Brigadier General Alexander Campbell, and acquaint him accordingly.[123]

General Carrera, the commander of the Spanish forces on the right flank of the Light Division, had received orders to withdraw to Alcantara once Ciudad Rodrigo had fallen. He left on 11 July and this did not bode well for the Light Division, for 'The enemy's attention being now of course entirely fixed upon the siege of Almeida, our utmost vigilance becomes extremely necessary, as we have no doubt of his soon forcing us over the Côa'.[124] The French wasted little time after capturing Ciudad Rodrigo to begin moving towards Portugal. On 12 July, they occupied Fuentes de Oñoro about 20km south of Fort Concepción.[125] The following day French cavalry was spotted between La Alameda de Gardón and Fuentes de Oñoro.[126]

---

122. Wellington is referring to his Instructions dated 3 July 1810.
123. *WD*, Vol. 6, p.249.
124. Shaw, p.227.
125. Simmons, p.74.
126. Tomkinson, p.32.

Upon receiving this intelligence Craufurd decided he could not delay the withdrawal of his infantry and on 14 July gave them orders to prepare to withdraw to Junça, Portugal, which is 7km south of Almeida. The French continued their probing of the lines and

> 7 squadrons of the enemy's cavalry having formed between Fuentes [de Oñoro] and Espeja, and having got near Fuentes. Major Napier and Captain Cotton[127] took a flag of truce into Gallegos this forenoon. Loison received them. He is quartered there, and they think about two regiments. There are some small camps in front of the village. Loison said that there was scarcely a house standing in Ciudad Rodrigo. He desired Cotton to tell Lord Wellington that he would bet his lordship 500 louis that he would not relieve Almeida, and that the Spaniards were very indignant with us for not relieving Ciudad Rodrigo. The enemy's vedettes were only about a mile on this side of Gallegos.[128]

The problem Craufurd faced was what to do about Fort Concepción. In order to deceive the French, Wellington did not want to destroy it until it was actually threatened. Even if he withdrew his infantry, Craufurd knew he still had to maintain communications and protect the explosives in the fort, until the time came to blow it up. On 16 July he finally ordered the infantry to withdraw but left Captain O'Hare's and one other company of the 95th Rifles at the fort.[129] That same day Wellington sent further instructions to Craufurd. Unfortunately, instead of clarifying what he wanted done, they were contradictory.

> It is desirable that we should hold the other side of the Coa a little longer, and I think that our doing so is facilitated by our keeping La Conception. At the same time I do not wish to risk any thing in order to remain at the other side of the river, or to retain that fort; and I am very anxious that when you leave it, it should be destroyed. I beg you, therefore, not to have any scruples about doing it too soon.

---

127. Captain Willoughby Cotton of the 3rd Foot Guards was the Light Division's DAAG.
128. Shaw, pp.228–9.
129. Costello, p.32. Shaw, p.229.

You may be certain, however, that when you do destroy that fort, you will be obliged to draw your cavalry into Almeida, etc; and the communication with the right of the Coa, excepting at that point, will be at an end.

If you have any further communication with Loison, send my compliments to him, and tell him that I gave money to the officers of the 1st Dragoons, and that sum which he sent shall be transmitted to them.[130]

On 17 July the cavalry outposts were reorganized. Craufurd ignored the orders to release the 16th Light Dragoons and sent them and the 1st KGL Hussars to San Pedro,[131] a village halfway between Almeida and Fuentes de Oñoro. These four squadrons were responsible for screening the southern approaches to Almeida. The 14th Light Dragoons were kept at Vale da Mula and continued to picquet the Dos Casas River. They were also responsible for maintaining communications with Fort Concepción.[132] On 19 July, Captain Cocks' troop, which included Lieutenant Tomkinson, were detached from the regiment and sent 30km south to Vila Mayor to screen the southern flank of the army.[133]

For the riflemen who were guarding Fort Concepción, the duty was not strenuous, but there was a sense of anticipation that something was going to happen at any moment.

. . . it was generally expected we should be attacked on the morrow. I think the intelligence was brought by a deserter. The fort contained a great quantity of rum and biscuit, which Captain O'Hare allowed the men of both companies to help themselves to and fill their canteens, upon their promise, which they kept, not to get drunk.[134]

The French continued to probe the outposts. On 19 July the Division HQ

received a report from the Officer on picquet at Fuentes [de Oñoro] at 8 o'clock a.m., saying that columns of the enemy

---

130. *WD*, Vol. 6, pp.264–5.
131. São Pedro do Rio Seco.
132. Tomkinson, p.33.
133. Cocks, pp.65–8. Tomkinson, pp.33–5.
134. Costello, p.32

were advancing. The General went off immediately towards Fuentes, and I went and turned out the infantry at Junca. This, however, proved to be only a strong patrol of the enemy, which drove our picquet back from Fuentes, but were driven back in their turn, and we took a prisoner. The General now establish the head-quarters of the division at San Pedro.[135]

Among those who were placed on alert was the 52nd Foot at Junça. Lieutenant Henry Dawson wrote home shortly afterwards that:

The French have been very busy in reconnoitring our right flank & this morning a strong patrol of them came in contact with our Drags at Villa Formosa who proved too strong for them & drove them back; it caused an alarm in camp, & of course we had a general turn-out, and remained under arms 'till all was quiet. We marched on the 16th from Val de la Mula to this place, & where we will remain. It is reported amongst us that our General has recd positive orders from Lord Wellington to remain in our present position 'till the French invest Almeida which I do not think will be done for some time.[136]

The Light Division did not sit passively waiting for the French to move. Lieutenant Shaw, in his capacity as the division's intelligence officer, not only analysed the reports from the picquets and the interrogation of deserters and prisoners, but he also sent out locals to gather information.

I went this morning to Aldeo Bispo to receive information from two spies whom I had sent on the 18th, the one to San Felices, and the other to Ciudad Rodrigo. By them it appears that the enemy have 4000 men in San Felices de Gallegos, and 3000 men in a camp about a league from it; in Castellejo and Silices Chico they have 1500 men; they also occupy Frexeneda; but the body of the enemy's army is encampted [sic] between Palacios, Carpeo, &c., and between that line and Gallegos.

The loss in the town, including both garrison and inhabitants, during the siege, was 500 killed and wounded. The garrison

---

135. Shaw, p.230.
136. Dawson, p.30.

(5300 men) the Governor, and the Junta, were all marched off prisoners to Salamanca. They made the members of the Junta walk; all priests and monks of the town are confined, also the writers of the *Diario*.[137]

The Destruction of Fort Concepción

The 14th Light Dragoons also actively patrolled in the no man's land on the other side of the Dos Casas River. On 21 July a dawn patrol had orders to see what French were in the vicinity of Barquilla about 10km to the east. With the patrol was Lieutenant Edmund Mulcaster, of the Royal Engineers.[138] The patrol made it to the three crosses north of Barquilla and then turned south. They had only gone a few kilometres when they came across a French force of two or three cavalry regiments with infantry in support moving west. The patrol raced back to Aldea del Obispo where Major Hervey and his squadron waited. Lieutenant Mulcaster was ordered back to Fort Concepción with a warning for Captain Burgoyne that the French were coming and to blow the mines.[139]

Captain Brotherton's 4th Squadron of the 14th Dragoons was responsible for the picquets covering the fort that morning and realized from the amount of the firing coming from the east that the French were advancing in force. He sent Lieutenant William Wainman, who was well mounted, to warn Captain Burgoyne that 'we were being driven back most rapidly, and that we had no time to lose'.[140] Lieutenant Wainman beat Lieutenant Mulcaster to the fort and upon hearing the news, Captain Burgoyne did not wait to begin destroying the fort. He sent the light dragoons who were part of his security force to warn everyone that the fort was about to blow. They did not, however, see Lieutenant Mulcaster. Captain Burgoyne was in Vale da Mula and saw the west side blow up

with success, as well as those in the outworks and detached redoubts. At the end of the saucisson three portfires were attached

---

137. Shaw, pp.230–1.
138. Why Lieutenant Mulcaster was riding out on patrol is unknown. It is possible he had no duties that day and, like many officers at the time, would join patrols out of boredom.
139. Mulcaster, Edmund, *The Peninsular War Diary of Edmund Mulcaster RE, 1808 – 1810*. Mark Thompson (ed.) Privately printed, 2015, p.114.
140. Brotherton, p.23.

at lengths, the ends being cut off slanting and then tied together; it was calculated these would give half an hour's law after being lighted last, however, exploded first, by some minutes. There were from 90 to 100 barrels of powder (Portuguese, of 64 lbs, each only), in each ravelin, divided in the two casemates between the flank and face, and they destroyed each ravelin, all but a very small bit at the salient angle. In the outer redoubt, which was large and high, the powder, 100 Portuguese barrels, was lodged in two small casemates, one at each angle of the front, and destroyed the whole front and part of the sides. In the middle small quadrangular fort, sixty Portuguese barrels were placed in one angle on the wooden floor dividing the casemate, and apparently cut the fort diagonally in two, throwing down the half where the powder was lodged. In the flanks were moderate breaches and in the face the wall opened, and the top tumbled down, making a good breach . . .[141]

Lieutenant Mulcaster did make it to the fort and upon his arrival found the fort had been abandoned. As he was '. . . riding up the ramp . . . I heard the burning of the portfire and saw the smoke issuing from the gallery. I therefore rode with all possible speed out of the fort to the dragoons who were continuing to skirmish. The fort exploded about quarter of an hour after I left it and the mines appeared to answer fully; all the flanks, one face and the outworks being breached.'[142]

Captain Brotherton continued to skirmish with the advancing French and had been pushed back to the east glacis when the mines exploded. He 'lost several horses and men by the explosion, besides the harrowing sight of poor Talbot's body being blown into the air. He was a delightful fellow, a friend (whose loss) I most deeply regretted, but singular and eccentric, particularly in his dress. He was dressed, the day he was killed, in nankeen pantaloons.'[143]

Upon receiving the word it was going to blow, the riflemen who were occupying the fort left none too soon, for 'A few minutes after our quitting the fort, its beautiful proportions, which had excited the admiration of so many beholders, was broken, as by the shock of an

---

141. Burgoyne, Vol. 1, pp.93–3.
142. Mulcaster, p.115.
143. Brotherton, p.24.

earthquake, into a blackened heap of ruins.'[144] The blast was heard for many miles and caused quite a bit of alarm. Lieutenant Simmons, who should have been in the fort with his company, was

> . . . lying under a tree in a sound sleep. I sprang up, thinking the French army had got into the camp, and seized my sword, which hung upon a bough of the tree, and proceeded to our alarm post. I found the same effect produced by the noise upon the whole of us, and the only feeling we had was to sell our lives at as dear a rate as possible. When the cause was known, and that the enemy had not driven in our outposts, we fell out and took our breakfast.[145]

Lieutenant Shaw was with General Craufurd at San Pedro, about 8km, when:

> About 5 o'clock this morning some firing was heard and soon after a report was received by the General that the picquet at Castellejo was engaged with the enemy. Before we got on horseback we heard an explosion at the fort; the General rode off immediately to Val de Mula, and while going there the whole of the mines of the Fort Conception went off. I believe nine in all. These explosions appeared to be quite successful. On our arrival at Val de Mula we found the 14th formed behind the villages, and the enemy's skirmishers on the right and left of Fort Conception. On our left of the fort we saw about a regiment of the enemy's cavalry and a battalion of infantry. On our right of the fort the enemy advanced with two regiments of cavalry and two battalions of infantry. They turned our left, and advanced into Val de Mula at the same time. The 14th retired (skirmishing with the enemy) to the stream between Val de Mula and Alameda, and about a mile and half from the former place. The guns were brought up in rear of this stream, and the 14th (who were now reinforced by a squadron of the 16th and one of the hussars) formed in front of the guns. Our skirmishers maintained themselves a long time among some rocks in front of the stream till the enemy came on with infantry. The enemy

---

144. Costello, p.32.
145. Simmons, p.75.

did not pass the stream, and about 10 o'clock they retired to Val de Mula. Upon the first alarm, the infantry marched into their position close to Almeida. While the cavalry were skirmishing, the 95th were ordered up, but they only got about half-way when the enemy retired, and were halted on the road, and hutted where they halted; the rest of the infantry hutted in the position, the left of which is within reach of the guns of the place, and the right in some enclosures.[146]

After the French withdrew, Craufurd rode to Junça. From there he rode to inspect the outpost line, which extended from Nave de Haver in the south to Malpartida in the north, a distance of 60km. He spent the night in Almeida. Lieutenant Shaw did not ride with him, but was ordered back to Almeida to send letters with the news to Wellington and Generals Picton and Alexander Campbell, who were on the far side of the Côa River.[147]

There was very little contact with the French over the next two days. Early in the morning of 22 July, Craufurd and Lieutenant Shaw did another inspection of the picquets near Vale da Mula '. . . and saw one or two of the enemy's videttes, but everything quite quiet. . . Our patrols which went this forenoon to Val de Mula, found none of the enemy there, but saw infantry and cavalry picquets in front of the fort.'[148] All was quiet the following day.

On 23 July, Lieutenant Simmons took the opportunity to visit Almeida where he

> spent a jovial evening with Lieutenants [Mathias] Pratt and [Robert] Beckwith in Almeida. About eight o'clock an officer told us that he had orders to clear the town of every person that was not to be employed in the siege, and regretted that we could not be allowed to remain longer within the walls. We drank success to their defence of the fortress, and that many Frenchmen might bite the dust before the place, shook him by the hand, and departed. We had scarcely left the town when the rain began to fall in torrents; thunder and lightning of that night was the most tremendously grand I ever beheld either before

---

146. Shaw, pp.231–2.
147. Ibid., p.232
148. Ibid.

or since. The Division, officers and men, had no shelter from this inclement night; as to lying down, it was nearly impossible, for the water ran in gutters amongst the rocks. I sat upon a stone like a drowned rat, looking at the heavens and amusing myself with their brilliancy and longing for the morning, which came at last, and the rain ceased. Our next consideration was to set the men to work to clean their arms and look after their ammunition.[149]

Rifleman Costello also wrote of this storm.

At night we experienced a storm that for violence, while it lasted, exceeded anything I had ever before beheld. The lightning, thunder, wind, and rain were absolutely awful. With a few other men, I had sought shelter in the hollow of a rock, where we were not a little amazed at the numbers of snakes and lizards which the occasional gleams of lightning exhibited to us running about in all directions, as though the tempest had the effect of bringing them all from their holes.[150]

Little did the men of the Light Division know that this storm was a harbinger of things to come.

---

149. Simmons, p.76.
150. Costello, p.32.

Chapter 8

The Fight on the Côa River, 24 July 1810

The destruction of Fort Concepción took the French by surprise and they were not sure what the British would do. Marshal Masséna wrote to Ney the next day that 'No doubt, if you press near the English, they will abandon Almeida or blow it up as La Concepción. Therefore, I desire that you support General Loison with other troops in order to push the enemy firmly on Almeida. I have no doubt that we will have a propitious success.'[1]

Intelligence was also coming in with reports that the morale among the defenders was very low. A rumour was circulating that '. . . Almeida would have opened its gates if the reconnaissance of the 21st had been a direct attack on the place'.[2] Another had that the governor of the city had sent a letter to Wellington 'cautioning that if the army did not march to support Almeida', it would open its gates 'without firing a shot'.[3]

Ney wrote back to Masséna the next day that he would attack the British on 24 July to 'invest Almeida and learn if the English wish to defend this fortress'.[4] He later amended his goal to 'cut the enemy off from the fortress and manoeuvre simultaneously to cut their retreat on the Coa'.[5] To do this, Marshal Ney had his whole corps of three infantry divisions and a light cavalry brigade, plus an attached dragoon brigade.

---

1. Horward, p.202.
2. General Loison to Marshal Ney dated 23 July 1810 in Horward, p.202.
3. Ibid.
4. Marshal Ney to Masséna 10 a.m. 23 July 1810 in Horward, pp.202–03.
5. Marshal Ney to Masséna 2 p.m. 24 July 1810 in Horward, p.209.

Marchand's 1st Division
Mermet's 2nd Division
Loison's 3rd Division
Lamotte's[6] light cavalry brigade (3rd Hussars and 15th Chasseurs-à-Cheval)
Gardanne's[7] dragoon brigade (15th and 25th Dragoons)

The British estimated that this force consisted of 22,000 infantry and 2,500 cavalry.[8] However, due to the restricted terrain, Ney decided to attack on a very narrow front with only Loison's 3rd Division and Lamotte's light cavalry brigade. The rest of the force would be in support. Furthermore, the initial attack would be conducted with the nine battalions of General Ferey's brigade and the hussars and chasseurs of the light cavalry. General Simon's brigade would follow behind them. The intention was to attack quickly, hit the left flank of the Light Division and use overwhelming force to roll up each battalion in succession before the battalions on the right flank could respond.

The French forces began to form up about 1 a.m. along the Tourões River just to the east of Vale da Mula. The heavy rains that night prevented the British outposts from spotting them.

The terrain just to the west of Vale da Mula is rolling farmland that drops about 10m as it gets closer to Almeida. About 500m south of Almeida is a long ridge that the road to Junça follows. On the northern end of this ridge was a stone windmill that overlooks the road to Vale da Mula. The western slope of this ridge is initially gentle, however within a kilometre it becomes very steep until it reaches the Côa River about 2km below. This area was divided into small sections of vineyards and pastures, each surrounded by stone walls whose height ranged from 1m to 2m. The main road from Almeida to Pinhel goes to the southwest for about 3km where it crosses the seventeenth-century bridge[9] over the Côa River. The first kilometre of this road goes down a gradual slope, but the last two kilometres is very steep, descending almost 200m to the river. On both sides of the road were walls that enclosed the vineyards and pastures. About 100m from the bridge is a large knoll that overlooks

6. Auguste Lamotte.
7. Claude-Matthieu, Comte de Gardane.
8. See Chapter 7 for the composition of each division and the cavalry.
9. The exact year the bridge was built is unknown. It was probably built around 1640, when the fortress of Almeida was built.

the road as it descends the ridge and the bridge. The road curves around this knoll to the south and once around it, goes north to the bridge. This knoll rises 50m above the river and blocks line-of-sight from the road to the bridge.

The Côa River runs through a steep gorge with its western slope steeper and 100m higher than the eastern side. The river bed is very rocky with large boulders. The river flows quickly through the gorge and its width is no more than 10m. For much of the year it can be crossed on foot at several fords upstream. In the vicinity of the bridge, the river is a major obstacle that is impassable to formed troops and artillery. During the dry season it would not be much of an obstacle for light infantry. The heavy rains on the night of 23 July turned the river into a raging torrent for several days, which made it impassable except at the bridge.

The bridge is made of cut granite. It is approximately 50m long and 4m wide. It has three arches and rises about 20m above the river.[10] As the bridge nears the western bank, it makes a 15-degree turn to the south, so that an individual standing on either end of the bridge cannot see the other end. Lining the sides of the bridge is a metre-high parapet.[11]

On the west side of the bridge, the road turns south and begins a sharp climb of 1.5km to the top of the gorge. The road has a metre-high wall along its river side. The western slope of the gorge is covered with large boulders and scrub.

Deployment of the Light Division

According to General Craufurd, on the morning of 24 July, the Light Division's

> cavalry out-posts formed a semicircle in front of Almeida, the right flank being appuyé [supported] to the Coa, near As Naves, which is about three miles above the place;[12] and the left flank

---

10. Garwood, F.S., 'The Royal Staff Corps: 1800 – 1837', *Royal Engineer Journal*, Vol. 57, 1943, p.88.
11. The bridge was partially destroyed by the French in 1811 when they blew up one of its arches. It was rebuilt in 1824–5. I could find no contemporary images of the bridge before it was rebuilt, so it is impossible to say if the bridge that stands there today is the same as it was in 1810. However, since only one arch was destroyed, the two are likely very similar.
12. The village is located about 5km south of Almeida and 2.5km east of the river.

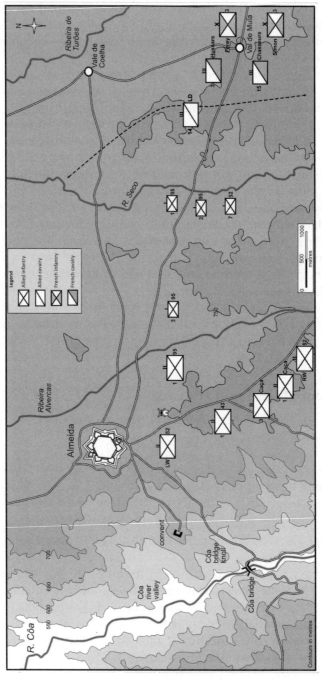

The Fight on the Coa River, 24 July 1810: Positions at 6 a.m.

also appuyé to the river, near Cinco Villas, which is about three miles below the fortress.[13] The centre of this line was covered by a small stream, and to the principal roads by which it was expected that the enemy would advance, namely, on the right and centre of this line, the cavalry posts were supported by piquets of infantry. The only road which our artillery, and the body of our cavalry could make use of to retreat across the Coa, was that which leads from Almeida to the bridge. The nature of the ground made it difficult for the enemy to approach this road on our left, that is to say, on the north side of the town, and the infantry of the division was therefore placed in a position to cover it on the right or south side, having its right flank appuyé to the Coa, above the bridge, its front covered by a deep and rocky ravine, and its left in some inclosures near a windmill, which is on the plain, about 800 yards south of the town.[14]

The 14th Light Dragoons were responsible for the picquets from Junça to Val da Mula to Cinco Villas. Captain Krauchenberg's and Captain von Gruben's squadrons of German hussars covered from Junça south to Naves, while Captain Ashworth's squadron of the 16th Light Dragoons had the outposts from Naves to Nave de Haver.[15]

The infantry was deployed with the 95th Rifles in the front along the road to Vale da Mula. Captain James Stewart's No. 1 Company and Captain Leach's No. 2 Company were responsible for the outlying picquets, while Captain O'Hare's No. 3 Company had the inlying picquets. Just to the right of the 95th Rifles' outlying picquets were Captain Robert Campbell's No. 7 Company of the 52nd Foot. With them were two guns from Captain Ross's RHA troop.[16] Captain Campbell, the senior officer with the picquets, was in command of all the outposts.[17] On the ridge behind the 95th was an old windmill

---

13. Cinco Villas is about 10km north of Almeida and 2km east of the river.
14. Craufurd, Robert, 'Action near Almeida', *Royal Military Chronicle*, January 1811, p.230.
15. Which squadrons of the 16th Light Dragoons covered the area is unknown, for Captain Cocks's troop, whom Lieutenant Tomkinson was a part of, was sent further south to screen in the vicinity of Vilar Mayor on 19 July.
16. Costello, p.32. Ross, p.10.
17. Dawson, p.33.

about 800m from Almeida which had two dismounted artillery pieces. Behind the windmill were four companies of the 52nd Foot. To the right of the windmill, along the western slopes of the ridge was the 43rd Foot, bivouacked 'amongst rocks, walls, and vineyards, on the slope of the hill which descends to the river Coa in the many walled enclosed fields'.[18] Down the ridge along the road to Junça was the 3rd Caçadores and to the right of them was the 1st Caçadores. On the far right, with its right flank anchored on the Côa River, was the 52nd Foot. The five battalions were covering about 5km of frontage.

As usual, the division stood-to at first light[19] and after the all clear was given, the troops began to clean their weapons and to dry their clothes from the night's heavy rains. Because their ammunition was damp due to the rain, fresh ammunition was distributed. The rain also caused problems with their weapons. Lieutenant Booth of the 43rd Foot wrote a few days later that '. . . after a dreadful stormy night . . . the fire-locks [were] nearly unserviceable'.[20] The day was also payday[21] and the regiments had a pay muster at 6 a.m.[22] The paymaster began to pay the soldiers by company and after two companies were paid, firing from the outposts raised the alarm and the formation was dismissed in order to move into their fighting positions along the ridge.

Leading this attack were the French 3rd Hussars and 15th Chasseurs-à-Cheval which moved around Vale da Mula, while the French Chasseurs de Siège moved through the village. This was an ad hoc battalion formed during the siege of Ciudad Rodrigo and consisted of the best marksmen from the light companies of infantry regiments of the 6th Corps. They were attached to General Loison's 3rd Division.[23]

---

18. Oglander, Henry, 'Diary'. Napier Collection, Bodleian Library, Oxford University. MS. Eng. misc. c. 471. Booth, Henry. 'Letter dated 30 July 1810' in Levine, p.132.
19. Nautical twilight was at 3:26 a.m.
20. Booth, Henry, 'Letter dated 30 July 1810' in Levine, p.132.
21. The British Army paid their soldiers on the 24th of each month.
22. Oglander, Diary entry 24 July. Green, p.28.
23. The exact composition of the Chasseurs de Siège is not known. It consisted of six companies. However, based on officer casualty reports, it included men from the 6th Light Regiment of the 1st Division, and the 27th and 50th Line Regiments of the 2nd Division, among others. Total strength was around 300 men. Its original commander was Captain François who was killed during the siege of Ciudad Rodrigo. Koch, Jean (ed.), *Mémoires*

Captain Brotherton's squadron of the 14th Light Dragoons was near Vale da Mula when the French began to advance. The cavalry was brought under fire and the captain ordered his men to retreat. Captain Stewart's Rifle company was quickly overrun and numerous men were killed or captured. Among them were Lieutenant John M'Cullock, who was caught in the open by the hussars and received seven sabre wounds.[24]

Captain O'Hare, who was commanding the inlying picquets, waited for orders, much to the impatience of Lieutenant Simmons.

> After smoking two pipes I damned them to my Captain for not coming on faster, who laughingly said. 'Stop, my boy, do not let us be in a hurry; there is time enough before night to get a broken head.' Soon after this observation the French appeared in great numbers, some singing, others screaming and howling like wild beasts, their drums also beating in every direction. Our company was ordered to advance with three companies of the 43rd Light Infantry. We soon came very near the enemy, who kept up a most desperate fire. We returned a steady fire. They now advanced very near, then retired a little, and came on again several times, until our ranks became much thinned, and in our turn we retired, moving more to the left of our line, as the enemy were now moving round and menancing [sic] our flank in in that quarter. Our Rifle Boys brought them down like wild ducks. At this moment a shot passed through the side of a brother officer in the same company with me. He exclaimed, 'Oh! Simmons, I am wounded.' A horse being near, we luckily got him away; he is likely to recover. In passing a road the fire was excessively hot from their cannons, their shells bursting continually above our heads in every direction.[25]

Rifleman Costello wrote later that

> Captain O'Hare accordingly placed us behind some dilapidated walls; we waited the approach of the picquet then under the Hon.

---

de Masséna rédigés d'après les documents qu'il a laissés et sur coux du dépôt de la guerre et du dépôt des fortifications par le général Koch: Avec un atlas, 7 vols. Paris: Paulin et le Chevalier, 1850. Vol. 7, pp.64–5.

24. Caldwell; Vol. 2, pp.86–7.
25. Simmons, pp.92–2.

Captain Stewart engaged about half a mile in our front, and slowly retreating upon us. They had already, as it afterwards appeared, several men killed, while Lieutenant M'Cullock[26] had been wounded and taken prisoner with a number of others. We could distinctly see the enemy's columns in great force, but had little time for observation, as our advance [picquets] ran in upon us followed by the French tirailleurs, with whom we were speedily and hotly engaged.[27]

The Portuguese in Almeida saw the danger that the riflemen were in and began firing artillery in support. However, their fire was not accurate and one round

burst so near, that it killed several of our men, and buried a sergeant so completely in mud, but without hurting him, that we were obliged to drag him out of the heap, to prevent his being taken by the enemy – at this moment also Lieutenant [Alexander] Coane, who stood close to me received a shot through the body. My old Captain, O'Hare, perceiving him roll his eyes and stagger, caught him by the arm, saying in a rather soft tone to the men about him: 'Take that poor boy to the rear, he does not know what is the matter with him,' and with the same characteristic coolness he continued his duties.[28]

The French also brought the company under fire and soon its position was untenable and 'we were ordered to retire half the company. Captain O'Hare's retired, and the remainder under Lieutenant [William] Johnston, still remained fighting for a few moments longer. I was with this party. We moved from the field in to the road, our men falling all round us. . .'[29]

The Attack of the French Cavalry

As the company was retreating French hussars came riding up from the south. The riflemen mistakenly thought they were 1st KGL Hussars

---

26. John Garlies McCullock.
27. Costello, pp.32–3.
28. Ibid., pp.32–3.
29. Simmons, p.77.

and this would cause them numerous casualties and practically destroy Captain O'Hare's company. Rifleman Costello heard

> a cry of 'The French cavalry are upon us' came too late as they charged in amongst us. Taken thus unprepared, we could oppose but little or no resistance, and our men were trampled down and sabred, on every side. A French dragoon had seized me by the collar, while several others, as they passed, cut at me with their swords. The men who had collared me had his sabre's point at my breast, when a volley was fired from our rear by the 52nd, who by this time had discovered their mistake, which tumbled the horse of my captor. He fell heavily with the animal on his leg, dragging me down with him. It was but for a moment nevertheless; determined to have one brief struggle for liberty, I freed myself from the dragoon's grasp, and dealing him a severe blow on the head with the butt of my rifle, I rushed up to the wall of our 52nd, which I was in the act of clearing at a jump, when I received a shot under the cap of my right knee and instantly fell. In this emergency, there seemed a speedy prospect of my again falling into the hands of the French, as the division was in rapid retreat, but a comrade of the name of Little[30] instantly dragged me over the wall, and was proceeding as quick as possible with me, on his back, towards the bridge of the Coa, over which our men were fast pouring, when he, poor fellow! also received a shot, which passing through his arm smashed the bone, and finally lodged itself in my thigh, where it has ever since remained. In this extremity, Little was obliged to abandon me. . . I must not forget a singular escape that occurred; a man of the name of [Rifleman Thomas] Charity, of my own company, when the cavalry first rushed upon us, had fallen, wounded in the head by a sabre; while on the ground, he received another severe sword slash on the seat of honour, and a shot through the arm, the latter, no doubt from the 52nd. Yet after all this, he managed to escape, and 'Clothed in scarlet lived to the tell the tale,' as a pensioner in Chelsea Hospital.[31]

---

30. Robert Liddle.
31. Costello, pp.33–4.

Lieutenant Simmons also was almost caught,

> ... when a body of Hussars in bearskin caps,[32] and light-coloured pelisses got amongst the few remaining Rifle Men and began to sabre them. Several attempted to cut me down, but I avoided their kind intentions by stepping on one side. I had a large cloak rolled up and strapped across my body; my haversack was filled with little necessary articles for immediate use; thus I got clear off. A volley was now fired by a party of the 43rd under Captain [Joseph] Wells, which brought several of the Hussars to the ground. In the scuffle, I took to my heels and ran to the 43rd, Wells calling out, 'Mind the Rifle Man! Do not hit him, for heaven's sake.' As I was compelled to run into their fire to escape, he seized me by the hand and was delighted beyond measure at my escape.[33]

Simmons wrote to his parents a few weeks later a slightly different version.

> In passing a road the fire was excessively hot from their cannons, their shells bursting continually above our heads in every direction. I was coming over with the rear section of the company when suddenly 300 or more French Dragoons dashed in among us, knocked down my sergeant, and cut down three or four men. A fellow brandished his sword in the air, and was going to bring it down upon my head. I dropped mine, seeing it was useless to make resistance. He saw I was an officer, and did not cut me. I looked round me to see if I had the least chance of escaping, and pulled my boat cloak off, which was buckled round me, when fortune favoured me; some of the 43rd and our own men gave them a volley. I took advantage of their confusion, rushed through them, and got through a breach in a wall our men were firing from, pleased enough at my good fortune.[34]

---

32. This would have been the 3rd Hussar's Elite Company, which wore bearskin busbies.
33. Simmons, pp.77–8.
34. Ibid., p.92.

Captain Leach's company was in a similar situation. Rifleman Green found:

> We had bad ground to form a line upon, and it was found necessary to move over the river, where there was a good position for artillery and infantry. My company was an out-lying picquet, and we had to remain. We were formed into four sections; the French infantry were in line. They were so near to us that we could discern their features. They were not twenty paces from us when our officer gave the word 'right about face!' As soon as we obeyed his order, we were surrounded by a troop of French hussars; they had come from behind a hill, and our company only 80 men, were thus hemmed in by horse and foot, and were all made prisoners. Their infantry did not fire, if they had they would have killed their own hussars, who were cutting us down with their swords. Some of us fired, and thus lowered some of them. It was a great field, and very bad ground to make our retreat. There was an enclosure near us of a stone wall and a pair of gates. We made our retreat through the gates, as the hussars were cutting at us with their swords. We were so jammed up at the gateway, they took 40 prisoners, rank and file. The pay-sergeant, who had the company's books, and three lieutenants . . . five men, and a sergeant were wounded in making for the bridge, where the light division had crossed the river. I carried a poor fellow on my back about half a mile, who had a musket ball through his thigh. An artillery officer, on horseback, was near the bridge; he said to me 'Is that lad wounded?' I said 'Yes sir.' 'Put him behind me on the horse;' but seeing him bleeding very much, he said 'I will dismount; he shall have the saddle!' We put him on, and I was glad to be relieved from my burden.[35]

Shortly after the battle began Captain Ross received orders to bring the remaining guns forward to support the two guns with the outposts.

> I joined the guns on piquet [sic] with two more, sending Jenkinson to the right, on the road to Junca, with the 2nd Division. The enemy advance rapidly, and take possession of

---

35. Green, pp.28–9.

a commanding height with their cavalry and two guns, from whence they return the fire which we had opened upon them, but without doing us any mischief from this ground.[36]

It was not long before Captain Campbell's Company of the 52nd Foot was sucked into the fighting. Lieutenant Henry Dawson wrote home five days later that

> we immediately stood by our arms & were placed so as to protect 2 Guns of the Horse Artillery, we had also in advance with us 500 Cavalry, we immediately threw out a few skirmishers, and before they were driven in upon us, 4 more Guns came to us, from superiority of numbers we retired, keeping up however a very heavy fire and join'd the Division in their position who were waiting ready to receive the enemy. Altho' we had retired 2 long miles, firing the whole way, only 3 men were wounded of the 95th & a few of the Cavalry.[37]
>
> As soon as the Picquets had retired upon the Division we were divided and sent to different places, that required strengthening; with a section of the Company, I was placed on the outer ditch of a small Tower[38] to protect the Artillery who were placed about ½ a mile from Almeida, on the left of our position; I saw nothing of the Battle of the Division except where the Artillery were engaged. Genl Craufurd had given particular orders for the Artillery to stand to the last; they certainly did their duty, & served their Shrapnels in beautiful style. The force of the French before they attacked the Division was upwards of 10,000, besides what they had in their rear to support them.[39]

The Withdrawal to the River

General Craufurd rode forward to assess the situation and realized that his decision to stay on the east bank of the river in support of Almeida might see the destruction of his division. Their only route to safety was across a narrow bridge over an otherwise impassable river.

---

36. Ross, pp.10–11.
37. Lieutenant Dawson was obviously mistaken.
38. The windmill.
39. Dawson, pp.32–3.

General Ferey was attacking on a very narrow front along the main road leading to the bridge. Because the division was deployed on a 5km front, it could only bring to bear a battalion at a time to stop the 4,000 men of General Ferey's brigade. There was a real danger that the French may make it to the bridge before the Light Division's battalions in the centre and left of the line could. Craufurd had no choice but to order an immediate withdrawal across the bridge. First to go would be the cavalry, artillery and wagons. Once they were across, the 1st Caçadores were to go next, followed by the 3rd Caçadores, the 52nd Foot and the 43rd Foot. The 95th Rifles were to be the last to cross.

Craufurd instructed Major Charles Napier, who was acting as a voluntary ADC, to tell Colonel Barclay,[40] who was on the far right flank of the division '. . . to fall back from the plain and regain the enclosures behind him, which he did, and the fire became very heavy: Barclay's horse was killed, mine was wounded. And threw me, but I remounted and rejoined Craufurd. . .'[41]

Once Major Napier reached Craufurd, he was sent to '. . . tell the 52nd, 43rd and 95th to maintain the enclosures until he got the cavalry and guns over the Coa, leaving two pieces to cover the retreat. I gave Barclay, and Major McLeod,[42] and Colonel Beckwith,[43] these orders, but they were all hotly engaged and could no longer keep their ground, lest the enemy should turn their flanks and reach the bridge before them.'[44]

After passing the new orders to Lieutenant Colonel Barclay, Major Napier returned to the Left Wing of the 52nd Foot's position where he found Captain Robert Campbell, wounded. The major was afraid that the captain would be captured and gave him his horse. Major Napier stayed with the 52nd Foot until they made it down the hill.[45]

As the riflemen passed through their ranks, soon it was the 43rd Foot's turn to try and slow the advancing French. Lieutenant Henry Oglander, who had just arrived from England the night before, wrote in his diary:

> About 8 a m, the Left Wing was ordered to advance up the
> hill before us, and as soon as we attained its summit, we took

---

40. Lieutenant Colonel Robert Barclay, commander of the 52nd Foot.
41. Napier, Charles, p.137.
42. Major Charles McLeod, commander of the Right Wing of the 43rd Foot.
43. Lieutenant Colonel Thomas Beckwith, commander of the 95th Rifles.
44. Napier, Charles, p.137.
45. Ibid., pp.137-8.

shelter under a wall, from which we commenced a fire against the approaching enemy. There we immediately retired, and again made a stand behind the walls of our old position, from which we were driven skirmishing through corn fields & vineyards to the top of some hills; and there into the road leading down the mountain to the bridge.[46]

Lieutenant John Brumwell's company was among those sent forward.

Our Left Wing was ordered out and I am in the left company, therefore I had an opportunity of seeing the whole. We were ordered to extend our companies and move on at 'double quick' and meet the enemy which was coming on at 'double quick,' and in a very large force. We skirmished with them for about half-an-hour in which we both lost a good many men. They sent cavalry and infantry to get round our flanks, which was soon observed and we were immediately ordered to retreat. The French pushed on in a very dashing way, the situation then became general, the whole of the troops were then keeping up a very sharp fire but still retreating.

I must now tell you what sort of ground we had to retreat over. There was a number of stone walls, which were very high, and we had to scramble over them and grade fields and all sorts of disagreeable places to pass through before we could reach the bridge. The enemy were pushing in very close and their balls flying round us like hailstones . . .[47]

The high walls, while providing cover, made it almost impossible for the 43rd Foot to form into a line. However, there were other problems with the position. Craufurd saw that

some companies, which formed the left of our line, were in a vineyard, which had been so completely inclosed by a high stone wall, that it was quite impossible for cavalry to get into it; but the preceding night having been excessively bad, some of the troops who had been stationed in this vineyard, had unfortunately pulled down the wall in many places, to make use of the

---

46. Oglander, Diary entry dated 24 July 1810.
47. Brumwell, pp.48–9.

stones to form a shelter against the rain, which was most violent. This wall, which Brigadier-general Craufurd had considered a complete defence, was therefore no longer such, and after our artillery and cavalry had moved off, the enemy's cavalry broke into the inclosure, and took several prisoners.[48]

Lieutenant John Hopkins, who was commanding one of the companies, was discussing the situation with Lieutenant Henry Booth, when he was seriously wounded and was evacuated to the rear. Lieutenant Booth assumed command of the company[49] and received orders

> to retire in line – very wisely and properly ordered! But unfortunately, from the vast quantity of high walls, six feet high generally, the number of rocks, vineyards, and broken ground which continued down to the water's edge, our line was soon broken, past all chance of being formed again, till we had crossed the bridge. In this manner the whole division retired down this tremendous hill. This was fine fun for the French skirmishers, who were following us closely from rock to rock, pelting us pretty handsomely down to the river! However, in all this confusion, our fellows behaved nobly, and retired fighting inch by inch, which in the end proved our misfortune; for had we made the best of our way over the bridge, and occupied the hills on the other side as soon as possible, we should have suffered less, and precisely the same position would have been gained.[50]

Major Patrickson, who led the Left Wing of the battalion, was ordered to form the rearguard with the five companies of his wing, while the Right Wing was told to retreat across the bridge.[51] The major and his five companies soon found themselves almost surrounded by the French. Private Thomas Garretty was with the rearguard and found that they were

---

48. Craufurd, Robert. 'Action near Almeida', pp.230–1.
49. Mockler-Ferryman, Augustus. 'Three Brothers in the Light Division', *Forty-Third and 52nd Light Infantry Chronicle*, Vol. III, p.180.
50. Letter from Lieutenant Henry Booth dated 30 July 1810, in Levine, pp.132–3.
51. Fergusson, p.9.

unaccountably placed within an enclosure of solid masonry at least ten feet high, situated on the left of the road, with but one narrow outlet about half musket-shot down the ravine. While thus shut up the firing in front redoubled, the cavalry, the artillery, and the caçadores successively passed by in retreat, and the sharp clang of the 95th Rifle was heard along the edge of the plain above. A few moments later and we should have been surrounded; but here, as in every other part of the field, the quickness and knowledge of the battalion officer remedied the faults of the General. In little more than a minute, by united effort, we contrived to loosen some large stones, when, by a poweful [sic] exertion we burst the enclosure, and the regiment, reformed in column of companies, was the next instant up with the riflemen. There was no room to array the line, no time for any thing but battle; every Captain carried off his company as an independent body, the whole presenting a mass of skirmishers, acting in small parties and under no regular command, yet each confident in the courage and discipline of those on his right and left, and all regulating their movements by common discretion. Having the advantage of ground and number, the enemy broke over the edge of the ravine; their guns ranged along the summit, played hotly with grape; and their hussars galloped over the glacis of Almeida, poured down the road, sabring everything in their way. The British regiments, however, extricated themselves from their perilous situation. Falling back slowly, and yet stopping and fighting whenever opportunity offered, they made their way through a rugged country, tangled with vineyards, in despite of the enemy, who was so fierce and eager, that even the horsemen rode in among the enclosures, striking at us, as we mounted the walls, or scrambled over the rocks.

Just then, I found myself within pistol-shot of the enemy, while my passage was checked by a deep chasm or ravine; as not a moment was to be lost, I contrived to mount to the edge, and, having gained the opposite side, put myself in a crouching position, and managed to slide down the steep and slippery descent without injury . . .[52]

---

52. Garretty, pp.91–2.

About the same time Major Patrickson received orders to form the rearguard, Captain Ross, commanding the artillery, was ordered

> to retire by General Crawford [sic]. We occupy a rocky height in front of the town for some time, but the French kept beyond our reach, sending their riflemen close up to our position, when General Crawford directed me to retire upon the town. About this time the guns under Captain Jenkinson were ordered from the right to join me at the town, and immediately afterwards the enemy's columns of cavalry and infantry advanced upon our right, occupying the ground just vacated . . . Lieut. Bourchier, of the Artillery, brought me the order 'to retire as rapidly as in my power across the bridge, and to get my guns into position on the opposite heights.' At this time we had five guns in action, firing upon a heavy column of cavalry moving apparently with the intention of charging us down the Junca road. Our fire was excellent, and broke them two or three times. Upon receiving the order to retire, I instantly sent to desire the Quartermaster to move off with the waggons, which were still under the walls of Almeida; for notwithstanding that I requested General Crawford's leave twice during the morning to send them across the river, he would not permit me to do so.[53]

The Withdrawal of the Artillery

As the artillery wagons were coming down the steep road, one of them flipped over close to the entrance to the bridge, blocking access for the guns and wagons that were following behind them. Behind the guns, the companies of the Left Wing of the 52nd Foot were filtering down the steep slopes and they provided protection to the overturned wagon. One company was detailed to help right it, although Captain Ross claimed it was due to the efforts of '. . . [Lieutenant Alexander MacDonald] M'Donald and [Lieutenant Daniel Macnamara] Bourchier, it was got safe off. During the time we were passing down the hill and up the heights on the other side, the enemy kept up an incessant but ineffectual fire upon us.'[54] Once the guns were up the hill, they quickly deployed along the top to bring the advancing French under fire.[55]

---

53. Ross, p.11.
54. Ibid.
55. Lipscombe, Nick, *Wellington's Guns: the Untold Story of Wellington and His Artillery in the Peninsula and at Waterloo*. Oxford: Osprey, 2013, p.125.

Lieutenant Dawson of the 52nd Foot, who had been left with a sergeant and twenty men to protect the artillery near the windmill, was still there when the artillery was ordered to withdraw. Lieutenant Bourchier, who had brought the orders for the guns told him

> make the best of your way to your Regt. To join it, I said, was an impossibility, you must attempt it, was my orders. It was impossible for me to keep up with Cavalry & flying Artillery, therefore I made the best of my way to some Vineyards and made three attempts to get to the bridge of The Coa, below Almeida, but every time always found the French between me and the party of the 95th who were quite on the left of the Division & almost 20 times my number. After a little consideration I determined to retire among the Rocks below Almeida, which I did unperceived & after having collected my party & a few stragglers of the 43rd & 95th in the all about 30 men.[56]

The 14th Light Dragoons and some of the KGL Hussars followed the guns down the hill and were the next to cross the river. The 14th Light Dragoons took a few casualties, including 'Cornet John Blackford, who was hit by a fragment of shell in the posterior, and as he was rather a soft sort of fellow, I thought, at first, that he made too great a fuss about it, though he turned deadly pale'.[57] Captain Brotherton, seeing many of the wounded infantry making their way down the hill, stopped to help Lieutenant Roger Frederick of the 43rd Foot who was shot in the leg.

> Happening to be close to him, I jumped off my horse to assist him. He was bleeding profusely and no surgeon (being) immediately at hand to stop it, I had my canteen slung round me full of strong wine, and put it to his mouth, and made him take a copious draught of it. Just as I had done this the surgeon of the regiment came up, and I told him what I had done, at which he expressed himself displeased, saying that probably I should be the cause of his death; but he (Frederick) always said afterwards to everybody that I had saved his life by giving him

---

56. Dawson, p.33.
57. Brotherton, p.24.

the wine, as he felt so faint that he felt he was dying. He lived afterwards in excellent health till the 21st June 1854.[58]

The 1st KGL Hussars were spread out on a wider front than the 14th Light Dragoons and had more trouble making it to the bridge. While most of Captain Krauchenberg's squadron made it to the bridge without incident, part of it was '. . . obliged to swim across the river, exposed to the enemy's fire, and narrowly escaping capture. . . the hussars had only a few horses killed and wounded'.[59]

The 1st Caçadores were the next to withdraw. Once they reached the bridge, which was still clogged with the artillery and cavalry, many soldiers pushed their way over the bridge instead of waiting for it to clear. Once on the other side of the river, they continued up the hill until they reached the crest and re-formed into a line. This would cause quite a bit of controversy over the next month.

Instead of sticking to the original plan, the Left Wing of the 52nd Foot crossed over next. They followed the road a little bit up the hill and lined the wall to provide supporting fire to the troops still on the other side of the river. Captain George Napier's company was sent upriver to the right to defend a shallow part of the river.[60]

As the Right Wing of the 43rd Foot reached the bottom of the hill, General Craufurd met Lieutenant Richard Brunton who

> had the honour to carry one of the Colours and the care of it when retiring with the Regiment broken up nearly into Skirmishing order, by the difficult nature of the ground, and the necessity for repelling attacks in various directions; was a duty of no small anxiety, difficulty and exertion. On being forced back in some disorder on the narrow and rocky road leading down to the Bridge, General Crawford came up to me, and the other Ensign and desired us to cross the Bridge, take up a conspicuous position on the opposite side as near the Bridge as possible, and display the Colours for the Regiment to rally on. This was done and we remained standing under a tremendous fire of musquetry from the opposite side which was precipitous and

---

58. Brotherton, p.24.
59. Beamish, Vol. 1, pp.282–3.
60. Napier, George, p.130.

well within range until the Regiment had passed the Bridge and rallied.[61]

When the Left Wing of the 43rd Foot reached the bottom of the hill, Major Patrickson was ordered to occupy the high hill that overlooked the bridge. He was supported by at least one company of riflemen. This was supposed to be the final position on the east bank. The French continued to press hard on the retreating British and Portuguese troops, and the fight for the hill began. Captain Leach, who commanded the riflemen, noted that the position was

> overhung by huge rocks in many places, from which, had our pursuers been permitted to possess themselves of them, they might have annihilated the troops underneath, without their being able to retaliate; and thus, the only option left them would have been a walk to Verdun as prisoners of war, or an instantaneous passage across the Styx instead of the Coa . . . As the rear-guard approached the Coa, we perceived that a part only of our cavalry, infantry, and artillery, had yet crossed the bridge; it became, therefore, indispensably requisite for us to keep possession of a small hill looking down on, and perfectly commanding the bridge, until everything had passed over, cost what it might. I trust I shall be pardoned for saying that the soldiers of the old and gallant 43d, and that part also of our own battalion whose lot it was to defend this important hill, against a vast superiority of numbers, proved themselves worthy of the trust. In ascending the hill, a musket-shot grazed the left side of my head, and buried itself in the earth close by.[62]

The Counter-Attack of the Rearguard

General Craufurd was on the west bank of the river and as the senior officer left on the east side, Lieutenant Colonel Beckwith assumed command of the troops remaining there. He ordered the 3rd Caçadores to withdraw and then the 95th Rifles. Once they were across, Craufurd

---

61. Brunton, Richard, 'A Narrative of the Services of Lieutenant Colonel Richard Brunton of the 13th Light Dragoons'. National Army Museum. File # 1968-07-461.

62. Leach, *Rough Sketches. . .*, pp.148–9.

sent word for the forces on the hill to retreat across the river. As the British withdrew from the hill, the French immediately occupied it and began to fire on them. While this was happening, Lieutenant Colonel Beckwith was standing with Major Napier at the bridge and realized that Lieutenant Colonel Barclay and the Right Wing of the 52nd Foot were still fighting in the hills upstream of the bridge and were in danger of being trapped on the wrong side of the bridge.

Beckwith ordered Major Napier to ride to the 52nd Foot and get them to move as quickly as possible. Napier, mounted on his third horse of the day, believed he 'had little hope of reaching the 52nd alive, but escaped, though a dragoon horse I had caught and mounted was shot in the leg just as I reached Barclay, and at the same moment his [Barclay's] cap was shot off'.[63] Barclay quickly replaced his missing hat with his night cap, which he wore for the rest of the day. It was during this fighting that he was shot in the foot.[64]

Beckwith crossed the bridge and met with Major McLeod of the 43rd Foot. The day started with the battalion commanded by Lieutenant Colonel Edward Hull who had arrived at their cantonments the night before. The colonel had been killed in the fighting and Major McLeod had assumed command. The situation was critical and the lieutenant colonel and major organized a force to retake the hill. In this force were Captains Robert Dalzell's, Thomas Lloyd's and William Napier's companies of the 43rd Foot, Captains O'Hare's and Leach's of the 95th Rifles, and some 3rd Caçadores.[65] The size of this force is unknown. Most sources give the numbers between 100 and 200 men. Considering there were at least six companies involved, the number was likely about 250 men.

Major McLeod, mounted on his horse, led the force in a wild charge across the bridge and up the 50m-high hill. There was little control of the companies by their officers and it quickly turned into an unorganized mass as they charged up the hill. Captain Leach, who had been wounded in the head when they abandoned the hill watched the charge go in.

---

63. Napier, Charles, pp.13–19.
64. Barlow, George Ulrich, *A Light Infantryman with Wellington: The Letters of Captain George Ulrich Barlow, 52nd and 69th Foot, 1808–1815.* Gareth Glover (ed.). Solihull (UK): Helion, 2018, p.44.
65. Napier, Charles, p.138. Simmons, p.78. Leach, *Rough Sketches. . .*, pp.149–50. I have not been able to identify which companies from the 3rd Caçadores were involved.

If any are now living of those who defended the little hill above the bridge, they cannot fail to remember the gallantry displayed by Major M'Leod [sic], of the 43d, who was the senior officer on the spot. How either he or his horse escaped being blown to atoms, when, in the most daring manner, he charged on horseback, at the head of a hundred or two skirmishers of the 43d and of our regiment mixed together, and headed them in making a dash at a wall lined with French infantry, which we soon dislodged, I am at a loss to imagine. It was one of those extraordinary escapes tending strongly to implant in the mind some faith in the doctrine of fatality.[66]

Captain William Napier, who participated in the charge, wrote:

M'Leod, a very young man, but with a natural genius for war, immediately turned his horse around, called to the troops to follow, and, taking off his cap, rode with a shout towards the enemy. The suddenness of the thing, and the distinguished action of the man, produced the effect he designed; a mob of soldiers rushed after him, cheering and charging as if a whole army had been at their backs, and the enemy's skirmishers, astonished at this unexpected movement, stopped short.[67]

Private Garretty of the 43rd Foot also took part in the charge.

The conflict was tremendous; thrice we repulsed the enemy at the point of the bayonet. M'Leod was in the hottest of the battle, and a ball passed through the collar of his coat; still he was to be seen with a pistol in his right hand, among the last to retire. At length the bugle sounded for retreat; just then, my left-hand man, one of the stoutest in the regiment, was hit by a musket shot, – he threw his head back, and was instantly dead. I fired at the fellow who shot my comrade, and before I could re-load, my pay-sergeant, Thomas,[68] received a ball in the thigh, and earnestly implored me to carry him away. As the enemy was

---

66. Leach, *Rough Sketches. . .*, pp.149– 50.
67. Napier, William, *History*. Vol. 3, p.291.
68. In December 1810 there were two Sergeants Thomas: Thomas and Edward. Neither are listed as pay sergeant.

not far off, such a load was by no means desirable; but he was my friend; I therefore took him up; and though several shots were directed to us, they all missed, and I was able, though encumbered with such weight, to carry him safely over the bridge. At length the assistance of another soldier was procured; we then carried the wounded man between us, when he was placed on a car. He returned me sincere thanks, and, what was just then much better, gave me his canteen, out of which I was permitted to take a draught of rum; how refreshing it was, can be fully known only to myself.[69]

Lieutenant Simmons of the 95th Rifles once again was in the thick of things and paid for his impetuosity.

A party of the 43rd, with Major M'Leod at their head and several of their officers, as well as our men and officers, ran up the hill, exposed to a desperate fire, as the enemy had a strong wall to fire over. They did us much mischief before we got at them. It was a grand sight. Our brave boys would face anything. They shouted. The French became panic-struck. At this moment I had nearly come to the wall. A musket ball hit me in the middle of my left thigh, and passed through a little upwards; being so near the man that favoured me with the shot, it luckily went directly through, and took a small piece of cloth trousers with it, at the same time I was also slightly hit in the leg. I staggered on a little, but fell; the blood spouted out on both sides. I put my hand into my pocket for a tourniquet, but fainted. Captain Napier of the 43rd, being near, twisted his handkerchief round my thigh. A sergeant of the 43rd, with three of their men, carried me off. By the time I got to the bridge, I came to myself; there was a desperate fire at it. A sergeant and three of my company, came to my assistance and relieved the other men.[70]

This fierce counter-attack stopped the French in their tracks and the force held the hill long enough for the Right Wing of the 52nd Foot to make it to safety on the other side of the bridge. Then Major McLeod and his men raced back down the hill and across the bridge. The attack

---

69. Garretty, p.93.
70. Simmons, p.93.

was not without consequences. Casualties among the officers were quite high. In addition to Lieutenant Simmons, Captain Thomas Lloyd was shot in the leg, while Lieutenant Thomas Smith of the 95th Rifles was severely wounded. Lieutenant Harry Smith, Thomas's brother, was leading the last section of the force across the bridge when he was shot in the leg. He would have been captured except for Major McLeod, who dismounted from his horse and gave it to him.[71]

The Assault on the Bridge

By 2 p.m. the Light Division was safely across the river and most were waiting for orders. A light rain began to fall as the battalions tried to sort themselves out and evacuate their wounded. The 43rd Foot held the western side of the bridge and to their right was the 3rd Caçadores. Further along the road and along the river banks was the 52nd Foot. Intersperse among them were the depleted companies of the 95th Rifles. Many were lining the walls, others were along the banks, while some were among the rocks on the slopes above the road. Near the bridge was an old stone house with a superb field of fire, which Captain John Cameron, of the 95th Rifles, placed his company.[72] Both sides continued to fire across the river at each other with small arms and artillery fire. Captain Jenkinson of Ross's RHA troop, was on the hill and found it

> the most delightful positions for our guns having greatly the advantage of ground on the left bank, we then opened our fire upon their advancing infantry with spherical case, which cut them up and broke them perpetually, and occasionally gave their artillery such discharges of it as compell'd them to shift their ground seven times and then retire altogether, they having fired several times in vain attempt to annoy us.[73]

The French were able to drag four guns up to the top of the hill near the river, which the British had re-taken and then withdrew from 30 minutes before. Captain Ross also saw these guns more of an annoyance than a threat for 'they could not stand our fire, being obliged to shift

---

71. Beamish said it was Sergeant Augustus Fischer of the 1st KGL Hussars who gave him his horse.
72. Smith, p.31.
73. Lipscombe, p.125.

their ground without firing more than three rounds in any one position they took up, and at last gave it up altogether, leaving us the power of commanding their infantry without interruption'.[74]

Having forced the Light Division back across the river with a minimum of casualties, Ney could have ended the operation at this point. However, he misread the situation and thought the British and Portuguese were too disorganized and disheartened to prevent him from seizing the far side of the bridge. He ordered General Ferey's brigade of General Loison's 3rd Division to take the bridge. The attacking force consisted of two grenadier companies from the 66th Line Regiment led by Captain Bonamaison and one grenadier company from the 82nd Line Regiment led by Captain Ninon.[75] They were formed behind the high hill that the Light Division had just abandoned. The assault caught the Light Division by surprise and the three companies initially made good progress. However, it was not long before the Light Division began to fire and between the rifles, muskets and artillery the French were stopped and the survivors dispersed into cover along the eastern bank of the river. Both Captain Bonamaison and Ninon were wounded.

Captain Leach, despite his wound, witnessed it.

> The whole of General Crawford's [sic] corps at length gained the opposite bank of the Coa, and was strongly posted near the bridge, behind walls, rocks, and broken ground The torrents of rain which fell the night before had so swollen the river, that all the fords were at that moment impassable; a fortunate circumstance, as the only way by which we could now be attacked was over the narrow bridge, on which we could bring a destructive fire; and we likewise commanded the approach to it from the opposite side with musketry. An incessant fire was kept up across the river by both parties, and after it had been continued some time, the French sent a party of grenadiers to storm the bridge, with the vain hope of driving us from our new position. They advanced most resolutely in double-quick time, and charged along the bridge; but few, if any, went back alive, and most of those who reached our side of it unhurt were killed afterwards.[76]

---

74. Ross, p.10.
75. Horward, p.213.
76. Leach, *Rough Sketches* . . ., p.150.

Rifleman Green was one of the defenders.

> Our troops had a good position on high ground, and there were
> some stone walls for shelter. We made loop-holes as we had
> done before. The French made a charge to cover the bridge three
> different times but were prevented. It was warm work! Here
> poor Captain Cray,[77] Lieutenant Riley,[78] and the Hon. Aberthnot,[79]
> were all killed and buried in one grave, with their clothes on,
> and without coffins! Our artillery had got their guns on rising
> ground, with good range, and well served; they swept the enemy
> down as fast as they made the attempt to get over![80]

Ney, having witnessed the failure of Ferey's troops to take the bridge,
turned to his ADC, Colonel Emmanuel Sprünglin, and ordered him
to lead the Chasseurs de Siège and take the bridge. These men had
distinguished themselves during the siege and the marshal thought they
were up to the task. Captain William Napier in the 43rd Foot described
this attack:

> . . . a second column, more numerous than the first, again
> crowded the bridge. This time, however, the range was better
> judged, and ere half the distance was won, the multitude was
> again torn, shattered, dispersed, and slain; ten or twelve men
> only succeeded in crossing, and took shelter under the rocks at
> the brink of the river. The skirmishing was then renewed, and
> a French surgeon coming down to the very foot of the bridge,
> merely waved his handkerchief and commenced dressing the
> wounded under the hottest fire; nor was this touching appeal
> unheeded, every musket turned from him . . .[81]

Colonel Sprünglin was more terse in his description of the attempt.

> At noon I received from M. le Marechal himself the order to carry
> at all costs the Coa bridge, whence two companies of Grenadiers

---

77. Captain Jasper Creagh died of his wounds on 25 July.
78. Lieutenant Peter Reilly died of his wounds on 30 July.
79. Rifleman Green was mistaken. Lieutenant Duncan Arbuthnott was
    neither wounded or killed. He was killed at Sabugal on 3 April 1811.
80. Green, pp.28–9.
81. Napier, William, *History*. Vol. 3, p.293.

had just been repulsed. I had 300 men; I formed my battalion in column, and approached the English with bayonets, and with the cry of Long live the Emperor. The bridge was carried away, but I had 4 officers and 89 soldiers killed, and 3 officers and 144 wounded soldiers. On the 25th the battalion, being destroyed, was dissolved.[82]

After seeing the failure of the second attempt, Ney sent staff officers out to find other crossing sites. One approached the river on the far right of the Light Division's line, where Captain George Napier, of the 52nd Foot was.

Where I was the French only came half-way down to the bank of the river from the opposite height, and then a fine dashing fellow, a French staff officer, rode down just opposite my position to try if the river was fordable at that part. Not liking to fire at a single man I called out to him, and made signs that he must go back; but he would not, and being determined to try it, he dashed fearlessly into the water! It was then necessary to fire at him, and instantly both man and horse fell dead, and their corpses floated down the river . . . The rain during the night had so swollen the river that the French were not sure that it was passable, and would not attempt the passage till an officer had been sent to try it. Now, had I permitted the officer to cross and then made him a prisoner, it would have proved that the river could be forded, and of course a strong force would soon have crossed and obliged me to retreat, and at the same time have turned the position of the brigade on its right flank at the same moment that every effort was being made to force the passage of the bridge . . . and his horse also, for had the animal crossed without his rider it would have served the enemy's purpose just the same, so the poor horse was shot![83]

Not finding another crossing site, Ney decided to make one last assault on the bridge. This met with even less success than the previous two, for the 'bridge was literally piled with their dead and they made

---

82. Sprünglin, Emmanuel, 'Souvenirs d'Emmanuel-Frédéric Sprünglin', *Revue hispanique*, Vol. 11, 1904, pp.439–40.
83. Napier, George, pp.131–3.

breastworks of the bodies'.[84] By 4 p.m. the assault was called off and a truce was arranged to gather the dead and wounded. The casualties were not all one-sided. Among those wounded in the 43rd Foot was Captain William Napier, who was shot in the hip.[85] Many of the Light Division officers could not believe that the French continued to attack after the first assault to capture the bridge failed. Captain Leach was very vocal in his damning of the French leadership.

> This experiment was repeated, and it is almost needless to add, that it met the same fate each time. The French officer who directed those attacks on the bridge, might have known, before he caused the experiment to be made, that a few hundred French grenadiers, advancing to the tune of 'Vive l'Empereur!' 'En avant, mes enfans!' and so forth, were not likely to succeed in scaring away three British and two Portuguese regiments, supported by artillery. It was a piece of unpardonable and unjustifiable butchery on the part of the man who ordered those brave grenadiers to be thus wantonly sacrificed, without the most remote prospect of success. They deserved a better fate, for no men could have behaved with more intrepidity.[86]

The gathering of the wounded was hampered by the rain, which had gone from a light drizzle to heavy downpour by the time the last attack had petered out. Rifleman Green, one of the few chroniclers of the battle who survived it unscathed, help to evacuate the casualties.

> There was what I had never seen before, French and English all mixed, carrying their comrades that were wounded to the rear! Amongst the French who came on this errand of mercy, was an Irishman. He belonged to the Irish Brigade in the French service. He was a deserter from our army, and said in good English 'Well Rifle Brigade, you will remember the 24th of July. We came to muster you this morning.' We replied, 'We had been mustered early, before the action began; we have thinned your ranks pretty well, and if we had been allowed to keep on firing we would have thinned them a little more!' He nodded

---

84. Smith, p.31.
85. Napier, Charles, p.140.
86. Leach, *Rough Sketches . . .*, pp.150–1.

his head and said 'He liked the French service better than the English,' and then turned away; if he had stayed until the time had expired he would doubtless had a ball from some of our rifles for his pert language.[87]

Once the wounded had been evacuated, around 6 p.m. Craufurd gave the order to withdraw. The 43rd Foot was left in place overlooking the bridge to prevent the French from advancing unopposed.[88] By midnight they were on their way in the heavy rain to Freixedas via Pinhel, a distance of 36km. The initial stopping point was Valverde, about 5km to the west. There they bivouacked in the rain among granite boulders, battered but unbowed.[89]

87. Green, p.29.
88. Oglander, Diary entry 25 July 1810.
89. Leach, *Rough Sketches* . . ., p.152.

Chapter 9

The Casualties at the Côa

'. . . our company sustained a very severe loss; our return was one officer, Lieutenant Coane, quite a youth, dangerously wounded, eleven file killed and wounded, and forty-five taken prisoners. My old Captain O'Hare had only eleven men on parade next day.'[1]

Rifleman Costello, 95th Rifles

The Near Misses

Once the battle is over or at least the immediate danger is past, a soldier will often check himself and his equipment to see what damage has been done. Sometimes the soldier will find that he was hit several times but has survived with no visible injuries. This appears to have happened to many individuals. Lieutenant William Freer of the 43rd Foot 'had two shots hit me one on the sole of my shoe the other went thro' the sleeve of my Jacket & gave me a smart rap'.[2] Private Anthony Hamilton of the 43rd Foot found 'in this engagement a musket ball struck my knapsack, went through my great-coat and blanket, and through a piece of bent leather that we carry for soles and into my shaving dish, and lodged there, breaking the glass. It did not sound in the least like a shot, but on examination I found it was.'[3] This introspection will often make him wonder how he survived. Lieutenant Richard Brunton, who carried the 43rd Foot's colours during the battle, had had enough of being shot at and as soon as the battle was over 'handed them over to Ensign [James] Considine'.[4]

---

1. Costello, p.34.
2. Freer; 'Letter dated 24 August 1810'.
3. Hamilton, Anthony, *Hamilton's Campaign with Moore and Wellington during the Peninsular War.* Staplehurst: Spellmount, 1998, p.84.
4. Brunton, 'A Narrative . . .'.

French Casualties

Most of the French infantry casualties were caused by the attempt to take the bridge. Unfortunately there are no definitive sources for their numbers. Emmanuel Koch, who edited Marshal Masséna's papers, gives the number at 117 men and 92 horses killed, and 410 men wounded.[5] Colonel Sprünglin, who commanded the Chasseurs de Siège, said they had 4 officers and 89 men killed, and 3 officers and 144 men wounded for a total of 93 killed and 233 wounded.[6] At 2 p.m. Marshal Ney wrote to Masséna that he had between 400 and 500 casualties and this was before the Chasseurs de Siège made their attempt to seize the bridge.[7]

According to Aristade Martinien's *Tableaux par Corps et par Batailles des Officiers Tués et Blessés*, the French had the following officer casualties:

Table 9.1: French Officer Casualties on the Côa River, 24 July 1810

Unit		Killed	Died of Wounds	Wounded	Total
Cavalry	3rd Hussars	2	–	–	2
	15th Chasseurs	–	–	1	1
Ferey's Brigade	66th Line Infantry	3	2	11	16
	82nd Line Infantry	1	–	2	3
Chasseurs de Siège[8]	6th Light Infantry	1	1	4	6
	27th Line Infantry	–	–	1	1
	50th Line Infantry	–	–	1	1
Total		7	3	20	30

Not surprisingly, since they were in both the first and third assaults on the bridge, the 66th Line Infantry Regiment took the heaviest officer casualties. Among them was its commander Colonel Jean Béchaud, who was seriously wounded, and Chef-de-Bataillon Stavelot who was wounded.

---

5. Koch, Vol. 7, p.117.
6. Sprünglin, p.440.
7. Horward, p.216.
8. Some of the 66th Line Infantry Regiment's officer casualties would probably include those who were serving with the Chasseurs de Siège.

A French infantry battalion in 1810 had an authorized strength of 19 officers and 810 men or a ratio of one officer per forty men.[9] General Loison's division had a strength of 302 officers and 11,948 men on 15 January 1810, which is also a ratio of one officer per forty men. By 15 September his division had 239 officers and 6,587 men, which is a ratio of one officer per twenty-eight men; by 1 January 1811 the ratio was one officer per twenty-six men; and by 15 March 1811, it was one officer per twenty-five men. For the cavalry, the ratio was one officer per twenty-two men. Using these figures the infantry lost about 700–800 officers and men, while the cavalry lost about 70 officers and men.

Light Division Casualties

Considering the wealth of available information, determining the Light Division's casualties should be relatively simple. Unfortunately this is not true. One factor affects the accuracy of the information. The returns were completed on 25 July and reflect what they knew at the time. As the days went by, men thought to be missing or captured returned to the ranks. Additionally some men were listed as wounded when the initial returns were compiled, but a number would die from their wounds over the next few months.

There are a couple of examples of men being listed as missing in the initial returns but then turning up after they were completed. The best example is Lieutenant Henry Dawson of the 52nd Foot. Early in the battle, his section was protecting the flank of the artillery by the windmill. Soon orders were received to withdraw. The cavalry and horse artillery were able to make it through to the bridge, but Lieutenant Dawson and his men were cut off. The battalion reported that Lieutenant Dawson and his men were either killed or captured. Yet Lieutenant Dawson refused to surrender and he spent the next 24 hours evading the French by proceeding down river to the bridge at Cinco Villas. He wrote home that 'On my arrival at Cavahal [Carvalhal] on the 25th, where the Division was quarter'd, I found the returns of our loss just going to be sent off. Genl Craufurd order'd them to be made out afresh and to take out our names as Prisoners.'[10]

The returns were corrected for Lieutenant Dawson and his men before being submitted to Army Headquarters, but in the case of the 1st Caçadores they were not. The initial returns had two privates killed, seven wounded and seven missing. However, returns submitted to the

---

9.   Haythornthwaite, Philip, *Napoleon's Line Infantry*. London: Osprey, 1983, p.4.
10.   Dawson, pp.32–3.

Table 9.2: Light Division Casualties Submitted by the Army Headquarters dated 25 July 1810[14]

	Killed					Wounded					Missing				Total
	Off	SGT	Drum	OR	Horses	Off	SGT	Drum	OR	Horses	Off	SGT	Drum	OR	
Staff	–	–	–	–	–	1	–	–	–	–	–	–	–	–	1
43rd Foot	3	2	–	13	–	10	8	–	77	–	–	–	1	14	128
52nd Foot	–	–	–	1	–	2	–	–	–	–	–	–	–	3	6
95th Rifles	1	–	–	11	–	8	1	–	54	–	1	1	–	52	129
1st Caçadores	–	–	–	2	–	1[14]	–	–	7	–	–	–	–	7	16
3rd Caçadores	–	–	–	2	–	1	1	–	23	–	–	–	–	2	29
14th Light Dragoons	–	1	–	–	–	1	–	–	1	4	–	–	–	–	3
16th Light Dragoons	–	–	–	–	–	–	–	–	–	3	–	–	–	–	–
1st KGL Hussars	–	–	–	–	1	–	–	–	2	3	–	–	–	2	2
Artillery	–	–	–	–	2	–	–	–	–	2	–	–	–	2	2
Total	4	3	–	29	3	23	10	–	164	12	1	1	1	80	316

14. *Cobbett's Political Register* Vol. 18, July–December 1810, p.223.

Portuguese Army Headquarters on 29 July had two privates killed, nine wounded and none missing. There was an 'Observation' with the 29 July returns that the seven missing privates had returned to the ranks on 25 July. There was no information on where they had been.[11]

Another issue that is difficult to reconcile is what counts as a wound. Did an individual have to be evacuated to be considered wounded? Did the standard vary from unit to unit? For example there is much anecdotal evidence that many men were hit but were not reported as being wounded. For example Captain Leach of the 95th Foot says he was shot in the head, but his name is not in any of the lists of the wounded. The most obvious case is the 52nd Foot. They had two officers listed as wounded, yet we know its battalion commander, Lieutenant Colonel Robert Barclay, was shot in the foot. If he was not reported as wounded, how many others were not? The ratio of officers to other ranks for the British Army is about one officer for every thirty men. Although the 52nd Foot was divided into wings posted on the opposite side of the battlefield, their casualties could have been higher based on the number of officers wounded.

The official return of casualties for the Light Division dated 25 July has a total of 316 casualties: 36 killed, 196 wounded, and 83 missing, plus an unidentified Portuguese officer wounded (see table opposite).

Charles Oman provides different numbers.

Table 9.3: Light Division Casualties Submitted by the Army Headquarters dated 25 July 1810[12]

Unit	Killed		Wounded		Missing		Total
	Officers	Men	Officers	Men	Officers	Men	
Staff			1	–	–	–	1
43rd Foot	3	15	10	86	–	15	129
52nd Foot		1	2	16	–	3	22
95th Rifles	1	11	8	55	1	53	129
1st Caçadores	–	2	–	7	–	7	16
3rd Caçadores	–	2	1[13]	24	–	2	29
Cavalry	–	1	1	3	–	2	7
Total	4	32	23	191	1	82	333

---

11. Portuguese Military Archives. AHM-DIV-1-14-270-01_m0043.
12. Oman, Vol. 3, p.544.
13. A Portuguese officer was listed as being wounded, but neither his name and rank, nor his battalion was given.

George Caldwell and Robert Cooper have been able to fill out more information on the 95th Rifles casualties.[15]

Table 9.4: 95th Rifles Casualties on the Côa River, 24 July 1810

	Officers	Sergeants	Buglers	Riflemen	Total
Killed	1	–	–	11	12
Died of Wounds	3	1	–	–	4
Wounded	5	–	–	54	59
Missing	1	1	–	52	54
Total	10	2	–	117	129

Yet the August 1810 Theatre Returns gives a much different number.

Table 9.5: 95th Rifles Casualties on the Côa River 24 July 1810 Based on August 1810 Returns

	Officers	Sergeants & Corporals	Buglers	Riflemen	Total
Killed	1	1	–	8	10
Died of Wounds	3	–	–	–	3
Wounded	6	1	1	11	19
Missing	1	2		47	50
Total	11	4	1	66	82

Missing
Captain Stewart's No. 1 Company: 1 lieutenant, 1 corporal, and 14 riflemen.
Captain O'Hare's No. 3 Company: 1 sergeant and 32 riflemen.
Captain Balvaird's No. 5 Company: 1 rifleman

Table 9.6: 43rd Foot Casualties on the Côa River 24 July 1810, Based on August 1810 Returns

	Officers	Sergeants	Corporals	Drummers	Privates	Total
Killed	3	2	–	–	12	17
Died of Wounds	–	–	–	1	10	11
Wounded	10	6	6	–	47	69
Missing	–	–	1	–	12	13
Total	13	8	7	1	81	110

---

15. Caldwell, Vol. 2, pp.86–7.

Table 9.7: Light Division Officer Casualties on the Côa River, 24 July 1810

Unit	Position	Name	KIA	DoW	WIA Severely	WIA Slightly	MIA
HQ	ADC	LT James Shaw	–	–	X[16]	–	–
43rd Foot	Battalion Cdr	LTC Edward Hull	X	–	–	–	–
	Company Cdr	CPT Ewan Cameron	X	–	–	–	–
	Company Cdr	CPT Peter Deshon	–	–	–	X	–
	Company Cdr	CPT James Hull	–	–	X[17]	–	–
	Company Cdr	CPT Thomas Lloyd	–	–	–	X[18]	–
	Company Cdr	CPT William Napier	–	–	X[19]	–	–
	Company Cdr	LT Horatio Harvest	–	–	–	X[20]	–
	Company Cdr	LT John Hopkins	–	–	X[21]	–	–

(continued)

16. The official sources has Lieutenant Shaw as being slightly wounded, but his wound caused him to be an invalid until late 1811.

17. Shot in the mouth. Garretty, p.95.

18. In a letter dated 30 July 1810 Lieutenant Henry Booth states that Captain Lloyd was severely wounded. If he was, he was recovered enough to lead his company at Busaco on 27 September 1810. Levine, p.134.

19. Shot in the hip. Napier, Charles, p.140.

20. The extent of his wound is unknown, but he had recovered in time to lead his company at Busaco on 27 September 1810.

21. Despite being seriously wounded twice he had recovered enough to lead his company at Busaco on 27 September 1810.

231

Table 9.7: Continued

Unit	Position	Name	KIA	DoW	WIA Severely	WIA Slightly	MIA
	Company Cdr	LT George Johnson	—	—	—	X[22]	—
		LT Roger Frederick	—	—	X[23]	—	—
		LT John M'Dermid	—	—	X	—	—
		LT John Stephenson	—	—	X	—	—
52nd Foot	Battalion Cdr	LTC Robert Barclay	—	—	—	X[24]	—
		Maj Henry Ridewood	—	—	—	X[25]	—
	Company Cdr	CPT Robert Campbell	—	—	—	X	—
95th Rifles	Company Cdr	CPT Jasper Creagh	—	X[26]	—	—	—
	Company Cdr	CPT Samuel Mitchell	—	—	X[27]	—	—
	Company Cdr	LT Alexander Coane	—	—	X[28]	—	—
		LT John M'Cullock	—	—	X[29]	—	X
		LT Donald McCloud	X[30]	—	—	—	—
		LT Mathias Pratt	—	X[31]	—	—	—
		LT Peter Reilly	—	X[32]	—	—	—
		LT George Simmons	—	—	X[33]	—	—
		LT Harry Smith	—	—	X[34]	—	—
		LT Thomas Smith	—	—	X[35]	—	—

22. In the left arm. He was well enough to lead his company at Busaco on 27 September 1810. Hall, John, *A History of the Peninsular War Volume VIII: The Biographical Dictionary of British Officers Killed and Wounded, 1808 – 1814. London: Greenhill, 1998, p.310.*

23. Shot in the leg. It was amputated on 29 July 1810. Levine, p.134.

24. He was wounded in the foot, but continued to command. Barlow, p.44.

25. According to Captain Barlow, he was shot through the head. Ibid.

26. Was shot in the lower body and died of his wounds that night. Simmons, p.82.

27. In the right arm. He would spend the next five months recuperating. Hall, p.412.

28. Wounded in the side. Simmons, p.82.

29. He was wounded seven times by sabre cuts. Caldwell. Vol. 2, p.86.

30. Killed instantly when he was shot through the heart. Simmons, p.82.

31. Shot in the neck and died on 30 July 1810. Costello, p.32.

32. Shot in the lower part of the body and died on 28 July 1810. Simmons, p.82

33. Shot in the thigh which injured the bone. Simmons, p.76. Hall, p.518

34. Shot in the left ankle. Smith, p.31.

35. Shot in the leg which left him lame. Hall, p.523.

Loss of Commanders

The real impact of casualties was on the Light Division's command structure. Within the three British infantry battalions two of three battalion commanders were casualties, while eleven of eighteen company commanders were. Particularly hard hit was the 43rd Foot which lost its battalion commander and eight company commanders. Compounding the problem, only seven captains were listed being with the battalion at the end of June, and one of them, Captain Duffy, was in the hospital with malaria. Four of its companies were commanded by lieutenants on the morning of the battle, but by the end of the day eight of the companies were commanded by lieutenants, seven of whom had not been in command at the beginning of the day. Among the new acting commanders was Lieutenant Richard Brunton, who carried the colours during the battle. He was given command of Captain Cameron's company.[36] Although these figures show that the Light Division officers believed in leading from the front, incurring the loss of so many senior officers was not sustainable in the long run. Although junior officers could be promoted to take their place, their experience could not be easily replaced.

Table 9.8: Light Division Senior Officer Casualties on the Côa River, 24 July 1810

	Killed	Wounded
Battalion Commander	1	1
Majors	–	1
Company Commanders	2	9

Evacuation of the Casualties

If a soldier was wounded on the east side of the river and was incapable of walking, he might have been carried back across the bridge to the

---

36. Brunton, 'A Narrative . . .'. Lieutenant Brunton being given command is a bit curious. He was the tenth senior surviving lieutenant and there were only seven vacancies. Why he was chosen over lieutenants who were senior to him is not known. It is possible that he was the senior officer left in his company.

safety of the other side. However, it was dependent on how intense the fighting was at the time. Rifleman James Tomlinson was 'surrounded by three French hussars, that he shot one, and parried off the swords of the other two for some time, until one of them made a blow at his head and cut his left eye out; and the other cut him on the thick part of his right arm, and being thus disabled he was compelled to surrender'.[37]

Otherwise he was probably left on the field to be captured by the French or died from the lack of treatment. Once across the river, the usual practice was to have an assistant surgeon treat him, before sending him to the rear for further medical attention. There is no evidence this is what happened. The medical staff was likely taken by surprise like everyone else and immediately retreated across the river and up the hill. There they set up a field hospital in a chapel. The wounded soldier had to make his way along the road to the top of the hill where the field hospital was. There were no ambulances to help move the wounded.

Rifleman Costello, who was abandoned on the east side of the river when the soldier who was helping him was shot, knew he had to help himself otherwise he would be left behind.

Urged by a strong desire to escape imprisonment, I made another desperate effort, and managed to get over the bridge, from the other side of which Captain Ross's guns were in full roar, covering our retreat; in this crippled state and faint through the loss of blood, I made a second appeal to a comrade, who assisted me to ascend the hill on the other side of the river. On the summit, we found a chapel which had been converted into a temporary hospital, where a number of wounded men were being taken to have their wounds dressed by the surgeons. Fortunately, I had not long to wait for my turn, for as we momentarily expected the coming of the French, everything was done with the greatest dispatch.[38]

Lieutenant Simmons, also of the 95th Rifles, noted:

a sergeant of the 43rd, with three of their men, carried me off. A sergeant and three of my company, came to my assistance and

---

37. Green, p.29.
38. Costello, p.34.

relieved the other men. They dragged me up the hill, which was nearly a mile, up a very rocky and steep place. The blood kept pouring from my wounds. I fainted several times. The Colonel of the German Hussars gave me some wine and put me on a horse, an Hussar also with me. I sent my men back. In this way I was conveyed about a league, and put into a church, where I met with numbers of men and officers in the same plight.[39]

The lieutenant's trip to the rear was not without some mishap. On the way up the hill they met General Craufurd 'I passed him in the blanket. The General had still in his remembrance the loss of his light cart. He told the men this was no time to be taking away wounded officers, and ordered them back. They observed, "This is an officer of ours, and we must see him in safety before we leave him."'[40]

Lieutenant Harry Smith was taken up the hill by

> Serjeant Augustus Fischer, 1st Hussars. In the combat near Almeida July 1810, when the English light division and the first hussars were driven by the enemy over the Coa, serjeant Fischer rescued lieutenant-colonel [sic] Smith of the English rifle-corps, who was severely wounded, and would certainly have fallen into the enemy's hands, had not Fischer, at the risk of his own personal safety, given him his horse, and submitted to make his own way on foot. General Craufurd, who was witness to this occurrence, sent a handsome remuneration to the serjeant on the following day.[41]

At this field hospital[42] were the medical staff from each battalion and regiment. An examination of various sources put the number of surgeons and assistant surgeons at the field hospital at seventeen.

---

39. Simmons, pp.93–4.
40. Ibid., p.79.
41. Beamish, Vol. 2, p.506. The incident is based on the testimony of Adjutant Friedrich Baertling.
42. I have not been able to determine where the exact location of the field hospital was. An examination of a 1:25,000 map of the area shows no chapel or ruins of a chapel on it. The hospital was probably in the church at Val Verde which was 3.5km from the summit.

Table 9.9: Medical Personnel with the Light Division, 24 July 1810[43]

Unit	Surgeons	Assistant Surgeons	Total
43rd Foot	1	1	2
52nd Foot	–	2	2
95th Rifles	1	1	2
1st Caçadores	1	2	3
3rd Caçadores	1	2	3
14th Light Dragoons	–	2	2
16th Light Dragoons	–	1[44]	1
1st KGL Hussars	1	1	2
Total	5	12	17

They treated the wounded as quickly as possible and sent the walking wounded on their way to Pinhel. Rifleman Costello was one of them.

There were of our regiment about seventy or eighty disabled, a number of those hobbled onwards assisting each other by turns. We commenced our slow and painful march, and with the help of a couple of rifles that served as crutches, I managed to reach the first village where the Juiz [de Fora] or chief magistrate selected and put the worst of our wounded into bullock carts. Amongst those I fortunately was one; and although crammed with six others into a wretched little vehicle, scarcely capable of accommodating more than two, I thought it a blessing for which I could not feel sufficiently thankful. In this manner, we were dragged along all night, and by the following daylight we halted at another village, where I felt so dreadfully faint from loss of blood and my confined position, that I could not move at all. While refreshing our parched lips with some water that had been eagerly demanded, Lord Wellington and some staff galloped up. Glancing his eye at us for a moment, and seeing our crowded condition in the carts, he instantly gave an order to one of his aides-de-camp to obtain additional conveyance from the Juiz

---

43. 'Theatre Returns for the British Army in Spain and Portugal' July 1810. Rawkins, William, *The Army of Portugal 1793 – 1814*. Maidenhead: History Bookman, 2017, p.77. Challis, 'The Peninsular Roll Call'.
44. The 16th Light Dragoons had only one squadron with the Light Division, so they might have had an assistant surgeon with them.

de Fora, and also bread and wine. His Lordship then rode off towards Almeida. Although neither bread nor wine made their appearance, a few additional carts were procured, into one of which I was transferred with four other men.[45]

Lieutenant Simmons was one those who were considered too badly wounded to send on his own and was kept in the hospital overnight.

I found a number of poor fellows as bad, and some worse wounded, laid in every direction upon the stone floors. A poor fellow, who died some time after I entered, begged of me to lie upon a paillasse beside him, as I was upon the bare stones; he divided it with me. This soldier belonged to the 43rd Light Infantry. I was on the ground, and very ill from loss of blood; he had been placed on a paillasse of straw and was dying, but his noble nature would not allow him to die in peace when he saw an officer so humbled as to be laid near him on the bare stones. I have experienced many such kindnesses from soldiers, and indeed if I had not, I should not be alive to tell the tale . . . I was anxious to see my wound, and on examining it I thought directly I should soon want a billet in another world, but fortune has since favoured me. The large artery in my thigh is not injured. After being dressed I was put upon a car drawn by bullocks, and got into Pinhel about 10 o'clock at night, having had nothing to eat all day except some wine; it rained frequently, which made me uncomfortable.[46]

The situation in Pinhel was not much better. Sergeant Robert Grant of the 74th Foot was there when the casualties started arriving.

About 1½ hour after the action, all that was wounded and some not quite dead was brought in here. There the numbers at upwards of 500 wounded. They were the most shocking spectacle ever I beheld – many without arms, hands, legs, and wounded in the head, body, and every other part. They were the most piercing syte [sic] I ever saw – colonels, officers, and private men . . . They are all carried on carts and conveyed from

---

45. Costello, pp.34–5.
46. Simmons, pp.80 & 94.

the field with all possible haste. The cries of them would pierce the heart of a slave. There was upwards of 47 officers, in all 24 of whom was killed on the spot. The rest I saw carried in here in a shocking state. [The following morning, Grant went to an unroofed convent where the wounded had been laid] and there I beheld a sad scene – officers and men lying in their wet and bloody clothes. Clothed the same way as they were carried from the field and the ground on which they were lying without straw or any covering whatever, many of them dead of their wounds and lying almost naked . . . Even when they were coming in, in numbers notwithstanding the loss on our side being very great, yet General Craufurd swears he will never give up when he has a British soldier left . . . Heaven only knows the issue of this dreadful carnage. I send this by express. The moment I have time I will acquaint you of the events of the dreadful day.[47]

Pinhel was the headquarters of Picton's 3rd Division. Lieutenant Harry Smith said that they were treated like princes while there,[48] but the resources of the village were quickly overwhelmed. The next day, the wounded were ordered to Freixedas 15km to the south west. Once more oxcarts were provided, but most were overcrowded with the wounded and dying. For Rifleman Costello it was a nightmare.

After we had been driven some miles further, one of my wounded comrades, who was shot through the body, and whose end seemed momentarily approaching, at length in a dying state relaxed his hold from the cart sides and fell across me as I lay at the bottom, whilst foam mixed with blood kept running from his mouth. This with his glass eyes fixed on mine made me very uncomfortable. Being weak and wounded myself, I had no power to move him, and in this situation, the horrors of which survived for some time in my mind, death put an end to his sufferings, but without granting me any respite for some hours. His struggles having ceased, however, I was enabled to recover myself a little, and called to the driver to remove the body. But the scoundrel of a Portuguese, who kept as much ahead of the bullocks as possible, was so afraid of the French, that I could get on other answer

---

47. Horward, p.215. Sergeant Grant's letters have never been published.
48. Smith, p.31.

from him than 'non quire', 'Don't bother me,' and a significant shrug of the shoulder which bespoke even more than his words.[49]

From Freixedas, the wounded were sent to Celorico 30km to the southwest. Lieutenant Harry Smith was the senior officer in the convoy and thus responsible for it.

> In collecting transport for the wounded, a sedan chair between mules was brought, the property of some gentleman in the neighbourhood, and, fortunately for me, I was the only person who could ride in it, and by laying my leg on the one seat and sitting on the other, I rode comparatively easy to the poor fellows in the wretched bullock-cars, who suffered excruciating agony, poor brother Tom (who was very severely wounded above the knee) among the rest. This little story will show what wild fellows we were in those days. George Simmons' (1st Rifles) bullocks at one stage had run away. As I was the spokesman, the surgeon in charge came to me in great distress. I went to the village magistrate, and actually fixed a rope in my room to hang him if he did not get a pair of bullocks (if the Duke of W. had known he would have hung me). However, the bullocks were got and off we started. The bullocks were not broken, and they ran away with poor George and nearly jolted him to death, for he was awfully wounded through the thick of the thigh.[50]

At Celorico, boats were procured to take the wounded to Figueira da Foz, a town at the mouth of the river where it empties into the Atlantic Ocean. On 31 July they

> descended the Mondego by boats, landing every night. At one house a landlord was most insolent to us, and Lieut. [Mathias] Pratt of the Rifles, shot through the neck, got very angry. The carotid artery must have been wounded, for it burst out in a torrent of blood, and he was dead in a few seconds, to our horror, for he was a most excellent fellow. On the same bed with

---

49. Costello, p.36.
50. Smith, p.32.

me was a Captain [James] Hull of the 43rd Regiment with a similar wound. I never saw any man in such a funk.[51]

For Rifleman Costello, river travel was much better than by ox cart, but there was no medical treatment for them while they were travelling.

Sick and ill as I was, I well recollect the exquisite scenery that met our gaze on the banks of that beautiful river, as we floated over its surface to our destination. The heat of the weather was intense and dreadfully affected our wounds. The scarcity of doctors too, and fear of falling into the hands of the enemy, spurred everyone forward, and so took up the moments that the surgeons had not time sufficient nor opportunity to look after us. The consequence was, that this neglect caused maggots to be engendered in the sores, and the bandages, when withdrawn brought away on them lumps of putrid flesh and maggots. Many died on board, and numbers were reduced in consequence to the necessity of amputation. By care and syringing sweet oil into my wounds, I however had managed to get rid of them.[52]

Once at Figueira da Foz, ships were arranged to take them to Lisbon. The Rifles officers were embarked on the *Nestor* and they disembarked in Lisbon on 7 August. The ships were met by Portuguese militia who took the enlisted soldiers on stretchers to a hospital.[53] The officers were placed in private homes. Lieutenant Simmons

after some trouble, got into an empty house; there is a mattress and sheets, things I have seldom of late been used to. My Colonel sent my servant after me. He is a trusty and good fellow. I have him here. As I have the house to myself, I have no one to disturb me. The people are not worthy of notice. I met with great barbarity all the way. They would let you die in the streets before they would assist you. If any of them come near to pity, it is only to rob you, if possible. I have several times on the road

---

51. Ibid., pp.32–3.
52. Costello, p.37.
53. Ibid.

been robbed of the bread I was going to make a poultice of, and not had an opportunity of buying more.[54]

Lieutenant Smith and his brother Thomas were 'were billeted in Buenos Ayres, poor Tom and I in awful agony in our miserable empty house. However, we got books, and I, although suffering got on well enough. But poor Tom's leg was in such an awful state he was sent home. George Simmons's wound healed. My ball was lodged on my ankle-joint, having partially divided the tendo Achillis.'[55]

Burying the Dead

Because the battle was a fighting retreat, the Light Division was not able to bury most of their dead. This was left to the French or the local peasantry. General Loison claimed in two letters to Marshal Ney on 26 July that:

> Parties of French infantry had begun to bury the enemy dead even before dusk on the day of the battle. The Bodies of 80 men of the Light Division were buried, or if the terrain was too rocky, thrown directly into the Coa from the right bank. The following morning, 25 July, 40 bodies were heaved into the river from the left bank; 57 were buried where they had fallen on the heights of Cabeço Negro that evening while 24 enemy bodies were laid to rest in a vineyard behind Ferey's position. On 26 July the remains of approximately 100 more enemy were interred, the majority wearing the green uniforms of light infantry interspersed with cavalrymen; they were buried in a ravine approximately 825 yards from the fortress.[56]

The British were able to retrieve the body of Lieutenant Colonel Hull, of the 43rd Foot. Private Garretty

> 'saw his body, with the face downwards, thrown across the back of a mule, for conveyance to some place of interment. . .'.[57]

---

54. Simmons, p.94.
55. Smith, p.33.
56. Horward, p.216. General Loison was clearly exaggerating.
57. Garretty, p.95.

Chapter 10

Fallout from the Action on the Côa

'Craufurd remained much too long before a vast superiority of the Enemy; we have lost in killed and wounded 30 officers & 400 men to no purpose whatever.'[1]
Major Alexander Gordon[2] to Lord Aberdeen 25 July 1810

Despite the heroic efforts of the officers and men of the Light Division, there was much criticism about the affair. Most centred on General Craufurd's decision to deploy on the east bank of the Côa River and his handling of his division during the battle. This criticism came from many sources, including Wellington, his staff and even publicly from the officers and men within the division. Additionally the conduct of the 1st Caçadores during the battle came under close scrutiny. This chapter explores four issues:

1. Who was responsible for the Light Division being deployed in such a precarious position?
2. Should Wellington have relieved Craufurd of his command?
3. Did Craufurd lose the confidence of his officers and men?
4. Were the accusations of cowardice against the 1st Caçadores justified?

Who Was Responsible for the Light Division Being Deployed in such a Precarious Position?

For some on the staff, the responsible officer was General Craufurd. For Major General Charles Stewart, the army's Adjutant General, the fault

---

1. Gordon, Alexander, *At Wellington's Right Hand: the Letters of Lieutenant-Colonel Sir Alexander Gordon, 1808 – 1815.* Rory Muir (ed.) Phoenix Mill: Sutton, 2003, p.99.
2. Major Gordon was Wellington's aide-de-camp.

was totally Craufurd's. In a letter to his half-brother Lord Castlereagh[3] on 29 July, he wrote that:

> There is no doubt that all the responsibility of what took place on the 24th lies with Craufurd. He had Lord Wellington's orders repeated twice to him not to engage, and to return across the Coa. However, he thought the enemy would respect the fortress of Almeida and not push him rapidly when they advanced, that he would have time to make a regular and orderly retreat, and that it was more becoming to do it in the presence of the enemy than to go off before their arrival.[4]

The army's Quartermaster General, Colonel George Murray, was equally harsh. He wrote to General Alexander Hope[5] on 25 July 1810: 'The Question naturally asked is, why was this loss incurred? And why did not the Corps cross the river, on it being ascertained that the Enemy were advancing with such a strong force . . .'[6]

Wellington's letter to his brother William Wellesley-Pole, the Chief Secretary of Ireland, was even more damning.

> Although I shall be hanged for them, you may be very certain that not only I have had nothing to do with, but had positively forbidden, the foolish affairs in which Craufurd involved his outposts. Of the first, indeed, in which Talbot was killed, I knew nothing before it happened. In respect to the last, that of the 24th, I had positively desired him not to engage in any affair on the other side of the Coa; and as soon as La Concepcion [*sic*] was blown up on the 21st, I had expressed my wish that he should withdraw his infantry to the left of the river; and I repeated my injunction that he should not engage in an affair on the right of

---

3. Robert Stewart, Viscount Castlereagh, had been the Secretary of War the year before, but was replaced by Lord Liverpool in 1810.
4. Charles Stewart to Castlereagh, dated 29 July 1810 quoted in Muir, Rory, *Life of Wellington*. www.lifeofwellington.co.uk. 2019.
5. General Sir Alexander Hope was the half-brother of General Sir John Hope, 4th Earl of Hopetoun.
6. George Murray to Alexander Hope, dated 25 July 1810 quoted in Muir, Rory, *Life of Wellington*.

the river in answer to a letter in which he told me that he thought the cavalry could not remain there without the infantry. After all this, he remained above two hours on his ground after the enemy appeared in his front before they attacked him, during which time he might have retired across the Coa twice over, where he would have been in a situation in which he could not have been attacked.[7]

However, an examination of the correspondence between Wellington and Craufurd tells a different story, because Wellington left the final disposition of the Light Division up to him.

On 2 July 1810 Wellington told him:

In case the enemy should attack[8] General Craufurd with a superior force, I wish him to retire upon Almeida, and eventually, should he find it necessary, across the Coa, holding the high grounds on the left of the river and Valverde, and keeping open the communication with the fort as long as may be practicable.[9]

On 11 July 1810, Wellington changed his mind and wrote to Craufurd that 'I do not wish to risk any thing beyond the Côa, and indeed, when Carrera is clearly off, I do not see why you should remain any longer at such a distance in front of Almeida.'[10] Yet in the same letter he waffles a bit and says:

It is desirable that the communication with Almeida should be kept open as long as possible, in order that we may throw into that place as much provisions as possible, and therefore I would not wish you to fall back beyond that place, unless it should be necessary. But it does not appear necessary that you should be

---

7. *Supplementary Dispatches, Correspondence, and Memoranda of Field Marshal Arthur Duke of Wellington, K.G.* Edited by the 2nd Duke of Wellington. London: John Murray, 1860–71. Vol. 6, pp.563–4. The letter was dated 31 July 1810. Hereafter referred to as *WSD*.

8. This was changed to 'In case the enemy should threaten to attack . . .' in a letter from Wellington on 11 July 1810.

9. *WD*, Vol. 6, p.230.

10. Ibid., p.259.

so far, and it will be safer that you should be nearer, at least with your infantry.[11]

Three days later Wellington provided Craufurd with further guidance. 'I think you will do well to move your infantry to Junca [Junça], but you had better retain all your cavalry till you shall withdraw across the Coa.'[12] Junça is 7km south of Almeida and 10km west of Fort Concepción, on the east side of the Côa River. Within a day of receiving these instructions, Craufurd had moved his infantry to the ridge line that ran from Junça to Almeida.

On 16 July, Wellington once again wrote to Craufurd, but this time qualified his instructions.

> It is desirable that we should hold the other side of the Coa a little longer, I think that our doing so is facilitated by our keeping La Concepcion. At the same time I do not wish to risk any thing in order to remain at the other side of the river, or to retain that fort . . . .[13]

It was not until 22 July that Wellington sent more empathic instructions, but even then he left the decision to withdraw across the Côa up to Craufurd:

> I have ordered two battalions to support your flanks; but I am not desirous of engaging an affair beyond the Coa. Under these circumstances, if you are not covered from the sun where you are, would it not be better that you should come to this side with your infantry at least? Let me know how your division is situated as soon as you can, and I will answer you by the parte [sic] tomorrow, or earlier.[14]

These often-contradictory instructions gave Craufurd wide latitude. If Wellington had wanted him to withdraw across the Côa he could have given him orders to do so, but instead he left it to his own judgment.

---

11. *WD*, Vol. 6, p.259
12. Ibid., p.267.
13. Ibid., p.275.
14. Ibid., pp.285–6.

In hindsight, this was a mistake that almost saw the destruction of the Light Division.

Should Wellington have Relieved Craufurd of His Command?

Wellington let his superiors know that he was displeased with Craufurd. Lieutenant Colonel Henry Torrens, the Military Secretary to the Commander-in-Chief of the Army General Sir David Dundas, wrote to William Wellesley-Pole on 11 August about the matter.

> Dispatches have been received from Lord Wellington of the 25th. There has been a sharp action between Craufurd's Brigade and the advance of The Enemy in which we have suffered rather severely for what can only be deemed an outpost skirmish. And it is much to be regretted that such occurrence was allowed to take place, as it can form no feature one way or another in the general result of the campaign. Lord W. is between ourselves much dissatisfied with Craufurd who, let his talents be what they may certainly does not possess either temper or genius to conduct the details of an outpost![15]

Despite his displeasure, there were several reasons why Wellington did not relieve or publicly censure Craufurd. The first is that he recognized that he too was at fault for not ordering him to withdraw. Wellington wrote to his brother on 31 July his feelings about the situation.

> You will say, if this be the case, why not accuse Craufurd? I answer, because if I am to be hanged for it, I cannot accuse a man who I believe has meant well, and whose error is one of judgment, and not of intention; and indeed I must add that although my errors, and those of others also, are visited heavily upon me, that is not the way in which any, much less a British army can be commanded.[16]

Wellington could have publicly censured Craufurd, but this could also have caused major problems. Historian Rory Muir summed it up neatly:

---

15. Unpublished letter provided to the author by Rory Muir.
16. *WSD*, Vol. 6, pp.563–4.

Alexander Craufurd declares: 'Actual censure Craufurd never could have borne; he would have given up his command at once'.[17] Of course, that is speculation and it underlines what a difficult subordinate Craufurd was, but it may well be true.

Venting his feelings by abusing Craufurd might have given Wellington some immediate satisfaction, but it would either cost him that officer's services or make him a bitter enemy and encourage the creation of factions of those who condemned and those who sympathised with Craufurd. Besides, Wellington still clearly valued Craufurd despite Barquilla and the Coa, although he could not discount the evidence they provided that 'Black Bob' was not at his best under fire, at least without a superior officer present to give him directions.[18]

In the end, Wellington decided to keep Craufurd in command. However, in a way of rebuking him without formally doing so, Wellington praised the actions of the battalion commanders in his official dispatch home about the action, but conspicuously left out Craufurd's name.[19]

Did Craufurd Lose the Confidence of His Officers and Men?

Although the officers and men of the Light Division performed quite well, the performance of General Craufurd was considered by many of his subordinates to be very poor. The criticism focused on two points: why was the division fighting in such an exposed position on the east bank of the Côa River, and his handling of the battle. The criticism was at all levels from his personal staff to junior officers to the other ranks and is indicative of a loss of confidence in their general.

Lieutenant John Cox of the 95th Rifles wrote in his diary that '. . . all this blood was shed for no purpose whatsoever a rearguard should have occupied the ground and the whole Division withdrawn over the river when such a superior force was seen advancing',[20] while Captain Henry Mellish, the Light Division's DAAG, wrote home on 1 August: 'You will of course have heard of the commencement of our operations.

---

17. Craufurd, *General Craufurd and His Light Division*, p.155.
18. Muir, Rory, *Life of Wellington*, www.lifeofwellington.co.uk. 2019.
19. *WD*, Vol. 6, pp.292–4.
20. Cox, John, 'Extracts from John Cox's Diary of the Peninsula War', p.5.

The affair of the 24th at the bridge of the Coa is much to be lamented as we lost several officers & men to no purpose. We might ought to have retired without the loss of ten men. The worst of it is that it gives the Enemy confidence against us.'[21]

Lieutenant Henry Booth of the 43rd Foot wrote home on 30 July:

> But why did our General wait for the attack in so infamous a position? It was impossible for us to keep our ground, nor was it intended that we should. We remained, as it were to be fired upon, without the means of defending ourselves till we could cross the bridge. Would it not have answered the purpose if General Craufurd had at first occupied the hills on the other side of the bridge, advancing his pickets some distance in front, which could have retired on the approach of the French, covered by the fire of our line on the hills, and then defend the bridge, as we might have done against a much superior force? Every one asks the same question.[22]

Captain Jonathan Leach of the 95th Rifle pulled no punches in his opinion of Craufurd in a letter written soon after the battle:

> You will have heard how universally General Craufurd was hated and detested in the retreat from Coruña. If possible he is still more abhorred now and has been ever since we landed in Portugal. He is a damned tyrant and has proved himself totally unfit to command a Company much less a Division. I understand he has just got into a scrape with Lord Wellington for pitching on ground for his position which the most uninstructed boy of one month's standing would have known better to have taken up.[23]

The captain appeared to have mellowed a bit in time, for 16 years later he wrote in his memoirs:

> We had here time to reflect on the events which the last twenty-four hours had produced, and were extremely puzzled to

---

21. Letter from Henry Mellish to his sister Anne Chambers dated 1 August 1810.
22. Levine, p.133.
23. Verner, Vol. 2, pp.129–30.

conjecture why General Craufurd, if he was determined to give battle with the Light Division, consisting of four thousand men, to Marshal Ney's whole corps of twenty-five thousand, did not cross the Coa, without waiting to be forcibly driven over, and having taken up a position on the left bank, then and there challenge his opponent. The investment of Almeida was not retarded five minutes by our waiting under its walls for the approach of the besieging army.[24]

Within a few days rumours began to spread within the division that Craufurd was being relieved. Lieutenant Henry Booth wrote on 30 July that 'The General is universally blamed, and Lord Wellington is said to have expressed his disapprobation. In proof he has given Sir Brent Spencer the command of the Light Division.'[25]

The Napiers were vehement in their condemnation and often it was personal, with attacks on his fitness to command. Captain William Napier of the 43rd Foot wrote in his history:

On the 21st, the enemy's cavalry again advanced, Fort Conception was blown up, and Crawfurd [sic] fell back to Almeida, apparently disposed to cross the Coa, but nothing was further from his thoughts. Braving the whole French army, he had kept with a weak division, for three months, within two hours march, of sixty thousand men, appropriating the resources of the plains entirely to himself, and this exploit, only to be appreciated by military men, did not satisfy his feverish thirst of distinction. Hitherto he had safely affronted a superior power, and forgetting that his stay beyond the Coa was a matter of sufferance, not real strength, with headstrong ambition, he resolved, in defiance of reason and of the reiterated orders of his general, to fight on the right bank.[26]

Captain George Napier of the 52nd Foot wrote 'Craufurd, however, let his vanity get the better of his judgment, and delayed so long that

---

24. Leach, *Rough Sketches* . . ., pp.152–3.
25. Levine, p.133.
26. Napier, William, *History* Vol. 3, pp.287–8.

at last the enemy made a sudden attack, and it was with the utmost difficulty that the brigade made good its retreat over the bridge . . .'[27]

Major Charles Napier, the volunteer aide-de-camp to General Craufurd, went even further. Not only did he attack the general, he wrote in detail about what the general did wrong:

It was a fierce and obstinate combat for existence with the light division, and only Moore's regiments could, with so little experience, have extricated themselves from the danger into which they were so recklessly cast; yet it was their first battle, and Craufurd's demon of folly was strong that day: their matchless discipline was their protection – a phantom hero from Coruña saved them. . . His errors were conspicuous, and the most prominent shall be noted for my own teaching.

1st. He fought knowing he must retreat from an over-whelming force, and having no object in fighting.

2nd. He occupied a position a mile in front of the bridge: thus voluntarily imposing on himself the most difficult operation in war, viz. passing a defile in face of a superior enemy, and in the confusion of a retreat! The result might have been destruction – it was great loss.

3rd. He detained the cavalry and guns in a position where they could not act, till the infantry were beaten back on them; thus he risked the destruction of three; for the defile became choked, and had the French charged down the road, there would have been a bloody scene. This was so evident that I rode up to my brother William, and asked him to form a square with his company to resist cavalry; the idea had already struck him, and Major McLeod and Captain Patrickson also: it was general.

4th. The position was amongst vineyards, with walls averaging nine feet high, and he ought to have thrown down enough to open communications to the rear: the want of this caused our chief loss, for while we were pulling down the enemy were firing and followed our paths.

5th. He sent no guns over to defend the passage and cover the retreat, until after the troops had commenced retiring: had one gun broke down, or the horses been killed on the bridge, the

---

27. Napier, George, p.130.

troops would have been delayed and exposed to a destructive fire from the heights around, while in the mass of confusion.

6th. He suffered the 52nd to be nearly cut off, and never sent them an order to retire, after having given them one to defend their post obstinately: his small division was therefore disjointed and nearly paralyzed by extension.

7th. His retreat over the bridge was confused, though every officer and soldier was cool and ready to execute any order, and there was no excuse to hurry.

8th. When the passage of the bridge was made he left no man to defend it; and had I not halted some who were going up to join their colours the bridge would have been for a quarter of an hour without being enfiladed, or exposed to a single musket shot. This was afterwards rectified, but the 43rd were placed in a most exposed position, when a few breastworks previously made would have covered them.

9th. He made our guns fire at the enemy's guns instead of their men. In short there seemed a kind of infatuation upon him, and nothing but the excellence of his men and officers saved the division: and as it was, the rains, which had swelled the river and destroyed the many fords, saved him from a repetition of the Franciscan convent at Buenos Ayres! – Craufurd had surrendered there.[28]

Perhaps Lieutenant Booth summed up the feelings of the Division 'Is not this the pretty loss for one regiment, owing entirely to the blunders of _____ [Craufurd]? I hope we shall be better managed for the future.'[29] Despite their shaken confidence in the ability of their general, what came out of the battle was a belief in their leaders at all levels, but especially at the battalion level. Lieutenant Harry Smith of the 95th Rifles put it succinctly '. . . but for Colonel Beckwith our whole force would have been sacrificed'.[30] This belief would become the hallmark of the Light Division.

---

28. Napier, Charles, Vol. 1, pp.138–40.
29. Levine, p.134.
30. Smith, p.31.

Were the Accusations of Cowardice the 1st Caçadores Justified?

Within 24 hours of the battle rumours were racing through the army that the 1st Caçadores had abandoned their positions in the face of the enemy and raced as a mob across the bridge and up the road to the heights overlooking the river. As has been seen in Chapter 8, this was gossip and did not reflect the whole truth. Who spread the gossip is unknown, but it did reach Wellington, who reacted badly to the news. The question is who brought the news and when was it received?

The first news of the combat was received about 2 p.m. Wellington had just finished writing a letter to General Craufurd and amended it with 'I have heard both from Pinhel and Valverde that there was firing in your front as late as nine this morning but I conclude that I should have heard from you, if it had been serious.'[31] Shortly after sending the message off, he finally received a dispatch from Craufurd, written by Captain William Campbell, the Light Division's DAQMG, informing Wellington of the seriousness of the fight. This dispatch was written at 11:00 a.m. and reached Wellington sometime around 2:30 p.m.[32] This in itself was a feat of horsemanship, since Wellington was in the village of Alverca, 50km from the Côa River Bridge, which the dispatch rider[33] rode in less than 3.5 hours. Unfortunately Captain Campbell's message cannot be found.

The times written on these messages are important because the withdrawal of the 1st Caçadores occurred sometime after noon, well after Captain Campbell's original message was sent to Wellington. There is a possibility that one of the Army-level staff officers who had been exploring the front lines was the bearer of the news or it might have been a later dispatch from Craufurd. Regardless of the sender, Wellington knew about it by the next morning. He sent an angry letter to General Dom Miguel Forjaz, the Portuguese Secretary of War, complaining about the shameful conduct of the 1st Caçadores and linked its battalion commander, Colonel Jorge de Avilez, to their conduct.[34]

---

31. *WD*, Vol. 6, p.291.
32. Ibid.
33. He was probably from the 1st KGL Hussars who often had troopers assigned to Craufurd as orderlies.
34. A copy of this letter exists in the Portuguese Military Archives, but the ink is so faded that it is virtually illegible.

Wellington also wrote to Marshal William Beresford, the commander-in-chief of the Portuguese Army, ordering him to investigate the incident. The marshal appointed his ADC, Major William Warre, to conduct the investigation. The captain started the inquiry with a prejudiced mind. He wrote to his father on 25 July that:

> The 3rd Caçadores under Col. Elder behaved very well, and suffered some loss. I am sorry I cannot add as much for the 1st, who did not behave so, and ran off at the very beginning, though their Colonel d'Arilez [sic], a very fine young man, behaved very well, as also some of the Officers. So much for the want of discipline and confidence. I had before expressed my fears about them. I am just about setting off to enquire into the business, and I hope a most severe example may be made to prevent the recurrence of such horrid disgraceful business. If they will not fight from feelings of patriotism or honour, they must be made to do so from fear of a more infamous death, and a more certain one, if they deserve it.[35]

It was not long before the gossip reached Lieutenant Colonel de Avilez, the commander of the 1st Caçadores. He wrote to Beresford on 26 July asking for a court martial to clear his name.

> I, Jorge de Avilez Juzarte de Sousa Tavares, commander of the 1st Caçadores Battalion, having heard offensive reports on my conduct and that of the battalion under my command, during the action of the 24th instant, and believing that the battalion had an equal share, as the other corps of the division, on the glory but also on the disgrace gain on that day, I beg leave to request that you do me justice calling a court martial, before which I can justify myself. I ask also that you relieve me immediately of this command because I can't exercise it until clear my name of those unjust accusations.[36]

Beresford waited until he had the results of Major Warre's investigation, which were not long in coming. On 26 July, the marshal directed his

---

35. Warre, pp.94–5.
36. AHM 1-14-96-10 ms 2: Letter from Lieutenant Colonel de Avilez to Marshal Beresford.

Military Secretary, Brigadier António de Lemos Pereira de Lacerda, to reply to Lieutenant Colonel de Avilez.

> His Excellency Marshal Beresford, having received your letter from the 26th instant, instructed me to tell you that, being certain that the first news arriving to this Head Quarter respecting the conduct of the Battalion under your command in the action of the 24th, were very bad, your personal conduct and of part of your officers was recognized as distinguished.
>
> In consequence the Marshal ordered one of his Aides-de-Camp to verify the facts and had the satisfaction to be informed that the 1st Caçadores Battalion behaved with the great valour and honour that we expect from soldiers of the Portuguese nation. His Excellency assures you that he is completely satisfied and as soon as the enquiry ordered is closed he will publish his favourable opinion on an Order of the Day to be known to the Army and Nation.[37]
>
> I have the greatest satisfaction to announce to you this favourable expressions from our Commander-in-Chief and the honour to congratulate you and all my fellow officers serving under your orders.
>
> God save you, Sir.[38]

Surprisingly, Beresford waited a day before informing Wellington, who wrote back on 29 July.

> In consequence of the receipt of your letter of the 27th instant, I have made an inquiry into the conduct of the 1st caçadores in the affair of the advanced guard with the enemy on the 24th instant.
>
> It appears that this battalion did not quit its post on the right of the Coa, till it received orders to retire from Colonel Beckwith of the 95th regiment, then fell back upon the bridge of the Coa at an accelerated pace, and a part of the battalion crossed the bridge, mixed with the cavalry and artillery, and ascended the hill on the left of the corps; the remainder of the

---

37. This Order of the Day was published on the 3 August 1810.
38. AHM 1-14-96-10 ms 3-4: Brigadier Lemos de Lacerda, Beresford's Military Secretary to Lieutenant Colonel de Avilez dated 26 July 1810.

infantry of the division, and a part of the 1st caçadores still continuing to occupy the ground on the right of the Coa, and in front of the bridge. After the whole division crossed the Coa, the 1st caçadores again took its position on the right of the 52nd.

It appears that the conduct of that part of the battalion which crossed the Coa mixed with the cavalry and artillery, has been the cause of the unfavourable impression has been created respecting them in the affair; but they had no orders to halt on the right of the Coa when they were ordered to retire, and they saw the artillery and cavalry crossing.

Upon the whole, although the reports which have been circulated are exaggerated, there appears to have been some grounds for the complaints made of the conduct of the caçadores in the premature and accelerated passage of the river by some of them; but I am convinced that if the officers, on whose statement I had formed my opinion of the conduct of the 1st caçadores, had known of the orders the caçadores had received to retire, of the conduct of the whole before they retired, of part when some had crossed the Coa, and of the whole afterwards, these statements, however well founded, would not have been made.

Every report which I have received, and every inquiry which I have made, has tended to raise still higher the opinion which I had formed of the conduct of the commanding officer.[39]

On the same day, Wellington wrote to the Portuguese Minister of War, General Dom Miguel Pereira Forjaz, informing him that the initial reports of the conduct of the 1st Caçadores were incorrect.

If you hadn't yet laid before the Government my letter of the 25th instant, marked confidential, I request you to not do it because I have reasons to believe that the part respecting the conduct of the 1st Caçadores Battalion on the 24th instant is not supported by facts.[40]

On 1 August, Wellington also wrote a longer letter to General Forjaz, with the specific details of the investigation.

---

39. *WD*, Vol. 6, pp.306–07.
40. AHM 1-14-11-56 ms 1-2: Wellington to Dom Miguel Forjaz dated 29 July 1810.

In my letter of the 25th last month I reported on the shameful conduct of the Portuguese 1st Caçadores Battalion on the action against the enemy of the 24th; on the 29th I wrote requesting that you delay the presentation of that letter to the Government until I had made a thorough enquiry on the circumstances.

In consequence I enclose a copy of a letter I wrote to Marshal Beresford in which I informed him of the result.

It's my opinion that if all the circumstances of the case were known there were no reason to complain about the conduct of the 1st Caçadores and looking at the nature of the attack made against the advanced guard in that day with superior numbers, and at the difficulties of the terrain by which the light troops retired under enemy fire, it's admirable to see that a corps so newly raised as the 1st Caçadores behaved so well.[41]

Within the army, this put the matter to rest. However, within the British government it did not. On 25 July, Wellington wrote to the Earl of Liverpool,[42] the British Secretary of State for War and the Colonies, about the battle and the conduct of the infantry.

I am informed that throughout this trying day the Commanding Officers of the 43rd, 52nd, and 95th regiments, Lieut. Colonel Beckwith, Lieut. Colonel Barclay, and Lieut. Colonel Hull, and all the officers and soldiers of these excellent regiments, distinguished themselves. In Lieut Colonel Hull, who was killed, His Majesty has lost an able and deserving officer. Brigadier General Craufurd has also noticed the steadiness of the 3rd regiment of caçadores, under the command of Lieut. Colonel Elder.[43]

Noticeably absent was any mention of the 1st Caçadores. He also wrote a separate letter to Liverpool the same day on the reports of their ill behaviour. The information in this letter became widespread and its contents were not well received.[44] Lieutenant Colonel Henry Torrens

---

41. AHM 1-14-11-56 ms 3-4: Wellington to Forjaz dated 1 August 1810.
42. He had replaced Lord Castlereagh on 1 November 1809.
43. *WD*, Vol. 6, p.293.
44. Unfortunately this letter cannot be found, but Wellington referenced it in his 1 August 1810 letter to Liverpool.

commented in a letter on 11 August to William Wellesley-Pole that: 'The only thing that I don't like in the news with regard to our ultimate prospects is that a Portuguese regiment after the first shot being fired ran off and dispersed all over the country.'[45] Colonel James Willoughby Gordon told Charles, 2nd Earl Grey, a Whig Member of Parliament. on 18 August 'In the last affair under Craufurd, two Portuguese Battalions were present, the one, under Lt-Col Elder, an English officer, behaved steadily enough, but the other, on the first shot, took to its heels, and dispersed'.[46]

On 1 August Wellington wrote to the Earl of Liverpool on the results of his investigation, which seemed to calm things down in London.

> In a dispatch which I wrote to your Lordship on the 25th of July, I informed you that the 1st battalion of Portuguese caçadores had behaved ill in the affair of the 24th.
>
> I have since made further inquiries upon that subject and I enclose your Lordship the copy of a letter to Marshal Beresford, in which I informed him of their result.
>
> My opinion is, that if all the circumstances of the case had been known, there would have been no complaint of the conduct of the 1st caçadores; and adverting to the nature of the attack made upon the advanced guard on that day, to the superior numbers of the enemy, and to the difficulties of the ground over which the troops had to retreat, I am surprised that any part of a corps newly raised, as the 1st caçadores, should have conducted itself so well.[47]

The real question is what did the men of the Light Division think? I have found no accounts by officers and men of the Light Division that criticized the behaviour of the 1st Caçadores. Most writers focused only on their own regiment. Those who did mention the caçadores did so in a positive manner. Lieutenant Henry Oglander possibly summed it up the best: 'I myself saw many of the Portuguese Cazadores conduct themselves so as to rival our own men.'[48]

---

45. Horward, p.363.
46. Earl Grey Papers, Durham University Library GRE/B19/53 quoted in *Life of Wellington*, www.lifeofwellington.co.uk. 2019.
47. *WD*, Vol. 6, p.317.
48. Oglander, Diary entry dated 24 July 1810.

Chapter 11

25 July–25 September 1810

'Having lost our communication with Almeida and the other side of the Côa, there was no use in contesting the passage of that river, in which we might be turned at almost all points; and I therefore yesterday withdrew our posts from the Côa.'[1]

Wellington

The Withdrawal of the Light Division

The division spent all of 25 July in Valverde re-organizing itself, tending to the wounded and preparing to withdraw further into Portugal. For the officers and men of the 43rd Foot who were still guarding the bridge on the Côa, it was relatively quiet and only disturbed by French picquets who occupied the hill opposite of them. Word reached them that the division would begin to withdraw at midnight, so Major McLeod ordered the regimental baggage to move out as soon as it was dark.[2] By midnight the division was on its way in the heavy rain to Freixedas via Pinhel, a distance of 30km. From Valverde they marched 5km to Carvalhal.[3] The going was very slow due to the rain and the muddy roads were clogged with baggage. The first to leave was the artillery, followed by the infantry. From Carvalhal they headed 13km north to Pinhel. There the wounded remained, while those still fit for duty continued on to Freixedas, 13km to the southwest. The main force made it to Freixedas around 8 a.m. Captain Leach of the 95th Rifles noted that:

1. Wellington to his brother Henry Wellesley dated 27 July 1810. *WD*, Vol. 6, p.288.
2. Oglander, Diary entry 25 July 1810.
3. Carvalhal de Atalaia.

Here we had the luxury of a roof over our heads, – quite a novelty in those times; and we lost no time in making ourselves as comfortable as circumstances would admit. One night of sound sleep in an old uninhabited house, and dry clothes, put us in condition again for whatever may be forthcoming.[4]

The division stayed in Freixedas for two days and then at daybreak marched to Alverca, but bypassed Bouça Cova on its way to Celorico about 35km to the southwest.[5] The route of its march took it through several villages that had been abandoned due to a fear of the French. The division stopped at Celorico for several days. However, the town was where the Army's HQ was located and no billets were available. They were sent a few kilometres south of the town where they bivouacked in huts made 'of the branches of trees in some woods near the town . . . the rains fell almost without intermission, accompanied by lightning and thunder. As we were at this time vegetating under some huts made of the branches of trees, which kept out about as much rain as a large sieve would have done, we had the full benefit of this shower-bath.'[6]

Despite the wet conditions, the mood of the soldiers improved for

unremitted exertions were made by the Commissariat to provide us with necessaries. Grapes were plentiful; vegetables also were within reach. Bread in sufficient quantities, with a pipe of wine in front for regimental use, afforded an agreeable prospect; and the evening after the arrival of this welcome reinforcement was spent in a good-humoured review of the dangers gone by.[7]

Duty was light, but the division was required to maintain company-size picquets at the two bridges across the Mondego River: one on the road to Pinhel and the other on the road to Trancoso to the north. The bridges were about 2km on the other side of Celorico, so the duty companies had a 5km march from their bivouacs.

One major change came out of the fight on the Côa. Wellington finally realized that the Light Division was too large for one man to

---

4. Leach, *Rough Sketches* . . ., p.153.
5. Oglander, Diary entry 28 July 1810.
6. Leach, *Rough Sketches* . . ., pp.153 & 155. Oglander, Diary entry 28 July 1810.
7. Garretty, p.95.

command without any subordinate command structure. In July General Craufurd was trying to control five infantry battalions, three cavalry regiments and a horse artillery troop. Yet to do this, all he had were two ADCs and two staff officers. He needed a brigade structure within his division, and on 4 August 1810, Wellington issued a General Order creating one. The new structure for the Light Division was to consist of two infantry brigades, each commanded by the senior battalion commander in the brigade. Each brigade would consist of one British infantry battalion, one Portuguese caçadore battalion and four companies of the 1st Battalion 95th Rifles.[8]

Lieutenant Colonel Thomas Beckwith's Brigade:
1st Battalion 43rd Foot
3rd Caçadores Battalion
Right Wing of the 1st Battalion 94th Rifles (4 companies)[9]

Lieutenant Colonel Robert Barclay's Brigade
1st Battalion 52nd Foot[10]
1st Caçadores Battalion
Left Wing of the 1st Battalion 94th Rifles (4 companies)[11]

Two days later, Lieutenant James Stewart of the 95th Rifles was assigned as Lieutenant Colonel Beckwith's Brigade Major, while Captain Charles Rowan of the 52nd Foot was assigned as Lieutenant Colonel Barclay's Brigade Major.[12] Rowan was the more experienced of the two brigade majors, having been the brigade major to the infantry since the three British battalions came to Portugal in late June 1809.

In the same general order that appointed them commanders of the brigades, the two lieutenant colonels were authorized to receive staff pay, equal to their regimental pay. This in effect doubled their daily pay from 17 shillings per day to £1 14 shillings.[13]

---

8. *General Orders: Spain and Portugal*. Vol. 2. London: Egerton Military Library, 1811, p.124.
9. Commanded by Major Dugald Gilmour.
10. Commanded by Major Hugh Arbuthnott.
11. Commanded by Major John Stewart.
12. *General Orders*, p.127.
13. Ibid., p.125. This was unprecedented. Prior to the creation of the brigade structure in the Light Division, no lieutenant colonels were permanently

The Strategic Situation

Despite having forced the Light Division back across the Côa River, the French were slow to exploit the situation. Wellington hoped that their next objective was to take Almeida. His goal was to delay the invasion of Portugal as long as possible, while he evacuated the people from the countryside all the way to Lisbon. Once the civilian population was gone, his plan was to destroy any food, crops and livestock that was left behind. This scorched-earth policy was designed to starve the French army rather than fight them. Napoleon's policy was that his armies were to live off the land while on campaign rather than depending on long supply lines. Wellington knew that he was not strong enough to stop the French at the border. However, if he could draw them deeper and deeper into Portugal, their strength would begin to erode with their inability to find food and supplies. Every day he avoided a battle, the weaker the French would become. His plan was to withdraw all the way to Lisbon knowing the French would follow his army.

The longer he avoided fighting, the more convinced Masséna would become that Wellington planned to evacuate his army back to England rather than risking its destruction. But Wellington had no intention of abandoning Portugal. His goal was to force the French to leave Portugal by starving them out. To do this he had to get the French to follow him all the way to Lisbon. There he had a surprise waiting for Masséna and his army. These were the fortifications that were being built around Lisbon, known as the Lines of Torres Vedras. They consisted of three separate sets of interconnecting forts, strongpoints and entrenchments, all mounted with numerous artillery pieces. The French could try to take the lines by assault, but trying to starve them out was impossible because the British and Portuguese armies, as well as the civilians, could be supplied and reinforced by sea. With little food available, the French would be dependent on a 400km supply line through hostile country.

Almeida was key to this plan. Its governor had no illusions about holding out until the French gave up, but there was enough food in the fortress to last 90 days.[14] The longer they held out the better it would serve Wellington's plan. Each day the French army was forced to besiege Almeida

---

assigned to command brigades. There was nothing in the army regulations that provided for their staff pay. The regulations did provide for a colonel on the staff and they received a per diem of £1 2 shillings 6 pence in addition to the pay they received for their regimental rank.

14. *WD*, Vol. 6, p.351.

the more they consumed the supplies in the local area. Furthermore, it allowed Wellington to continue to strip the countryside of food the French would depend on when they invaded. Additionally, the longer the delay, the more the Lines of Torres Vedras could be strengthened.

Masséna could bypass Almeida, but that would leave an enemy fortress along his army's line of communications. So he decided to take the fortress first. Once it was taken he would march his army into Portugal.

Plans for the Light Division

Wellington's intention was to give the Light Division some well-deserved rest. Most of their outpost duties were assumed by Lieutenant General Stapleton Cotton and his cavalry, with the Light Division in support. Wellington wrote to Craufurd on 26 July that 'That is very important that we should not allow them [the French] to make the siege of Almeida without keeping their army collected; at the same time we must not allow them to push us too hard in our retreat.'[15] Forcing their army to concentrate on the siege would cause them to deplete the resources in the area quicker.

Only the infantry of the Light Division were given a rest. Initially the 1st KGL Hussars were kept under Craufurd's control and they had the responsibility of covering the road in the vicinity of Freixedas. It is unclear exactly when, but about this time all the cavalry that had been attached to the Light Division was returned to their own division. Major General Anson's cavalry brigade[16] now had the responsibility for observing along the front. The Light Division was directly behind them. To the south, were Generals Slade's and Fane's cavalry brigades, supported by Major General Cole's 4th Infantry Division, which was at Guarda. The rest of the army had pulled back 150km from Almeida to the area between Celorico and Pinhanços. This would allow the army to withdraw unopposed when the French advanced.[17]

On 5 August the Light Division was ordered to march east towards the border with Spain. The 1st Brigade was initially billeted in Vale de Azares about 6km from Celorico. On the morning of 7 August a punishment parade was ordered that went on for several hours. On 17 August a general court martial, presided over by Major General

---

15. *WD*, Vol. 6, p.285.
16. 1st KGL Hussars and the 16th Light Dragoons.
17. Ibid., p.286.

Stafford Lightbourne was held. Several cases were heard, the last being that of Private John Hands of the 43rd Foot, who was accused of attempting to desert to the enemy while on picquet duty at the Molinos dos Flores Ford on or about 19 June.

> The Court having considered the evidence against the Prisoner, together with what he offered in his defence were of opinion, he was guilty of the charge exhibited against him, being in breach of the Articles of War, and do by virtue thereof sentence him, the Prisoner, Private John Hands, 43d Regiment, to be shot to death, at such time and place as His Excellency the Commander of the Forces shall think fit.
>
> Which sentence has been confirmed by His Excellency the Commander of the Forces.
>
> The sentence of the General Court Martial on the prisoner, John Hands, 43d Regiment, is to be carried into execution in the presence of the 43d Regiment and the other Troops of the Light Division at the same station, to be paraded for that purpose, on to-morrow evening, by a party of the 43d Regiment, under the direction of the Assistant Provost attached to the Light Division.[18]

Private Hands's execution was delayed for a day, because the 1st Brigade was on the move. On 19 August they marched 15km northeast to Açores where he was executed by a firing squad.[19] The next day the 1st Brigade marched eastward and stopped a few kilometres to the east of Alverca. The 2nd Brigade continued on until it reached Freixedas.[20]

Although the Light Division was supporting the cavalry, life was good compared to what it had been for the previous seven months. Captain Leach wrote that:

> Notwithstanding that we were night and day on the qui vive, sleeping in our clothes, and liable to be under arms at the shortest notice, some sportsmen amongst us contrived to slay many hares,

---

18. *General Orders*, pp.136–7.
19. Oglander, Diary entry 20 August 1810.
20. Ibid., Diary entries 7–28 August 1810. Dawson, p.39.

partridges, quails, and rabbits, which proved a happy addition to the lean ration beef.[21]

When he was not on duty, which was most days, Lieutenant Henry Oglander of the 43rd Foot spent his time exploring the countryside riding for many kilometres in every direction.[22]

The French Advance

The French crossed the Côa River on 26 July and quickly occupied Pinhel and Valverde. This force consisted of General Loison's division, General Lamotte's light cavalry brigade[23] and General Jean-Baptiste Lorcet's dragoon brigade.[24] Their mission was to determine where the British were and then to provide outposts to provide early warning should Wellington advance to relieve Almeida. The rest of the army spent much of the first two weeks of August preparing for the siege of Almeida. On the night of 15 August the first trenches were dug. Ten days later the French siege guns were in place and the bombardment began at 5 a.m. the next morning. Firing on the fortress continued all day and around 7 p.m. disaster struck for the defenders. An artillery shell exploded in the main magazine of the fort, blowing up almost all of the defenders' ammunition. Two days later, on 27 August, the garrison surrendered. Wellington had hoped that the garrison would hold for 90 days. He got 34.

The Army Withdraws

Wellington knew that the time had come to withdraw and gave orders to do so. The Light Division was ordered to take the main road to Coimbra that ran just east of the Serra da Estrela Mountains.[25] The 2nd Brigade led the march, while the 1st Brigade formed the rearguard. The march was not strenuous at the beginning and the division marched only 150km in 28 days.

---

21. Leach, *Rough Sketches . . .*, pp.154–5.
22. Oglander, Diary entries 7–28 August 1810.
23. The 3rd Hussars and 15th Chasseurs-à-Cheval.
24. The 3rd and 6th Dragoons.
25. The modern road is the N17.

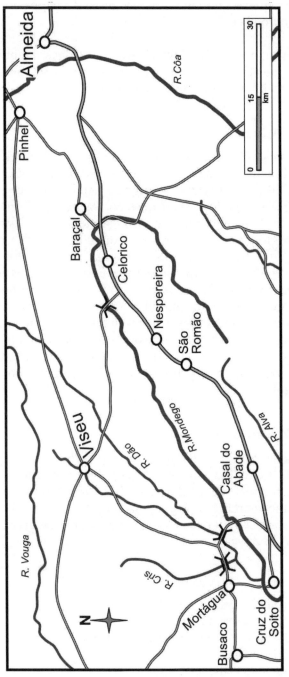

The Retreat to Busaco: 25 July–25 September 1810.

Table 11.1: March of the Light Division, 28 August – 25 September 1810

Day	Starting Location – Route – Ending Location	Distance
28 August	Baraçal[26]	
29 August–1 September	Forno Telheiro, Portugal	6km
2 September	Celorico (outside same camps 52nd were in previously)	6km
3 September	Cortico da Sera – Carrapichana – Vila Cortez da Sera – São Paio	24km
4 – 8 September	Nespereira, Gouviea	4km
9 September – 15 September	Vinhó, Portugal – Moimenta da Serra – Paços da Serra	6km
16 September	Paços da Serra – Pinhanços – São Romão	20km
17 September	Bivouacked in the woods halfway between São Romão and Galizes.	10km
18 September	Casal do Abade	20km
19 September	Cruz do Soito	20km
20 September	Cruz do Soito – crossed the Mondego at ford 2km below Oliveira do Mondego – Marmeleira – Mortágua, Portugal	27km
21–24 September	Mortágua	
25 September	Busaco	15km

The initial marches were leisurely and some officers took the time to play tourist. Captain Leach and another officer explored the Serra do Estrela Mountains, looking for a mythical bottomless lake that was connected to the sea. After searching for several hours they spent the night in the mountains and returned the following day without finding it.[27] Captain Joseph Wells and Lieutenant Henry Oglander took several trips into the mountains and occasionally westward to follow the Mondego River.[28]

If the day's march was short, the departure time was often later in the day. But as the enemy came nearer, the marches started early and often were of 20km or more. On 16 September the division left Paços da Serra at 4:30 a.m. and marched 5km northeast to Moimenta da Serra, where they stayed in some woods until 2 p.m. They then marched 18km

---

26. Baracal, Freches, Portugal.
27. Leach, *Rough Sketches . . .*, pp.156–7.
28. Oglander, Diary entries for 6, 11 and 12 September 1810.

southeast to their new billets in São Romão. The further south they went, the rougher the terrain became. Lieutenant Oglander blamed the bad roads on poor staff work and even General Craufurd. He noted in his diary on 20 September that they

> passed Mondego by a ford a little below a place called Olivarez, thence proceeded over a very hilly and barren country to a village called Mortagõa,[29] 7 leagues distant from Vizeu & 6 from Coimbra. The road was in parts exceedingly bad, and had not been previously reconnoitred to ascertain whether it was passable for the artillery, a duty which ought to be performed by the QrMrGl[30] department any negligence on its part ought to be corrected by the Genl of Division. Ours however looks rather to trifles than essentials.[31]

Captain Leach was a bit more philosophical about the march.

> On the 20th of September we commenced our daily labours before daybreak, and, by a movement to the right, we left the road leading from Celorico to Coimbra, crossed the Mondego by a ford, after having marched along its beautiful serpentine banks several miles, and found ourselves on the main road leading from Vizeu to Coimbra. General Pack's Portuguese brigade, and some cavalry were likewise on this road, by which the mass of the French army was moving down on Coimbra. The four following days we were constantly getting under arms, owing to the incessant arrival of reports from our cavalry pickets in front. In short, we slept with one eye open the whole time, and the men were always accoutered.[32]

Despite the month-long rest in the vicinity of Celorico, the past seven months of outpost duty was beginning to take its toll. Captain George

---

29. Mortágua.
30. The Quartermaster General Department was responsible for assigning routes and bivouacs. Captain Burgoyne of the Royal Engineers did survey this route.
31. Oglander, Diary entry for 20 September 1810.
32. Leach, *Rough Sketches . . .*, p.158.

Napier of the 52nd Foot was worn out and sick, but continued to do his duty. He wrote:

> Every night I suffered from fever or ague during this retreat; but what is very curious, as showing the effect of the mind has upon the body, the moment we engaged with the enemy the ague left me, and I was quite strong and able to do my duty, and go through my day's work as well as any officer in the regiment, without the least feeling of illness or weakness; but when we halted at night I lost all energy, and was as suffering and miserable a wretch as can well be conceived.[33]

The Light Division stopped at Mortágua where they linked up with Brigadier General Denis Pack's 1st Portuguese Infantry Brigade. The town sat 'on a small plain formed by the hill, which are parallel with the Serra de Busaco, and another ridge which takes the same direction, leaving an interval of flat ground of half a league in breadth'.[34] There the Light Division waited for the French to draw closer. Screening to the front of them were their comrades from the 14th and 16th Light Dragoons and the 1st KGL Hussars. The following day, the 43rd Foot had picquet duty and Lieutenant Oglander was sent to a chapel on a hill overlooking the village. He was relieved at 6 a.m. the next morning. He had about 12 hours' rest before he was sent as the outlying picquet to the village of Barril about 500m east of Mortágua along the road to Viseu, which the French were expected to march down. He and his picquet rejoined the battalion at 6:30 a.m. just in time to march with them to a wooded area about a 2km north of the town. They stayed there until 1 p.m. when they

> moved down to Mortagōa [sic], in consequence of the Enemy appearing in sight upon the opposite heights & obliging our dragoon picquets to give ground. As they pushed on in force on the high ground towards the chapel, out flanking us on our right, we retired to our alarm post where we (the division) remained til the infantry and artillery had gone to the rear: we then nigh having meanwhile come on, retired about a ¼ a league to a wood, when together with the 52nd and Caçadores the regt past [sic] the night.[35]

---

33. Napier, George, p.138.
34. Oglander, Diary entry for 22 September 1810.
35. Ibid., Diary entry for 23 September 1810.

Lieutenant William Tomkinson of the 16th Light Dragoons had just gotten off piquet duty when:

> Everyone expected the enemy to move on this morning. At daylight all was quiet, and the piquets being relieved, we returned to our camp ground on the plain. About 3, the enemy drove back our piquets near to the village of Mortiagua [sic], which General Crawford [sic] wished to dispute. Sir Stapleton ordered him out to the rear of the plain, forming the three light regiments as a covering party to him. The enemy contented themselves with the heights above the village, and at night we retired, leaving a squadron from each regiment with the Light Division.[36]

Assistant Commissary General Augustus Schaumann was with a detachment of the 1st KGL Hussars foraging for food to the northwest of Mortágua, when he heard gunfire from the village. He rushed back and could see in the distance:

> Our troops were standing formed up in large masses, while the French, whose muskets shone in the evening sunlight like distant lightning, were coming on in dark columns slowly down the hills and getting into formation. We could actually see one of their generals on a white horse, for he was particularly conspicuous as he rode up and down the dark lines. It was a grand, but at the same time gruesome, sight. Probably the French had been held up in the hills by some obstacle and were now trying to make up for lost time . . .[37]

Wellington had arrived about the time Craufurd was deciding to give battle to the advancing French. Not wanting to lose men to contest ground he had no intention of holding, Wellington ordered 'Generals Crawford [sic] and Pack, and the whole of the cavalry, except a few squadrons, to retire by the road leading towards the Sierra de Buzaco [sic]'.[38]

---

36. Tomkinson, p.41.
37. Schaumann, August L., *On the Road with Wellington: the Diary of a War Commissary in the Peninsular Campaigns.* New York: Alfred A. Knopf, 1925, p.244.
38. Leach, *Rough Sketches . . .*, p.158.

Each brigade left a battalion in the woods on the west side of Mortágua and sent the 95th Rifles and the Caçadores to the ridge behind the woods. No one slept well that night. Captain Leach and his men

> . . . bivouacked that night on a bleak cold hill, covered with heath; and having no provisions, nor any fluid stronger than water to counteract the effect of the dews and piercing wind, we were not sorry when ordered to stand to arms as usual an hour before daybreak on the 24th. We then moved a short distance to the rear, and took up our ground in some pine-woods; several of our companies being posted as pickets to support those of the cavalry in their front.[39]

It was worse for the 43rd Foot who were still in the woods.

> A most ridiculous alarm, proceeding from a trifling cause, threw the whole camp, into complete confusion during the night. A few horses got loose and getting among the Arms, threw them down; this frightened them and caused them to gallop thro the wood, overturning the piles of arms and trampling over the men. The noise and the darkness of the night, preventing people suddenly awakened from discovering the real source of the disturbance, created in their minds the most extraordinary fears. The most prevalent idea was that the enemy had surprised us, and that their cavalry was in the midst of the wood. The men rushed in crowds from the spot where the alarm first arose forgetting their arms, individually trying to escape. It was not til some minutes had passed that they recovered from their alarm, and its cause was discovered. How ridiculous so ever the whole occurrence may appear, it served to show how much a surprise from the enemy at night ought to be guarded against as even the bravest troops, when suddenly wakened without having any time for reflexion, may fall into the most dangerous confusion.[40]

The next morning, the Light Division moved a kilometre to the rear where they waited in woods for the enemy to advance. About 3 p.m.

---

39. Ibid., pp.148–9.
40. Oglander, Diary entry for 23 September 1810.

French cavalry[41] came forward and skirmished with the British light cavalry. On 24 September, Wellington rode to the Light Division and ordered Craufurd to retreat to Busaco. The 2nd Brigade, minus the 1st Caçadores, would form the rearguard. About 1 p.m. the 1st Brigade

> retreated with much expedition from the ground we occupied to the grand position on the Serra de Busaco, which we reached about ½ past 2. The enemy pursued us closely and showed particular alertness in bringing up their artillery. The retreat however was conducted by Ld Wellington in person with the utmost skill and regularity, the enemy being held completely in check until the whole of our troops arrived in their stations. The skirmishing commenced with the retreat, continued til dark. The 52nd and 95th together with some cavalry and artillery formed the rearguard & were the only troops engaged.[42]

Captain Leach was with the rearguard and saw

> the French again come on with such a numerous and combined force of cavalry, infantry, and artillery, that the Light Division, General Pack's brigade of Portuguese, and the small cavalry force with us, immediately commenced their retreat towards the Sierra de Buzaco, on which the whole of the allied army, including General Hill's division from Alemetjo, was now assembling in a position covering Coimbra.
>
> The French adopted a very efficacious plan in their pursuit of our rear-guard, by sending forward light infantry and light cavalry to skirmish, intermixed, side by side; thus affording mutual support to each other, as the ground became either open or intersected. By those means, and aided by their flying artillery, the French pressed our rear-guard closely, which was formed by a squadron or two of the cavalry, and some companies of our battalion and of the 52nd regiment. We continued to be engaged until we reached the position at Buzaco. Nothing could exceed the regularity with which this retreat was conducted; and it was effected without much loss.[43]

41. General of Brigade Pierre Soult's brigade consisting of the 1st Hussars and 8th Dragoons.
42. Oglander, Diary entry for 25 September 1810.
43. Leach, *Rough Sketches . . .*, pp.159–60.

Chapter 12

The Battle of Busaco,
26–27 September 1810

The French army had moved slowly from the Spanish border, but Wellington had no illusions about what their short-term goals were. He wrote to the Earl of Liverpool on 20 September that:

The enemy's intention in these movements is apparently to obtain possession of Coimbra, with a view to the resources which that town and the neighbouring country will afford them. The movements, however, which I had previously made to enable me to withdraw the army without difficulty from a position in which I did not consider it advisable to risk an action, enabled me to secure Coimbra against the attack of any small corps; and the whole of that part of the army which has been under my immediate command, with the exception of five regiments of cavalry, has passed to the right of the Mondego, and in front of Coimbra, Brigadier General Pack's brigade of Portuguese infantry being at St. Cambadaõ[1] with the Royal Dragoons, and Brigadier General Craufurd's division at Mortagoa.[2]

As the French advanced, Wellington did everything he could to slow them down, including destroying bridges, attacking foraging parties and maintaining a heavy cavalry screen to prevent them from seeing his dispositions. He wanted to avoid a battle at all costs unless he was assured he could win. This meant finding favourable ground to fight on.

---

1. Santa Comba Dão is about 10km from Mortágua and is situated between the convergence of the Cris and Dão Rivers.
2. *WD*, Vol. 6, p.432.

He found it just to the northeast of Coimbra along a high ridge called Serra de Busaco.[3] If the conditions were right, he would halt his army's retreat there and fight.

On the morning of 26 September, Wellington's army was deployed on the Serra de Busaco.[4] In a letter to the Earl of Liverpool dated 30 September 1810, Wellington described it as

> . . . a high ridge which extends from the Mondego in a northerly direction about eight miles. At the highest point of the ridge, about two miles from its termination, is the convent and garden of Busaco. The Serra de Busaco is connected by a mountainous tract of country with the Serra de Caramula, which extends in a north easterly direction beyond Viseu, and separates the valley of the Mondego from the valley of the Douro. On the left of the Mondego, nearly in a line with the Serra de Busaco, is another ridge of the same description, called the Serra de Murcella, covered by the river Alva, and connected by other mountainous parts with the Serra d'Estrella.[5]

In the same letter, he went on to explain the importance of this position.

> All the roads to Coimbra from the eastward lead over the one or the other of these Serras. They are very difficult for the passage of an army, the approach to the top of the ridge on both sides being mountainous.[6]

The ridge towers above the valley 1.5km below. In some places it is over 300m higher with a slope of 15 degrees. In 1810 the ridge had few trees and was covered with rocks, scrub brush, heather and gorse. Behind the crest there was a plateau that could not be seen from its north.

Although the ridge was an excellent defensive position, as late as 21 September, Wellington still had not made up his mind on whether to fight a battle there. He wrote to the commander of his cavalry, Lieutenant General Stapleton Cotton that

---

3. Also known as the Serra do Buçaco.
4. It was 30km from Coimbra and 225km from Lisbon.
5. *WD*, Vol. 6, p.445.
6. Ibid.

We have an excellent position here, in which I am strongly tempted to give battle. Unfortunately Hill[7] is one day later than I expected; and there is a road upon our left by which we may be turned and cut off from Coimbra. But I do not yet give up hopes of discovering a remedy for this last misfortune; and as for the former the enemy will afford it to us, if they do not cross the Criz[8] to-morrow.[9]

The road Wellington was referring to was scouted by Lieutenant John Bell of the 52nd Foot, who was serving as the Light Division's DAQMG. His report, dated 22 September, read:

This road[10] is completely concealed, except in passing the small ridge between Mora[11] and Mortagoa. From the crossing near Parada[12] to Villa Nova,[13] it follows the course of a small stream in a deep ravine, which cuts the Sierra de Busaco at its northern extremity, about two miles and a half from the wall of the Convent park. Villa Nova is in the open country in the rear of the Sierra, and only one league from Mealhada.[14]

The road is an excellent car road, but perhaps hardly wide enough in some places for British artillery. At present, and during all the dry season, it affords an easier and quicker line of march for troops than the road by the convent, as it is neither so steep nor so winding as the other.[15]

If Marshal Masséna discovered this road he would be able to bypass Wellington's position on the Serra de Busaco. As important to Wellington

---

7. General Hill was the commander of the 2nd Division.
8. The Cris River runs north–south and is about 10km east of Mortágua and 20km from Busaco.
9. *WD*, Vol. 6, pp.434–5.
10. This road is about 30km long and generally follows modern roads M38 to CM1694 from Mortágua to Trezói to Parada Anadia to Algeriz Anadia to Vila Nova de Monsarros to Mealhada.
11. Moura, Mortágua.
12. Parada Anadia.
13. Vila Nova de Monsarros.
14. Mealhada is about 10km due west of the Convent.
15. Chambers, George, *Bussaco*. Felling: Worley, 1994, pp.182–3.

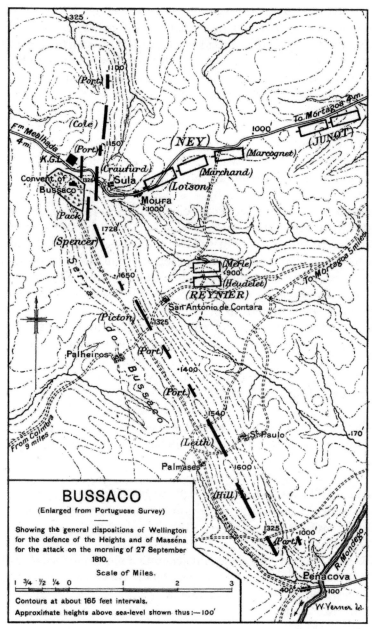

Battle of Busaco: Disposition of Forces 27 September 1810.
(From Willoughby Verner's *History and Campaigns of the Rifle Brigade*)

in his decision to fight a battle was the location of Lieutenant General Rowland Hill and the 10,000 men[16] with him. Wellington would fight if he had Hill. On 11 September Hill was 170km away in the vicinity of Castello Branco keeping an eye on Lieutenant General Reynier's 2nd Corps. By 21 September, Hill was at Foz de Arouce less than 40km from Busaco. Wellington knew that he could be there within a day,[17] so he chose to stand and fight.

Disposition of Wellington's Army

Although Busaco Ridge was an excellent fighting position, it was 13km long which would be difficult to completely cover with 50,000 infantry. The least likely place for the French to attack was on the right and Wellington had General Hill and his men cover 6km of frontage. A kilometre to his left was General Leith's 5th Division, then General Picton's 3rd Division and to the left of them was General Spencer's 1st Division. These three divisions covered about 6km of front. To the left of Spencer was General Pack's Portuguese brigade and then the Light Division, which covered the main road from Mortágua. On the left of the Light Division was General Cole's 4th Division. Directly behind the Light Division, was Brigadier General Francis Colman's Portuguese brigade

Supporting the Light Division's position were four artillery batteries. On their left, with the 4th Division was Captain Robert Bull's RHA troop of light 6-pounders. To the immediate right of the 43rd Foot was Captain Ross's RHA Troop of light 6-pounders. To his right was Captain Andrew Cleves' King's German Artillery troop of light 6-pounders and Captain Antonio de Sousas Passos's Portuguese company of light 6-pounders. On the right flank of General Pack's Portuguese brigade was Captain Robert Lawson's company of 9-pounders.[18]

The Light Division's position was about 300m in front of the Convent of Busaco. It covered the main road[19] from Mortágua that ran through Moura to the small village of Sula. Lieutenant Colonel Beckwith's 1st Brigade was to the right of the road. The 43rd Foot was in line and the 3rd Caçadores

---

16. General Hill's force consisted of his own 2nd Division and Major General John Hamilton's Portuguese division.
17. General Hill showed up on the morning of 26 September.
18. Lipscombe, pp.125 & 132.
19. Modern road N234.

were behind them. The Right Wing of the 95th Rifles, commanded by Major Dugald Gilmour, was to the right of the 3rd Caçadores. Lieutenant Colonel Barclay's 2nd Brigade straddled the road with the 52nd Foot, commanded by Major Hugh Arbuthnott, in a line in the front. Directly behind them were the 1st Caçadores. The Left Wing of the 95th Rifles, under the command of Major John Stewart, was to the left of the 1st Caçadores. The whole division was behind the crest of the ridge and was not visible to the French below.

September 26th: a Day of Skirmishing

Although Wellington's army had withdrawn to the top of the Busaco Ridge, it continued to contest the approach with a strong skirmish screen. The Left Wing of the 95th Rifles and the 3rd Caçadores had the duty. Captain Leach's company was among them.

> Along the base of the Sierra ran an extended chain of our infantry pickets; and in like manner at the foot of the French ridge of mountains their pickets were thrown out. The valley therefore, which divided us, was considered neutral ground . . . Early in the morning the French cannonaded our four companies again, which were advanced into the village of Sula, but could not dislodge us. Massena then sent out a cloud of light infantry, who engaged our pickets all along the line; and under cover of this fire he reconnoitred [*sic*] our position. This fire of the light troops lasted without intermission until night. . . The fire of the light troops throughout the 26th having been kept up without intermission, we relieved our companies at this duty every hour or two. The situation of a light bob, or a rifleman, was found to be no sinecure. The blaze of musketry with which the mountains and valleys had rung for twelve hours, ceased with night; and every thing was as quiet as if the two armies had been in their own countries profound peace.[20]

Captain George Napier's company of the 52nd Foot was sent down the hill early in the evening to reinforce the skirmish line. With him came his 24-year-old cousin Captain Charles Napier of the Royal Navy, who

---

20. Leach, *Rough Sketches* . . ., pp.161–83.

after being placed on half-pay decided to visit the rest of the clan in Portugal.[21]

> He had gone out with me the evening before the battle to skirmish a little with the French pickets, as General Craufurd thought they had advanced rather closer to the foot of our position than was right, so I was ordered to move down and push them a little farther off. Charles Napier our cousin would take a little white pony I had, to ride with us, notwithstanding I told him it was very foolish for most certainly he would get hit, being the only person on horseback. But he chose to go his own way and in less than half an hour he got shot in the calf of the leg, but very slightly; and I was delighted at it, the obstinate dog, he deserved it well! However, he was very good-humoured and laughed as much as anyone at his own folly. [22]

Although not in the Light Division, Ensign William Grattan of the 88th Foot, who was about to fight in his first battle, left a vivid description of the night before the battle.

> . . . During the evening we could perceive the enemy occupying the different stations in our front, and the light troops of both armies were warmly engaged along the entire of the line. At night we lay down to rest; each man, with his firelock in his grasp, remained at his post, anxiously waiting the arrival of the morrow, which was destined to be the last that many amongst us were to behold. We had no fires, and the death-like stillness that reigned throughout our army was only interrupted by the occasional challenge of an advanced sentry, or a random shot fired at some imaginary foe.[23]

---

21. He is not to be confused with their brother, Major Charles Napier of the 50th Foot, who was serving as a volunteer ADC to General Craufurd. Apparently battlefield tourism was popular in the clan.
22. Napier, George, pp.146–7.
23. Grattan, William, *Adventures with the Connaught Rangers: 1809 – 1814.* London: Greenhill, 1989, pp.28–9

The French Attack

From the French perspective, Wellington's position on the ridge was formidable. Chef-de-Bataillon Pelet wrote afterwards that:

> The enemy crowned the summit of the mountain, where the walls of the convent of Bussaco could be seen, with artillery along a line more than eight or even ten thousand yards. To the right, beyond the road of San Antonio de Cantaro and extending quite far through the posts and militia units was General Hill's division, which had just joined the army within the past few days. The centre was near the convent and straddled the road to Coimbra. The left was also extended very far up to a detached abutment that was almost perpendicular and slightly in front of the summit; the enemy had placed a redoubt at its extremity. When our army advanced, we saw a full line whose deployment indicated at least sixty thousand men and consequently the greatest part of Wellington's army.[24]

Masséna's plan was fairly simple. He did not expect much resistance. Wellington had been falling back for over two months so why would he fight now? His reconnaissance of Busaco Ridge revealed Wellington's army spread over a large area. A heavy assault concentrated in one or two areas should be sufficient to break their line. General Reynier and his 2nd Corps would attack the left centre of Wellington's line. Once they achieved a lodgment on the ridge, Marshal Ney and the 6th Corps would assault up the road from Moura to Sula.[25]

The Attack of General Reynier's 2nd Corps

General Reynier had his 16,000 men formed up and ready to attack by first light.[26] A heavy mist had formed in the valley so covered up the ridge towards the British and Portuguese. His attack was aimed at the low ground on the ridge that was about 4km to the right of the Light Division. The approach was along a country road that ran from the village of Santo António de Cantara up the ridge to the village of Palheiros which was on the plateau. It was not far to the top of the ridge – less than 500m – but the

---

24. Pelet, pp.173–4.
25. Ibid., p.175.
26. Nautical twilight was at 5:19 a.m. and sunrise was at 6:19 a.m.

climb would be very difficult for the ridge at this point was 160m above the valley.[27]

Général de Division Pierre Merle's 6,000-man 1st Division would attack up the hill about a kilometre from the road, while Général de Division Étienne Heudelet de Bierre's 10,000-man 2nd Division would use the road as its axis of advance. Both divisions attacked in regimental columns, each column three or four battalions strong, but only a company wide. The attack was preceded by hundreds of skirmishers, who hoped to prevent the British and Portuguese light troops from decimating the columns as they advanced up the hill.

Initially the heavy mist covered the French advance, but about half-way up the ridge, the mist lifted and soon the columns were brought under heavy artillery fire. The columns started off in good order, but the steepness of the slope and the rough terrain wreaked havoc and it was not long before the battalions became a mass of disorganized troops. Despite the terrain and the fire of the enemy, Général de Brigade Antoine Anaud's brigade of Heudelet's division was almost to the crest of the ridge when the British 74th Foot and the Portuguese 21st Infantry Regiment halted them with their musket fire. General Merle's division faced the same obstacles, but persevered and made it to the top of the ridge unopposed, but exhausted. The troops did not have time to even catch their breath when they were counter-attacked by the 45th and 88th Foot of General Picton's 3rd Division and the 8th Portuguese Infantry Regiment from the 5th Division. After a bitter fight, Merle's division was chased back down the hill. While the counter-attack against Merle's division was going on, General Heudelet's other brigade, led by Général de Brigade Maximilien Foy, arrived and broke through the Allied line on the ridge. Its success was short lived for they were quickly attacked by General Leith's 5th Division and forced down the hill. This ended the 2nd Corps' attack.

The Attack of Marshal Ney's 6th Corps

Ney's forces were deployed close to the village of Moura, less than 2km from the Anglo-Portuguese forces on the ridge. His plan was to send the 6,000 men of General Loison's 3rd Division up the road to Sula and then to the top of the ridge. The 6,000 men of General Marchand's 1st Division would climb the ridge to the left of the 3rd Division. General Mermet's 2nd Division would be kept in reserve. In accordance with his orders,

---

27. A 36 per cent of slope or 20 degrees.

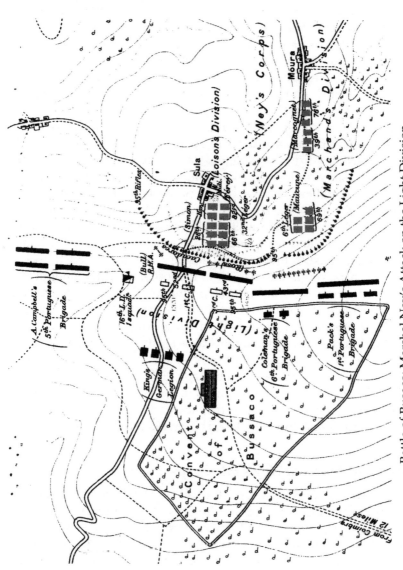

Battle of Busaco: Marshal Ney's Attack on the Light Division.
(Based on Willoughby Verner's *History and Campaigns of the Rifle Brigade*)

Ney did not give the order to attack until he saw General Reynier's troops reach the top of the ridge. The 6th Corps' attack started about 8 a.m.[28]

Marchand's 1st Division began their climb with General Maucune's brigade in front, followed by General Marcognet's brigade. Maucune had his brigade deployed in two regimental columns, with the 69th Line Regiment on the left and the 6th Light Regiment on the right. Each regiment was in a battalion of columns. The 69th Line had three battalions, and the 6th Light had two. The frontage of each battalion column was about 35 men (20–25m) and it was 15–18 men deep. Marcognet's Brigade advanced in a single column, with the 39th Line Regiment in front, followed by the 76th Line Regiment. The path of their march would take them to the right of the Light Division, where they would encounter the 1st and 6th Portuguese Brigades.

Loison's 3rd Division attacked with his two brigades abreast, each in a column of battalions. The total frontage of the division was 50–100m wide. Général de Brigade Édouard Simon's brigade was on the right, while General Ferey's brigade was on the left. Leading Simon's brigade were the three battalions of the 26th Light, followed by the two battalions of the Hanoverian Legion and then the Légion du Midi. To the left of them was General Ferey's brigade, led by the three battalions of the 66th Line and then the two battalions of the 82nd Line. In an effort to protect his left flank, Loison had the 2nd Battalion of the 32nd Light deployed as skirmishers. Like the columns of the 2nd Corps, as the 6th Corps' divisions marched up the steep ridge, their columns lost their cohesion and they were more a mass of troops than a unit with parade-ground precision.

As Ney's corps marched up the ridge, he deployed a massive skirmish screen consisting of all the light companies from each of his battalions, plus the 2nd Battalion of the 32nd Light Regiment, about 1,500 men in all. To oppose them were the 95th Rifles and 3rd Caçadores. This was the first time that the 95th Rifles had been deployed as a battalion in a skirmish line. Captain Leach wrote in a letter that 'the French in their advance to the attack could see nothing but our green jackets peeping out from among the rough and broken ground and making every shot tell amongst them without their being able to do us any material injury.'[29] Despite this bravado, the Allied skirmish line was in danger of being overwhelmed, and Craufurd sent forward the 1st Caçadores to help out.

---

28. Oglander, Diary entry 27 September 1810.
29. Verner, Vol. 2, p.148.

The Light Division now had 2,000 men in the skirmish line. Sixty per cent of the division had been committed and only the 43rd and 52nd Foot were still in line. A skirmish line could never stop a determined column and when the columns were within 150m of the crest, Craufurd pulled his men back.

As the French moved up the hill they were brought under heavy fire from the Allied artillery. Captain George Napier wrote that '. . . the brigade of horse artillery under Captain Hugh Ross threw such a heavy fire of shrapnel-shells, and so quick, that their column, which consisted of about eight thousand men, was put into a good deal of confusion and lost great numbers before it arrived at a ledge of ground just under the brow of the hill, where they halted a few moments to take breath. . .'[30] Twenty-three years later George's brother, Captain William Napier of the 52nd Foot, wrote in his history:

> General Simon's brigade, which led Loison's attack, ascended with a wonderful alacrity, and though the light troops plied it unceasingly with musketry, and the artillery bullets swept through it from the first to the last section, its order was never disturbed, nor its speed in the least abated. Ross's guns were worked with incredible quickness, yet their range was palpably contracted every round, and the enemy's shot came singing up in a sharper key, until the skirmishers, breathless and begrimed with powder, rushed over the edge of the ascent, the artillery suddenly drew back, and the victorious cries of the French were heard within a few yards of the summit.[31]

Waiting for the French columns on the crest of the hill were the 43rd and 52nd Foot. The two British battalions were deployed in a line with only a space of about 25m between them. General Simon's brigade was headed straight for the junction of the two battalions and if not stopped, would hit two companies from both battalions at the same time. In a strange twist of fate, the two Napier brothers were close to each other. Captain William Napier's company of the 43rd Foot was on the left of his battalion's line, while Captain George Napier's company of the 52nd Foot was one company over on the right of his battalion.

---

30. Napier, George, pp.141– 2.
31. Napier, William, Vol. 2, p.334.

Only Captain Thomas Lloyd and his company stood between them.[32] General Ferey's brigade would hit the 43rd Foot.

As the columns reached the top of the ridge, they paused for a moment to catch their breath and to re-organize themselves. Craufurd, who was standing on a rock in front of his division, turned around, waved his hat to his troops, and shouted 'Remember Sir John Moore & revenge his Death'.[33] The waiting troops 'answered by a shout that appalled the enemy, and in one instant the brow of the hill bristled with two thousand British bayonets wielded by steady English hands, which soon buried them in the bodies of the fiery Gaul!'[34]

The French were taken by surprised and chaos ensued. Most British accounts agree on what happened next. Lieutenant Oglander of the 43rd Foot wrote in his diary that night that

> the French were charged by the 43rd and 52nd Regts. They however did not think proper to await us, but fell into confusion and fled the moment our men, advancing with a loud shout, appeared over the brow of the hill. They retired in such a hurry that we were obliged to halt and fire, not being able to overtake them with our bayonettes [sic].[35]

Lieutenant Charles Booth, also of the 52nd Foot, wrote:

> The front of their columns alone – chiefly composed of officers – stood the charge; the rest took to their heels, throwing away their arms, pouches, etc. Our men did not stand to take prisoners; what were taken were those left in our rear in the hurry of pressing forward in the charge. The flanks of the 43rd and 52nd in their charge met only the enemy's skirmishers who had by superior numbers driven in the 95th Rifles but a few seconds before the charge of the division. These poor fellows were all glad enough to give themselves up as prisoners, our men not being allowed to fire a shot at them. The advanced part of the charging line – the four companies first mentioned – after throwing themselves into the midst of the enemy's

---

32. Napier, George, p.142. Levine, p.138.
33. Dawson, pp.40–1.
34. Napier, George, p.142.
35. Oglander, Diary entry 27 September 1810.

retreating columns, killing, wounding, and in short felling to the ground lots of them, were with great difficulty halted, and then commenced from the flanks of the whole division the most destructive flanking fire that I believe was ever witnessed. Not a tenth part of their whole force would have escaped had not the four companies, by precipitating themselves too far in front of the general line, exposed themselves to the fire of their comrades, and thus prevented more than 300 firelocks on each flank of the division from being brought into action. The flanks, and in fact every other part of the division (except the four centre companies), had to pass over in the charge some very steep rugged ground, where, not meeting with anything but the enemy's skirmishers, they pushed on head-over-heels, until the descent became almost perpendicular. At this time they were halted, and had a fine view of what was going on in the centre.[36]

Lieutenant Charles Booth's brother, Henry, was in Captain Lloyd's company on the left of the 43rd Foot. Charles noted in the same letter that Harry

was in Captain Lloyd's – the left-hand company of the 43rd – in one of those who met the head of the French column in the charge. His captain, who was close to him at the time they reached the enemy's columns, was on the point of being bayoneted, but knocked down the fellow attempting it. Harry must have had a shave or two, as he could not prevent himself from being in the very thick of them, but he speaks only of the actions of others.[37]

Captain George Napier of the 52nd Foot wrote from the perspective of a company commander and gives a slightly different account. According to him, despite the shock of seeing the British rise out of the ground, the French did not break immediately.

My company met the head of the French column, and immediately calling my men to form column of sections in order to give

---

36. Levine, pp.136–8.
37. Ibid., pp.137–8.

more force to our rush, we dashed forward; and as I was by this movement in front of my men a yard or two, a French soldier made a plunge at me with his bayonet, and at the same time his musket going off I received the contents just under my hip and fell. At the same instant the French fired upon my front section, consisting of about nine men in the front rank, all of whom fell, four of them dead, the rest wounded, so that most probably by my being a little advanced in front my life was saved, as the men killed were exactly those nearest to me. Poor Colonel Barclay also received a wound . . .[38]

While Captain Napier and the company to his left stood there and shot it out with the French, in a brilliant show of initiative the two companies of the 43rd, commanded by his brother William and Captain Lloyd,

seeing that the French were still in column and in great confusion from the unexpected suddenness of the charge and the shout which accompanied it, had wheeled up their companies by the left, and thus flanked the French column and poured a well-directed fire right into them. Major Arbuthnott,[39] who was on my left, did the same with the remaining companies of the 52nd, so that the enemy was beset on both flanks of his column, and, as you may suppose, the slaughter was great. We kept firing and bayoneting till we reached the bottom, and the enemy passed the brook and fell back upon their main body, which moved down to support them and cover their retreat. All this was done in a very short time – that is, it was not above twenty minutes from the charge till the French were driven from the top to the bottom of the mountain like a parcel of sheep. I really did not think was possible for such a column to be so completely destroyed in a few minutes as that was, particularly after witnessing how gallantly they moved up under a destructive fire from the artillery and a constant galling one from our sharpshooters.[40]

---

38. Napier, George, pp.142– 3.
39. Major Hugh Arbuthnott was the acting commander of the 52nd Foot.
40. Napier, George, pp.143–4.

Captain Leach, who was in the Right Wing of the 95th Rifles and assigned to the 1st Brigade, was watching the retreat of the French when orders were received to pursue them.

> The instant the attacking columns were turned back, they were exposed to the fire of our whole division; whilst our battalion and some caçadores were ordered to pursue, and to give them a flanking fire, and the horse artillery continued to pour on them a murderous fire of grape, as they were struggling through the narrow streets of Sula, and trampling each other to death in their great haste to escape. Men, muskets, knapsacks, and bayonets, rolled down the side of the mountain in such a confused mass, as it is impossible to convey a just idea of. The village of Sula, and the ground on each side of it, as also the road by which the columns of attack advanced, were heaped with killed and wounded, all lying within a small space of ground.[41]

Among the first French casualties was General Simon. He was shot in the mouth by a 23-year-old Irishman from County Derry, named Alexander Hopkins[42] of Captain Robert Campbell's company of the 52nd Foot. He and Private Matthew Harris[43] then took him prisoner. They were escorted back up the hill by Lieutenant James F. Love, who watched them capture the general, and the prisoner was brought to General Craufurd.[44]

General Maucune's Assault

While the fight between General Loison's men and the Light Division was going on, General Marchand's 1st Division reached the Allied line to the right of the Light Division. There the men from General Maucune's brigade reached the crest of the hill only to run into Pack's Portuguese brigade. Captain Leach was delighted with what happened next.

---

41. Leach, *Rough Sketches* . . ., p.166.
42. Private Hopkins was from Coleraine in County Derry. At 5ft 11¾in (182cm), he was tall for a light infantryman. He had grey eyes, light brown hair, and a swarthy complexion.
43. Private Harris was from Herefordshire and had enlisted in 1799 at the age of 24.
44. Dawson, p.41. Moorsom, pp.124–5.

General Pack's Portuguese brigade formed line and charged in a most regular and spirited manner under a cannonade of round-shot from the enemy's batteries. It shows what improvement they had made since British officers and good discipline have been introduced amongst them. I was quite hoarse with cheering and halloing. Whenever we saw the Portuguese about to charge, who were nearly a mile distant, we all set up a howl which undoubtedly spirited them on and they behaved uncommonly well, much better than the most sanguine could have expected.[45]

As the Light Division chased the French down the hill they soon started coming across wounded Frenchmen. Captain George Napier wrote that:

As I went down the hill following the enemy, I saw seven or eight French officers lying wounded. One of them as I passed caught hold of my little silver canteen and implored me to stop and give him a drink, but, much as it pained me to refuse, I could not do it, being in full pursuit of the enemy, and it was impossible to stop for an instant. This may be thought hard-hearted, but in war we often do and must do many harsh and unfeeling things. Had I stopped to give him a drink I must have done so for the others, and then I should have been the last at the bottom of the hill instead of one of the first in pursuit of the enemy; and recollect my boys, that an officer should always be first in advancing against the enemy and last in retreating from him. When we got to the bottom, where a small stream ran between us and the enemy's position, by general consent we all mingled together searching for the wounded. During this cessation of fighting we spoke to each other as though we were the greatest friends and without the least animosity or angry feeling![46]

The Withdrawal to the Ridge

After about 30 minutes, the bugles were sounded for the men in the valley to return to their positions on the ridge. It was much harder going back up the hill than it was going down. Lieutenant Booth probably

---

45. Verner, Vol. 2, p.150.
46. Napier, George, p.145.

summed it up the best: 'we were not five minutes in the charge down the hill, it cost us more than half an hour to get up into our first position again.'[47] George Napier, who was wounded in the groin, found he could not make it back and got the battalion's adjutant, Lieutenant John Winterbottom, to help him. When he reached the top, he found that his brother, Major Charles Napier, was badly wounded.[48]

During the withdrawal some soldiers took the opportunity to look for some loot. Private Anthony Hamilton of the 43rd Foot was among them.

> We pursued them into the village, when we were stopped by some artillery which they had there in reserve. While endeavouring to regain the hill, I ran into a house which was deserted, in order to avoid their fire, for a moment, and while there, I observed the end of a sword hanging from the chimney just below the jamb. Thinking them must be an owner to it, I looked up the chimney and discovered a French officer, who had hid there to escape pursuit. I immediately pulled him down and told him that he was my prisoner, upon which he took a gold watch and gave it to me if I would release him. I immediately took the watch, and was leaving in a hurry, when unfortunately for the Frenchman, I met another soldier at the door, who however consented to let him go upon his giving him his gold epaulets.[49]

The Attack on Sula

By 11 a.m. the French attacks had ended. However during this period of quiet, a French infantry company was sent into Sula and 'refused to retire, which so incensed Crawfurd that, turning twelve guns on the village, he overwhelmed it with bullets for half an hour. After paying the French captain this distinguished honour, the English general, recovering his temper, sent a company of the forty-third down, which cleared the village in a few minutes.'[50]

---

47. Levine, p.136.
48. Instead of continuing as a volunteer ADC to General Craufurd, Major Napier had attached himself to Wellington's staff.
49. Hamilton, pp.89–90.
50. Napier, William, Vol. 3, pp.335–6.

The Search for Casualties

In the early evening, Masséna sent an officer under a white flag to arrange a truce so that the wounded and dead could be evacuated. Captain Leach and other officers decided to go back to the valley. They were shocked by what they found.

> During this cessation we went down amongst them for the sake of curiosity and as you may imagine it was a sad carnage. By Heaven! one little village was full of killed and wounded. The attacking Division was composed of the following French regiments, as I was enable to ascertain from their buttons. The 6th, 26th, 66th, 82nd, a Battalion of their Hanoverian Legion and the Légion du Midi. Those regiments had nearly reached the summit of the hill when they were attacked. On the day after the battle we got the return of the 26th regiment which was 700 killed and wounded. A deserter from the Hanoverian Legion told me in English 'My Company come up the hill one hundred and he come back with twenty-two men only,' from those remarks you may suppose their loss in this attack was immense. The French 82nd and Légion du Midi are old Vimiera[51] friends. The 26th, 66th, and 82nd are Bridge of Lodi[52] boys, but of the Heights of Busaco I daresay they will be less proud.[53]

Light Division Casualties

Compared to the combat on the Côa, the Light Division had few casualties, with only 24 dead and 152 wounded. Captain Leach explained why.

> You will naturally wonder to see by the returns that our regiment lost no officers. I will account for it in two ways. In the first place we lost so many officers at the Côa which have not yet joined in consequence of their wounds (and three of whom are since dead) that we had a great scarcity, scarcely enough to do the duty. In the second place the hills occupied by the Light Division were extremely high and the approach to them near the summit full of craggy rocks. Amongst these and some fir

---

51. Battle of Vimeiro, Portugal was fought on 21 August 1808.
52. The Battle of Lodi was fought on 10 May 1796. Lodi is in northern Italy.
53. Verner, Vol. 2, p.149.

trees our Companies lay scattered and had such excellent cover that I am puzzled to conceive how we contrived to lose forty-one men. Not an officer was hit.[54]

Table 12.1: Light Division Casualties at Busaco, 27 September 1810[55]

	Officers		Other Ranks			Total
	Killed	Wounded	Killed	Wounded	Missing	
1st Battalion 43rd Foot	–	–	–	8	–	8
1st Battalion 52nd Foot	–	3	3	10	–	16
1st Battalion 95th Foot	–	–	9	32	–	41
1st Caçadores	–	–	2	20	1	23
3rd Caçadores	–	3	10	76	–	89
Total	–	6	24	146	1	177

Of the six officer casualties, Ensigns Alfonso Botelho and Joaquim Segurada, both from the 3rd Caçadores, were severely wounded.[56] Captain George Napier was slightly wounded in the groin. Lieutenant Charles Wood of the 52nd Foot was also slightly wounded in the shoulder. Lieutenant Colonel Robert Barclay, the commander of the 2nd Brigade, was slightly wounded just below the right knee and in the foot.[57] Craufurd was faced with a dilemma. If he sent Barclay back to Lisbon, who would replace him? The next senior officer was Lieutenant Colonel Jorge de Avilez, commander of the 1st Caçadores. It is unknown whether Craufurd trusted de Avilez to command the brigade. The easiest solution was to have Barclay remain in command. This would be a costly mistake.

French Casualties

It is very difficult to determine the French casualties at Busaco. Focusing on just General Loison's division is a bit easier, but even then there are problems. Sir Charles Oman states it was 1,252 or about 20 per cent of those who made the assault. However, this was only for the killed and wounded. It does not include those taken prisoner.

---

54. Verner, Vol. 2, p.148.
55. Oman, Vol. 3, p.551.
56. AHM-DIV-1-14-256-02 Casualty Returns for 3rd Caçadores Battalion dated 27 September 1810.
57. Dawson, p.41.

Table 12.2: Casualties in General Loison's Division on 27 September 1810 According to Sir Charles Oman[58]

	Officers		Other Ranks		Total
	Killed	Wounded	Killed	Wounded	
Simon's Brigade					
26th Line	6	37	15	225	283
Légion du Midi	1	32	5	273	311
Hanoverian Legion	4	26	5	182	217
Ferey's Brigade					
32nd Light	2	13	3	95	113
66th Line	5	15	15	123	158
82nd Line	3	18	4	145	170
Total	21	141	47	1,043	1,252

If these numbers are correct 162 officers were killed or wounded out of 239 who were reported in the 15 September 1810 muster rolls. This was a staggering 68 per cent of all the officers in the division. Yet the numbers by name count of the officers listed in Aristide Martinien's *Tableaux par Corps et par Batailles des Officiers Tués et Blessés pendant les Guerres de l'Empire* gives a far different total.[59]

Table 12.3: Officer Casualties in General Loison's Division on 27 September 1810 According to Aristide Martinien

	Killed	Wounded	Died of Wounds	Total
Simon's Brigade				
HQ	–	1	–	1
26th Line	6	12	3	21
Légion du Midi	1	5	–	6
Hanoverian Legion	4	5	–	9
Total	11	23	3	37

(Continued)

---

58. Oman, Vol. 3, p.553.
59. It is difficult to reconcile the two different casualty figures. However, Martinien's figures are based on the names of the officer casualties reported by each regiment. Oman does not give his source for his.

Table 12.3: Continued

	Killed	Wounded	Died of Wounds	Total
Ferey's Brigade				
32nd Light	1	4	1	6
66th Line	5	5	–	10
82nd Line	3	4	–	7
Total	9	13	1	23
Loison's Division Total	20	36	4	60

The sixty officer casualties is 25 per cent of the total officers reported present for duty in the 15 September 1810 muster rolls. Although significantly lower than Oman's figures, they still represent a serious loss, especially among the senior leadership. One general was wounded and captured, while a regimental commander and three battalion commanders were wounded. This was 25 per cent of the regimental and battalion commanders. Hardest hit was the 66th Line Infantry Regiment which lost its regimental commander[60] and one of its battalion commanders.[61] Compounding the problem was there no chance for replacements for the army was over 1,000km from France.

The Aftermath

Night finally fell and Wellington was still unsure what Masséna would do. He wrote to Charles Stuart, the British Envoy Extraordinary and Minister Plenipotentiary to Portugal, that night. 'We have been engaged with the enemy for the last three days, and I think we shall be attacked again tomorrow; as I understand they must carry our position, on which, however, they have as yet made no impression, or starve. Our loss has been trifling.'[62]

---

60. Colonel Jean Béchaud.
61. Chef-de-Bataillon Vivarès
62. *WD*, Vol. 6, p.441.

Chapter 13

The Retreat to Lisbon, 28 September–10 October 1810

The night after the battle was spent evacuating the wounded, burying the dead and preparing for the next day. Dawn broke at 5:49 a.m. and after the morning stand-to the question on everyone's mind was would the French attack. Deserters had come in throughout the night and soon rumours began to spread that 'General Junot, whose corps had not been engaged the day before, had volunteered to storm, with fifteen thousand grenadiers, that point of the position where the Light Division stood'.[1] Although no French attack took place, they were not quiet. Instead 'Massena let slip swarms of light troops, as heretofore, and kept us eternally at work with them, until night put an end to the contest. The French erected a half-moon battery on a hill immediately fronting us and our artillery endeavoured to throw shells on their working parties, but the distance was rather too long.'[2]

Captain Leach of the 95th Rifles had picquet duty in Sula on the night of 28 September and '. . . seven deserters came in during different periods of the night, all agreeing in the same story, that the French army had broken up, and was marching away to turn our left'.[3] This news was passed up through the chain of command to Wellington and he knew that the time to withdraw had come. Orders were sent out and once again the Light Division was ordered to cover the retreat with the cavalry.

No one got much sleep that night while the army made preparations to march. Lieutenant Oglander of the 43rd Foot noted in his diary that they 'got under arms at ½ past 1 A.M. and continued in constant

---

1. Leach, *Rough Sketches . . .*, p.168.
2. Ibid., p.169.
3. Ibid.

expectation of marching till 6, during which time other corps & baggage past us; we then commenced our march thro the wood of the convent of Busaco, and passing thro two villages the names of which I could not learn, we halted at Botao,[4] which is a considerable place'.[5]

Captain Leach confirms what Lieutenant Oglander wrote. 'When day dawned on the 29th, we found that the reports of the deserters were correct, and that the whole allied army, except the Light Division and a small force of light cavalry, which were left on the position as a rear-guard, was already retiring on Coimbra. About nine o'clock in the morning we followed the main body, and bivouacked at night in a wood some miles from Buzaco [sic].'[6]

Craufurd was near the convent watching his troops withdraw when the 52nd Foot came marching by. He saw Captain George Napier and pulled him out of the formation and

> ordered me to post myself in the garden of it, which overlooked the late position of the army and commanded the road by which the troops were retiring, and there to remain and defend it as long as I had a man left! This I should have done, for I was determined to keep my post if I lived as long as I had a cartridge left to load with; but as no enemy appeared I had no opportunity of showing what good stuff an English company of light infantry was made of. It was ascertained in about an hour that the enemy had moved off also and were marching by another road to Coimbra, which they expected to reach before us and so cut off the British army, or at least a large portion of it, from the retreat to the lines.[7]

After marching about 16km, the Light Division spent the night in Botāō and the next morning continued south for another 20km to Coimbra. The march to the city was '. . . over a mountainous country, abounding with olive plantations. The road was bad & in wet weather it was scarcely be passable. The Regt halted for the night in an olive ground near Coimbra. We now found that there could be no intention of opposing the enemy on the right bank of the Mondego as part of

---

4. Botāo, a town about 13km southwest of Busaco Ridge.
5. Oglander, Diary entry 29 September 1810.
6. Leach, *Rough Sketches . . .*, p.169.
7. Napier, George, p.148.

the Army had already passed the river, and we saw a division crossing at a ford below the town.'[8] The Light Division spent the night of 30 September camped on the north side of the city.

Coimbra, a once-thriving university city, was quickly becoming a ghost town. Although the civilians had been given orders to evacuate it, many had waited until the last minute to begin the 250km trip to Lisbon. Lieutenant James Fergusson of the 43rd Foot wrote home that:

> It was a distressing sight to see the inhabitants of that large town obliged to abandon their houses and property and fly for their lives; many of the better class, accustomed to every luxury, obliged to travel on foot night and day suffering every description of misery, until they arrived at Lisbon; many died from want and fatigue. The miseries of war never struck us so forcibly; we felt for the poor creatures, but it was not in our power to relieve them. We were hard pressed by the crowd, and with difficulty made our way through them to Condeixa, and escaped.[9]

It was at Coimbra that the Light Division began to receive replacements for its losses over the previous seven months. Lieutenants John Woodgate and Charles Kinloch, and Ensigns Samuel Pritchard, George Love, Charles Kenny, John Barrett, Richard Lifford and George Cleghorn, all of the 52nd Foot, joined them there. Additionally Captain Charles Beckwith's company of the 2nd Battalion 95th Rifles arrived at Coimbra on 30 September with three officers,[10] six sergeants, two buglers and 102 rifleman. The company left England in late August and made it to Lisbon on 15 September. They stayed there about five days and were sent by sea to Figueria da Foz, arriving there eight days later. There was no docking facilities but they were greeted by a 'hundred hideous looking Portuguese women, whose joy was so excessive that they waded up to their arm-pits through a heavy surf, and insisted on carrying us on shore on their backs!'[11] They then marched 50km to joined the Light Division in Coimbra. They were assigned to the 1st Brigade.

---

8.   Oglander, Diary entry 30 September 1810.
9.   Levine, pp.138–9.
10. Captain Charles Beckwith, First Lieutenant Walter Bedell and Second Lieutenant John Kincaid.
11. Kincaid, *Adventures. . .*, pp.6 & 8.

The replacement officers came in a various state of readiness for the rigours of a campaign. Despite being a veteran of the 1809 Walcheren Campaign, Lieutenant John Kincaid was totally unprepared and would pay for it over the next two weeks.

> ... as our route lay through the city of Coimbra, we came to the magnanimous resolution of providing ourselves with all manner of comforts and equipments [sic] for the campaign on our arrival there; but, when we entered it, at the end of the second day, our disappointment was quite eclipsed by astonishment at finding ourselves the only living things in a city, which ought to have been furnished with twenty-thousand souls.
>
> The difficulties we encountered were nothing out of the usual course of old campaigners; but, untrained and unprovided as I was, I still looked back upon the twelve or fourteen days following the battle of Busaco as the most trying I have ever experienced, for we were on our legs from day-light until dark, in daily contact with the enemy; and, to satisfy the stomach of an ostrich I had, as already stated, only a pound of beef, a pound of biscuit, and one glass of rum. A brother-officer was kind enough to strap my boat-cloak and portmanteau on the mule carrying his heavy baggage, which, on account of the proximity of the foe, was never permitted to be within a day's march of us, so that, in addition to my simple uniform, my only covering every night was the canopy of heaven, from whence the dews descended so refreshingly, that I generally awoke, at the end of an hour, chilled, and wet to the skin . . .[12]

The next morning,[13] the Light Division could see the French army approaching in the distance. The order came to continue their march southward, and by 8:00 a.m. they were on the road.[14] As the officers and men marched through the city they passed the local prison, which also served as the insane asylum. When the orders came to evacuate the city, the prison officials quickly obeyed them. Having no means of transporting a large number of felons and the insane, they left them locked up. They must have thought the French would take

---

12. Kincaid, *Adventures* . . ., pp.10–12.
13. 1 October 1810.
14. Kincaid, *Adventures*. . ., p.17. Oglander, Diary entry 1 October 1810.

Côa terrain uphill from the east side of the bridge. The ridge in the distance was the where the Light Division was initially deployed. (Nicholas Haynes collection)

Côa terrain just north of the knoll. Note the high wall in the foreground. (Nicholas Haynes collection)

The old road from Almeida down to the bridge. Notice the height of the old wall. (Nicholas Haynes collection)

View of the Côa River from the bridge. (Author's collection)

View of the Côa River Bridge from the east side. (Nicholas Haynes collection)

View of the Côa River Bridge from the west side. The author is standing on the bridge. He is 1.8m (5ft 10in) tall. It shows how narrow the bridge is. (Author's collection)

View from the Côa knoll that the French occupied. Notice how it dominates the approaches to the bridge. (Nicholas Haynes collection)

View of the Côa knoll that the British rearguard charged up in order to give the 52nd Foot time to get to the bridge. (Nicholas Haynes collection)

View from Moura Windmill of the Anglo-Allied positions on Busaco Ridge. This is where Masséna had his HQ during the battle. In 1810 the ridge was not covered with trees. (Author's collection)

View of the French avenue of approach from the Anglo-Allied positions on Busaco Ridge. (Author's collection)

Busaco Ridge just to the right of the Light Division's position. The ridge would have looked like this at the time of the battle. (Author's collection)

The rock that General Craufurd stood on to watch the French climb Busaco Ridge. The grove of trees was not there in 1810. (Steve Brown collection)

The Lines of Torres Vedras: view from Arruda of Fort # 9. (Nicholas Haynes collection)

The Lines of Torres Vedras: View from Fort #9 northwest towards Fort # 10 which is on the hill to the left. (Nicholas Haynes collection)

The Lines of Torres Vedras: View to the northeast from Fort # 10 Carvalho. Arruda is on the right horizon. (Nicholas Haynes collection)

The Lines of Torres Vedras: the Arruda church where Lieutenants Kincaid, Simmons and Strode buried the old woman. (Nicholas Haynes collection)

care of them. James Clark, the Quartermaster of the 95th Rifles, took a party of men to break open the doors and release those locked inside.[15] Captain George Napier witnessed it and years later wrote:

> We who were the last of the troops were passing by the prison, which was also the madhouse, the unfortunate inmates, prisoners and maniacs, were all at the grated windows rending the air with wild shrieks of despair at seeing the whole population of the city driven before us through the gate, and these unfortunate wretched creatures all locked in, and a fire having broken out in some houses close by them which they with reason expected every moment to communicate with the prison, and that they must all perish in the flames! The British officers and soldiers could not stand this sight, and we soon broke open the gates and let them all loose; the maniac, the murderer, and the thief were turned adrift without a moment's hesitation or an instant's thought, by which many a villain of the deepest dye was again let loose upon society and escaped the punishment due to his crimes. But what else was to be done? We had no time to make inquiries, their keepers or jailers had left them, the flames were fast approaching, and the enemy entering the town! If we did wrong, it was from motives of humanity and under circumstances that those only who were present can appreciate, and I feel confident that no man of feeling could for one moment blame us. As we moved along, driving this immense multitude of unhappy people before us, houseless, penniless, and hungry, I could not help cursing war and all its dreadful attributes, and inwardly feeling that I was myself one of the instruments by which so much misery and injustice was inflicted on a poor guiltless race of inoffensive human beings, not one of whom most probably ever had a voice in the decision of peace or war, and who were scourged so severely for what?[16]

Coimbra was also a forward supply depot for the army and despite knowing for many weeks that the army would be retreating, the Army's Commissary Department was unable to evacuate all their stores. Tons of food and equipment was destroyed or left for the French. The quickest

---

15. Kincaid, *Adventures. . .*, p.17.
16. Napier, George, pp.149–51.

The Retreat to Lisbon, 28 September–10 October 1810.

way to destroy the alcohol was to cave in the ends of the casks. By the time the Light Division marched through the city the streets were literally running with rum and wine.[17]

Although their next stop was Condeixa, about 15km to the south, the pace was very slow, due to the large number of refugees clogging the road. The officers and men were not prepared for the sea of human misery that preceded them.

> We arrived some hours sooner than the French at Coimbra, from which Lord Wellington had ordered all the inhabitants to withdraw and carry all their property and provisions with them; but as they had unfortunately delayed doing this till we were actually on the march through the town, the hurry, fright, and confusion were beyond description, and I never witnessed so heart-rending a scene! Beautiful women and young children, the aged, the decrepit, the sick, the poor, the rich, nobles and peasants, all in one dense mass of misery, wretchedness, and confusion; some barefoot, others crying, women tearing their hair with loud lamentations, and calling on every Saint in the calendar, many of them running to the officers for protection and food, the weather bad, and all drenched with rain . . .[18]

The Light Division eventually reached Condeixa and found more chaos. Like Coimbra, the town was also an army supply depot and as the troops were passing by, the commissary officers

> handed out shoes and shirts to any one that would take them, and the streets were literally running ankle deep with rum, in which the soldiers were dipping their cups and helping themselves as they marched along. The commissariat, some years afterwards, called for a return of the men who had received shirts and shoes on this occasion, with a view of making us pay for them, but we very briefly replied that the one half were dead, and the other half would be d----d before they pay anything.[19]

---

17. Oglander, Diary dated 1 October 1810.
18. Napier, George, p.149.
19. Kincaid, *Adventures. . .*, p.18.

Lieutenant James Fergusson of the 43rd also noticed the large amount of stores being destroyed, including cavalry equipments [sic], hospital supplies, tea, brandy, shirts, shoes, troswers [sic], and tobacco . . .'[20]

Lieutenant Oglander was incensed at what he perceived as wanton destruction of supplies due to the incompetence and corruption of the commissary officers.

> At Condexa considerable stores of liquor, salt provisions and tents were destroyed. The destruction and abandonment of stores is probably to be attributed not as the fault of the commander in chief, who cannot overlook the execution of every minute detail but to the ignorance and carelessness not say disinterest of the Commissariat. The later motive indeed I much fear had its weight, as any irregularity in their accounts may be easily concealed by adding the deficiencies caused by these scams to the list of articles destroyed already, which, I should think from the hurry and confusion inevitable in such circumstances, it would be next to impossible to discover. Their neglect of the publick interest however is quite apparent from the circumstance of salt provisions not having been issued to the troops, which passed thru Condexa this day. The Light Division 3500 strong, Genl Pack's brigade of Portuguese 3000, the cavalry and Artillery might have received a least two days provisions of salt meat from the store which would have made a material difference in the quantity destroyed. And the Bullocks killed for the days [sic] supply of the troops would of course have been driven on with the rest of the Herds. So self evident a saving was notwithstanding neglected for which the commissary is highly culpable. Another instance of want of consideration is shown in their conduct at this town. The 43rd and probably the other regts did not get their ration of wine, tho the streets of the place were flowing with liquor and considering the fatigue, which the men had undergone, it would not have been improper to have given them an extra allowance.[21]

It was here that Captain Napier of the 43rd Foot finally could go no further due to his wound.

---

20. Levine, p.139.
21. Oglander, Diary entry 1 October 1810.

I was so ill and still with my wound that I could no longer sit my horse, and was forced to get into a cart and make the best of my way to Lisbon, in the progress of which one cold, dark, rainy night the Portuguese driver decamped and left his cart and myself sticking in the mud. Seeing a light at some distance I got out of the car and made my way to it, but so exhausted with pain and illness (having the ague also) that I sank down perfectly done up at the door of the house from whence the light had proceeded. And luckily for me this was the quarter of my friend Sir [Galbraith] Lowry Cole, commanding the 4th division, who, upon being informed that a wounded officer was at his door, instantly came out, had me carried in, gave me his own bed, had a surgeon sent for to dress my wound (which was very severe) and then sent me a good dinner; after which I fell asleep, and awoke the next morning at daybreak quite refreshed and able to get on with General Cole's staff to the Lines . . . From the Lines I went to Lisbon, which was so crammed with troops, sick and wounded soldiers, the commissaries and their clerks, all the skulkers and riff-raff of the army, besides thousands of Portuguese driven in from the country towns, that it was hardly possible to get a place to lodge in. But good luck attended me here also, for by accident I found the house where my brother Charles was quartered and who arrived some days before, having suffered much from the pain of his wound (which was very severe) . . . I found Charles in bed very ill, his face so dreadfully swollen that I could neither see eyes nor nose, and having only heard that 'he was dreadfully wounded in the face' when I beheld him this horrid-looking figure, I really thought his nose had been shot off! . . . The ball had entered on one side of his nose and passing through had lodged in the jawbone of the opposite side, from whence it was abstracted with much difficulty, great part of the jaw coming away with it as well as several teeth.[22]

October 2nd found the Light Division marching at 6 a.m.[23] Their destination was Pombal 27km south. Their route took them through Redinha,

---

22. Napier, George, pp.151–5.
23. Oglander, Diary entry 2 October 1810.

a town on the south bank of the Redinha River.[24] Like Coimbra and Condeixa, Pombal was also a supply depot. Knowing what happened in the previous two places and afraid that the men would straggle to loot and pillage the remaining supplies, Craufurd had the division bivouac on the south side of the city. Despite these measures, which Captain Leach thought were a good idea, 'so inveterate is the propensity of drink in the soldier, that, in spite of every precaution, many of them contrived to get drunk by dipping rum out of the streets, on our march through the town, in tin cups, or in any vessel nearest at hand.'[25]

The division was up and ready to march at daybreak and left Pombal at 6 a.m.[26] They marched about 15km before bivouacking for the night in a evergreen forest. The division stayed there for two nights and on 5 October marched to 25km to Batalha, via Leiria. Discipline had broken down within the army and looting by stragglers was rampant. Wellington had had enough and in 'consequence of the irregularities committed by the English and Portuguese troops in Leyria [sic], Lord Wellington ordered the Provost martial to seize and hang one of each nation, whom he should first find in the act of plundering or straggling, which order was carried into immediate execution as an example. The corps which had misbehaved were forbidden to enter any village or town till further orders.'[27] The 95th Rifles were the last of the Light Division to march through Leiria and as he approached the entrance to the city, Lieutenant Kincaid 'saw an English and a Portuguese soldier dangling by the bough of a tree, the first summary example I had ever seen of martial law'.[28]

The Light Division reached Batalha early enough for the officers to do some exploring. In the city was the fourteenth-century Dominican monastery of Saint Mary of the Victory, the burial site of King João the First and his English wife, Queen Philippa. Captain Leach and Lieutenant Kincaid decided to visit the monastery. There they found 'I know not who the culprits were, nor to what division of the army they belonged; but in going into the cathedral, I saw the coffin of the said King John open, and the body, which was of course embalmed, exposed to view, wrapped in rich robes of crimson velvet and gold. By way of a relic, I cut off a button and some gold fringe from his robes; whilst others,

---

24. A battle would be fought there five months later on 12 March 1811.
25. Leach, *Rough Sketches* . . ., p.170.
26. Kincaid, *Adventures*. . ., p.20.
27. Oglander, Diary entry 4 October 1810.
28. Kincaid, *Adventures*. . ., p.18.

more ambitious, could be satisfied with nothing less than a royal finger.'[29] Lieutenant Kincaid claimed that the culprit was a Rifle officer, but was quick to point out to his readers that '. . . point not thy finger at me, for I am not the man'.[30]

The French advance guard was only a day behind and 6 October the Light Division was on the road by 5 a.m. The day's march was to Condeeiros via Cavalhal Turquel a distance of 30km. The terrain had gradually changed as they marched south and even water was scarce.

> There is a remarkable want of water throughout the whole district, thro which we passed today. The olive plantations are almost uninterrupted and tending from Carvalhos to Rio Maior; and on the left side of the road there runs a chain of hills parallel with it and nearly the same height and steepness throughout. The land which is not planted with Olives is generally barren being covered with heath & furze excepting in the immediate vicinity of the villages, thinly scattered by the road side and near to which are some cork lands.[31]

The division continued its practice of beginning to march early in the day. On 7 October it started its march at 6 a.m. and went 12km to Rio Maior and then another 14km to Alcoentre, where it bivouacked in an olive grove. They continued to have good weather, with very little rain. Lieutenant Oglander wrote in his diary that:

> I must here observe that from the 23rd of Sept to this day the whole brigade constantly bivouacked with the exception of the 29th of Sept to 5th Oct when there was a little rain. The fineness of the weather was a fortunate circumstances for us as the great regularity of the retreat may in a great measure be attributed to the very favourable state of the weather which saved the men from the variety of disorders that would otherwise have attacked them; and lessened the fatigue of marching by the excellent state in which we found the roads. And by being able to remain out at night we avoided being quartered in the villages in which the men

---

29. Leach, *Rough Sketches* . . . , p.170. Ironically, he did not see anything wrong with desecrating the corpse of King João.
30. Kincaid, *Adventures*. . ., p.20.
31. Oglander, Diary entry 6 October 1810.

would have got new wine in spite of any precautions to prevent it. Fortunate as this was for us, it was doubly so for the inhabitants, who loaded with their property and unable to procure the means of conveying their burdens would have sank under the fatigue of the journey and have been obliged to remain behind in a country destitute of the means of furnishing them with subsistence and exposed to the cruelty of an enemy exasperated at their flight.[32]

Unfortunately for them, this was the last day of good weather.

In Lisbon, Lieutenants Harry Smith and George Simmons, both of the Rifle Battalion, believed they had sufficiently recovered from their wounds and were anxious to rejoin the battalion, Lieutenant Smith having

> heard of the army having retired into the celebrated lines of Torres Vedras, and nothing would serve us but join the Regiment. So our medical heroes very unwillingly sent us off to Belem,[33] the convalescent department under Colonel [Captain John] Tucker, 29th Regiment, a sharp fellow enough. When I, George Simmons, and Charlie Ecles [sic],[34] 3rd Battalion, just arrived sick from Cadiz, waited on him to express our desire to join he said, 'Oh, certainly; but you must be posted to do duty with convalescents going up the country.' I was lame and could not walk. George Simmons cantered on crutches, and Charlie Ecles was very sick. However, go or no go, and so we were posted to 600 villains of every Regiment in the army . . .[35]

Lieutenant Simmons provided more detail on this detachment. It

> was formed at Belem under the command of Major [Barnaby] Murphy of the 88th Regiment; he had men belonging to every regiment in the country, amongst whom several who had much rather remained at Belem than have paraded their bodies in a field to be shot at. We marched off about seven o'clock in the morning. The men of the Light Division who had been wounded with us

---

32. Ibid; entry 7 October 1810.
33. Belém is a suburb of Lisbon and was the site of the main British hospital in Lisbon.
34. Lieutenant Charles Eeles.
35. Smith, pp.33–4.

and were well again, formed the rear-guard, and I travelled with it; but in spite of all my precautions several men skulked away unobserved, slipping to houses and other places. When we halted and called the rolls, 100 out of 800 that had marched off were missing, which sadly annoyed Major Murphy. He asked my how many of mine were gone. 'Not one,' was my answer, 'and depend upon it none will leave now.' 'Well, then, sir take the rear-guard to-morrow and make any straggler a prisoner, and I will bring him to a Drumhead Court-Martial'; which order he made known to the detachment The rain had fallen heavily all day. We got under shelter into miserable houses that had been left by their inhabitants at Lumiar.[36]

Major Murphy became sick and because he was the next senior officer, Lieutenant Smith took charge.

The command devolved on me, a subaltern, for whom the soldiers of other corps have no great respect, and such a tasks I never had as to keep these six hundred rascals together. However, I had a capital English horse, good at riding over an insubordinate fellow, and a voice like thunder. The first bivouac I came to was the Guards (these men were very orderly). The commanding officer had a cottage. I reported myself. It was raining like the devil. He put his head out of the window, and I said, 'Sir I have 150 men of your Regiment convalescent from Belem.' 'Oh send for the Sergeant-major,' he very quietly said; – no 'no walk in out of the rain.' So I roared out, 'We Light Division men don't do duty with Sergeant-majors, nor are we told to wait. There are your men, every one – the only well-conducted men in 600 under my charge – and these are their accounts!' throwing down a bundle of papers and off I galloped to the Household man's astonishment.[37]

The continuous marches and bivouacking every night began to take its toll on the men and their equipment. Private Thomas Garretty wrote

---

36. Simmons, p.110. Lumiar is just north of Lisbon, near the airport. It is about 35km from Arruda dos Vinhos.
37. Smith, pp.33–4.

25 years later in his memoirs about the hardships the men of the Light Division endured.

> One day a bullock was killed for our use, and afforded a luxurious repast; but we were obliged to make haste about it. Scarcely had we finished a hasty meal, when the advance of the enemy was announced. The men were unwilling to lose even a fragment of viands so scarce; and several were afterwards observed, collecting bundles of the long dry grass and making a fire, over which they frizzled pieces of meat, impaled on the end of a ramrod. The hardships we endured in the prosecution of this retreat were increasingly severe. Personal comforts were out of the question. No change of linen could be procured; and as to a pair of stockings, the luxury was not to be thought of. As mine were worn to tatters, I contented myself without a new supply. Snatches of broken slumber were all we could obtain, though ready to stumble with weariness. The physical energies both of myself and comrades, have since that period, often appeared wonderful, even to myself. Many a time I have marched eight or ten miles on the nourishment afforded by a little water; and even then, with a pipe and good company, we talked away dull care, and were able with three cheers to face about, and with a determined volley warn away the following foe. We were much hurt by exposure to extreme. After the exhaustion arising from a forced march, pursued for hours, during the meridian heat of this burning climate, we lay down to rest for the night; and on the following morning such was the copiousness of the fallen dew, that our blankets appeared as if dipped in water.[38]

October 8th saw the end of the good weather and early in the morning the rain came down in torrents. The 95th Rifles, which was bringing up the rear, spent the night on the south side of Alcoentre, while the 43rd Foot was in the vicinity of Vila Nova de São Pedro, about 15km to the east.[39] Whenever possible the troops were billeted in towns or villages. However, at times that did not mean much. Captain Leach

---

38. Garretty, pp.97–8.
39. Leach, *Rough Sketches. . .*, p.171. Oglander, Diary entry 8 October 1810.

halted one night in an uninhabited cottage with only half a roof on it, in which four of us, besides our servants, horses, mules, and donkeys, were huddled together. In endeavouring, by dint of a fire, to dry our clothes, which were fairly rusted on us by constant exposure to the weather by day and night, the remnant of the cottage, as the devil would have it, caught fire; and with great difficulty we succeeded in dragging forth from the flames and smoke our miserable quadrupeds and the baggage, and depositing them in the street, under as tremendous a torrent of rain as would have satisfied old Noah himself. With the assistance of the soldiers, aided also by the continued rain, the flames were got under, and we-entered our hut, where we passed the night.[40]

The rain also affected the detachment of Lieutenants Smith and Simmons and despite their efforts men slipped away when they were not looking. 'Marched under continued rain to Cabeza de Monchique, meeting numbers of poor people, making their way to Lisbon in the most wretched plight, telling us the British army were in full retreat before the French. At the end of this day's march, another one hundred heroes had disappeared . . .'[41]

Although the Light Division was the rear infantry division as the army marched to Lisbon, the rearguard was under the command of General Stapleton Cotton and consisted of General Slade's brigade[42] and General George Anson's brigade.[43] Anson's was the army's rearmost brigade. A picquet, consisting of the Left Squadron of the 16th Light Dragoons, commanded by Captain George Murray who had been slightly wounded three days before in a skirmish at Leiria, were left in Rio Maior while the rest of the cavalry withdrew to Alcoentre. The cavalry had been covering the withdrawal of the army for ten days and were exhausted. On this day General Cotton made a serious mistake.

Captain Murray's squadron had withdrawn from Rio Maior, but

about twelve the enemy attacked them but though our general was apprised of this he conceived they would halt short as they

---

40. Leach, *Rough Sketches*. . ., p.171.
41. Simmons, p.111.
42. The 1st Royal Dragoons and the 14th Light Dragoons.
43. The 16th Light Dragoons and the 1st KGL Hussars.

had done the two preceding days. Perhaps we forgot that we had been making short marches and that it was not certain the enemy would do likewise. Besides, the country after Leyria had become so barren and so short of forage and water it was almost necessary for them to push on.[44]

The two cavalry brigades continued through Alcoentre and bivouacked a few kilometres away. General Cotton had decided to spend the night in the town, as did Generals Slade and Anson. With them were Captain Bull's Royal Horse Artillery troop, and the baggage of the two cavalry brigades. For all practical purposes, the only thing between them and the enemy was Captain Murray's squadron of less than 100 men. Lieutenant Tomkinson was with Captain Cocks's squadron, which had the duty for the day.

About 2 we heard some shots fired near the village, and Captain Cocks' squadron, being the first for duty, moved down as quickly as possible with the first mounted dragoons we could collect, in all not fifty men. On our way down we met five of the guns coming up in the greatest confusion, some with four, some with six horses to them, having got away how they could. On the other side the village ran a considerable brook, which was not passable excepting at the bridge on the entrance into the town. The enemy had two regiments of cavalry close up,[45] and Captain Murray's people were all withdrawn over the bridge. Our party formed up ready to charge down the street. There was a howitzer and two ammunition waggons without a horse to them, commissariat mules and men in the street in the greatest confusion. The enemy did not long remain idle, and detached two squadrons from the 14th Dragoons into the village; they passed the bridge, driving in Captain Murray's people, and came half-way up the street to where we were formed. The enemy's two squadrons were close to each other, in sixes, completely filling up the street. From the bridge to the where we were formed, the street makes a right angle; the head of the column passed the turning, the other squadron in the rear,

---

44. Cocks, p.85.
45. Tomkinson is mistaken. They were the 500 men of the 3rd Provisional Dragoon Regiment, consisting of the 3rd and 4th Squadrons of the 14th and 26th Dragoons, which was part of General Sainte-Croix's Brigade.

not seeing how we were formed. In this situation they halted, when we charged them; they instantly went about and wished to retire. There was the greatest noise and confusion with the enemy, their front wishing to get away, and their rear, not seeing was going on, stood still. They got so close together that it was impossible to get well at them. We took twelve and killed six, driving them over the bridge again, and by this means allowing time for what remained in the town to get clear away. . . . It was a dead surprise; and had the French dashed into the town without waiting a moment, they would certainly have got the two guns and some of the general's baggage.[46]

The cavalry continued to skirmish until night fell.

The next day, 9 October, the Light Division was on the move at 5:30 a.m.[47] It was still raining and they had a long march of 40km to Alemquer[48] via Carregado, a town near the Tagus River. Contact had been broken with the enemy and they were hoping to for a quiet night in the town. There they 'enjoyed the supreme luxury of a roof over our heads, and made up for lost time by a good night's sleep. The town was deserted by the inhabitants, through fear of the invading army.'[49]

Lieutenants Smith and Simmons continued their march through the pouring rain with their detachment. At Sobral de Monte Agraço they were informed that the division was going to Arruda,[50] so they marched their detachment 'and arrived in that place about eight o'clock wet through. The Quartermasters of regiments came in soon after, and then the town was divided; the troops followed. I took possession of a good house for Captain O'Hare's officers and had a good fire against their arrival.'[51]

Now that they had broken contact with the enemy, Craufurd had decided to rest the division in Alemquer for a day. It was still raining on the morning of 10 October and the officers and men were enjoying the rest and a chance to dry their clothes. In what had to be a mistake by the army staff, the cavalry of the rearguard upon reaching Carregado

---

46. Tomkinson, pp.50–1.
47. Oglander, Diary entry 9 October 1810.
48. Modern-day Alenquer.
49. Leach, *Rough Sketches. . .*, p.172.
50. Also known as Arruda dos Vinhos.
51. Simmons, p.111.

were ordered to march 27km south towards Póvoa de Santa Iria e Forte da Casa. No word was sent to Craufurd that the cavalry screen had been withdrawn. Compounding the problem, the division staff thought that the division was safe and the normal precautions of sending out outlying picquets was not taken. Lieutenant Henry Booth with a section from Captain John Hopkins's company of the 43rd Foot, had an inlying picquet.[52] This was noted by several officers including Lieutenants Fergusson and Oglander.[53] Private Garretty was nervous because 'no guards were posted, no patroles [sic] sent forward, nor any precautions taken against surprise, although the town, situated in a deep ravine was peculiarly favourable for such an attempt. It was clear to me, and others, that our officers were uneasy at this posture of affairs; the height in front was anxiously watched. . .'[54]

About 3 p.m. Lieutenant Kincaid of the 95th Rifles was ready to eat a much anticipated hot meal inside a house when

> we saw the indefatigable rascals, on the mountain opposite our windows, just beginning to wind round us, with a mixture of cavalry and infantry; the wind blowing so strong, that the long tail of each particular stuck as stiffly out in the face of the one behind, as if the whole had been strung upon a cable and dragged by the leaders. We turned out a few companies, and kept them in check while the division was getting under arms, spilt the soup as usual, and transferring the smoking solids to the haversack, for future mastication.[55]

It was much the same throughout the town. Captain Leach was about to sit down to a hot turkey dinner when the alarm was sounded,[56] while Private Garretty of the 43rd, who was serving as his company commander's batman, was preparing dinner for his captain.

> Three or four officers messed together; and on that day another or two were expected, by way of a small party. Culinary preparations on a moderate scale were going on, and I had just

---

52. Mockler-Ferryman, Augustus, 'Three Brothers in the Light Division', *Forty-Third and 52nd Light Infantry Chronicle*, Vol. III. Page 180
53. Levine, pp.139. Oglander, Diary entry 10 October 1810.
54. Garretty, p.106.
55. Kincaid, *Adventures. . .*, pp.20–1.
56. Leach, *Rough Sketches. . .*, p.172.

opened the Captain's trunk, and taken out some table-linen, when lo! The well-known bugle sounded to arms. Aware that something unexpected had happened, I ran up stairs, and on looking out at a back-window, I saw the enemy on the brow of a mountain, a column of whom were rapidly descending into the town. Coming down in haste I found the dinner ready, but there is many a slip between the cup and the lip; and, reaching across the table, which was ready garnished, I swept the whole – utensils, food, and all – into the orifice of a large travelling-bag, and made my way with it into the street. Confusion and disorder are terms too weak to describe the condition of the public thoroughfare. This time, thought I, we shall be surely taken. The Captain clamoured for his horse; I was as urgent for a mule to carry the baggage; every minute of delay seemed an hour. At length by uncommon effort, we cleared the town . . .[57]

Captain William Napier of the 43rd Foot recalled that:

The alarm was instantly given, and the regiments got under arms; but the principal post of assembly had been marked on an open space, very much exposed to an enemy's guns, and from whence the road led through an ancient gateway to the top of the mountain behind. The enemy's numbers increased every moment, they endeavoured to create a belief that their artillery was come up; and although this feint was easily seen through, but the General desired the regiments to break and reform on the other side of the archway, out of gun range; and immediately all was disorder. The baggage animals were still loading, the streets were crowded with the followers of the division, and the whole in one confused mass rushed, or were driven headlong into the archway. Several were crushed, and with worse troops a general panic must has ensued; but the greatest number of the soldiers, ashamed of the order, stood firm in their ranks until the confusion abated.

Nevertheless the mischief was sufficiently great; and the enemy's infantry descending the heights, endeavoured some to turn the town on the left, while others pushed directly through the streets in pursuit . . .[58]

---

57. Garretty, p.109.
58. Napier, William, Vol. 3, pp.351–2.

Craufurd wasted no time in ordering the retreat to Sobral, 16km to the southwest. By the time they reached the village the sun had set. Lieutenant Henry Booth and his picquet tried to provide some cover and fired '. . . away in all directions in order to keep them in check, so great was their impudence and spirits at seeing us retreat in so confused a manner'.[59] There would be a full moon in three days, but with the continuous heavy rains, the night was pitch black. The men were allowed to rest briefly in Sobral, but it was only a temporary halt. Soon the word came to march to Arruda, 9km to the southeast. The march in the pouring rain, with the possibility of the enemy in close pursuit, had to be miserable. Yet Captain Leach painted a different portrait of it.

> A few shots from the pickets soon explained how matters stood; and in less than ten minutes the whole division was under arms, and some companies engaged with the French advanced guard at the outside of the town. We were forthwith put in march towards Arruda, where, after wading through oceans of mud and water, and with an incessant shower-bath from above, we arrived after night fall. The raging of the elements rendered our retreat comparatively quiet and comfortable; as the French were glad enough, no doubt, to shelter themselves from the storm in our late quarters at Alemquer, and to allow us to proceed unmolested . . . when we reached Arruda in a dark tempestuous night, soaked with rain, half-famished with hunger, bitterly cursing the fellow who had, a few hours before, turned us out of our comfortable quarters, and expecting neither more nor less than to bivouac in some snipe-marsh.[60]

Lieutenant John Bell, the Light Division's Deputy Assistant Quartermaster General, the brigade majors[61] and the regimental quartermasters[62] preceded the main body. Upon arriving at Arruda Lieutenant Bell began allocating billets.

---

59. Mockler-Ferryman, p.180.
60. Leach, *Rough Sketches* . . ., pp.172–3.
61. Lieutenant James Stewart of the 95th Rifles was the 1st Brigade's and Captain Charles Rowan of the 52nd Foot was the 2nd Brigade's.
62. David Fraser of the 43rd Foot, George Woods of the 52nd Foot and James Clark of the 95th Rifles. I was not able to find the name of the

... After marking off certain houses for his general and staff, split the remainder of the town between the majors of brigades: they in their turn provided for their generals and staff, and then made a wholesale division of streets among the quarter-masters of the regiments, who, after providing for their commanding officers and staff, retailed the remaining houses, in equal proportions, among the companies; so that, by the time that the regiment arrived, there was nothing to be done beyond the quarter-master's simply telling each captain 'here's a certain number of houses for you.'[63]

Most of the officers could not believe what was waiting for them in Arruda. Lieutenant Fergusson of the 43rd wrote home that it was 'was beautifully situated, and a favourite retreat of the rich merchants of Lisbon – their quintas being splendidly furnished, and made as luxurious as possible'.[64] Captain Leach was amazed 'at finding, not only a roof over our heads in Arruda, but a prospect of not going to bed supperless. We consoled ourselves for the loss of the turkey at Alemquer with some fowls, and a good allowance of capital wine, which we found in the house allotted to myself and my subalterns.'[65]

As they rested the officers reflected on what happened in Alemquer and how they were caught by surprise. Lieutenant Oglander was quite adamant about who was to blame.

It appears extraordinary that General Craufurd, who was the commandant in the town, should have suffered himself to be so completely taken by surprise. Under any circumstances, it is a fault that can hardly be excused in any general; but in the present case I do not think it possible to find a palliation for this neglect. The heights above the place were so lofty that a picquet must have seen the enemy's approach and parties might have been stationed upon the road a mile without the town for the same purpose. He also had cavalry under his command which might have patrolled the roads; whether any other these precautions were taken, I do not know; but with such means under proper

---

quartermasters for the 1st and 3rd Caçadores Battalions.
63. Kincaid, *Adventures. . .*, pp.22–3.
64. Levine, p.139.
65. Leach, *Rough Sketches . . .*, p.174.

directions, timely notice ought to have been obtained. And it is evident that no inferior officer was in fault as Genl C. (who is always ready to sacrifice another, if he can thereby save himself, and who magnifies trifles into the most serious crimes) would doubtedly have made it known to the army by bringing the offender to a court martial. The whole blame must therefore fall upon him.[66]

They did not know it at the time, but after marching 250km in the past 13 days, they had made it to their destination. Arruda would be their home for the next month.

---

66. Oglander, Diary entry 10 October 1810.

Chapter 14

The Lines of Torres Vedras, 11 October–14 November 1810

Now that they were close to Lisbon, the question for the officers and men was what did the future hold. Were they staying or evacuating the country? Some might have heard rumours about the Lines of Torres Vedras, but most had been upcountry for a year and had not heard anything. Lieutenant Fergusson of the 43rd Foot wrote home that 'This was the first knowledge we had of the famous lines of Torres Vedras'.[67] Now, seeing them in person was another matter. When daylight broke, many of the officers and men were surprised at the extent of the fortifications that awaited them and knew that they would not be leaving the country.

The Lines of Torres Vedras

In 1809 Wellington realized that should Napoleon decide to invade Portugal he would not be able to effectively defend the country. Eventually he would have to evacuate the British army. There had to be a way to prevent the country from falling. After performing a reconnaissance of the terrain just north of Lisbon, he realized that it strongly favoured the defenders. After consulting his engineers he devised a plan to fortify the approaches to Lisbon and make it costly or impossible for the French to take the city. He laid out his concept in a memo dated 20 October 1809 to Lieutenant Colonel Richard Fletcher, his senior engineer. 'The detailed design of the Lines was developed over the coming months by Fletcher

---

67. Levine, p.139.

and the British, Portuguese, and German engineers. Each redoubt was individually designed to fit the terrain and its operational needs.'[1]

The defences would be in a series of four lines. The First and Second Lines would protect Lisbon. The Third Line would be around St. Julien,[2] a fortified harbour about 20km west of Lisbon. This would be the last defence for the British army, in case they were forced to evacuate by sea. The Fourth Line was on the left bank of the Tagus and was designed to protect the seaborne approaches to Lisbon, should a French force attack on the side of the river. Each Line had numerous forts and redoubts, and all were mounted with guns.

Table 14.1: Number of Forts in the Lines of Torres Vedras[3]

Line	Forts	Guns	Troops
First Line	70	319	18,700
Second Line	69	215	15,000
Third Line (St. Julian)	13	94	5,300
Fourth (Almada)	17	86	7,500

Complementing these forts was landscaping done to make the approach to them very difficult. Dams were built to flood low-lying areas, slopes were cut to make steep escarpments, and dense tangles of abattis were constructed to block approaches that could not be flooded or cut.

Chef-de-Bataillon Pelet, Marshal Masséna's ADC, left a description of the Lines from the French side.

> The English Lines, enveloping twenty or twenty-four thousand yards,[4] barred the terrain between the Tagus and the sea. The right extended from Alhandra; the centre was at Monte Agraço, or mountain of Grace, facing Sobral;[5] and the left reached through

---

1. Thompson, Mark, *Wellington's Engineers: Military Engineering in the Peninsular War 1808 – 1814*. Barnsley: Pen & Sword, 2015, p.49.
2. Modern-day São Julião da Barra.
3. Thompson, p.50.
4. 18–20km.
5. Also known as Sobral de Monte Agraço.

Torres Vedras to the sea. There was a very narrow defile in front of Sobral and beyond the mountain rose up again suddenly like a gigantic wall of rocks extending on both flanks; it was this formidable barrier that the English had crowned with works. On both sides of the passage two deep valleys full of ravines opened out and extended all the way to the sea and the Tagus. They served as the first obstacle of the primary defence line and as a kind of ditch at this line. These were the valleys where the rivers of Arruda and Torres Vedras flowed. Thus the terrain we occupied was joined at only one point to the range of mountains not covered by rocks or absolutely inaccessible, all the avenues, and all of the small detached abutments useful for observation or flanking the base and slopes, had been carefully entrenched to form their first line. One could find every type of field fortification among the thirty-two works. The works were armed with 141 pieces in position, manned by 10,040 Portuguese troops; and they were surrounded by with unattached militia and a multitude of ordenanza.[6] Finally the first line was defended more particularly by the English army.[7]

In his report to Masséna, he described the terrain around Sobral similar to that of the Busaco Ridge. 'The mountains on which we find the principal work of the enemy rises before Sobral as that of Bussaco above Moura.'[8]

Wellington's plan was to man the forts with Portuguese militia and keep the British and Portuguese regulars as mobile reserves that could be moved quickly to reinforce any threatened area, the idea being that the French would take heavy casualties attacking the fortified positions and should they break through they would be easily defeated by the British and Portuguese army.

---

6. The ordenanza was similar to a peasant levy. Every able-bodied male was required to enroll in it. They were called out to defend the country when invaded. The best men would eventually go into the militia and from there into the army. The ordenanza were armed with personal weapons and whatever could be spared from the militia and the regular army. Rawkins. William, *The Army of Portugal 1793 – 1814*. eBook. Maidenhead: History Bookman, 2017, p.108.

7. Pelet, pp.224–5.

8. Ibid., p.230. 'Report to Masséna dated 7:00 p.m., 13 October 1810'.

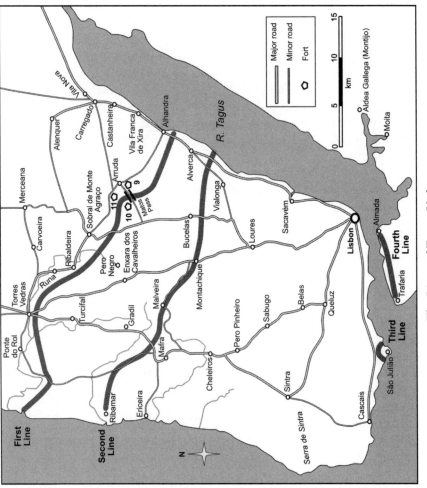

The Lines of Torres Vedras.

Wellington's Plans for the Light Division

Wellington knew where he wanted the Light Division positioned within the Lines, prior to their arrival at Arruda. They would be in the centre between Sobral and Arruda. To their right would be Lieutenant General Rowland Hill's 2nd Division, which had the responsibility for securing the right flank of the Lines. To the left of the Light Division would be General Pack's Portuguese brigade.

In a letter dated 11 October 1810, Wellington laid out his concept of what he wanted the Light Division to do.

> The paved road which leads through Aruda [sic] passes on to Alhandra,[9] in front, and under fire of the Serra of Alhandra; there are roads of communication with this road on its left, going to Alhandra, with Villa Franca,[10] and I believe Castaneira,[11] but these are at present impracticable; and on its right with Loureiro[12] and Calhandria,[13] in the valley of Calhandriz, by which Hill's position on the Serra of Alhandra may be turned. These roads are, however, not paved, and are, of course, now impracticable, and there are redoubts upon the heights on both sides of the valley of Calhandriz, and the village itself is prepared.
>
> In the present state of the weather the enemy may certainly get light troops upon the paved road from Aruda to Alhandra, without passing through Aruda, but they positively cannot get guns there; and as the only paved or at all practicable road to Aruda, from this side of the river of Aruda, passes through Sobral, I hope that the point is, for the present at least, pretty secure.
>
> From this statement, however, you will see how important the situation of Aruda and the possession of the pass of Matos (which, by the by, itself turns Hill's position) are to our operations. Aruda itself, I do not think, could be held for any great length of time

---

9. Alhandra is about 10km to the southeast of Arruda and on the Tagus River.
10. Vila Franca de Xira is about 5km north of Alhandra along the Tagus River.
11. Castanheira do Ribatejo is 12km north of Alhandra along the Tagus River.
12. A small village about 500m from Calhandria.
13. Modern-day Calhandriz. It is 7km south of Arruda along Highway A10.

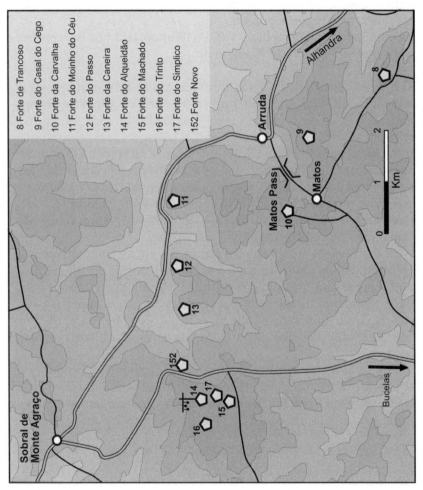

8 Forte de Trancoso
9 Forte do Casal do Cego
10 Forte da Carvalha
11 Forte do Moinho do Céu
12 Forte do Passo
13 Forte da Caneira
14 Forte do Alqueidão
15 Forte do Machado
16 Forte do Trinto
17 Forte do Simplico
152 Forte Novo

The Light Division's sector of the Lines of Torres Vedras.

against a superior force, but the pass of Matos can, defended as it is by the two redoubts.[14]

I understand from Fletcher also that the redoubts command the road going out of Aruda towards Alhandra. So that if you should find it most advantageous to give up Aruda, the enemy could not make much use of that road, at least by daylight.

I need say nothing to you about the defence of the pass of Matos. I think it would be desirable, however, that you should occupy, with the 52nd or 43rd, the high ground which continues from the right of the right hand redoubt, looking from Matos towards Aruda.

As soon as the attack upon Hill shall be absolutely decided, I shall move Sir B. Spencer's division upon St Iago dos Velhos,[15] about two or three miles to the south of Matos, on the road from Matos to Burcellas.[16] He will then occupy the heights of St. Romão[17] on your right, bringing his right to the redoubts which protect the left of the valley of Calhandriz. I do not like to move him yet however, because I will think it possible that the enemy may turn himself this way; and if he does, I have another arrangement prepared for him, upon which I shall write to you hereafter. I wish you, however, with a view to this arrangement, to look out for the roads of communication from Matos to the high road from Sobral to Bucellas.[18]

Initially the French movements in the vicinity of the Lines of Torres Vedras caused Wellington to send reminders to all of his division

---

14. The Pass of Matos is a narrow defile that leads from Arruda through the lines for about 1km to the southwest to the village of Mata. On a hill to the southwest, overlooking Mata, was Fort #10 Forte da Carvalho, armed with two 14-pounder guns and 400 militiamen. To the east of the pass was Fort #9 Forte do Casal do Cego, armed with three 9-pounder guns and 280 militiamen. Jones, John, *Journal of the Sieges Carried on by the Army under the Duke of Wellington between the Years 1811 & 1814*. 3 vols. Cambridge: Ken Trotman, 1998, Vol. 3, pp.94–5.
15. Santiago dos Velhos is about 5km south of Mata.
16. Bucelas is 15km south of Arruda.
17. São Romão is akm east of Santiago dos Velhos.
18. *WD*; Vol. 3, p.475.

commanders. For example on 17 October 1810 he wrote to General Craufurd:

> The positions which the enemy have taken up in our front and the measures which they are adopting to fortify themselves on our right, induce me to believe that their attack will be principally directed upon our right.
>
> I see that they have troops encamped on the heights above Villa Franca; and Hill[19] tells me, in a letter of last night, that, there were large fires on the heights near Alhandra, from which his piquets were obliged to withdraw in the evening.
>
> I have brought General Leith's division to the rear of this fort,[20] where part of it is encamped. General [William] Spry's Portuguese brigade will be cantoned this night in a village in the rear of the redoubts Nos. 12 and 13. The Hanoverian legion[21] are in the villages behind no. 11; to all of which the British brigades in General Leith's division will be a reserve.
>
> If the enemy should make their attack between this and Aruda, I think these arrangements will make us tolerably secure, and will give time to make a further movement of troops to the right. On the other hand, if he should make his attack upon the centre or left wing of the army, with all the troops in front of this place, I shall be able to transfer General Leith's division to be the reserve of the right of the centre, for which I originally intended him.
>
> The disposition which I have above described will show you what line I wish you to take. If the enemy attack Hill's right, and our line to the left of this redoubt, my intention is to employ you in an offensive movement. If they attack Hill's left, by Trancoso[22] or the valley of Calhandriz, and at the same time the ground on the right of this redoubt, I should prefer that you should look to Hill, rather than to the redoubts Nos. 11, 12,

---

19. Lieutenant General Hill, the commander of the 2nd Division.
20. The Great Redoubt at Sobral.
21. The King's German Legion, not the Hanoverian Legion that was in General Loison's Division of the French 6th Corps.
22. Trancoso de Baixo, about 5km south of Arruda.

and 13.[23] It would be necessary, however, for you to observe the ground between Nos. 10 and 11.[24]

However, as the days went by and it became apparent that Masséna had no intention of attacking the Lines, the number of letters written to Craufurd by Wellington tapered off.

Daily Life within the Lines of Torres Vedras

The Light Division did not remain very long in Arruda, because the town was outside the Lines. Tents were sent from Lisbon and the division went under canvas. These tents were Portuguese army ones and of poor quality. It was not until 2 November that 'English bell-tents arrived for the Light Division, to replace the poor and small Portuguese ones, which proved a great luxury'.[25] Each battalion was assigned a sector of the lines to outpost, with Arruda being in the centre of the picquet lines. The 43rd Foot's position was in the vicinity of Fort #10.[26] Every morning the division would form up and stand-to before sunrise.[27]

Picquet duty rotated between the companies and usually began at 11 a.m. and lasted 24 hours. The outposts changed every day due to probes by French. Lieutenant Oglander of the 43rd Foot wrote in his diary on 13 October that 'We relieved Capt [John] Swinburn's Company on picquet to the right of the town; we remained quiet till towards dark, when, on account of the French appearing in force & skirmishing with our picquets on the left, we were reinforced by Capt [William] Napier and a new arrangement for defence took place.'[28]

When not on picquet duty, the companies were sent to the different redoubts to improve the defences. Captain O'Hare's company of the 95th Rifles was attached to the 3rd Caçadores to dig defensive positions on the heights above Arruda, while the 52nd Foot was sent with

---

23. Respectively Forte Do Moinho do Céu, Forte Do Passo and Forte da Caneira.
24. *WD*, Vol. 3, pp.489–90.
25. Simmons, p.115.
26. I have not been able to identify where the other battalions' positions were.
27. Oglander, Diary entry for 18 October 1810.
28. Ibid., Diary entries for 13 and 14 October 1810.

entrenching tools to Fort #9 Forte do Casal do Cego.[29] Improving their positions never stopped. When one was considered done, the work parties were moved to another. By early November, work was switched from improving the redoubts to creating obstacles in the terrain behind their positions in the First Line. The Pass of Matos became the focus of the 43rd Foot, when on 1 November the battalion was moved there to create a double line of abattis.[30]

Fraternizing with the French

During the first few weeks in the Lines, the Light Division had occasional contact with French patrols and foragers. By late October, most contact had petered out because the farms and houses had been thoroughly picked over. Captain Leach noted that 'A wide open valley, which divided the pickets of the two armies, in the immediate front of the Light Division, the French frequently made foraging parties into; but after the first week, I do not believe as much provision could have been found for man or horse in the whole valley, as would have rationed half a squadron of Lilliputian cuirassiers for twenty-four hours.'[31]

Fraternizing between the armies was forbidden, and it appeared that when an officer was present, it was enforced. On 23 October, Lieutenant Simmons of the 95th Rifles had command of a picquet when he saw:

> Two French soldiers entered a house in our front. [Lieutenant John] Hopwood and myself with three men crawled from our post into an avenue of trees, which covered us from the immediate view of the French vedette posted on a little eminence to apprise his friends of any danger. We succeeded in entering the house unobserved, and surprised the two Frenchmen, who were filling some canteens with wine, but sprang to their arms. One of them snapped his firelock, but it did not go off. They were instantly taken from them. A moment after, one soldier offered me some brandy he had in a calabash slung across his shoulders. I gave both a large goblet of wine, sent a soldier to get all the canteens he could muster from the piquet and return, we keeping a good look-out. We filled sixty, then destroyed the

---

29. Simmons, p.112. Oglander, Diary entry for 18 October 1810.
30. Oglander, Diary entry for 1 November 1810.
31. Leach, *Rough Sketches . . .*, p.177.

hogshead,[32] took our prisoners to the piquet, and sent an escort with them to the General.[33]

When no officers were present, however, the picquets were friendlier. Rifleman Costello recalled that:

> It was a common thing for us to meet each other daily at the houses between our lines, when perhaps both parties would be in search of wine and food. In one of the houses so situated, I remember once finding Crawley[34] in a drunken state with a couple of French soldiers. I was mortified by the merriment his appearance had excited, and could with difficulty get him away, as he stripped, and offered to fight the whole three of us for laughing at him.[35]

French Deserters

As food and supplies became scarce for the French, the number of deserters appearing before the lines increased. Lieutenant Simmons captured a few and they 'informed us that the enemy were losing a number of men from disease, and that there was a great scarcity of provisions; that Colonel [Nicholas] Trant had assembled the Portuguese Militia in large force and had entered Coimbra, and had taken a number of sick and wounded officers and men and stopped the communications with Spain, cutting off the supply of provisions.'[36]

Maintenance of the Quarters

When not on duty, the officers tried to improve their quarters and to find things to do to relax and entertain themselves. It rained incessantly and they were

---

32. A hogshead can hold 238.7 litres or 63 gallons.
33. Simmons, p.113.
34. Private Thomas Crawley.
35. Costello, p.42.
36. Simmons, p.114.

seldom dry. . . between constantly strengthening our position; endeavouring to keep off agues by dint of cigars, and of such fluids as were sometimes attainable from the sutlers who paid us a visit from Lisbon; reconnoitring our French neighbours with telescopes; trying to keep our horses, mules, and donkeys alive during the inclement weather, with chopped straw, or what little herbage the hills afforded, with, now and then, a very diminutive allowance of barley or Indian corn; and the occasional arrival of letters and newspapers from England – we passed some five or six weeks, wondering whether Massena would attack us, or walk away from our front.[37]

Maintaining their quarters was a constant struggle due to the rain, which continued almost the whole time they were in the Lines. Many officers abandoned the tents for better accommodation, but at times they must have questioned this decision. Lieutenant Oglander thought he had built a very good hut, but after a night of rain, part of it collapsed.[38] Lieutenant William Freer of the 43rd Foot and his messmates built a turf house complete with glass windows and a fireplace.[39] Lieutenant Kincaid and his friends found a cattle shed

which we cleaned out, and used as a sort of quarter. On turning out from breakfast one morning, we found that the butcher had been about to offer up the usual sacrifice of a bullock to the wants of the day; but it had broken loose, and, in trying to regain his victim, had caught it by the tail, which he twisted round his hand; and, when we made our appearance, they were performing a variety of evolutions at a gallop, to the great amusement of the soldiers; until an unlucky turn brought them down upon our house, which had been excavated out of the face of the hill, on which the upper part of the roof rested, and in they went, heels over head, butcher, bullock, tail and all, bearing down the whole fabric with a tremendous crash. It was very fortunate that we happened to be outside; and very unfortunate, as were now obliged to remain out.[40]

---

37. Leach, *Rough Sketches. . .*, pp.176–7.
38. Oglander, Diary entry dated 29 October 1810.
39. Freer, William, unpublished letter dated 10 November 1810.
40. Kincaid, *Adventures. . .*, pp.27–8.

Much to the chagrin of the officers, their billets changed on a regular basis. On 6 November, the 43rd Foot was ordered to abandon their encampment on high ground and moved into the Pass of Matos. It meant that they moved from relatively dry quarters into 'wet ground, pitching out tents in the rain and leaving behind us all the comforts which a few days quiet had enabled us to obtain'. They remained in the wet lowlands for five days before being allowed to return to their former billets. No reason was given for their move.[41]

Free Time

Lieutenants Kincaid, Simmons, and John Strode spent their time off duty exploring Arruda. Once they looked

> into the church, which was in nowise injured, and was fitted up in a style of magnificence becoming such a town. The body of a poor old woman was there, lying dead before the altar. It seemed as if she had been too infirm to join in the general flight, and had just dragged herself to that spot by a last effort of nature, and expired. We immediately determined, that as hers was the only body that we had found in the town, either alive or dead, that she should have more glory in the grave than she appeared to have enjoyed on this side of it; and, with our united exertions, we succeeded in raising a marble slab, which surmounted a monumental vault, and was beautifully embellished with armorial blazonry, and depositing the body inside, we replaced it again carefully. If the personage to whom it belonged happened to have a tenant of his own for it soon afterwards, he must have been rather astonished at the manner in which the apartment was occupied.[42]

In early November, Wellington issued an invitation to all the officers in the army to attend a party to celebrate Marshal Beresford's investiture as a Knight of the Bath. The party was held at the Mafra Palace, about 45km from Arruda. Some officers from the Light Division attended. Captain Henry Mellish, who was sick in Lisbon, received a copy of the invitation but decided not to attend.

---

41. Oglander, Diary entries dated 6 & 11 November 1810.
42. Kincaid, *Adventures. . .*, pp.25–6. Simmons, p.113.

> Lord Wellington will be happy to see such officers of the Army as can make it convenient to come to a Dinner & Ball at Mafra when he proposes to invest Marshal Beresford with the order of the Bath. He requests the General Officers comg Divisions of the Army will make arrangements that a major general & a sufficient number of officers for the Duty of the Division may remain with each. As Lord W intends returning at night to his Quarters at Pero Negro he trusts all other officers will do the same.[43]

Captain Mellish was amazed at these arrangements and wondered what would have happened if the French had attacked.

> By this arrangement no harm can happen in the event of a night attack & indeed at Mafra he is scarcely further from the lines than at Pero Negro. It would be rather entertaining if there should be an alarm & the knights, red ribbon & all were obliged to take to horse in the middle of the first dance. It is expected to be very splendid. I shall not go.[44]

Wellington did not anticipate the large number of officers and civilians who would attend and it was not the dignified affair that one would have expected. Lieutenant Freer had picquet duty that night, otherwise he would have gone. He did talk to those who went and it

> was attended by several hundred officers both British & Portuguese but the wording [of] the invitation misled several of the visitants who went off expecting it was a dinner party they waited and waited till two o'clock in the morning thinking dinner a long time coming & when nearly starved to death they were ushered into the supper room and the bolting occasioned by their long fast no doubt astonished his Lordship. The supper was not long disappearing.[45]

While the gala at Mafra was the exception, the officers and men found amusements wherever they could. Lieutenant Harry Smith and Colonel Beckwith were observing work being done on their positions when

---

43. Mellish,Henry, unpublished letter dated 22 November 1810.

44. Ibid.

45. Freer, William, unpublished letter dated 10 November 1810.

. . . it came on to rain, and we saw a Rifleman rolling down a wine-cask, apparently empty, from a house near. He deliberately knocked in one of the heads; then – for it was on the side of a rapidly shelving hill – propped it up with stones, and crept in out of the rain. Colonel Beckwith says, 'Oh, look at the lazy fellow; he has not half supported it. When he falls asleep, if he turns around, down it will come.' Our curiosity was excited, and our time anything but occupied, so we watched our friend, when in about twenty minutes the cask with the man inside came rolling down the hill. He must have rolled over twenty times at least before the rapidity disengaged him from his round-house, and even afterwards, such was the impetus, he rolled over several times. To refrain from laughing excessively was impossible though we really thought the noble fellow must be hurt, when up he jumped, looked round and said 'I never had any affection for an empty wine-cask, and may the devil take me if ever I go near another – to be whirled round like a water-mill in this manner!' The fellow was in a violent John Bull passion, while we were nearly killed with laughing.[46]

Some officers took the time to visit friends and relatives in other divisions. Lieutenant Simmons rode one day to visit his brother Joseph, who was in the 23rd Foot and billeted in Bucelas, which was about 10km away. 'He was delighted to see me, little expecting, from accounts he had received, to shake me by the hand again. I dined with him, spent the day; he would give me a bottle of cherry brandy.'[47]

Free Time for the Other Ranks

Although much time was spent on picquet and guard duty, building fortifications and maintenance of their equipment and uniforms, the other ranks did have time when they were not closely supervised. Much time was spent in unauthorized foraging for alcohol and searching for items that could be converted into money or exchanged for food, alcohol or a woman. Lieutenant Kincaid recalled observing one such incident.

---

46. Smith, pp.36–7.
47. Simmons, p.121.

While we remained in the lines, there was a small, thatched, mud-walled, deserted cottage under the hill near our company's post, which we occasionally used as a shelter from the sun or the rain, and some of our men in prowling about one day discovered two massive silver salvers[48] concealed in the thatch. The captain of the company very properly ordered them to be taken care of, in the hope that their owner would come to claim them, while the soldiers in the meantime continued very eager in their researches in the neighbourhood, in expectations of making further discoveries, in which however they were unsuccessful. After we had altogether abandoned the cottage, a Portuguese gentleman arrived one day and told us that he was the owner of the place, and that he had some plate concealed there which he wished permission to remover. Captain ---- immediately desired the salvers to be given to him, concluding that they were what he had come in search of, but on looking at them he said that they did not belong to him, that what he wished to remove was concealed under the dunghill, and he accordingly proceeded there and dug out about a cartload of gold and silver articles which he carried off, while our unsuccessful searchers stood by, cursing their mutual understandings which had suffered such a prize to slip through their fingers, and many an innocent heap of manure was afterwards torn to pieces in consequence of that morning's lesson.[49]

The Destruction of Arruda

'This was the only instance during the war in which the light division had reason to blush for their conduct. . .'
Lieutenant John Kincaid, 95th Rifles[50]

Although the Light Division was not billeted in Arruda because it was outside the Lines of Torres Vedras, it was used as their base of operations during their time there. Lieutenant Fergusson of the 43rd Foot described it as a 'pretty little town of Aruda was beautifully situated,

---

48. A flat tray.
49. Kincaid, *Random Shots . . .*, pp.60–1.
50. Kincaid, *Adventures . . .*, p.25.

and a favourite retreat of the rich merchants of Lisbon – their quintas being splendidly furnished, and made as luxurious as possible. It was altogether a little paradise. . .'[51] It would not be so for long.

The town appeared to be deserted when the Light Division entered it and the officers and men of the division decided to take what they could to make their life easier. Captain Leach observed that 'Never was a town more completely deserted than Arruda. The inhabitants, dreading the approach of the French, had taken flight to Lisbon, leaving their houses, many of which were magnificently furnished, without a human in them. The chairs and tables were subsequently carried up to the camp, which was formed on the fortified ridge of hills running from the Tagus to the sea. . . and they proved highly useful to us in our canvass habitations.'[52]

Lieutenant Kincaid provided more detail about what they did.

> Like all other places on the line of march we found Arruda totally deserted, and its inhabitants had fled in such a hurry, that the keys of their house doors were the only things they carried away; so that when we got admission, through our usual key,[53] we were not a little gratified to find that the houses were not only regularly furnished, but most of them had some food in the larder, and a plentiful supply of good wines in the cellar . . . Unfortunately for ourselves, and still more so for the proprietors, we never dreamt of the possibility of our being able to keep possession of the town, as we thought it a matter of course that the enemy would attack our lines; and, as this was only an outpost, that it must fall into their hands; so that, in conformity with the system upon which we had all along been retreating, we destroyed every thing that we could not use ourselves, to prevent their benefiting by it. But, when we continued to hold the post beyond the expected period, our indiscretion was visited on our own heads, as we had destroyed in a day what would have made us luxurious for months . . .
>
> In very warm or very wet weather it was customary to put us under cover in the town during the day, but we were always

---

51. Levine, p.139.
52. Leach, *Rough Sketches* . . ., p.174.
53. 'Transmitting a rifle-ball through the key-hole: it opens every lock.' Kincaid, *Adventures* . . ., p.23.

moved back to our bivouac, on the heights, during the night; and it was rather amusing to observe the different notions of individual comfort, in the selection of furniture, which officers transferred from their town house to their no house on the heights. A sofa, or a mattress, one would have thought most likely to be put in requisition; but it was not unusual to see a full-length looking-glass preferred to either.[54]

Rifleman Costello told of how they kept their picquet fires going.

For a few days after our arrival, it presented a picture of most wanton desolation. Furniture of a more splendid description in many instances was laid open to the spoliation of the soldiery. Elegant looking-glasses wrenched from the mantelpieces were wantonly broken to obtain bits to shave by, and their encasures [*sic*], with chairs, tables, &c. &c., used as common firewood for the picquets. . . the philosophical reader will perhaps admit of the plea, that if we had not, the French would have done it for us, an event which we expected, though it fortunately never was realized.

Tom Crawley was particularly pre-eminent in this havoc; his enormous strength and length fitting him especially for the pulling down and 'breaking up' department.

Our company was one night on picquet at Arruda; we had, as usual, made a blazing fire close to the stable of a very large house, which in the morning we had noticed contained a very handsome carriage. . . Rather late in the evening we missed Tom – who, by the way, had a great love of exploring the houses of the village, and whom we imagined to be employed in his favourite amusement 'looking for wine'. After having consumed sundry chairs to keep alive our fire, we found it necessary to obtain fresh fuel, and while consulting where it was to come from, one man, with an oath, proposed to burn the Portuguese coach. The novelty of the thing among our thoughtless fellows was received with acclamations, and as our officers were absent in a house close by, several started up on their legs for the purpose. The stable-doors were immediately opened, and the coach wheeled backwards into the large blazing fire. 'This

---

54. Kincaid, *Adventures . . .*, pp.23, 24 & 27.

will make a jolly roast!' exclaimed several of the men, as the paint and paneling began to crack under the influence of the heat. Our scamps were laughing and enjoying what they called a capital joke, but just as the flames were beginning to curl up around the devoted vehicle, a roar like that of a bull came from its interior, and threw us for a moment into consternation; immediately afterwards one of the glasses was dashed out, and Tom Crawley's big head was thrust through the window, amid shouts of laughter from the men, as he cried out—'Oh bad luck to your sowls [sic]! Are you going to burn me alive?' At the same moment, urged powerfully by the heat of his berth, he made the most violent efforts to open the door, which from the handle being heated, was a difficult and painful operation. We had some trouble ere we could extricate the poor fellow, and then not before he was severely scorched. It afterwards appeared he had gone half tipsy into the carriage, and was taking a snooze, when he was so warmly awoke. After this occurrence, Crawley used to boast of going to sleep with one eye open.[55]

By 12 November, the town had been thoroughly looted. Lieutenant Oglander claims that it was not just the Light Division who was involved and blamed General Craufurd for not taking steps to prevent it.

The state of the town of Arruda on our return was shameful to the English whose character thereby will probably suffer in the opinion of the Portuguese, tho the blame certainly attaches but to one individual. Every article of furniture had either been removed from the houses or had been destroyed. The system of plunder had even been carried to such an extent that in some houses not a window or door remained. The depredations were carried on by Portuguese of all Regts who were allowed to take what they chose and also by countrymen, who came under pretence of removing property by the direction of the owners, but who were frequently robbers that converted the whole to their own use and emolument. Even worse than this,

---

55. Costello, pp.41–2. Rifleman Crawley was in Captain O'Hare's No. 3 Company, the same as Rifleman Costello. He was hospitalized from 22–24 October 1810. Whether it was for his burns or something else, is not recorded.

the soldiers both of the cavalry and infantry were permitted without any restraint to enter the houses and by their wantonness a great deal of valuable property was destroyed. General C. might easily have prevented this by directing the picquets to furnish patrols to prevent the removal or destruction of any thing whatever; and the duty would not have been any hardship to the men, as there was till very lately, a cmpy [sic] stationed in the town to the right, which only furnished one double sentry.[56]

The extent of the destruction hit many of the officers and soon they were wondering how they would justify it if word got out. 'We were in hopes that, afterwards, the enemy would have forced the post, if only for an hour, so that we might have saddled them with the mischief; but, as they never even made the attempt, it left it in the power of ill-natured people to say, that we plundered one of our own towns . . . and even in that we had the law martial on our side, whatever gospel law might have said against it.'[57] This seemed to be a common theme, for Lieutenant Fergusson, said it also. 'It was plundered, burnt, and utterly destroyed; all the valuable furniture of the houses thrown into the picket fires, to the disgrace of our army; but unfortunately we did not permit the enemy to get possession of it, even for a moment to have shared the stigma.'[58]

Enforcement of Discipline

General Craufurd never let up on his high standards and expected his officers to adhere to them, regardless of the situation. Lieutenant Oglander ran afoul of him on 16 October and was placed under arrest for what he thought was a trivial offence.

Moved early in the morning from Arruda to a spot on the hill about ½ mile beyond the village of Matta [Mata]. In the morning the compy went to reinforce the outlying picquet but after remaining with it about ¼ of an hour, it was ordered to collect all the intrenching tools in the quarters of the Regt and proceed with them to join it. During our march, the rain fell

---

56. Oglander, Diary entry dated 12 November 1810.
57. Kincaid, *Adventures. . .*, pp.2–5.
58. Levine, p.139.

in torrents. In marching off the Compy this evening I omitted to give the word of Shoulder, which the general observing, he ordered the command to be taken from me and also put me under arrest. It is to be observed, that he was then in a great passion (occasioned probably by the French having effected a reconnaissance of force of our position)[59] and when he is in that state, his spleen must find a vent somewhere! Woe to the man who first comes within his reach![60]

The lieutenant was kept under arrest for six days, essentially confined to his quarters. He was not allowed to go on picquet duty or supervise work parties. Oglander was furious with Craufurd and lost all respect for him. On 22 October:

The General thought proper to release me this evening alleging as a reason for having put me under arrest, that he was determined not to overlook the smallest faults the better to support that system of discipline, which he had been at such pains to establish in his English brigade.!!! Thrice admirable. This system, the merit to establishing which he so boldly arrogate to himself, originated with Sir John Moore, beyond all comparison his superior in every respect; unless indeed, he means certain voluminous regulations of his making, many of which are impracticable, more frivolous, and few good. But if he meant these rules, he contradicted himself, as he asserted at the time, that he put me under arrest to shew his determination to support his majesty's regulations, which I had broken through by omitting the word to Shoulder. But be this as it may; his correction of my omission affords a convincing proof of the folly of visiting the most trifling faults with severe corrections. In my case, he could only have had recourse to a Court martial though I might have offended in a hundred times higher degree. An arrest which might only to be used in cases of an aggravated nature is considered ridiculous by his injudicious application of it. Numbers of officers have been put under arrest by him; of which only one was brought to a court martial, and he was honourably acquitted.[61]

---

59. This reconnaissance occurred on 13 October 1810.
60. Oglander, Diary entry 16 October 1810.
61. Ibid., Diary entries for 21 and 22 October 1810.

Changes in the Light Division

Upon linking up with the 1st Brigade on 10 October, Lieutenant Harry Smith met with his brigade commander, Lieutenant Colonel Beckwith who told him. "'You are a mad fool of a boy, coming here with a ball in your leg. Can you dance?" "No, I can hardly walk but with my toe turned out." "Can you be my A.D.C.?" "Yes; I can ride and eat . . .'"[62] Thus the lieutenant joined his brigade commander's staff as his unofficial ADC.[63]

Lieutenant Colonel Barclay's light wound refused to heal properly and by the time the Light Division reached the Lines of Torres Vedras it was badly infected. He was forced to return to England in mid-October to recover.[64] The 2nd Brigade needed a new commander. The only possible candidate within the division was Charles M'Cleod who had been promoted to lieutenant colonel on 16 August, but he was too junior to be given command of a brigade.[65] Wellington knew that he had gotten away with giving the brigades to lieutenant colonels in August, but several colonels had recently arrived in the Peninsula, among them Brevet Colonel James Wynch, the commander of the 4th Foot. Upon his arrival in Portugal in late October, he became the senior colonel who was not commanding a brigade. He had been seriously wounded in the Den Helder Campaign of 1799, shot through the body at Corunna on 16 January 1809 and, despite his wound having not fully healed, participated in the Walcheren Campaign later in the year. As the commander of the 4th Foot, he and his battalion had been trained to be light infantry by Sir John Moore at Shorncliffe and Hythe in 1803 and 1804.[66] The only possible drawback for him taking command of the 2nd Brigade was that he had still not fully recovered from the wound he received at Corunna the year before.[67] On 14 November, Colonel Wynch was appointed the commander of the 2nd Brigade.[68]

---

62. Smith, p.35.
63. Only general officers were authorized an ADC. LTC Beckwith was responsible for providing him with a billet, forage and rations.
64. Lieutenant Colonel Barclay was in Portsmouth by 29 October 1810. *London Chronicle*, 29 October 1810, p.416.
65. An infantry brigade was authorized a major general as its commander.
66. The 43rd and 52nd Foot, as well as the 95th Rifles, went through the same training with them.
67. *Gentleman's Magazine*, February 1811, p.188.
68. General Orders; dated 14 November 1810.

Once within the safety of the Lines of Torres Vedras, Craufurd wrote to Wellington about expanding the Light Division. But again Wellington was faced with the problem that Craufurd was only a brigadier general. He had seven major generals who were either on the staff or commanding brigades.[69] All of them had a valid claim to the command of the Light Division, by rights of seniority. Wellington wrote to him on 23 October that 'I should be happy to make your division stronger, and I have had in contemplation various modes of effecting that object; but you must see the difficulty which is created by the arrival of General Officers, of rank superior to yours. However, I hope that I shall be able, in some manner, to increase your force.'[70]

Wellington did not forget his promise and on 12 November wrote again to General Craufurd and offered him the Brunswick Oëls Battalion.

> I have been thinking for some time of reinforcing your division, and you see what I have been able to do in this way this day. The truth is, that if I should make you as strong as I could wish, there will be other claimants for the command of the division; and I think it much better to keep a Portuguese brigade in reserve and unattached, to be attached to you when it is necessary to reinforce you, than to place one permanently under your command which would give claims to others.[71]
>
> In the mean time I wish to know from you in what manner you will dispose of the Brunswick Light Infantry between your brigades, that I may put your distribution of them in orders.[72]

---

69. Charles Colville, James Dunlop, Daniel Hoghton, Sigismund von Low, William Lumley, John Sontag and Charles Stewart.
70. *WD*, Vol. 3, pp.503–04.
71. Wellington never said which brigade he was thinking about. It was likely General Pack's Independent Brigade consisting of the 1st and 16th Line Regiments and the 4th Caçadores. This brigade was just to the right of the Light Division at Busaco, and preceded them during the retreat to Torres Vedras. At the time they were the next unit over on the left of the Light Division in the Lines of Torres Vedras. General Pack was also junior to General Craufurd, which would forestall any questions on seniority.
72. *WD*, Vol. 3, p.580.

However, there was a slight catch. The Brunswick Oëls were authorized twelve companies of light infantry, but the Light Division would only get nine of them,[73] or about 500 other ranks. These were the 1st, 4th, 5th, 6th, 7th, 8th, 9th, 11th and 12th Companies The other three companies were assigned to different divisions.[74] The Brunswickers were assigned to the 2nd Brigade.[75]

The Brunswick Oëls were raised in 1809 by Frederick William, Duke of Brunswick. He had been deposed by Napoleon in 1806, when his lands were incorporated into the Kingdom of Westphalia. He reached an agreement with the Austrians to raise a Brunswick Corps to support them in their invasion of central Germany in April 1809. After the defeat of the Austrians by Napoleon in July 1809, the Duke of Brunswick retreated with his corps through Germany to the north, where they were evacuated by the Royal Navy. He offered his services to the British government. The infantry were formed into the Brunswick Oëls Jägers,[76] while the cavalry were called the Brunswick Oëls Hussars. They disembarked in Portugal in October 1810 and were initially assigned to the 4th Division.[77]

Initially, all of the officers in the Brunswick Oëls were German and this presented a language problem. When the regiment arrived in Lisbon, Lieutenant Ernest Olfermann of the 97th Foot, a German officer who was fluent in English, was assigned to them as their Brigade Major. In a letter dated 14 October 1810, his duties were explained to him by Major General Charles Stewart, the Adjutant General of the Army: '. . . if you act as a Brigade-Major to the latter corps, explaining to them such instructions as the Colonel commanding may think proper to issue, as also pointing out to them the states and returns they are to furnish this department

---

73. von Kortzfleisch, Gustav, *Geschichte des Herzoglich Braunschweigischen Infanterie–Regiments und seiner Stammtruppen 1809–1867*. Braunschweig: Albert Limbach, 1896. Vol. 1, p.158.
74. General Orders, dated 12 November 1810. The 3rd Company went to Colonel Edward Pakenham's Brigade in the 4th Division. In the 5th Division, Major-General Dunlop's Brigade received Company No. 2, while Company No. 10 went to Brigadier General Andrew Hay's Brigade.
75. Ibid., dated 16 November 1810.
76. The regiment was usually called the Brunswick Oëls and quickly picked up the nickname 'The Owls'.
77. Haythornthwaite, Philip, *The Napoleonic Source Book*. New York: Facts on File, 1990, pp.147–8.

Table 14.1: Organization of the Light Division, 14 November 1810

Division HQ	Brigadier General Robert Craufurd	Commander
	Captain William Campbell 23rd Foot	ADC
	Captain Henry Mellish 87th Foot	DAAG
	Lieutenant John Bell 52nd Foot	DAQMG
	Charles Purcell	ACG
1st Brigade	LTC Thomas Beckwith	Commander
	Lieutenant Harry Smith 95th Rifles	Unofficial ADC
	LT. James Stewart 95th Rifles	Brigade Major
1st Bn 43rd Foot	LTC Charles McLeod	Commander
Right Wing 95th Rifles	Major Dugald Gilmour	Commander
Company 2nd Bn 95th Rifles	Captain Charles Beckwith	Commander
Company 3rd Bn 95th Rifles	Captain William Percival	Commander
3rd Caçadores Bn	LTC George Elder	Commander
2nd Brigade	Colonel James Wynch	Commander
	Captain Charles Rowan 52nd Foot	Brigade Major
1st Bn 52nd Foot	Major Hugh Arbuthnott	Commander
Left Wing 95th Rifles	Major John Stewart	Commander
1st Caçadores Battalion	LTC Jorge de Avilez	Commander
Brunswick Oëls	LTC Georg de Korfes	Commander

with from time to time, his Excellency will take a proper opportunity of taking your services into consideration.'[78] When the Brunswick Oëls were assigned to the Light Division, Lieutenant Olfermann went with them.[79]

After the Light Division arrived in the Lines of Torres Vedras, they were reinforced with Captain William Percival's company from the 3rd Battalion 95th Rifles. It was stationed at Cadiz, but came to Portugal at Wellington's request. It disembarked in Lisbon about the time the Light Division was nearing Arruda. Captain Percival and his company were on its way to join them and were at Sobral, when they were shanghaied by Lieutenant General Spencer, the commander of

---

78. *WSD*, Vol. 13, pp.471–2.
79. General Orders, dated 12 November 1810.

the 1st Division. They were part of the attack on the advanced guard of Junot's corps. The fighting was heavy and mostly among the light troops. Captain Percival's company took many casualties.[80] Lieutenant Charles Eeles 'was shot through the body and put on the road to Lisbon; also Captain Percival, who commanded the company shot through the wrist. The 3rd Battalion Company behaved like Rifle Men and were complimented . . .'[81]

---

80. Verner, Vol. 2, p.167. The 24 October 1810 returns showed twenty-nine other ranks listed as sick and two dead. The dead were probably casualties from the fight. I have been unable to determine if the other twenty-nine were wounded or ill.

81. Simmons, p.112.

Chapter 15

The Pursuit of the French to Santarém, 15 November–31 December 1810

Sunrise on the morning of 15 November was at 6:40 a.m. The temperature had dropped overnight and the colder night air passing over the wet ground had produced a dense fog. Visibility of the French positions was obscured. Around 10 a.m. the fog had lifted and Captain Leach and his riflemen who

> happened to be on picket in front of Arruda on the night of the 14th; and looking as usual, with our eyes, in the twilight of the following morning, towards our opponents, the French sentries, we thought could be discovered as heretofore; but when day broke thoroughly, we found that the cunning rogues had played us an old trick of theirs, by placing figures of straw upright, with a soldier's cap on each, and a pole by the side to represent a musket. Their whole army had retired, during the night, in the direction of Santarem . . .[1]

Word reached Wellington at Sobral, who rode there every morning, and he wrote a dispatch to General Craufurd at 10:20 a.m. explaining what he wanted the Light Division to do.

> You will observe that the enemy have retired from the ground they occupied with their right, about Sobral, and I think it most

---

1.   Leach, *Rough Sketches . . .*, p.177.

probable that they will have retired their whole army towards Santarem.

Sir B. Spencer's division[2] is now feeling its way on towards Alemquer, and a patrole of our cavalry is just gone to the wood in front of No. 11.[3]

If you should find that the enemy have retired their left, as well as their right, I beg you to cross the river at Aruda [sic], and feel your way on towards Alemquer, by the direct road leading from Aruda.

Send this note on to General Hill, by the direct communication from Aruda [sic] to Alhandra. I wish him to feel his way on by the high road to Villa Franca and Castanheira, to Carregado, with the advanced guard of his corps.

I shall soon have some British cavalry at Sobral and Alemquer, and General Hill had better get some of the 13th Light Dragoons from St. Antonio de Tojal, to observe in his front.

We must make our first movements with caution, as I heard last night that the enemy had a reinforcement[4] on the frontier of Upper Beira[5] on the 9th.[6]

It is unclear when the dispatch reached the Light Division's HQ or where Craufurd was when it arrived. Furthermore, although the distance was less than 15km, Wellington might not have had an ADC to take the message immediately. It probably did not reach the Light Division HQ before noon. There is no evidence that Craufurd was there to read it, because he was not one to sit around his headquarters. He was likely on the road visiting his subordinates at the time. What we do know is that Lieutenant Harry Smith, who was serving as Lieutenant Colonel

2. The 1st Division.
3. Redoubt #11.
4. This would have been Lieutenant General Jean-Baptiste Drouet's 9th Corps of about 12,000 men. How accurate Wellington's information was is open to question. Chef-de-Bataillon Pelet, Masséna's ADC, claimed that about this time, a British officer came under a flag of truce and 'asked if Drouet's corps had arrived at Sabugal, in order to learn no doubt if we had any news.' Pelet, p.299.
5. Modern-day Beira Alta, the area in the vicinity of Viseu, Guarda and Coimbra.
6. WD, Vol. 6, pp.594–5.

Beckwith's unofficial ADC, was there. Sometime in mid-afternoon he was ordered to ride the 15km to General Hill's HQ at Sobralihno[7] with a copy of the dispatch. When Lieutenant Smith arrived there is unknown, but it was late in the afternoon. He wrote about his ride several years later.

> This dispatch I was doomed to carry. It was one of the utmost importance, and required a gallop. By Jove, I had ten miles to go just before dark, and when I got to Colborne's[8] position, who had a Brigade under Lord Hill, a mouse could not get through his works. . . Such a job I never had. I could not go in front of the works – the French had not retired; so some works I leaped into, and led my noble English horse into others. At last I got to Lord Hill, and he marched immediately, night as it was. How I got back to my Division through the night I hardly know, but horse and rider were both done . . .[9]

Wellington did not wait to see if Craufurd had received his orders and rode to the heights just south of Alemquer to assess the situation. At this point it was just him and his retinue of a few ADCs and an orderly. He sent another dispatch to Craufurd at 3:15 p.m. clarifying his original orders.

> I enclose a letter in triplicate, which I wrote you this morning, and I hope that somebody at Aruda will have opened it, and will have acted upon it in your absence. You see the enemy at Villa Nova, I conclude, and I request you to communicate with the officer in command of General Hill's outposts, who will, I hope,

---

7. Hill, Rowland, *Lord Hill's Letters from the Peninsula*. Darlington: Napoleonic Archive, ND, pp.12–13. The letters state that it was written from Lobral Pequeña, but there is no village by that name. Sobralihno is located about 1.5km southwest of Alhandra. 'Ihno' is a Portuguese suffix meaning little/small in English. Pequeña also means small in Portuguese.
8. Lieutenant Colonel John Colborne of the 66th Foot was the acting commander of the 1st Brigade, 2nd Division.
9. Smith, p.37. There is an element of truth in Lieutenant Smith's account. Sunset was at 4:49 p.m. and the moonrise was at 8:31 p.m. This might explain Wellington's frustration on arriving at Alemquer and not finding General Hill's troops.

be this night at Carregado. In the morning I wish you to feel your way cautiously to Villa Nova, and thence on the road to Santarem.

I shall move General Spencer's division in the morning to Alemquer, and General Hill's Corps I shall close up on the high road along the Tagus. I shall be up here very early in the morning.[10]

When word reached the Light Division's HQ that the French positions appeared to be abandoned, Craufurd issued a warning order that the division was to be ready to march at a moment's notice. However, as pointed out above, the order to advance was slow in coming. It was after 3 p.m. before the Light Division began its march. The division went north through the Lines and marched 15km to Alemquer. It was not the orderly movement that the division was known for. Part of the problem with the march was that the Light Division had to make their way through the obstacles that had been built to keep the French from marching south. Lieutenant Oglander described in his diary how

the 1st Brigade marched and was followed by the 2nd. After the 1st Brigade had marched about 2 miles, it was halted to wait the coming up of the 2nd and on moving forward, darkness came on, by which we lost our road several times and the division was only kept together by sounding the bugles many part of it separated. We passed in the dark through a deserted camp and halted next to the road a within a mile of Alemquer. This night the whole division bivouacked. It fortunately was remarkably fine and warm; we therefore passed it without much inconvenience.[11]

The day's march took them through the positions that had been occupied by the French. Lieutenant Simmons of the 95th Rifles took the opportunity to examine them and was shocked by what he found. They were 'in a most filthy state, and in several huts I found dead men who had fallen victims to the inclement weather'.[12] In the following days he would find far worse. He wrote a graphic description of the destruction in Alenquer to his parents a month later that:

---

10. WD, Vol. 6, pp.595–6.
11. Oglander, Diary entry for 15 November 1810.
12. Simmons, p.115.

The first night we passed through several French camps and found a number of dead bodies. We halted near a large village, and lay down for the night in the fields. In the morning we marched through a place, Alenquer, which was entirely sacked by the enemy, the windows and doors torn down and burnt, as well as most of the furniture in each house, beautiful china, pier-glasses and chandeliers all dashed to pieces, and every kind of devastation that is possible for savages to be guilty of. They had left numbers of miserable objects behind them in the houses, that were so ill as not to be able to march; these were of course put to death by the Portuguese when we happened to miss finding them out.[13]

The next morning they marched at daybreak[14] heading to Vila Nova via Carregada and then to Azambuja. The French tried to destroy the bridge at Vila Nova, but had to retreat as the Light Division came up. The Light Division made it to Azambuja around 1:30 p.m. after a march of 20km.[15] The countryside and villages they passed were devastated by the French. Captain Leach wrote that:

The road from Alemquer to Azimbjua was covered with horses, mules, and asses, belonging to the French, which had died from want of forage. We passed many French soldiers lying dead by the road-side, whose appearance indicated that disease and want of food had carried them off. Every house in every town or village which lay in their line of retreat was thoroughly ransacked. Desolation and devastation marked their track.[16]

Lieutenant Oglander noted that '. . . the number of dead animals was astonishing and especially disgusting. Part of them must have died during the advance of the French Army . . . The towns which had been occupied by the enemy were very much injured. Some houses

---

13. Ibid., pp.121–2. Letter to his parents dated 16 December 1810. His outrage is a bit hypocritical considering the damage done to Arruda by the Light Division.
14. Sunrise was at 6:41 a.m.
15. Oglander, Diary entry for 16 November 1810. Simmons, p.115.
16. Leach, *Rough Sketches. . .*, p.179.

were quite destroyed; others completely gutted, and very few had any furniture left in them. They were also in general excessively filthy.'[17] Lieutenant Simmons recorded in his diary that 'We took a number of stragglers this day who had been suffering sadly from starvation and disease. The road was found strewn with rags and pieces of Frenchmen's appointments and caps, and occasionally a dead horse, mule, or jackass to enliven the scene.'[18]

That night it began to rain heavily and the weather would be bad for almost the rest of the year. The next day, 17 November, the Light Division was up well before dawn and on the road in pursuit of the French. On the far side of Azambuja, they ran into a French picquet, which quickly retreated. After marching about 13km they came across a French force on a ridge outside of Cartaxo, consisting of three infantry battalions and a regiment of cavalry. General Craufurd '. . . conceiving it to be only a small rear-guard, the whole of which was exposed to view, instantly made dispositions for the attack, by forming the Light Division into a single line, which, with the troop of Horse Artillery and one squadron of the 14th Light Dragoons, constituted his whole force'.[19]

About this time Wellington appeared and stopped the attack, because he did not know what was on the other side of the ridge. It turned out the ridge concealed the rest of General Junot's 8th Corps. Initially the officers and men could not understand why they were halted but they changed their minds upon learning that a

French corps, numbering, it was believed, eighteen thousand infantry, and two to three cavalry, with a due proportion of artillery. We could, undoubtedly, have given a good account of the troops which the French general thought proper to expose to our view; but that we could have also mastered the remainder which were in reserve behind the brow, I will not undertake to say. Had other divisions of our army been sufficiently advanced to have aided in the attack, it is more than probable that Lord Wellington would have tried his hand at them.[20]

---

17. Oglander, Diary entry for 16 November 1810.
18. Simmons, p.115.
19. Leach, *Rough Sketches* . . ., pp.179–80.
20. Ibid., p.180.

Lieutenant Oglander, a strong critic of Craufurd, thought it was a good idea to halt the attack.

> After several formations, we were preparing to advance in columns of sections to attack, when fortunately Ld Wellington arrived and put a stop to the movement. We otherwise should with 3000 infantry and some cavalry have attacked an enemy's corps of superior strength formed on the plain near Val and which might have been reinforced from Santarem to almost any number. It was ground that the enemy evidently was not interested to keep & which therefore would probably be resigned without a contest. The utmost therefore that could be gained by an attack on that corps would have been the earlier possession of the tract on the right bank of the Rio do Val from which the French retired this evening and the following morning.[21]

Craufurd was not happy about having his orders changed by Wellington and formed the division up on the plain outside of Cartaxo and read them the riot act about how poor their march discipline had been over the past two days. He told them that:

> If I ever have occasion to observe any man of the Brigade pick his road on the march and go round a pool of water instead of marching through it I am fully determined to bring the officer commanding the Company to which that man belongs to a Court Martial. Should the Court acquit the officer it shall not deter me from repeating the same ceremony on the other officer again and again. Every halting day (if necessary) I will bring an officer to a Court Martial who shall presume to allow the men of his Company to go out of the way of a pool of water I will insist on every soldier marching though water and I will flog any man attempting to avoid it.[22]

It rained through much of the night, but that did not keep the Light Division from starting its advance at daybreak on the morning of 18 November. With them was Captain Ross's Royal Horse Artillery

---

21. Oglander, Diary entry for 17 November 1810.
22. Verner, Vol. 2, pp.172–3. The speech is from Captain Leach's unpublished diary. It did not make it into *Rough Sketches*.

troop, while out front of the division was the 14th Light Dragoons. The terrain they crossed was very flat and with all the rain over the past several weeks it was flooded. It was not long before they came into contact with the French rearguard crossing a causeway to get to the bridge over the Rio Maior. The cavalry had dismounted and began to engage the French but could do not do much with their short-range carbines. Lieutenant Simmons was sent forward with a section of rifleman and found the British light dragoons were

> highly pleased to see me arrive with some Rifle Men and take the post of honour from them, as the company I belonged to was sent on piquet, with orders to remain at the bridge. The French sent a few men forward to commence a fire upon us. I crawled on the bridge with three men, and lay down by a dead mule, where we had a good rest and took deliberate aim. The Frenchmen soon became wary of showing themselves, which convinced me we had hit some of them. The company had a hard day's work, were relieved at night by a company of the 52nd, but we were ordered to remain near at hand during the night as a reserve to it.[23]

The division halted for the day and bivouacked in the numerous olive groves in the area. It provided some protection from the rain and the troops found that olive 'wood is very hard and so greasy that it is as flammable as coal, so that, in spite of the rain, we managed to have good fires'.[24] In a truly bizarre incident, Craufurd, possibly having drunk too much wine and still stung by Wellington's refusal to let him attack the day before, 'seized a musket, and, followed only by a serjeant, advanced in the night along the causeway; thus commencing a personal skirmish with the French picquets, from whose fire he escaped by miracle . . .'.[25] Lieutenant Simmons, who was part of the force guarding the causeway, recorded in his diary that:

> General Craufurd, over his wine, took it into his head that the enemy was moving off and he was anxious to be the first to find it out. He came to the piquet and took three soldiers and

---

23. Simmons, pp.116–17.
24. Ibid., p.117.
25. Napier, William, Vol. 3, p.388.

walked cautiously along the causeway until the French sentry challenged and fire. The General ordered his men to fire and retire. This circumstance created so much alarm in the enemy's camp, who imagined that the British army was passing the bridge and falling upon them, that they became panic-struck and commenced a tremendous fire in every direction for some time. The balls came rattling in among the trees, and General Craufurd was sadly annoyed at being deceived in his conjectures and having caused such an uproar, with a great chance of foolishly throwing away his life.[26]

The heavy rains continued through the night. The next morning, the division stood-to before sunrise in case the French attacked. When it was light enough for the picquets to see the across the river, Lieutenant Simmons 'found that during the night they had been very busy cutting down olive-trees and forming abatis [sic] on the position. This they had every appearance of occupying for some time; it was a most commanding one, the left upon the Tagus, the swampy Rio Mayor all along its front, with a tête de pont at the end of the bridge over the river.'[27]

The rains continued and the division move back to what all hoped would be dryer ground. They bivouacked in

a large pine-wood, to make ourselves as comfortable as we could; but in which we passed as cheerless a night as one uninterrupted deluge of rain might be supposed to produce. Hoping to escape in some measure from the fury of the storm, many of us crept into an old water-course in the wood, in which, rolled up in our cloaks, and doubled up with wet and cold, we did contrive, nevertheless, to fall asleep. But it is impossible to forget the being suddenly awoke, a short time afterwards, and feeling myself all at once buoyed up and floating down the little ravine, in the same plight as if I had been dragged under a ship from stem to stern. There was a general outcry from all the party who had sought refuge in this water-course, and a scramble to get on terra firma took place. Taking a few mouths-ful [sic] of rum and a cigar, the remainder of the night was spent at the

---

26. Simmons, p.117.
27. Ibid.

foot for a fir-tree, smoking, shivering, and cursing our stupidity for having taken up so injudicious a position.[28]

The morning of 20 November saw no letup in the rain. Wellington had decided to force the French from their position and planned a concerted attack with the 1st and Light Divisions, and General Pack's Portuguese brigade.

> The First Division made demonstrations near the causeway, as in like manner did the other troops further to their left. The Light Division and some cavalry at the same moment crossed the Rio Maior, by a narrow bridge behind Vallé, and advanced along the enemy's position, which rested on the Tagus. We were soon engaged with their picket, with whom we kept up a skirmish for some hours, and in such rain as might be supposed to have rendered fire-arms useless. Numbers of their light troops were scattered along the base of the position, ready for our reception, if we should advance to attack; but Massena concealed his masses behind the brow.[29]

Lieutenant Harry Smith was at the Light Division HQ when Wellington arrived. There was much concern among the officers about the attack because the French position

> was bristling on our right with abattis, three or four lines. We felt the difficulty of carrying such heights, but towards the afternoon we moved on. On the Duke's staff there was a difference of opinion as to the number of the enemy, whether one corps d armée or two. The Duke, who knew perfectly well there were two, and our move was only a reconnaissance, turned to Colonel Beckwith. 'Beckwith, my Staff are disputing whether at Santarem there is one corps d'armée or two?' 'I'll be d----d if I know, my Lord, but you may depend on it, a great number were required to make those abattis in one night.' Lord Wellington laughed, and said, 'You are right, Beckwith; there are two corps d'armée,' The enemy soon showed themselves. The Duke, as was his wont, satisfied himself by ocular demonstration, and the

28. Leach, *Rough Sketches . . .*, pp.182–3.
29. Ibid., p.184.

Division returned to its bivouac. Whilst here, Colonel Beckwith was seized with a violent attack of ague.[30]

It was thought best to get the troops out of the rain and the order was given to withdraw into the village of Vale de Santarém a kilometre to the rear. The 2nd Brigade was placed in the village, while the 1st Brigade was dispersed in farms and villages close to the Rio Maior. The 43rd Foot made its camp in a large quinta[31] on a hill a little way up stream from the bridge. The 3rd Caçadores were billeted in a village close to the Ponte do Celeiro, which was about 3km upstream of the Ponte do Seca Bridge.[32] The 95th Rifles were dispersed into the farm buildings that lined the Rio Maior.[33]

Wellington's purpose for ordering the attack was to determine if the French were just temporarily halting in Santarém or moving into cantonments that provided better access to food supplies while they awaited reinforcements. He did not want to risk a battle that would cause heavy casualties. He knew that the scarcity of supplies in the area would eventually force the French to retreat. Chef-de-Bataillon Pelet confirmed Wellington's suspicions about why Masséna had ordered his army to withdraw to Santarém.

> Considering its position, the French army's only goal for the time being was to maintain itself in the heart of Portugal as long as possible and wait for orders and all the reinforcements that it had requested. Until they arrived, it could only prepare for new operations by producing resources to build bridges on the rivers and to reinforce its position and defensive system in a way to extend itself to gather food. While waiting, we could study the countryside, gather materials and information, and prepare the course for insuring its conquest. Rumours on the approach of the 5th Corps[34] continued to circulate, although it was still quite distant. There was talk about the 9th Corps [commanded by Lieutenant General Drouet, Comte d'Erlon].[35]

---

30. Smith, pp.37–8.
31. A large country estate.
32. Modern-day Ponte D'Asseca.
33. Oglander, Diary entry for 20 November 1810. Simmons, p.118.
34. Commanded by Marshal Édouard Mortier.
35. Pelet, p.299.

The French position was very strong and appeared to be as formidable as the Lines of Torres Vedras.

The front was covered by the river Maior, which, during the winter months, is not fordable. The bridge and causeway, leading across it to the foot of the heights of Santarem, are exceedingly long and narrow; and a smaller hill, detached as if it had been placed there for the express purpose, looks down on the causeway, which the French artillery and musketry stationed there completely enfiladed. The French formed breast-works for their infantry in various places near the head of the causeway, and abattis on it.

Rising boldly, and somewhat abruptly, from their end of the causeway, is a high hill, on the top of which stands Santarem . . . In that town were Massena's head-quarters during the whole winter.

The extensive woods of olive which clothed the sides and summit of the hill the year before . . . were cut down in less than forty-eight hours by the French, who constructed with them a double row of most formidable abattis across the whole of the ridge.

The right extended towards a country difficult of approach in the winter months, from the wretched state of the roads in the neighbourhood.[36]

After a few weeks the position was made even stronger. On 25 November, Lieutenant Oglander went for a ride and close to the bridge he

had a good view of part of the enemy's position at Santarem. The bridge and causeway leading to and from it are in length about 800 yards, passing over a small river, and marsh, which is now flooded. It is commanded in its full by a hill on the enemy's side, of which are planted 4 pieces of artillery. At its termination, the road turns suddenly to the left, and passes on the edge of the marsh at the bottom of three other hills, which overlook it. These must be gained before the high and almost uninterrupted ridge on which the town is situated can be approached by this road. The ascent up this range is very long

---

36. Leach, *Rough Sketches. . .*, pp.181–2.

and steep, and it is broken by an abattis which stands along the whole brow of the hill. This however once past, the Town of Santarem is gained, unless indeed the French have taken any measures for defending the streets. Our artillery is planted on the top of another high hill on our side, within cannon shot of that which commands the bridge on the enemy's. The fire from our Artillery might indeed silence that opposed to it, and thereby facilitate the passage of troops over the causeway, which however could not be affected without great loss. Our guns wont [sic] after that be of little or no use, and every thing must be gained at the point of the bayonette [sic]. The above description relates only to the position as viewed from the bridge. Our advance sentries are posted by an abattis just past the last arch of the bridge and a viditte [sic] is pushed across the river close to the causeway on the right. The sentries of both parties are within shot of each other.[37]

After the weeks of rain, the normally narrow river had become a major obstacle.

The river is formed by two streams, which run nearly parellel [sic] with each other, at the distance of perhaps 200 yards, and join close to the causeway. These two streams having overflowed their banks, and laid under water the intervening lands, appear as one river of vast breadth; and any attempt to pass by throwing over it a bridge, when the waters are all high would thereby be rendered very difficult . . . The river may be passed everywhere, excepting the Ponte da Seca, without being exposed to the fire from the enemy's position. The two arches of the Ponte do Saleira are still complete, but the causeway between them is still under water; a few parts of it however just rize [sic] above the stream and prove that it is in ruins.[38]

Over the next week the division settled into a routine as they tried to dry out. Every morning there was a stand to at dawn, after which the outposts were relieved. Lieutenant Charles Kinloch of the 52nd Foot wrote home on 24 November that:

---

37. Oglander, Diary entry for 25 November 1810.
38. Ibid., Diary entry for 15 December 1810.

Nothing has been done on either side since we came here 19th Nov except a little skirmish. The French have received a reinforcement of about 15,000 men & we have now given up all idea of attacking them in their position which is very strong, if they attempt to move forward which is expected everyday [sic] we shall of course move back to our position, in which the only fear is that they will not venture to attack us. Our sentries are at present within 150 yards of each other & their advanced battalion within less than a mile of us, so much so that we see everything they do & hear their bands playing quite plain.[39]

Steps were taken to improve their living conditions, especially in the 43rd Foot, whose 800 men were crowded into one large farm complex. On 23 November three companies 'moved into the village of Val, a circumstance which much increased the comfort of, and indeed was necessary for the health of the whole, the Quinta being previously very much crowded'.[40] However, 10 days later the three companies were moved to Pov de Exerta.[41]

The division was responsible for providing an outpost at the Ponte de Seca. It consisted of 'three hundred men being always on picket at the head of the bridge, and several more on inlying picket near at hand. On the bridge (which was mined and charged) we constructed abattis; and to render our post at the causeway more secure, we made covert ways and traverses. . . The sentries of the two armies were so near each other on the bridge, and the videttes of the cavalry so closely advanced on the marsh on the right, that they might have conversed without exalting their voices much.'[42] The duty lasted for 24 hours and the outposts were generally relieved after morning stand-to.[43]

On 26 November, Craufurd inspected the position at the bridge and 'ordered the abatis to be advanced some yards upon the bridge in case we should have occasion to blow up the principal arch, which would then be clear. I got over the parapet on the enemy's side and went forward to the place the General had ordered the abatis to be moved to.

---

39. Kinloch, p.61.
40. Oglander, Diary entry for 23 November 1810.
41. Possibly Póvoa da Isenta which was 4km northwest of Vale de Santarém, Portugal. Oglander, Diary entry for 3 December 1810.
42. Leach, *Rough Sketches . . .*, p.186.
43. Oglander, Diary entries for 14 and 15 December 1810.

Three of my men began to pull it to pieces and bring the wood. I expected the French would fire at me from the tête de pont, and I was suffering so much from disease that I was really careless what happened, but I was allowed to finish my job without interruption.'[44]

Rifleman Costello, who was in Lieutenant Simmons's company, described the defences of the bridge as 'double sentries, and abbatis [sic] of fallen trees. But the better to foil the incursions of the enemy, the arches had been undermined, and the powder secured from the wet by bullocks' hides, trained ready for explosion.'[45]

The duty was fairly easy, with few incidents. Neither side was inclined to go looking for trouble. An occasional French deserter or a flag of truce that would approach the outposts and some false alarms that caused the division to turn out. Skirmishing between the outposts did occur, but it was rare. On 15 December, the French made a reconnaissance in force with two cavalry regiments and two infantry battalions, near the town of Rio Maior, a village 30km to the northwest. Upon notification of the excursion, the division immediately turned out and stood at its positions until sunset. Two weeks later, on 28 December the heavy baggage at Cartaxo and the commissary stores at Valada, which was 14km south of Val de Santarém, were ordered to the rear. The only impact on the division was their daily ration of wine and rum was stopped because it was too far in the rear to bring forward.[46]

Discipline did not appear to be a problem within the division, but there were habits throughout the army that were frowned upon. For example, firewood was in short supply and the soldiers took to cutting down olive and fruit trees. Wellington noticed this and in a general order forbade the practice.[47] Complaints were also received that the troops were using doors, window frames and furniture for their fires and Wellington had to issue another general order forbidding this practice. He also appealed to their sense of honour and said he 'is ashamed to acknowledge, that the British troops have, in many instances done more mischief to the country in this manner, than had been done by the enemy'.[48]

In December numerous courts-martial were held throughout the army. The charges ranged from robbery to desertion. Major General

---

44. Simmons, p.119.
45. Costello, p.43.
46. All of these incidents were recorded by Lieutenant Oglander in his diary.
47. General Order dated 5 December 1810.
48. Ibid., dated 12 December 1810.

Charles Colville, a brigade commander in the 4th Division, convened an army-wide court martial on 21 December that sat until 27 December. Its purpose was to try soldiers accused of desertion. All but one was found guilty. Those convicted were sentenced to 1,000 lashes.[49] Although none of the court-martialled soldiers were from the Light Division, Craufurd wanted it to be clear what would happen to any soldier from his division who was caught deserting. On 30 December he inspected the 1st Brigade at Quinta do Valle and then 'addressed them in a speech of considerable length, relative to the pardon of two men, who had been guilty of a great excess against some natives and of military insubordination; and also relative to the desertions which had occurred in the English Regts'.[50]

Christmas came and went, with a large horse race on the plains at Val de Santarém to break the monotony. It was attended by Wellington and the Marquis de la Romana.[51] Despite the easy duty, morale began to flag. The division had been on the front line for almost a year and they were tired. A good night's sleep was a luxury as they slept fully clothed and their equipment at hand in case of an attack.[52] Lieutenant Kinloch wrote home on 7 December describing the mood of the officers.

> A great majority of the officers of the army are most heartily tired of this sort of life & long most anxiously for home, none more than the Light Division. Would you believe it, that not a soul has had their clothes off for these eight months except to change. Perhaps when I have been two years in the country, as many of them have, my military ardour may be a little damped, however I have nothing yet to give me the home sickness. We are all under the greatest uneasiness respecting Colonel Barclay whom we understand to be in a very bad way, there could not be a man more beloved by both officers and men than he was.[53]

Not helping the situation was the constant rain. After a year of hard campaigning clothing and equipment was beginning to fall apart.

---

49. General Orders, dated 18, 27, and 29 December 1810.
50. Oglander, Diary entry for 30 December 1810.
51. Pedro Caro, 3rd Marquis de la Romana.
52. Leach, *Rough Sketches . . .*, p.187.
53. Kinloch, p.62.

Lieutenant Kincaid of the 95th Rifles, who had been in country for only three months, described the condition of his clothes.

> We had the utmost difficulty, however, in keeping up appearances in the way of dress. The jacket, in spite of shreds and patches, always maintained something of the original about it; but woe befel [sic] the regimental smallclothes,[54] and they could only be replaced by very extraordinary apologies, of which I remember that I had two pair at this period, one of a common brown Portuguese cloth, and the other, or Sunday's pair, of black velvet. We had no women with the regiment; and the ceremony of washing a shirt amounted to my servant's taking it by the collar, and giving it a couple of shakes in the water, and then hanging it up to dry. Smoothing-irons were not the fashion of the times, and, if a fresh well-dressed aide-de-camp did occasionally come from England, we used to stare at him with about as much respect as Hotspur did at his 'waiting gentlewoman'.[55]

In addition to problems with uniforms and equipment, officers and men began to fall ill. After seeing the squalid and filthy buildings that the French had abandoned during their retreat, Wellington was concerned that they might cause his own troops to get sick. He issued a general order to his regimental commanders requesting the they 'be very cautious in occupying the quarters in which the French troops may have been quartered, to make their men clean them well out before they sleep in them; and, if possible, to have fires lighted in them, but care must be taken not to burn the houses'.[56] This was to clean the houses of fleas and lice. Although unknown at the time, they are carriers of typhus. The next day he issued orders in regards to horses. They were not to 'be put into any stables or places which have been occupied by the enemy, without very carefully cleaning and washing the mangers, &c. to take every precaution against glanders'.[57]

---

54. Breeches.
55. Kincaid, *Adventures*, pp.34–5. Hotspur and the waiting gentlewomen were from Shakespeare's play *Henry IV*.
56. General Order dated 16 November 1810.
57. General Order dated 17 November 1810. Glanders is a disease that affects the respiratory system of animals. At the time there was no known cure.

Exhaustion, harsh living condition, and constant exposure to rain and cold began to take a toll. On 24 November[58] 735 soldiers, or 20 per cent of the British and Brunswick other ranks[59] strength, were reported sick and unavailable for duty. The day before Christmas, the number was reduced to 652 or 17 per cent. During the period eighty-four soldiers died.

Table 15.1: Light Division Other Ranks Sick or Dead, November – December 1810[60]

	November				December			
Unit	Strength	Sick	% Sick	Died	Strength	Sick	% Sick	Died
43rd Foot	971	205	21%	16	967	167	17%	5
52nd Foot	998	158	16%	14	993	141	14%	10
95th Rifles[61]	911	175	19%	11	898	172	19%	4
Brunswick	915	197	22%	6	894	172	19%	18

It should be noted that the numbers may include the wounded from the Battle of Busaco. Yet there were only fifty wounded soldiers among the British battalions. Many of the wounded would have returned to their battalions by December.

Lieutenant Simmons, who had been seriously wounded at the Côa River on 24 July and had returned to his battalion in October, collapsed on 2 December and had to be evacuated to Lisbon for treatment. While recuperating, he wrote a long letter home in which he explains what happened to him.

> The excessive wet and bad weather has had great influence upon my constitution since I was wounded. I feel myself, I am sorry to say, quite a different man. This last march we have been exposed very much to the weather. We have had nearly a continuance of rain, and sleeping on the ground, the water

---

58. Each battalion was required to submit a strength report on the 24th of each month. It included the number of sick.
59. Enlisted soldiers who were not sergeants or musicians.
60. I could not find figures for the 1st and 3rd Caçadores Battalions.
61. Includes the 1st Battalion, and one company each of the 2nd and 3rd Battalions

making a gutter on both sides of one's body, was not pleasant to me. There was a time when I would not have cared a fig for it, but my leg, after lying thus became very painful, and I felt as though I had to drag a ten-stone weight about with me. In the morning, possibly obliged to march for miles through grape gardens, fighting with the enemy, I limping along, and often finding difficulty to keep up with my men. Only a little while back I could run miles, always the first to go through or over anything; judge how my feelings must be hurt at so serious a difference. I continued with my regiment as long as possible, until my mind became so much hurt and my body so much debilitated that I could hardly drag myself along. In this state I went on piquet; rain all night. I was stationed at the bridge of Valle with a section of the company. I lay down occasionally by the fire. I was so ill I could not smoke a pipe, the greatest luxury a man can have in bad weather. The next morning I was relieved and went to bed, not a feather bed, but some straw in the corner of an old stable, with knapsack for a pillow. I was recommended to start directly for Lisbon by my friend, the surgeon.[62] I argued against it and said, as I had got a good comfortable bed, I should soon come round. Here, for the first time in my life, I was attacked with dysentery and in indescribable torture. On the 3rd of December I found if I put off many days longer I should not be able to leave the regiment. . . I am nearly worn to a skeleton. I was laughing at myself when shaving in the glass this morning at my hollow eyes and squalid visage.[63]

It was not just the officers and men on the front line who were sick. Captain Henry Mellish, the Light Division's DAAG, had been sick in Lisbon since early November. On 16 November he heard that the Light Division had started advancing, got out of bed and rejoined the headquarters at Alenquer. His health continued to get worse and three weeks later he was back in Lisbon.[64]

Senior officers also began to fall sick. On 20 November, Lieutenant Colonel Beckwith was incapacitated with a fever and by the end of

---

62. Joseph Burke.
63. Simmons, pp.123–5.
64. Mellish, Henry, Unpublished letters 21 November and 8 December 1810.

the year was sharing a place in Lisbon with Lieutenant Simmons.[65] Lieutenant Colonel Georg de Korfes, the commander of the Brunswick Oëls, died on 30 December 1810 from an intermittent fever.[66] Compounding the chain-of-command problems was that Colonel Wynch, the commander of the 2nd Brigade, came down with typhus in late December and thought not likely to survive.

Craufurd was likely as exhausted, both physically and mentally, as the troops he commanded. He was willing to take risks not only with his command but himself. His desire to attack the French rearguard on 17 November, without first doing a proper reconnaissance, could have cost him his division. His irrational behaviour on the night of 18 November, when he led a four-man patrol of the French position and engaged in a skirmish with their outposts, could have cost him his life. At least one historian believes he was depressed.[67] More than anything he wanted to go home and on 8 December he sent a letter to Wellington requesting permission to return to England to see his wife. Wellington did not want him to go and told him that if he insisted on going that due to the '. . . number of General Officers senior to you in the army, it has not been an easy task to keep you in your command; and if you should go, I fear that I should not be able to appoint you to it again, or to one that would be so agreeable to you, or in which you could be so useful'.[68] Craufurd decided to stay.

By the end of December the Light Division's chain-of-command was in a shambles. Its senior leadership had been decimated by death, injury, and sickness. In additional to its commander who did not want to be there, both brigade commanders were too sick to command, and were replaced by the senior lieutenant colonels in their brigades. Of its battalions, only the 43rd Foot was still commanded by its lieutenant colonel. Fortunately for the division, both armies went into winter quarters. With no operations in the foreseeable future, there would be time for the Light Division to sort out its command problems. But that is a story for another time.

---

65. Simmons, p.131,
66. Von Kortzfleisch, p.163.
67. An unpublished paper by Nicholas Haynes lays out a strong case for him being so.
68. *WD*, Vol. 7, pp.34–5.

Table 15.2: Organization of the Light Division, 31 December 1810

Division HQ	Brigadier General Robert Craufurd	Commander
	Captain William Campbell 23rd Foot	ADC
	Lieutenant John Bell 52nd Foot	DAQMG
	Charles Purcell	ACG
1st Brigade	LTC George Elder	Acting Commander
	Lieutenant Harry Smith 95th Rifles	Unofficial ADC
	Lt. James Stewart 95th Rifles	Brigade Major
1st Bn 43rd Foot	LTC Charles McLeod	Commander
Right Wing 95th Rifles	Major Dugald Gilmour	Commander
Company 2nd Bn 95th Rifles	Captain Charles Beckwith	Commander
Company 3rd Bn 95th Rifles	Captain William Percival	Commander
3rd Caçadores Bn	Major Manuel Pinto da Silveira	Commander
2nd Brigade	LTC Jorge de Avilez	Acting Commander
	Captain Charles Rowan 52nd Foot	Brigade Major
1st Bn 52nd Foot	Major Hugh Arbuthnott	Commander
Left Wing 95th Rifles	Major John Stewart	Commander
1st Caçadores Battalion	Major John Alego	Commander
Brunswick Oëls	Major Frederick von Hertzberg	Commander

Chapter 16

What Happened to Them

It would be impossible to provide a biography of every officer and soldier who fought in the Light Division in 1810. As a reader I am always curious about what happened to those who are featured so prominently in the narrative. Most of the officers and men continued to fight with their regiments over the next 40 months. Some were killed, many were seriously wounded and others died from disease. Many of those who survived went on to senior rank in the British Army.

Division Staff

Bell, John. Although assigned to the 52nd Foot, he served as the division's DAQMG until July 1813 when he was appointed its AQMG. He served in that position until the end of the Peninsular War in April 1814. He was promoted through the ranks and was a full general in 1860. He was the senior general in the Army when he died on 20 November 1876 at the age of 90. During the 64 months he spent in the Peninsula, he was only wounded once, at Vimeiro on 21 August 1808. He was awarded the Army Gold Cross,[1] and the Military General Service Medal (MGSM) with six clasps.[2] He became a Companion of the Bath (CB) on 22 June 1815, a Knight Commander of the Bath (KCB) on 6 April 1852 and a Knight Grand Cross of the Bath (GCB) on 18 May 1860.

Campbell, William continued to serve as the DAQMG of the Light Division until the end of the Peninsular War in April 1814. He was

---

1. The Pyrenees, Nivelle, Orthes and Toulouse.
2. An individual could not receive both an AGM and a MGSM clasp for the same battle. The clasps were Vimeiro, Busaco, Ciudad Rodrigo, Badajoz, Salamanca and Vitoria.

promoted to brevet major on 12 April 1814. He served at Waterloo as an AQMG. He was promoted to brevet lieutenant colonel on 18 June 1815. He was promoted to colonel[3] on 10 January 1837 and major general on 9 November 1846. He died on 3 June 1852. He received the MGSM with eight clasps[4] and made a CB on 22 June 1815.

Craufurd, Robert was promoted to major general on 4 June 1811. He continued to command the Light Division until he was severely wounded in the storming of Ciudad Rodrigo on 19 January 1812. He died from his wounds on 24 January 1812 and was buried in the walls of Ciudad Rodrigo the next day.

Mellish, Henry was promoted to major in the Royal Sicilian Regiment in March 1811, but continued to serve as the DAAG until August 1811 when he returned to England. He served at Isle de France and died at his home in England on 24 July 1817 from congestive heart failure.[5]

Napier, Charles survived his wounds and re-joined his regiment[6] in March 1811 during the pursuit of the retreating French. He served with them until June 1811 when he became an exploring officer deep in Spain. He left the Peninsula in August 1811. He was promoted to lieutenant colonel in the 102nd Foot in 1811 and went with his regiment to Bermuda. He served in Chesapeake Bay during the War of 1812. He exchanged back into the 50th Foot in 1813. He was promoted to major general in 1837 and sent to India. He became famous as the conqueror of Sindh in 1843 and was appointed the Governor of the Bombay Presidency. He was removed from that position for clashing with the policies of the Directors of the East India Company. He was promoted to lieutenant general in 1846. He went home to England in 1847 but came back to India in 1849 as the Commander-in-Chief in India. He returned to England in 1851 and died on 29 August 1853. He was made a CB on 4 June 1815, a KCB on 19 July

---

3. He was never appointed a regimental colonel, but received a per diem, about £1 plus, as a general officer unattached not being a regimental colonel.
4. Busaco, Fuentes de Oñoro, Vitoria, the Pyrenees, Nivelle, Nive, Orthes and Toulouse.
5. Sheardown, William, *Records and Family Notices of Military and Naval Officers ... Connected with Doncaster and Its Neighbourhood*. Doncaster: Gazette, 1873, p.36.
6. The 50th Foot.

1838, and GCB on 4 July 1843. He received an AGM for Corunna and the MGSM with two clasps: Busaco and Fuentes de Oñoro.

Shaw, James served as the aide-de-camp to General Craufurd until his death in January 1812. He served as an extra-ADC to Major General Charles Baron Alten, who commanded the Light Division, until 1 November 1813 when he returned to England. He was promoted to captain on 16 July 1812. He was a Deputy Assistant Quartermaster General during the Waterloo campaign. After the occupation of France, he became a staff officer in England and eventually organized the Royal Irish Constabulary. In 1854 he was promoted to lieutenant general and in 1862 to general. He died in 1865 at the age of 77. He changed his name to Shaw Kennedy in 1834. He received the MGSM with three clasps: Ciudad Rodrigo, Badajoz and Salamanca. He was made a CB on 19 July 1838 and a KCB on 28 June 1861.

Wynch, James did not lead the 2nd Brigade for very long. He died from typhus in Lisbon on 6 January 1811.

43rd Foot

Booth, Henry stayed with the 1st Battalion until March 1811 when he returned to England due to poor health. In June 1812 he was promoted to captain and took command of a company in the 1st Battalion in Spain. He led them until October 1813. His whole military career was with the regiment and was promoted to lieutenant colonel in 1830. He commanded the regiment during the Canadian Rebellion of 1837–8. He died in 1841.[7]

Brumwell, John served with the 1st Battalion until he was severely wounded during the assault on Ciudad Rodrigo on 19 January 1812. He died from his wounds on 27 January 1812.

Duffy, John was striken with malaria in late June 1810 and was evacuated to Alverça. He went home in July to recover. He returned to the Peninsula in December 1810 and fought with the battalion until he was slightly wounded at the siege of Ciudad Rodrigo in January 1812. He was mentioned in dispatches for his role in the assault on the city.

---

7. Mockler-Ferryman, pp.173–83.

He returned to England in May 1812 and but came back to the Peninsula in February 1813. He was promoted to major on 13 June 1813. He was slightly wounded at Vitoria on 21 June 1813, but fought with the battalion in the Pyrenees, the Nivelle and Nive. He returned to England in January 1814. He died in 1855 having been promoted to lieutenant general in 1851. What was unusual about him was his family background. His father was a quartermaster sergeant in the 10th Foot. For his services he received the AGM for Badajoz, the MGSM with seven clasps,[8] and made a CB on 26 September 1831.

Fergusson, James led his company until December 1812 when he was promoted to major in the 79th Foot. A month later he exchanged into the 85th Foot. While commanding his company in the 43rd Foot he was severely wounded at Ciudad Rodrigo in January 1812 and at Badajoz three months later. He remained in the Peninsula until the end of the war in April 1814. Over the next 46 years he would be promoted through the ranks till he became a full general in 1860. From 1850–3 he was the regimental colonel of the 43rd Foot. He died on 4 September 1865. For his service he received the AGM for Badajoz and the MGSM with eight clasps.[9] He was created a CB on 26 September 1831, a KCB on 5 July 1855, and a GCB on 18 May 1860.

Frederick, Roger after losing his leg, was placed on the retired full pay list of the 7th Royal Veteran Battalion in 1814. Despite the administration of wine to him by Captain Brotherton he lived for another 44 years dying on 21 June 1854 at the age of 64 in Hersham, Surrey.

Freer, William continued to serve with the 1st Battalion until he lost his right arm at the assault on Badajoz in April 1812. He returned to the Peninsula in February 1813 and fought with the battalion until the war ended in April 1814. He was wounded at Nivelle in November 1813 and promoted to captain on 1 December 1813. William stayed on active duty and was eventually promoted to lieutenant colonel. He was in command of the 10th Foot on Corfu when he died on 2 August 1836.

---

8. Egypt, Fuentes de Oñoro, Ciudad Rodrigo, Vitoria, the Pyrenees, Nivelle and Nive.
9. Vimeiro, Corunna, Busaco, Fuentes de Oñoro, Ciudad Rodrigo, Salamanca, Nivelle and Nive.

Garretty, Thomas was with his company at Sabugal, Fuentes de Oñoro and the siege of Ciudad Rodrigo. He was seriously wounded in the left thigh at the assault on Badajoz on 6 April 1812. He returned to England in 1813. He was medically retired in 1817, when the regiment was reduced to a single battalion. He was recalled to duty in 1819 and found fit for service in a veterans battalion. He retired in 1823 after 17 years of service. His date of death is unknown, but he was still alive in 1848 and received the MGSM with clasps for Busaco, Fuentes de Oñoro, Ciudad Rodrigo and Badajoz.

Hamilton, Anthony fought with the Light Division until 1813 when he was captured on picquet duty during the siege of San Sebastian but eventually escaped captivity. He volunteered for duty with the York Chasseurs and went to the West Indies with it. He rejoined the 43rd Foot in 1819 and was discharged in Quebec, Canada where he first became a farmer and then an itinerant labourer. His memoirs were published in 1847. His date of death is unknown, but he never received the MGSM which was awarded in 1848.

Harvest, Horatio fought with his battalion through 1811 and early 1812. He was killed leading the Forlorn Hope on the assault on Badajoz on 6 April 1812.

Hopkins, John served with the regiment in the Peninsula until September 1813 and fought in eleven actions from 1811–13. He was promoted to captain on 29 August 1811 and major in 1824. He was a Military Knight of Windsor and selected to be the governor of all the knights. He died on 17 March 1875. He received the MGSM with seven clasps.[10]

Hull, James never recovered from his wounds on the Côa River and retired in May 1812. He was given a temporary pension of £100 pounds per year.

M'Dermid, John was back with the battalion by March 1811. He was killed at Sabugal on 3 April 1811.

---

10. Busaco, Fuentes de Oñoro, Ciudad Rodrigo, Badajoz, Salamanca, Vitoria and the Pyrenees.

McLeod, Charles went home to Great Britain in December 1810 but was back with his battalion in Portugal by May 1811. He was killed during the assault on Badajoz on 6 April 1812 and was buried in a cornfield on the slope of a hill overlooking the regimental camp.[11] As a battalion commander he received the AGM with two clasps for Busaco, Ciudad Rodrigo and Badajoz.

Napier, William stayed with the 1st Battalion throughout most of the Peninsular War. In March 1811 he was appointed the Brigade Major of the 1st Brigade of the Light Division and was in that position until he was forced to return to England due to poor health. He returned to the battalion in April 1812 and assumed command of it upon the death of its commander at Badajoz on 6 April. He was promoted to major in May 1812 and brevet lieutenant colonel on 22 November 1813. He remained in command of the battalion until March 1814. He went on half-pay in 1819 but continued to be promoted through the ranks and in 1841 was a major general. He died on 12 February 1860. William Napier received the AGM for Salamanca, Nivelle, and Nive and the MGSM with three clasps: Busaco, Fuentes de Oñoro and Orthes. He was made a CB on 4 June 1815 and a KCB on 27 April 1848. He is best remembered for writing the six-volume *History of the War in the Peninsula and in the South of France*.

Oglander, Henry continued to serve with the 1st Battalion until he was seriously wounded on 6 April 1812 during the assault on Badajoz, where he lost his left arm. He returned to the Peninsula as a captain in the 47th Foot and was seriously wounded during the siege of San Sebastian in 1813, where he was shot in the body and lost the index finger on his right hand. Due to his wounds he received a pension of £450 per year. He stayed in the Army and commanded the 26th Foot from 1817. He was on the staff at Cawnpore, Bengal from 1836 and a local major general in India. He was on sick leave when he resigned his command in 1840 to accompany his regiment to China. He died, of dysentery, at sea off the coast of China on 23 June 1840. He became a CB on 19 July 1838. He received an AGM for San Sebastian.

Stephenson, John was invalided home in December 1810 due to the wounds he received on the Côa River. He exchanged into the 6th Dragoon

---

11. Hall, p.380.

Guards, and was promoted to captain in 1812 and then to major in 1824. He never saw active service after 1810. He retired by the sale of his commission in 1837 and died on 27 July 1850.

52nd Foot

Barclay, Robert. Although only slightly wounded below the knee at Busaco on 27 September, the wound never healed properly and he returned to England in late October. He died of his wounds on 3 May 1811.

Booth, Charles fought with his regiment through all the actions in 1811 and the siege of Ciudad Rodrigo in January 1812. He volunteered for the storming party and was killed during the assault on Badajoz on 6 April 1812.

Campbell, Robert served with the 1st Battalion until September 1813. He was seriously wounded at Badajoz on 6 April 1812 and San Sebastian on 31 August 1813. For his service at San Sebastian he was promoted to Brevet Major and received the AGM. He transferred to the 13th Foot in July 1818 and a month later he transferred to the 28th Foot and went on half-pay. He received a pension of £200 per year for his wounds. He died in 1836.

Harris, Matthew continued to serve with the regiment until the war ended in 1814. On 25 October 1814 he transferred to the 45th Foot. He was medically discharged on 8 May 1815. Because of the wounds he received while serving with the 52nd Foot, including being shot in the side and the right hand, he was awarded a pension of shilling per day. He died on 28 November 1861 at the age of 81. He received the MGSM with six clasps.[12] According to regimental tradition he did not receive any recognition for his capture of General Simon at Busaco until 1843, when Lieutenant Love, now a lieutenant general, intervened on his behalf.[13] However, I could find no record of this award.

Hopkins, Alexander served with the 52nd Foot until he was wounded in the right leg on 6 April 1812 during the assault on Badajoz. His

---

12. Corunna, Busaco, Ciudad Rodrigo, Badajoz, Salamanca and Vitoria.
13. Moorsom, pp.124–5.

wound was severe enough that he was given a medical discharge from the army after eight years of service on 21 August 1813 with a pension of 1 shilling per day. According to regimental tradition he received a £20 pension for his capture of General Simon at Busaco.[14] However, I could find no record of this award.[15]

Napier, George was promoted to major in 1811 and continued to serve in the 1st Battalion until 1812 where he lost his right arm leading the Light Division's storming party in the assault on Ciudad Rodrigo on 19 January. He spent the next two years recovering. He returned to his battalion in the Peninsula in January 1814. He would move up through the ranks and was promoted to major general in 1837 and appointed the governor of the Cape Colony in 1839. He was promoted to general in 1854 and died on 16 September 1855. He received an AGM for Ciudad Rodrigo and the MGSM with four clasps: Corunna, Busaco, Orthes, and Toulouse. He was made a CB on 4 June 1815 and a KCB on 10 July 1838.

Ridewood, Henry served with the 1st Battalion until June 1811 when he transferred to the 2nd Battalion. However, he stayed with the 1st Battalion until August 1811 when he was promoted to lieutenant colonel in the 45th Foot and went home to England to command its 2nd Battalion. He returned to the Peninsula in July 1812 as commander of the 1st Battalion. On 21 June 1813 he was seriously wounded at Vitoria and died from his wound on 11 July 1813. He received an AGM for Salamanca.

95th Rifles

Beckwith, Thomas Sidney continued to command the 1st Brigade of the Light Division until August 1811 when he was sent home due to poor health. He was promoted to brevet colonel on 4 June 1811. On 7 January 1813 he was appointed the Assistant Quartermaster General of the British forces in Canada. He commanded a brigade in

---

14. Moorsom, pp.124–5.
15. Like Private Harris, the pension for his wound was equal to a little more than a shilling per day.

the 1813 Chesapeake campaign. He was promoted to major general on 4 June 1814 and was the Quartermaster General of the British forces in Canada. In 1829, he became the commander of the East India Company's Bombay Army and the following year was promoted to lieutenant general. He died of a fever on 19 January 1831. He was awarded three AGMs for his service in the Peninsula: Vimeiro, Corunna and Busaco. He was made a Knight Bachelor on 29 May 1813 and a KCB on 2 January 1815.

Coane, Alexander fought with the 1st Battalion through 1811 until he fell sick in early 1812. He was sent to Lisbon where he died from a fever on 14 February 1812.[16]

Costello, Edward fought with the 1st Battalion in the Peninsula until April 1814 when peace was declared. He ended the war as a sergeant. His trigger finger was shot off at Quatre Bras, two days before Waterloo, and he was pensioned out of the army in 1818. In 1835 he was commissioned as a captain in the British Legion and fought in Spain during the Carlist War. He returned to England in 1838 and was appointed a Yeoman Warder of the Tower of London. He died in 1869 at the age of 81. He was one of the most decorated soldiers in the 95th Rifles. He was awarded the Waterloo Medal and the MGSM with eleven clasps: Busaco, Fuentes de Oñoro, Ciudad Rodrigo, Badajoz, Salamanca, Vitoria, Pyrenees, Nivelle, Nive, Orthes and Toulouse.[17]

Cox, John stayed with the 1st Battalion in the Peninsula until the war ended in April 1814. He was severely wounded at Ciudad Rodrigo in January 1812 with a compound fracture of his left arm and at Tarbes in March 1814 when his left leg was broken by a musket ball. Despite five years of continual campaigning and fighting at Waterloo, he was not promoted to captain until 1819. Eighteen years later he was promoted to lieutenant colonel and in 1855 he was promoted to major general.

---

16. Gairdner, James P., *The American Sharpe: the Adventures of an American Officer of the 95th Rifles in the Peninsula & Waterloo Campaigns*. Gareth Glover (ed.). Barnsley: Frontline, 2017, p.235.
17. Only ten officers and riflemen in the 95th Rifles had more clasps than him.

He died in 1863.[18] For his service in the Peninsula, he received the MGSM with ten clasps.[19]

Green, William served in the Peninsula in the 1st Battalion until peace was declared in April 1814. In early 1811, he became his company's bugler. He was severely wounded in the thigh and left hand and wrist at the assault on Badajoz on 6 April 1812. He was evacuated to England and was declared unfit for duty on 9 December 1812. He was given a pension of 9 pence per day. He died in 27 January 1881 at the age of 97. He received the MGSM with clasps for Corunna, Busaco, Ciudad Rodrigo and Badajoz.[20]

Kincaid, John served with the 1st Battalion through the rest of the Peninsular War. He was its adjutant at Waterloo. He was finally promoted to captain in 1826 and retired by sale of his commission in 1831. For his service he was appointed Exon of the Yeomen of the Guard in 1844 and was made a Knight Bachelor on 30 June 1852. He died on 22 April 1862.[21] He received the MGSM with nine clasps.[22]

Leach, Jonathan commanded his company until the end of the Peninsular War. During that time he fought in twenty-one battles and sieges. Despite being wounded he assumed command of the 1st Battalion at Waterloo after the two senior officers above him became casualties. He was promoted to brevet major on 21 June 1813 and brevet lieutenant colonel on 18 June 1815. He was made a CB on 22 June 1815 and was promoted to major in the Rifle Brigade on 9 September 1819.

---

18. 'Orders, Decorations, Medals and Militaria: Major General John Cox, late 95th Rifles'. *Dix Noonan Webb Auctions*, 2019.
19. Roliça, Vimeiro, Busaco, Fuentes de Oñoro, Ciudad Rodrigo, Vitoria, the Pyrenees, Nivelle, Nive and Orthes.
20. Green, pp.36–7, 58–9. Mullen, A.L.T., *The Military General Service Roll: 1793 – 1814*. Dallington: Naval and Military Press, 1990, p.526.
21. Dalton, Charles, *The Waterloo Roll Call*. New York: Hippocrene, 1978, p.173.
22. Fuentes de Oñoro, Ciudad Rodrigo, Badajoz, Salamanca, Vitoria, Pyrenees, Nivelle, Nive and Toulouse.

He retired by sale of his commission on 24 October 1821. He received the MGSM with twelve clasps.[23] He died on 14 January 1855.

Maher, Thomas. After being captured at Barba del Puerco, he was sent to France where he remained a prisoner until peace was declared in 1814. He rejoined the regiment at Dover and went with them to Belgium the following year. Edward Costello wrote that he missed the battle because

> A quarrel had originated a few nights before the battle of Waterloo in a wine-house at Brussels, between some of our men, and the Belgian gens-d'armes; the consequence was, that the inhabitants were forced to send for the guards. These, of course, were soon on the spot, but were as soon attacked and beaten back by the Belgians, who would have driven them into the guard-house but for Meagher, who, suddenly turning to the assailants, levelled his rifle and shot the foremost through the body; on this, the whole of the gen-d'armes retreated, not, however, till after Meagher had received a cut on the side of the neck. For this affair he was put into prison, and a general court-martial honourably acquitted him, not until the battle had been fought which for ever destroyed Napoleon's hopes. Our company, to which Meagher belonged, soon after presented a requisition to Captain Leach, who then commanded us, and through his intercession, Meagher obtained a Waterloo medal.[24]

McCullock, John. After being captured on 24 July 1810 he refused to give his parole and was sent to Valladolid with the other men who had been captured. There he obtained clothing from a Spanish peasant and made his way back to the army. On 15 March 1811, at Foz do Arouce, he was shot in the shoulder joint and lost the use of his arm and was

---

23. Roliça, Vimiero, Busaco, Fuentes de Oñoro, Ciudad Rodrigo, Badajoz, Salamanca, Vitoria, Pyrenees, Nivelle, Nive and Toulouse.
24. Costello, pp.26–7. This may be a bit of a fantasy. According to the *Waterloo Medal Roll*, there was no Meagher or Maher who received a Waterloo Medal. However in the 2nd Battalion in Captain Eaton's Company, there was a Thomas McCann and a Patrick Maghan. Could they be the one he is referring to? *Waterloo Medal Roll*. Dallington: Naval and Military Press, 1992, pp.318 & 329.

sent back to England to recover. He was promoted to captain in 1813 and fought in the 1814 campaign in the Netherlands. At Waterloo he was shot in his other arm and, having told Wellington that although '. . . having no longer an arm to wield for his country, but being anxious to serve it', he was promoted to major in the 2nd Garrison Battalion in December 1815. He went on half-pay on 25 December 1816 and died in London in 1818.[25]

Mercer, James was killed at Barba del Puerco. He was providing the only support to his mother. She was awarded a £40 pension by the government on 25 December 1815 because she was living in poverty.[26]

Mitchell, Samuel transferred to the 2nd Battalion 95th Rifles when one company joined the Light Division in January 1811. He fought with the Light Division and was severely wounded at Ciudad Rodrigo on 16 January 1812. In April 1812 he was seconded to the Portuguese 6th Caçadores and promoted to major. He fought with them at Vitoria and the Pyrenees in 1813. He was promoted to major in the 95th Rifles in September 1813 and served with the regiment in the New Orleans Campaign in 1814–15. He was promoted to lieutenant colonel in the 31st Foot in 1829 and transferred to the 3rd Foot in 1830. He died in Berhampore, India on 3 June 1833. He was made a CB on 4 June 1815.

O'Hare, Peter was promoted to major on 11 April 1811 and died in the assault on Badajoz on 6 April 1812.

Simmons, George was promoted to 1st lieutenant on 25 July 1811 and fought with the battalion in Portugal, Spain and France until the end of the war in 1814. He was severely wounded at Waterloo but continued to serve with the 1st Battalion. Like his friend John Kincaid, he too was finally promoted to captain in 1828 and major in 1838. He retired by the sale of his commission in 1845 and died in 1858 at the age of 72. He received the MGSM with eight clasps.[27]

---

25. Kincaid, pp.205–06. Cope, p.210.
26. *Journal of the House of Commons*, Vol. 72, p.541.
27. Fuentes de Oñoro, Ciudad Rodrigo, Badajoz, Salamanca, Vitoria, Pyrenees, Nivelle and Toulouse.

Smith, Harry was appointed the Brigade Major of the 2nd Brigade of the Light Division in March 1811 and served in that position until the end of the war in April 1814. He was promoted to captain on 28 February 1812. After the Peninsular War was over, he went to North America and served on the staff during the Chesapeake and New Orleans campaigns. He returned to Europe in time to participate in the Waterloo campaign and was the Brigade Major of the 10th British Brigade.[28] He was promoted to major in 1826 and lieutenant colonel in 1830. From 1828–40 he served in South Africa and fought in the Kaffir War.[29] He was sent to India in 1840, where he served as the Adjutant General. He fought in the Gwalior Campaign of 1843 and commanded a division in the 1st Sikh War[30] and won the battle of Aliwal on 28 January 1846. He was promoted to major general and returned to South Africa in 1847, where he was appointed the governor of the Cape of Good Hope. He served in that position until 1852. During that time he led the British forces in the 7th and 8th Kaffir Wars[31] between 1847 and 1851. He returned to Great Britain and served on the Home Staff and promoted to lieutenant general in 1854. He retired in 1859 and died on 12 October 1860. For his service he was made a CB on 22 June 1815, a KCB on 2 May 1844, and a GCB on 7 April 1846. In July 1846 he was created a baronet. He received a MGSM with twelve clasps.[32] The city of Ladysmith, South Africa is named after his wife.

Stewart, James was killed in a skirmish at Freixadas, Portugal on 28 March 1811.[33]

Tomlinson, James was captured by the French and survived his wounds. He was sent to a prison in the Alps. He was repatriated to England when the war ended in 1814 and rejoined the regiment. He fought with

---

28. Part of Lieutenant General Sir Galbraith Cole's 6th Division.
29. 1834–5.
30. 1845–6.
31. Also known as the Xhosa Wars.
32. Corunna, Busaco, Fuentes de Oñoro, Ciudad Rodrigo, Badajoz, Salamanca, Vitoria, Pyrenees, Nivelle, Nive, Orthes and Toulouse
33. This was Lieutenant James Stewart, the Brigade Major of the 1st Brigade, not Captain James Stewart.

the 2nd Battalion at Waterloo and eventually retired to Hinckley with a pension of 9 pence per day.[34]

1st Caçadores

Algeo, John was promoted to lieutenant colonel on 12 April 1812 and assumed command of the battalion the same day. He was killed in action at the Bidassoa on 17 October 1813. He was awarded the AGM with two clasps for Badajoz, Salamanca and Vitoria.

de Avilez, Jorge was promoted to colonel and took command of the 2nd Portuguese Line Infantry Regiment in February 1812. He was promoted to brigadier general in 1816. He led the Portuguese Army during the Banda Oriental Campaign in Brazil from 1818–20 and was promoted to lieutenant general in 1821. During the Liberal Wars, he was a constitutionalist and was named the commander-in-chief of the Portuguese Army in 1823. After the coup-d'etat that ended the Liberal Wars, General de Avilez was stripped of his rank and imprisoned. In 1834 he was restored to his former rank and the following year was named a Peer of the Realm. He died on 15 February 1845 at the age of 60.

2nd Caçadores

Nixon, Robert served as the commander of the 2nd Caçadores until July 1811, when he returned to his regiment, the 28th Foot. He was promoted to brevet lieutenant colonel in the British Army on 30 May 1811. He fought with his regiment in the Peninsula until November 1813 when he returned to England. He was wounded at Waterloo and became a CB on 22 June 1815. He retired from the army in 1816. He died unmarried on 26 August 1826.[35]

3rd Caçadores

Elder, George led the 3rd Caçadores until April 1812. On 30 May 1811 he was promoted to brevet lieutenant colonel in the British Army. At the siege of Badajoz he led the 1st Brigade of the Light Division and was

---

34. Green, p.29.
35. Swanzy, Henry, *The Families of French of Belturbet and Nixon of Fermanagh.* Privately printed, 1907, p.74.

seriously wounded during the assault on 6 April and developed lockjaw. He was sent to home to recover. Before he went home he was made a Knight Commander of the Portuguese Tower and Sword. Upon his return to Portugal he was promoted colonel in the Portuguese Army on 10 July 1813 and given command of the 6th Portuguese Line Regiment. On 26 February 1814 he took command of the Portuguese 7th Line Regiment. At the end of the war in April 1814, Colonel Elder marched back to Portugal with his regiment and stayed with the Portuguese Army. He was promoted to brigadier general and in 1816 to major general in the Portuguese Army. He returned to England in 1823. In 1830 he was promoted to major general in the British Army. In 1836 he was sent to India to serve on the staff at Madras. A week after his arrival he was thrown from his horse and died from his injuries on 3 December. During the Peninsular War, George Elder was wounded nine times. For his service, he was mentioned in dispatches four times[36] and received an AGC for commanding at Busaco, Fuentes de Oñoro, Ciudad Rodrigo and Badajoz.[37] He was made a Knight Bachelor on 11 November 1813, a CB on 4 June 1815 and a KCB on 13 September 1831.

1st KGL Hussars

Aly, Wilhelm stayed with the regiment until he was promoted to major in the 2nd KGL Hussars in January 1814. He rejoined the Hanoverian Army in 1816 when the KGL was dissolved. He was promoted to colonel in the 6th Hanoverian Dragoons and commanded the 4th Cavalry Brigade. He died at Osnabruck on 26 March 1833.

Arentschildt, Friedrich led the 1st KGL Hussars until 26 January 1814 when he took command of the 3rd KGL Hussars. He led the 7th British Cavalry Brigade in the Waterloo campaign. Upon the disbanding of the KGL in 1816 he entered Hanoverian service and was promoted to major general commanding a cavalry brigade. He died at Northeim on 10 December 1820 at the age of 65.[38] He was created an Honourary KCB on 2 January 1815. He received the AGC with one clasp for Talavera, Fuentes de Oñoro, Salamanca, Vitoria and Toulouse.

---

36. The Côa, Sabugal, Ciudad Rodrigo and Badajoz.
37. *United Services Magazine*, 1837, Vol. 2, pp.233–9.
38. Beamish, Vol. 2, p.556.

Bergmann, Georg was severely wounded at El Bodón on 25 September 1811. He died from his wounds on 17 October 1811.

Cordemann, Ernst was promoted to captain on 20 June 1813 and served with the regiment throughout the Peninsular War and in the Waterloo campaign. By July 1815, in addition to numerous skirmishes, he had fought in sixteen battles. Upon the disbanding of the KGL in 1816, he returned to Hanover. For his service he received the Hanover Guelphic Order and the British Waterloo Medal. Rather than joining the Hanoverian Army, he chose to stay in the British Army and went on half pay as a lieutenant colonel. He died in Langenhagen on 27 September 1833.[39]

Krauchenberg, Georg served with the regiment until he was promoted to major in the 3rd KGL Hussars on 20 June 1813. He was wounded several times during the Peninsular War. He left the Peninsula in August 1813. He helped train the new Hanoverian Army and served in north Germany in 1814 and at Waterloo. After the KGL was disbanded in 1816 he rejoined the Hanoverian Army and eventually was promoted to major general. He served as the Inspector of Cavalry, commanded the 3rd Cavalry Brigade and the 1st Cavalry Division. He died at Hanover on 14 May 1843. He was made a CB on 4 June 1815. There is no record of whether the French returned his dog.[40]

14th Light Dragoons

Brotherton, Thomas went home to England in January 1811, but returned to Portugal by late April. He remained with the regiment until he was promoted to major in the 3rd Dragoon Guards on 28 November 1811. He returned to England again and exchanged back into the 14th Light Dragoons on 26 March 1812. In June 1812 he came back to the Peninsula and rejoined the 14th Light Dragoons. He fought with the regiment through the rest of the war. During the 52 months he spent in Portugal and Spain he fought in twelve battles and actions. He was wounded three times, the third at Nive in December 1813, where he was taken prisoner. He was promoted to brevet lieutenant colonel on 19 May 1814. He continued to be promoted over the years and in 1860 was made a general. For his service, he was made a CB on 3 February

---

39. Beamish, Vol. 2, p.549.
40. Ibid., Vol. 2, p.556.

1817, a KCB on 5 July 1855 and a GCB on 28 June 1861. He was awarded the MGSM with eight clasps.[41] General Brotherton died in Esher, Surrey on 20 January 1868 at the age of 85.

Hanley, William. By 1812 he had been promoted to corporal and was presented with a silver medal by the officers of the regiment for leading a patrol after the Battle of Salamanca that captured two French officers and several dragoons at Blasco Sancho.[42] He retired as the sergeant major of the regiment. After retiring, he became the foreman of the works at the Tower of London and was still alive in January 1855.[43] He was awarded the MGSM with eleven clasps.[44]

16th Light Dragoons

Cocks, Edward was promoted to brevet major in May 1811, when he became General Stapleton Cotton's ADC. He purchased a majority in the 79th Foot on 20 February 1812 and was killed at the siege of Burgos on 8 October 1812.

Tomkinson, William served with the 16th Light Dragoons until March 1812, when he purchased a captaincy in the 60th Foot. Three months later he exchanged into the 16th Light Dragoons and served with them until September 1813 when he returned to England. He fought with the regiment at Waterloo. He went on half pay in 1821. He was promoted lieutenant colonel in 1837. He retired by sale of his commission in 1849 and died in 1872. He received the MGSM with four clasps: Busaco, Fuentes de Oñoro, Salamanca and Vitoria.

Captain Ross's Royal Horse Artillery Troop

Jenkinson, George served in the Peninsula with Captain Ross's troop until the end of the war in 1814. During those 58 months he fought

---

41. Egypt, Busaco, Fuentes de Oñoro, Salamanca, Vitoria, the Pyrenees, Nivelle and Nive.
42. Tancred, George, *Historical Records of Medals and Honorary Distinctions*. London: George Murray, 1891, p.311.
43. Hanley, p.348.
44. Talavera, Busaco, Fuentes de Oñoro, Badajoz, Salamanca, Vitoria, Pyrenees, Nivelle, Nive, Orthes and Toulouse.

in fifteen actions and was promoted to brevet major on 21 June 1813. He commanded the troop at Orthes on 27 February 1814 and received the AGM for it. He was promoted to brevet lieutenant colonel on 12 April 1814 and to captain in the Royal Artillery on 20 December 1814. During the 100 Days in 1815 he was appointed a colonel on the staff and attached to the Württemberg Army as an observer.[45] He was a first cousin to Robert 2nd Earl of Liverpool, the Prime Minister. He died in London on 21 March 1823.

Ross, Hew Dalrymple commanded his troop for the 58 months it was in the Peninsula. Most of that time he was attached to the Light Division, during which he was in twenty-three battles or actions. He was promoted to major on 31 December 1811 and to brevet lieutenant colonel on 21 June 1813. He was mentioned in dispatches five times. He received the AGC with two clasps[46] and the MGSM with three clasps.[47] He and his troop fought at Waterloo. Over the next 39 years he was promoted through the ranks until he was promoted to general on 28 November 1854. On 1 January 1868, he became a field marshal and on 3 August he was appointed the lieutenant governor of the Royal Hospital at Chelsea. He died in Knightsbridge on 10 December 1868 at the age of 89. On 2 January 1815, he was made a KCB and on 28 June 1861 a GCB.

Smyth, George Barttelot served with Captain Ross's troop in the Peninsula until 1 December 1813 when he resigned his commission. During the 54 months he was in Portugal and Spain he fought in fourteen actions. After returning to England he became a magistrate and a Deputy Lieutenant of the County of Sussex. He changed his name to Barttelot in 1837. He died on 28 November 1872 at the age of 84.[48] He received the MGSM with five clasps.[49]

Royal Engineers

Burgoyne, John served in the Peninsula until the end of the war in April 1814. He was involved in every siege the British army undertook, except

---

45. *Royal Military Calendar*, 3 vols. London: Egerton, 1815. Vol. 3, pp.324–5.
46. Busaco, Badajoz, Salamanca, Vitoria, Nivelle and Nive. Due to multiple awards he received an Army Gold Cross with two clasps.
47. Fuentes de Oñoro, Ciudad Rodrigo and the Pyrenees.
48. Bromley, Vol. 2, p.295.
49. Busaco, Fuentes de Oñoro, Ciudad Rodrigo, Badajoz and Salamanca.

first Badajoz in 1811. He was awarded a brevet lieutenant colonelcy for his performance at the second siege of Badajoz in 1812. At the end of the war he was part of the army that was sent to North America and was the senior Royal Engineer during the New Orleans campaign. He missed Waterloo. In 1855, at the age of 72, he was with the British army in the Crimea. He was the first Royal Engineer to be promoted to field marshal. He died in 1871 at the age of 89. For his service in the Peninsula, he received an AGM with a clasp[50] and the MGSM with three clasps: Busaco, Ciudad Rodrigo and Nivelle. He became a CB on 4 June 1815, a KCB on 19 July 1838, and GCB on 31 March 1852.

Mulcaster, Edmund served during the first and second sieges of Badajoz, was wounded at the siege of Ciudad Rodrigo on 15 January 1812, and killed on 25 March 1812 during the third siege of Badajoz.

---

50. Badajoz, Salamanca, Vitoria, San Sebastian and Nive.

Appendix I

Strength of the Light Division, February–December 1810

Every infantry battalion and cavalry regiment in the British Army was required to submit a report to the Horse Guards of its strength on the 25th of each month. For those battalions in Great Britain, the strength return was submitted by the regiment. For battalions on active service, the return was sent up through its chain of command to the headquarters of the theatre where the battalion was assigned. A return was also sent to its regiment in Great Britain. The regimental returns usually did not contain as much information as those from the theatre headquarters. Furthermore, because of the delay of receiving the returns from the theatre, the information in the regimental returns could be one or two months out of date.

The returns are divided into four separate categories:

- Officers Present: this reflected the officers who were present for duty with the battalion. It did not include the officers who were assigned to the battalion but who were on the army staff.
- Staff Officers: like Officers Present, this section only included the officers who were present for duty with the battalion and not those who were performing temporary duty on the staff of the army.
- NCOs: this included sergeants, but not corporals. Additionally musicians, such as drummer, buglers and trumpeters, were also included in this section.
- Rank and File: this section included all soldiers who were not officers, sergeants or musicians. It did not differentiate by rank.

  - Fit for Duty: the total number of soldiers who were available to perform their duty. Some returns have this category as Present or Present Fit for Duty.

- Sick: the number of soldiers who were incapacitated due to injury, illness, or wounds. The returns did not break the numbers down by why the soldiers were incapacitated. In some returns it was further divided by those who were sick in their quarters and those who were hospitalized.
- On Command: the number of soldiers who were assigned to the battalion but were detached for duty in another location.
- Total: the total of rank and file soldiers assigned to the battalion, regardless of their status.
- Dead: the number of soldiers who died from disease, injury, or combat.
- Deserters: This section shows the number of deserters since the previous month. It also listed those soldiers thought to have been taken prisoner.

Abbreviations:

1LT	First Lieutenant
2LT	Second Lieutenant
Adj	Adjutant
Bu	Bugler
Cor	Cornet
CPT	Captain
Dr	Drummer
Ens	Ensign
LT	Lieutenant
Maj	Major
NCO	Non-Commissioned Officer
Pay	Paymaster
QM	Quarter-master
SGT	Sergeant
Tr	Trumpeter

Table A1.1: 1s: Battalion 43rd Foot, February–December 1810

Date	Officers Present							Staff Officers			NCOs		Rank and File					
	LTC	Maj	CPT	LT	Ens	Pay	Adj	QM	Surgeon	Assistant Surgeon	SGT	Dr	Fit for Duty	Sick	On Command	Total	Dead	Deserted
February	1	1	8	21	1	–	–	1	1	1	55	23	819	146	15	980	7	–
March	1	1	7	18	1	–	–	1	1	1	54	23	843	112	29	971	7	–
April	–	2	17	19	1	–	–	1	1	1	54	23	843	112	14	969	3	–
May	–	2	8	25	1	–	1	1	1	1	54	23	849	98	18	965	3	–
June	–	2	8	20	1	1	1	1	1	1	56	23	846	95	18	959	3	–
July	–	2	7	21	8	1	1	1	1	3	54	22	760	143	26	929	16	–
August	–	2	8	22	8	1	1	1	1	3	56	22	724	162	36	922	11	–
September	1	2	8	21	6	1	1	1	–	2	57	23	742	250	24	1016	5	–
October	1	2	8	21	6	1	1	1	1	2	57	22	679	306	23	1008	2	1
November	1	2	8	20	6	1	1	1	1	2	59	22	738	205	28	971	16	–
December	1	1	8	20	6	1	1	1	1	2	56	23	769	167	31	967	5	2

Table A1.2: 1st Battalion 52nd Foot, February–December 1810

Date	Officers Present					Staff Officers					NCOs		Rank and File					
	LTC	Maj	CPT	LT	Ens	Pay	Adj	QM	Surgeon	Assistant Surgeon	SGT	Dr	Fit for Duty	Sick	On Command	Total	Dead	Deserted
February	1	2	7	18	3	–	1	1	–	1	58	19	905	103	39	1047	11	1
March	1	2	7	19	1	–	1	1	–	1	56	20	929	98	15	1042	4	56
April	1	2	7	19	2	–	1	1	1	1	56	20	945	84	13	1042	1	56
May	1	2	7	19	1	–	1	1	1	1	56	21	940	88	15	1043	5	–
June	1	2	8	19	1	1	1	1	1	–	56	21	950	68	18	1036	1	1
July	1	2	9	19	1	1	1	1	1	1	55	21	928	82	18	1028	3	–
August	–	2	9	17	1	1	1	1	1	1	60	21	911	90	20	1021	1	1
September	–	2	9	17	1	1	1	1	1	1	59	21	862	135	21	1018	2	2
October	–	2	9	19	7	1	1	1	1	1	60	21	791	192	24	1007	8	–
November	1	1	8	20	7	1	1	1	1	2	60	21	817	158	23	998	1	9
December	1	1	8	20	7	1	1	1	1	2	60	22	829	141	23	993	3	0

Table A1.3: 1st Battalion 95th Rifles, February–December 1810

Date	Officers Present							Staff Officers			NCOs		Rank and File					
	LTC	Maj	CPT	1LT	2LT	Pay	Adj	QM	Surgeon	Assistant Surgeon	SGT	Bu	Fit for Duty	Sick	On Command	Total	Dead	Deserted
February	1	1	9	20	4	1	1	–	1	1	60	14	820	119	8	947	10	–
March	1	2	9	17	4	1	1	–	1	1	58	14	809	110	20	939	8	–
April	1	2	7	19	?¹	1	1	–	1	1	53	14	816	92	18	918	14	–
May	1	2	7	19	3	1	1	1	1	–	53	14	824	76	18	918	2	–
June	1	2	7	21	2	1	1	1	1	–	51	13	839	56	9	904	2	–
July	1	2	6	19	2	1	1	1	1	1	50	13	839	56	9	904	2	1
August	–	2	7	17	2	1	–	1	1	1	50	13	723	110	7	840	11	1
September	–	2	8	14	11	1	–	1	1	1	52	13	728	97	18	843	–	–
October	–	2	9	16	5	1	–	1	1	1	50	13	688	134	10	841	–	–
November	–	2	9	17	5	1	–	1	1	1	48	14	646	169	16	831	13	–
December	–	2	9	16	7	1	–	1	1	1	47	16	671	120	16	807	10	3

1. Information is not available.

389

Table A1.4: Captain Charles Beckwith's Company 2nd Battalion 95th Rifles, September–December 1810

Date	Officers Present					Staff Officers					NCOs		Rank and File					
	LTC	Maj	CPT	1LT	2LT	Pay	Adj	QM	Surgeon	Assistant Surgeon	SGT	Bu	Fit for Duty	Sick	On Command	Total	Dead	Deserted
September	–	–	1	2	1	–	–	–	–	1	6	2	99	3	0	102	–	–
October	–	–	1	1	1	–	–	–	–	1	6	2	81	19	2	102	–	–
November	–	–	1	1	1	–	–	–	–	1	6	2	83	17	1	101	1	–
December	–	–	1	1	1	–	–	–	–	1	6	2	70	29	0	99	2	–

Table A1.5: Captain William Percival's Company 3rd Battalion 95th Rifles, November–December 1810

Date	Officers Present					Staff Officers					NCOs		Rank and File					
	LTC	Maj	CPT	1LT	2LT	Pay	Adj	QM	Surgeon	Assistant Surgeon	SGT	Bu	Fit for Duty	Sick	On Command	Total	Dead	Deserted
November	–	–	1	2	2	–	–	–	–	–	6	2	68	27	2	97	–	–
December	–	–	1	3	2	–	–	–	–	–	6	2	65	30	2	97	–	–

Table A1.6: Brunswick Oëls, November–December 1810

Date	Officers Present								Staff Officers		NCOs		Rank and File					
	LTC	Maj	CPT	1LT	2LT	Pay	Adj	QM	Surgeon	Assistant Surgeon	SGT	Dr	Fit for Duty	Sick	On Command	Total	Dead	Deserted
November	1	1	10	23	8	1	1	1	1	1	54	22	700	197	18	915	6	24
December	1	1	9	21	9	1	1	1	1	1	53	23	684	172	38	894	16	2

Table A1.7: 1st KGL Hussars, March–July 1810

Date	Officers Present								Staff Officers			NCOs		Rank and File						Horses
	LTC	Maj	CPT	LT	Cor	Pay	Adj	QM	Surgeon	Ast Surgeon	Vet Surg	SGT	Tr Dr	Fit for Duty	Sick	On Cmd	Total	Dead	Deserted	Fit for Duty
March	1	1	5	6	6	–	–	1	1	1	1	37	8	389	53	87	459	4	2	458
April	1	1	6	6	6	–	–	3[2]	1	1	1	37	8	395	56	77	536	1	–	453
May	1	1	5	7	3	1	1	5[3]	1	1	1	36	8	426	72	25	523	–	–	538
June	1	–	6	6	7	–	1	3[4]	1	1	1	35	7	427	39	19	486	1	4	528
July	1	–	5	5	7	–	1	4[5]	1	1	1	35	7	421	42	19	482	1	2	512

2. Includes two Quartermasters of Cavalry, who were NCOs.
3. No Quartermaster but five Quartermasters of Cavalry, who were NCOs.
4. Includes two Troop Quartermasters, who were NCOs.
5. Includes three Troop Quartermasters.

Table A1.8: 14th Light Dragoons, June–July 1810

Date	Officers Present								Staff Officers			NCOs		Rank and File						Horses
	LTC	Maj	CPT	LT	Cor	Pay	Adj	QM	Surgeon	Ast Surgeon	Vet Surg	SGT	Tr	Fit for Duty	Sick	On Cmd	Total	Dead	Deserted	Fit for Duty
June	1	2	8	11	–	1	1	5[6]	1	1	1	39	7	499	26	49	574	5	1	540
July	–	2	8	11	–	1	1	3[7]	–	2	1	39	7	452	68	48	568	6	1	524

Table A1.8: 16th Light Dragoons, June–July 1810

Date	Officers Present								Staff Officers			NCOs		Rank and File						Horses
	LTC	Maj	CPT	LT	Cor	Pay	Adj	QM	Surgeon	Ast Surgeon	Vet Surg	SGT	Tr	Fit for Duty	Sick	On Cmd	Total	Dead	Deserted	Fit for Duty
June	–	2	7	13	4	1	1	5[8]	1	1	1	36	7	484	41	46	571	0	0	543
July	–	2	6	13	4	1	1	5[9]	1	1	1	35	7	490	34	43	567	1	1	532

2. No Quartermaster but five Troop Quartermasters.
3. No Quartermaster but three Troop Quartermasters.
4. No Quartermaster but five Troop Quartermasters.
5. No Quartermaster but five Troop Quartermasters.

Appendix II

Gazetteer of Place Names

Using modern maps to find places mentioned by the officers and men of the Light Division in their letters, diaries and memoirs can quite difficult. In the nineteenth century, spelling of these places was not standardized and often they spelled it the way it sounded to them, which varied depending on the writer. Sometimes the writer would spell the name differently when he wrote. Compounding the problem is that some of the names of the places have changed over the past 200 years. Below is a listing of the contemporary names as used by those in the Light Division and their twenty-first century names.

Nineteenth-Century Name	Modern Name
Alemquer, Portugal	Alenquer, Portugal
Alfayates, Portugal	Alfaiates, Portugal
As Naves, Portugal	Naves, Portugal
Arruda, Portugal	Arruda dos Vinhos, Portugal
Azaza River	Azaba River
Azeva, Portugal	Azevo, Portugal
Barraçal, Portugal	Baraçal, Portugal
Barba del Puerco, Spain	Puerto Seguro, Spain
Busaco, Portugal	Buçaco, Portugal
Bussaco, Portugal	Buçaco, Portugal
Calhandria, Portugal	Calhandriz, Portugal
Capilla, Spain	Capilla del Rio, Spain
Carboneros, Spain	Molino Carbonero, Spain
Carnathal, Portugal	Carvalhal de Atalaia, Portugal
Carpio, Spain	Carpio de Azaba, Spain
Carvalhal, Portugal	Carvalhal de Atalaia, Portugal
Castaneira, Portugal	Castanheira do Ribatejo, Portugal

Castello Branco, Portugal	Castelo Branco, Portugal
Castello Rodrigo, Portugal	Castelo Rodrigo, Portugal
Castillejo, Spain	Castillejo de dos Casas, Spain
Cavahal, Portugal	Carvalhal de Atalaia, Portugal
Celorico, Portugal	Celorico da Beira, Portugal
Cismeiro, Spain	Sexmiro, Spain
Coa River	Côa River
Condeixa, Portugal	Condeixa-a-Nova, Portugal
Convent of Busaco, Portugal	Convento de Santa Cruz do Buçaco, Portugal
Foz d'Arounce, Portugal	Foz d'Arouce, Portugal
Freixeda, Portugal	Freixedas, Portugal
Gallegos, Spain	Gallegos de Argañán, Spain
Izambuja, Portugal	Azambuja, Portugal
La Alameda, Spain	La Alameda de Gardón, Spain
La Calzada, Spain	Calzada de Oropesa, Spain
Ladocir, Portugal	Ladoeiro, Portugal
Lobral Pequeña, Portugal	Sobralihno, Portugal
Malpartida, Spain	Malpartida de Plasencia, Spain
Manzana, Spain	el Manzano, Spain
Marialva, Spain	Marialba, Spain
Molino Carboneros, Spain	Molino Carbonero, Spain
Molinos dos Flores Ford	Vado de Flores Ford
Orapeza, Spain	Oropesa, Spain
Palacios, Spain	Dehesa de Palacios, Spain
Pezerel, Spain	Dehesa del Pizarral, Spain
Ponte de Murcella, Portugal	Ponte da Mucela, Portugal
Ponte do Seca, Portugal	Ponte D'Asseca, Portugal
Ponte do Seleiro, Portugal	Ponte do Celeiro, Portugal
Ponto do Souro, Portugal	Ponte de Sor, Portugal
Puerto de Baños, Spain	Baños de Montemayor, Spain
Punhete, Portugal	Constância, Portugal
Sampayo, Portugal	São Paio, Gouveia, Portugal
Santarem, Portugal	Santarém, Portugal
St. Cambadaō, Portugal	Santa Comba Dào, Portugal
San Felices el Chico, Spain	Saelices el Chico, Spain
Serra de Busaco, Portugal	Serra do Buçaco, Portugal
Sobral, Portugal	Sobral de Monte Agraço, Portugal
St. Julien, Portugal	São Julião da Barra, Portugal
Sula, Portugal	Sula Mortágua, Portugal

394

Tourones River	Tourões River
Truxillo, Spain	Trujillo, Spain
Upper Beira, Portugal	Beira Alta, Portugal
Val de Mula, Portugal	Vale da Mula, Portugal
Val Verde, Portugal	Valverde, Portugal
Valle, Portugal	Vale de Santarém, Portugal
Venta de Bazagona, Spain	La Bazagona, Spain
Villa Franca, Portugal	Vila Franca de Xira, Portugal
Villa Mayor, Portugal	Vilar Maior, Portugal
Villa de Ciervo, Spain	Villar de Ciervo, Spain
Villa de Puerco, Spain	Villar de Argañán, Spain
Villa Novo, Portugal	Vila Nova de Foz Côa, Portugal
Villar Bridge, Spain	Casería Villar de Flores, Spain
Zibreira, Portugal	Zebreira, Portugal

Appendix III

Locations of Bridges and Fords across the Agueda and Azaba Rivers

Table A3.1: Agueda River Crossings

Nineteenth-Century Name	Modern Name	Geographical Coordinates	Military Grid Reference System with Map Name
Barba del Puerco Bridge	Puerto Seguro Bridge[1]	40°49'37.2'N 6°44'52.3'W	29TPF8990921993 Villar de Ciervo
Capilla Ford	Capilla del Rio Ford	40°38'09.9'N 6°37'10.7'W	29TQF0129701084 Ciudad Rodrigo
Ciudad Rodrigo Bridge	Ciudad Rodrigo Bridge	40°35'41.8'N 6°32'14.9'W	29TQE0837496708 Ciudad Rodrigo
La Caridid Trestle Bridge	La Caridid Trestle Bridge[2]	40°34'46.2'N 6°30'53.6'W	29TQE1033495047 Serradilla del Arroyo
Molino Carbonero Trestle Bridge	Molino Carbonero	40°36'26.1'N 6°35'11.7'W	29TQE0418197959 Ciudad Rodrigo
Molinos dos Flores Ford	Vado de Flores	40°37'29.0'N 6°38'57.3'W	29TPE9882799755 Ciudad Rodrigo
Molino de Copera Ford	Molino de Copera Ford[3]	40°42'51.7'N 6°39'31.8'W	29TPF9775109685 Villar de Ciervo
Molino de Valdespino Ford	Molino de Valdespino Ford[4]	40°43'35.1'N 6°40'09.2'W	29TPF9683811000 Villar de Ciervo

(continued)

---

1. Called Puente de los Franceses.
2. I have not been able to pinpoint exactly where this bridge was built, but the coordinates are the most likely location.
3. Located about 1.5km north-northeast of Serranillo.
4. Located about 2.5km north of Serrranillo.

Table A3.1: Continued

Nineteenth-Century Name	Modern Name	Geographical Coordinates	Military Grid Reference System with Map Name
Navas Frias Bridge	Navas Frias Bridge	40°17'45.5'N 6°48'57.6'W	29TPE8562562896 Gata
Pizarral Ford	Pizarral Ford	40°43'43.4'N 6°40'05.1'W	29TPF9692711258 Ciudad Rodrigo
Serranillo Ford	Serranillo Ford[5]	40°41'48.3'N 6°39'38.3'W	29TPF9765107726 Villar de Ciervo
Molíno de Gerbeduero Ford	Molíno de Gerbeduero Ford[6]	40°43'43.4'N 6°40'05.1'W	29TPF9692711258 Villar de Ciervo
Villar Bridge	Casería Villar de Flores[7]	40°19'40.6'N 6°44'02.6'W	29TPE9250066621 Gata

Table A3.2: Azaba River Crossings

Nineteenth-Century Name	Modern Name	Geographical Coordinates	Military Grid Reference with Map Name
Carpio Ford	Carpio de Azaba Ford[8]	40°34'36.7'N 6°39'38.0'W	29TPE9801294416 Ciudad Rodrigo
Carpio Ford	Carpio de Azaba Ford[9]	40°35'25.4'N 6°40'06.8'W	29TPE9729595900 Ciudad Rodrigo
Marialva Bridge	Marialba Bridge	40°37'28.2'N 6°39'38.7'W	29TPE9785599704 Ciudad Rodrigo
Marialva Ford	Marialba Ford[10]	40°36'50.7'N 6°40'30.8'W	29TPE9666198516 Ciudad Rodrigo

5. It is about 600m to the southeast of Serranillo. There is a bridge there now.
6. The ford is located 4km east of Villar de la Yegua.
7. The bridge is located where CV-199 crosses the Agueda, about 15km downstream of Navasfrias.
8. Located about 2.5km southwest of Carpio. There is a bridge there. It is where the Camino a Bodón crosses the river.
9. It is located 2km west of Carpio de Azaba. Also called the Don Clemente Arjona Ford. The E-80 bridge is there now.
10. Located about 1km southwest of the Marialba Bridge.

Appendix IV

General Craufurd's After-Action Report on the Combat at Villa de Puerco

Letter from Brigadier General Craufurd to Wellington dated Val de la Mula 12th July 1810[1]

The enemy had, during the last three or four days, been in the habit of coming with detachments of infantry and cavalry into Barquilla, and with infantry into Cesmiro and Villa de Puerco, and I was desirous of cutting them off. But considering the vicinity of the enemy's position, and his strength in cavalry, I did not think it prudent to send a small detachment, and I therefore ordered all that were off duty of six squadrons to assemble behind the Dos Casas at twelve at night, on the road which leads from La Conception to Alameda.

It was between one and two when we crossed the Dos Casas, and not a shot had then been heard since six or seven the preceding evening, from which circumstance, and the severe fire of the 9th and 10th, I felt apprehensive that Ciudad Rodrigo had surrendered.

Leaving Alameda on our right, and sending patroles on the road towards Gallegos, we went through the wood, and halted in a hollow within three quarters of a mile of Villa de Puerco. About sunrise, we marched off again; and I have to regret that I did not, as I originally intended, keep sufficiently to the right to come out of the wood between Cesmiro and Villa de Puerco; this would have prevented what happened. But the anxiety to do what we had to do, as quickly as possible, lest the enemy should have been advancing towards our position, (occasioned by the continued cessation of fire at Ciudad Rodrigo,) together with the

---

1. *WD*, Vol. 6, pp.252–3.

appearance of some cavalry making off, induced me to take the shorter road, which led us through a bad defile.

Immediately after the head of the column had come out of this defile, we discovered infantry, which, on account of a height and standing corn, were not seen until very close. The squadrons formed successively as they came out; and Krauchenberg's squadron of hussars, followed by the 16th, part of the former having gone off after some French dragoons. The hussars received the fire of the square; but being unable to penetrate it, they passed on, leaving it to their left. Had the 16th come straight upon it, the square being then without fire, it would probably have been broken; but they were too much to their left and passed it on the other flank. At this moment a most unfortunate mistake took place, to which alone is to be attributed the escape of the infantry.

Some French dragoons were seen coming out of Barquilla, and behind them was a body of Cavalry, which, from its position and manoeuvres, every one supposed to be French. Another body of cavalry was likewise seen marching towards Barquilla, upon the road which comes from Valdespino, and no doubt was entertained that these also were French. This drew off our attention from the infantry, and the 16th and hussars advanced towards the cavalry that were near Barquilla, which, except the first mentioned party of French dragoons, proved to be the squadron of the 14th from Aldea del Obispo. Still, no doubt was entertained that those coming by the Valdespino road were French, but they turned out to be Captain Gruben's squadron of hussars, who had been placed at night in the farm between Villa de Ciervo and Barquilla, in order to cut off the enemy's retreat. About the same time, a patrole from the Gallegos road brought the report of some squadrons of cavalry having entered Alameda.

Whilst this was passing, the 14th had come out of the defile; and I am informed by Major Harvey [sic] that the following circumstances took place.

Colonel Talbot, after the first squadron was formed, charged the square without effect, and was killed; and whilst Major Harvey was forming the other two, he received an order from Colonel Arenstschildt [sic] to march off from the left to oppose the cavalry near Barquilla which he also supposed to be French. The enemy's infantry, continuing its march, got into Cesmiro, which was too near to the enemy's position for it to be possible for me to think of attacking it, particularly as we were now convinced that Ciudad Rodrigo had fallen; although five companies of the 95th, and three of the 52nd, were in reserve between Castillejo and Barquilla.

We took two officers and twenty nine dragoons, as your Lordship knows. Our loss you are also acquainted with.

Return of the number of Killed, Wounded, and Missing of a detachment of the Army under the Command of his Excellency Lieut. General Viscount Wellington, K.B., in the affair near Villa de Puerco, on 11 July 1810

	Officers	Serjeants	Rank & File	Horses	Total loss of Officers, NCOs, and R&F
Killed	2	–	7	15	9
Wounded	–	2	20	16	22
Missing	–	–	1	1	1

General Craufurd's Report on the Combat of the Côa[1]

Marshal Massena, not content with the gross misrepresentations which were contained in the first official account of the affair of the 24th July, near Almeida, has in subsequent dispatch reverted to it in a tone of boasting, wholly unjustified by the circumstances, assuring the War Minister that his whole army is burning with impatience to teach the English army what they taught the division of Craufurd in the affair of Almeida. Brigadier-general Craufurd has therefore determined to give this public contradiction to the false assertions contained in Marshal Massena's report of an action, which was not only highly honourable to the light division, but which positively terminated in its favour, notwithstanding the extraordinary disparity of numbers. A corps of 4000 men remained during a whole day in presence of an army of 24,000 men; it performed in the presence of so superior a force, one of the most difficult operations of war, namely, a retreat from a very broken and extensive position, over one narrow defile. It defended, during the whole of the day, the first defensible position that was to be found in the neighbourhood of the place where the action commenced; and in the course of the affair, this corps of 4000 men, inflicted upon this army of 24,000 men, a loss equal to double to that which it sustained. Such were the circumstances of the action in which Brigadier-general Craufurd's corps was opposed to the army, commanded by Marshals Massena and Ney on the 24th of July, and it is therefore indisputable, that they had the best of it. From Marshal Massena's official dispatch, containing a statement of the force to which we were opposed, it appears

---

1. Craufurd, Robert, 'Action near Almeida', *Royal Military Chronicle* January 1811, pp.229–32.

that the cavalry consisted of the 3d hussars, 15th chasseurs, 10th, 15th, and 25th dragoons, and that the whole infantry of Ney's corps was present, except one regiment of the division of Marchaud [*sic*]. The infantry of Ney's corps according to the intercepted official returns, amounted at that time, to upwards of 22,000 effectives, and the cavalry regiments were certainly between 6 and 700 each. It therefore appears, that the force with which Marshals Massena and Ney advanced to attack the light division on the morning of the 24th July, consisted of 20,000 infantry, and between 3 and 4000 cavalry to which were opposed three English battalions, 43d, 52d, and 95th; two Portuguese battalions, (1st and 3d chasseurs) and eight squadrons of cavalry; making in the whole, a force of about 3200 British, and 1100 Portuguese troops. Almeida is a small fortress, situated at the edge of the declivity forming the right bank of the valley of the Coa, which river runs from the south to the north, and the bridge over which is nearly an English mile west of the town. From the 21st to the 24th of July, the chain of our cavalry out-posts formed a semicircle in front of Almeida, the right flank being appuyé [supported] to the Coa, near As Naves, which is about three miles above the place; and the left flank also appuyé to the river, near Cinco Villas, which is about three miles below the fortress. The centre of this line was covered by a small stream, and to the principal roads by which it was expected that the enemy would advance, namely, on the right and centre of this line, the cavalry posts were supported by piquets of infantry. The only road which our artillery, and the body of our cavalry could make use of to retreat across the Coa, was that which leads from Almeida to the bridge. The nature of the ground made it difficult for the enemy to approach this road on our left, that is to say, on the north side of the town, and the infantry of the division was therefore placed in a position to cover it on the right or south side, having its right flank appuyé to the Coa, above the bridge, its front covered by a deep and rocky ravine, and its left in some inclosures near a windmill, which is on the plain, about 800 yards south of the town. The Governor had intended to mount a gun upon the windmill, and one was actually in it, but it was useless, as it was not mounted, and another (also dismounted) was lying near the mill. These are the two guns which Marshal Massena says he took in the action. On the morning of the 24th, the centre of our line of piquets was attacked, namely, that which occupied the road leading from Almeida to Val de la Mula, which village is about four English miles east of the fortress. These piquets were supported by the 14th light dragoons and two guns, but when the head of a considerable column, with artillery, presented itself, and began to form on the other side of the rivulet, the piquets were withdrawn. The enemy then passed the rivulet, a cannonade took place, and the enemy formed a line of fifteen squadrons of cavalry, at a distance of about a mile from the above mentioned windmill, with artillery in its front, and a division of about 7000 infantry on its right; other troops were seen, though not so distinctly, advancing upon our right, It being now evident that we were opposed to a force as to render it impossible for Brigadier-general Craufurd to prevent the investment of the place, he determined to cross the Coa. He ordered the artillery and cavalry to move off by the road leading from the town to the bridge, and the infantry to follow, retiring across the vineyards towards the bridge. He directed that the infantry should move off in echelon from the left, it being necessary to hold the right till the last, in order to prevent the enemy approaching the bridge, by a road coming from Junca, and which runs in the bottom of the valley, close to the river. Some companies, which formed the left of our line, were in a vineyard, which had been so completely inclosed by a high stone wall, that it was quite impossible for cavalry to get into it; but the preceding night having been excessively bad, some of the troops who had been stationed in this vineyard, had unfortunately pulled down the wall in many places, to make use of the stones to form a shelter against the rain, which was most violent. This wall, which Brigadier-general Craufurd had considered a complete defence, was therefore no longer such, and after our artillery and cavalry had moved off, the enemy's cavalry broke into the inclosure, and took several prisoners. Our total loss, in prisoners and missing, amounted to about 60, after all those who were at first returned as such had joined their regiments. The 43d regiment having been on the left of the line, was the first that arrived near the bridge. The Brigadier-general ordered some companies of it to occupy a height in front of the bridge, and the remainder to pass over and form on the heights on the other side of the river. Part of the 95th regiment, and the 3d battalion of chasseurs, who arrived next, were formed on the right of these companies of the 43d regiment that were in front of the bridge. This position was maintained until every thing was over, and until one of the horse artillery ammunition waggons, which had been overturned in a very bad situation, was got up and dragged to the other side by the men. During the remainder of the day, the bridge was most gallantly defended by the 43d and part of the 95th regiments, and after it was dark we retreated from the Coa. To retire in tactical order over such ground, so broken, rocky and intersected with walls, as that which separated the first position from the second, would have been impossible, even if not under the fire of the enemy, and the ground on the other side of the river, was equally unfavourable for reforming the regiments. Whoever knows any thing of war, knows that in such an operation, and upon such ground, some derangement of regular order, is inevitable, but the retreat was made in a military, soldier-like manner, and without the slightest precipitation. In the course of it, the enemy, when he pressed was attacked in different places by the 43d, 52d, and 95th regiments, and driven before them. With respect to the enemy's loss, it is of course difficult to say what it was, because we know, that from the commencement of the revolutionary war to the present day, no French official report has ever contained a true account of their loss. Upon this occasion, Marshal Massena says – *'We have taken one stand of colours, four hundred men, and two pieces of cannon; our loss amounted to nearly three hundred killed and wounded.'* He took no colours, the cannon were the two dismounted guns belonging to the fortress, which were lying in and near the windmill, and instead of 400 prisoners, he took only about 60, supposing every one of those whom we returned as missing, to have fallen alive into the enemy's hands. Now, if in the same paragraph in which he states his own loss at 300, he calls 60 prisoners 400, we may fairly infer that he is not more accurate in the one than the other, and this circumstance, as well as the usual practice of their service, and the probability of the thing from what we could observe, fully justify us in assuming it to have been from 6 to 700; ours amounted, in killed, wounded, and prisoners, to 330. Such is the true account of this affair, upon which the Marshal prides himself so much, but in which it is certain, that the advantage was on our side. We could not pretend to prevent the investment of the place, but in our retreat, we did not lose a gun, a trophy, or a single article of field-equipage; and we inflicted on the enemy a loss, certainly the double of that which we sustained. The account contained in the commencement of the Marshal's dispatch, of what had passed on the 21st of July, is equally contrary to the truth. He talks of having forced the passage of the little rivulet that is between Almeida and Val de la Mula, on the 21st, whereas our piquets remained there, and not a single French man passed it until the morning of the 24th. He says, that many of our sharp-shooters fell into their hands on the 21st; the truth is, they did not take a single man. The retreat of the 14th dragoons from Val de la Mula, was conducted in the most slow and regular manner and all our intentions with respect to Fort Conception, were completely fulfilled.

(Signed) Rob. Craufurd, Brig. General.

Bibliography

British National Archives

WO12/6250 52nd Foot 1st Battalion 1810.
WO12/6313 52nd Foot 2nd Battalion 1810.
WO12/5573 43rd Foot 1st Battalion 1810.
WO12/5634 43rd Foot 2nd Battalion 1810.
WO12/9522 95th Foot 1st Battalion 1809.
WO12/9523 95th Foot 1st Battalion 1810.
WO12/9581 95th Foot 2nd Battalion 1810.
WO12/9586 95th Foot 3rd Battalion 1810.
WO12/1254 16th Light Dragoons 1810.
WO12/11652 Brunswick Light Infantry 1810.
WO12/11643 Brunswick Hussars 1810.

Portuguese Military Archive: Arquivo Histórico Militar (AHM)

AHM-DIV-1-14-270-01 Casualty Returns for 1st Caçadores Battalion dated 27 July 1810.
AHM-DIV-1-14-256-02 Casualty Returns for 1st Caçadores Battalion dated 27 September 1810.
AHM-DIV-1-14-256-02 Casualty Returns for 3rd Caçadores Battalion dated 27 September 1810.

Unpublished Sources

Brunton, Richard, 'A Narrative of the Services of Lieutenant Colonel Richard Brunton of the 13th Light Dragoons'. National Army Museum. File # 1968-07-461.
Cox, John, 'Extracts from John Cox's Diary of the Peninsula War'. Hampshire Archives. File # 170A12W/D/0021.

Cox, John, 'Extracts from William Cox's Diary'. Hampshire Archives.
Duffy, John, 'Diary'. National Army Museum. File # MS 9204-182-2.
Fergusson, James, 'Memoirs 1803 – 1818'. Typed transcription by Eileen Hathaway, 1999. Soldiers of Oxfordshire Museum. File # Sofo2135.
Freer Family Letters. Leicester Museum.
Henry Francis Mellish Papers. Nottingham University Archives.
Oglander, Henry, 'Diary'. Napier Collection, Bodleian Library, Oxford University. MS. Eng. misc. c. 471.

Print and Internet Sources

Amaral, Manuel, 'Jorge de Avilez', *O Portal da História*. Online, 2019.
Arentschildt, Friedrich von, *Instructions for Officers and Non-Commissioned Officers of Cavalry on Outpost Duty*. London: Parker, Furnivall, and Parker, 1844.
Bamford, Andrew, 'British Army Individual Unit Strengths: 1808–1815', *The Napoleon Series Online*, 2019.
Blakeney, Robert, *A Boy in the Peninsular War*. London: Greenhill, 1989.
Bromley, Janet and David, *Wellington's Men Remembered*. 2 vols Barnsley: Praetorian Press, 2015.
Brotherton, Thomas, *A Hawk at War: The Peninsular War Reminiscences of General Sir Thomas Brotherton*. Edited by Bryan Perrett. Chippenham: Picton Publishing; 1986.
Broughton, Tony, 'French Light Infantry Regiments and the Colonels who Led Them: 1791 to 1815', *The Napoleon Series Online*, 2019.
Brown, Steve, *Wellington's Red Jackets: The 45th (Nottinghamshire) Regiment on Campaign in South America and the Peninsula, 1805–14*. Barnsley: Frontline, 2015.
Brumwell, John, *The Peninsular War, 1808–1812. Letters of a Weardale Soldier, Lieutenant John Brumwell*. Edited by William Egglestone. Delhi: Facsimile Publisher, 2019.
Bruyère, Paul, *Historique du 2ᵉ Régiment de Dragons*. Chartres: Garnier, 1885.
Burgoyne, John, *Life and Correspondence of Field Marshal Sir John Burgoyne*. 2 vols. Edited by George Wrottesley. London: Richard Bentley; 1873.
Burnham, Robert, *Charging against Wellington: Napoleon's Cavalry in the Peninsular War 1807 – 1814*. Barnsley: Frontline, 2011.
Burnham, Robert and Ron McGuigan, *The British Army against Napoleon: Facts, Lists, and Trivia 1805 – 1815*. Barnsley: Frontline, 2010.
Buttery, David, *Wellington against Junot: the First Invasion of Portugal 1807 – 1808*. Barnsley: Pen & Sword, 2011.

Caldwell, George and Robert Cooper, *Rifle Green in the Peninsula*. 4 vols. Leicester: Bugle Horn, 1998.

Campbell, William and James Shaw, *Standing Orders as Given Out and Enforced by the Late Major-Gen. Rob Craufurd for the Use of the Light Division during the Years 1809, 10, and 11*. Godmanchester: Ken Trotman, 2006.

Challis, Lionel, 'British Officers Serving in the Portuguese Army, 1809 – 1814', *Journal of the Society for Army Historical Research*, Vol. 27, No. 110 (Summer, 1949), pp. 50–60.

Challis, Lionel, 'The Peninsular Roll Call', *The Napoleon Series Online*, 2019.

Chambers, George, *Bussaco*. Felling: Worley, 1994.

Cobbett's Political Register, various dates.

Cocks, Edward C., *Intelligence Officer in the Peninsula: Letters & Diaries of Major the Hon. Edward Charles Cocks 1786 – 1812*. Edited by Julia Page. New York: Hippocrene Books; 1986.

Compilação das Ordens do Dia, Quartel General do Exercito Portuguez Concenentes a Organização, Disciplina, e Economia Miitares na Campanha de 1810.

Combermere, Mary W., *Memoirs and correspondence of Field-Marshal Viscount Combermere*. 2 vols. London: Hurst and Blackett, 1866.

Cooke, John, *A Narrative of Events in the South of France and of the Attack on New Orleans, in 1814 and 1815*. London: T. & W. Boone: 1835.

Cope, William. *The History of the Rifle Brigade (the Prince Consort's Own) formerly the 95th*. London: Chatto & Windus, 1877.

Costello, Edward, *The Peninsular and Waterloo Campaigns*. Camden: Archon Books; 1968.

Craufurd, Alexander, *General Craufurd and His Light Division*. Uckfield: Naval and Military Press, 2004.

Craufurd, Robert, 'Action near Almeida', *Royal Military Chronicle*, January 1811, pp. 229–32.

Craufurd, Robert, *Standing Orders, as Given Out and Enforced by the Late Major-Gen. Robt. Craufurd for the Use of the Light Division during the Years 1809, 1810, and 1811*. Edited by William Pitcairn Campbell and James Shaw, Godmanchester: Ken Trotman, 2006.

Dalton, Charles, *The Waterloo Roll Call*. New York: Hippocrene, 1978.

Dawson, Henry and Charles, *'Every Implement of Destruction Was Used against Us': The Lives of Henry and Charles Dawson, 52nd Regiment of Light Infantry Based on their Peninsular War Letters*. Edited by Philip Abbott. Privately published, 2015.

de Brito, Pedro, *British Officers in the Portuguese Service 1809–1820*, Academia.edu. Accessed 7 March 2019.

de Miñano y Bedoya, Sebastián, *Diccionario geografico-estadistico de España y Portugal.* 11 vols. Madrid 1826–1829.

Dobbs, John, *Recollections of an Old 52nd Man.* Staplehurst: Spellmount; 2000.

D'Urban, Benjamin, *The Peninsular War Journal: 1808–1817.* London: Greenhill Napoleonic Library; 1988.

Dupuy, Raoul, *Historique du 3e Régiment de Hussards de 1764 a 1887.* Paris: Librairie Française, 1887.

European Magazine and London Review, various dates.

Fitzclarence, Frederick, *A Manual of Outpost Duties.* London: Parker, Furnivall, and Parker, 1851.

Garretty, Thomas, *Memoirs of a Sergeant Late in the Forty-third Light Infantry Regiment previous to and during the Peninsular War.* Cambridge: Ken Trotman; 1998.

Garwood, F.S., 'The Royal Staff Corps: 1800 – 1837', *Royal Engineer Journal,* Vol. 57, 1943.

Gates, David, *The British Light Infantry Arm c. 1790 – 1815.* London: B.T. Batsford, 1987.

General Orders: Spain and Portugal. Vol. 2. London: Egerton Military Library, 1811.

Gentleman's Magazine, various dates.

Glover, Gareth, *The Two Battles of Copenhagen 1801 and 1807: Britain & Denmark in the Napoleonic Wars.* Barnsley: Pen & Sword, 2018.

Glover, Michael, *Wellington's Army in the Peninsula 1808–1814.* New York: Hippocrene, 1977.

Gordon, Alexander, *At Wellington's Right Hand: the Letters of Lieutenant-Colonel Sir Alexander Gordon, 1808 – 1815.* Edited by Rory Muir. Phoenix Mill: Sutton, 2003.

Grattan, William, *Adventures with the Connaught Rangers: 1809 – 1814.* London: Greenhill, 1989.

Green, William, *Where Duty Calls Me: The Experiences of William Green of Lutterworth in the Napoleonic Wars.* Edited by John and Dorothea Teague. West Wickham: Synjon Books; 1975.

Grehan, John, *The Lines of Torres Vedras: the Cornerstone of Wellington's Strategy in the Peninsular War 1809 – 1812.* Barnsley: Frontline, 2015.

Hall, John, *A History of the Peninsular War Volume VIII: The Biographical Dictionary of British Officers Killed and Wounded, 1808–1814.* London: Greenhill, 1998.

Hamilton, Anthony, *Hamilton's Campaign with Moore and Wellington during the Peninsular War.* Staplehurst: Spellmount; 1998.

Hanley, William, 'Letter to William Napier dated 25 January 1856', *United Services Magazine* 1856, Part I, pp. 246–8.

Haythornthwaite, Philip, *Napoleon's Line Infantry*. London: Osprey, 1983.

Haythornthwaite, Philip, *The Napoleonic Source Book*. New York: Facts on File, 1990.

Hill, Rowland, *Lord Hill's Letters from the Peninsula*. Darlington: Napoleonic Archive, n.d.

Horward, Donald, *Napoleon and Iberia: the Twin Sieges of Ciudad Rodrigo and Almeida, 1810*. London: Greenhill, 1994.

Hulot, Jacques-Louis, *Souvenirs Militaires du baron Hulot*. Paris: Spectateur Militaire, 1886.

Jones, John, *Journal of the Sieges Carried on by the Army under the Duke of Wellington between the Years 1811 & 1814*. 3 vols. Cambridge: Ken Trotman, 1998.

Journal of the House of Commons, various dates.

Kincaid, John, *Random Shots from a Rifleman*. Philadelphia: E.L. Carey and A. Hart, 1835.

Kincaid, John, *Adventures in the Rifle Brigade in the Peninsula, France, and the Netherlands from 1809–1815*. Staplehurst: Spellmount, 1998.

Kinloch, Charles, *A Hellish Business: the Letters of Captain Charles Kinloch 52nd Light Infantry 1806 – 1816*. Edited by Gareth Glover. Godmanchester: Ken Trotman, 2007.

Koch, Jean (ed.), *Mémoires de Masséna rédigés d'après les documents qu'il a laissés et sur coux du dépôt de la guerre et du dépôt des fortifications par le général Koch: Avec un atlas*. 7 vols. Paris: Paulin et le Chevalier, 1850.

Leach, Jonathan, *Recollections and Reflections Relative to the Duties of Troops Composing the Advanced Corps of an Army*. London: T. and W. Boone, 1835.

Leach, Jonathan, *Rambles along the Styx. Being 'Colloquies between old soldiers who are supposed to have met in the Stygian Shades*. London: 1847.

Leach, Jonathan, *Rough Sketches of the Life of an Old Soldier*. Cambridge: Ken Trotman, 1986.

Leach, Jonathan, *Sketch of the Services of the Rifle Brigade*. London: T. & W. Boone, 1836.

Lemaitre, Louis, *Historique du 4ᵉ Régiment de Dragons*. Paris: Henri Charles-Lavauzelle, 1894.

Levine, Richard, *Historical Records of the Forty-third Regiment Monmouthshire Light Infantry 1739 to 1867*. Uckfield: Naval & Military, 2014.

Lievyns, A. et al, *Fastes de la Légion-d'honneur: biographie de tous les décorés*. 5 vols. Paris: 1847.

Lipscombe, Nick, *Wellington's Guns: the Untold Story of Wellington and His Artillery in the Peninsula and at Waterloo*. Oxford: Osprey, 2013.

Lista dos Officiaes do Exercito em 1811. Lisboa: Na Impressão Regia, 1811.

London Chronicle, various dates.

Martinien, Aristide, *Tableaux par Corps et par Batailles des Officiers Tués et Blessés pendant les Guerres de l'Empire (1805 – 1815)*. Paris: Éditions Militaires, n.d.

McGuigan, Ron, 'The British Army in Portugal and Spain: Its Order-of-Battle (June 1808 - April 1809)', *The Napoleon Series Online*. 2019.

McGuigan, Ron and Robert Burnham, *Wellington's Brigade Commanders*. Barnsley: Pen & Sword, 2017.

Mockler-Ferryman, Augustus, 'Three Brothers in the Light Division', *Forty-Third and 52nd Light Infantry Chronicle* Vol. III, pp. 173–83.

Money, John, *To the Right Honorable William Windham on a Partial Reorganization of the British Army*. London: T. Egerton, 1799.

Moorsom, William (ed.), *History of the 52nd Regiment: 1755 – 1816*. Tyne & Wear: Worley, 1996.

Muir, Rory, *Life of Wellington*, www.lifeofwellington.co.uk. 2019.

Muir, Rory, *Wellington*. 2 vols. New Haven: Yale University, 2013.

Muir, Rory et al, *Inside Wellington's Peninsular Army 1808 – 1814*. Barnsley: Pen & Sword, 2006.

Mulcaster, Edmund, *The Peninsular War Diary of Edmund Mulcaster RE, 1808 – 1810*. Edited by Mark Thompson. Privately published, 2015.

Mullen, A.L.T., *The Military General Service Roll: 1793 – 1814*. Dallington: Naval and Military Press, 1990.

Napier, Charles, *Life and Opinions of General Sir Charles James Napier*. 4 vols. London: John Murray 1857.

Napier, George, *Passages in the Early Military Life of General Sir George T. Napier*. London, John Murray, 1884.

Napier, William, *History of the War in the Peninsula and in the South of France*. 6 vols. New York: W.J. Widdleton, 1864.

Napier, William (ed.), *The Early Military Life of General Sir George T. Napier*. London: John Murray, 1886.

O Exército português em finais do Antigo Regime. Online.

Oman, Charles, *Wellington's Army, 1809 – 1814*. London: Greenhill, 1993.

Oman, Charles, *A History of the Peninsular War*. 7 vols. Oxford: AMS, 1980.

'Orders, Decorations, Medals and Militaria: Major General John Cox, late 95th Rifles', *Dix Noonan Webb Auctions*, 2019.

Pakenham Letters 1800 to 1815. Godmanchester: Ken Trotman, 2009.

Pelet, Jean, *The French Campaign in Portugal, 1810 – 1811*. Minneapolis: University of Minnesota, 1973.

Pérez de Herrasti, Andrés, *Relacion historica y circunstanciada de los sucesos del sitio de la plaza de Ciudad-Rodrigo en el año de 1810*. Madrid: 1814.

Rawkins, William, *The Army of Portugal 1793 – 1814*. Maidenhead: History Bookman, 2017.

Rifle Brigade Chronicle, various dates.

Ross, Hew D., *Memoir of Field-Marshal Sir Hew Dalrymple Ross, G.C.B., Royal Field Artillery with a New Introduction by Howie Muir*. Godmanchester: Ken Trotman, 2008.

Royal Military Calendar. 3 vols. London: Egerton, 1815.

Scarfe, Norman, *Letters from the Peninsula: the Freer family correspondence 1807–1814*. Leicester: University College, 1953.

Schaumann, August L., *On the Road with Wellington: the Diary of a War Commissary in the Peninsular Campaigns*. New York: Alfred A. Knopf, 1925.

Selin, Shannon, 'The Marriage of Napoleon and Marie Louise', *Imagining the Bounds of History*. Online. 2019.

Shaw, James, 'A Private Journal of General Craufurd's Out-Post Operations on the Coa and Agueda in 1810' in *A Manual of Outpost Duties*. London: Parker, Furnivall, and Parker, 1851.

Sheardown, William, *Records and Family Notices of Military and Naval Officers . . . Connected with Doncaster and Its Neighbourhood*. Doncaster: Gazette, 1873.

Simmons, George, *A British Rifleman: Journals and Correspondence during the Peninsular War and the Campaign of Wellington*. London: Greenhill, 1986.

Sinnott, John, *A Manual of Light Infantry and Other Duties*. London: Parker, Furnivall, and Parker, 1849.

Smith, Harry, *The Autobiography of Sir Harry Smith: 1787 – 1819*. London: Constable, 1999.

Sprünglin, Emmanuel, 'Souvenirs d'Emmanuel-Frédéric Sprünglin', *Revue hispanique*. Vol. 11, 1904, pp. 299–547.

Summerfield, Stephen, *Coote Manningham's Shorncliffe Lectures of 1803 and the Origins of the 95th Rifles*. Godmanchester: Ken Trotman, 2001.

'Sunrise and Sunset Calculator', *Time and Date Online*, 2019.

Surtees, William, *Twenty-five Years in the Rifle Brigade*. London: Greenhill, 1996.

Swanzy, Henry, *The Families of French of Belturbet and Nixon of Fermanagh*. Privately published, 1907.

Tancred, George, *Historical Records of Medals and Honorary Distinctions*. London: George Murray, 1891.

Tennant, Richard, 'Wellington's Mules', *Napoleon Series Online*, 2019.

Thompson, Mark, *Wellington's Engineers: Military Engineering in the Peninsular War 1808 – 1814*. Barnsley: Pen & Sword, 2015.

'Three Brothers in the Light Division', *The 43rd & 52nd Light Infantry Chronicle* Vol. 3. London: Eyre and Spottiswoode: 1894, pp. 173–83.

Tomkinson, William, *The Diary of a Cavalry Officer in the Peninsular War and Waterloo: 1809–1815*. London: Frederick Muller, 1971.

United Services Journal, various dates.

United Services Magazine, various dates.

'Used Port Wine Barrels', *Luso Barrel: Specialty Wooden Barrels from Portugal*. Online. 2019.

Vane, Charles (ed.), *Correspondence, Despatches, and Other Papers of Viscount Castlereagh, second Marquess of Londonderry*. London: William Shoberl, 1851, Vol. 7

Verner, Willoughby, *History & Campaigns of the Rifle Brigade: 1800 – 1813*. 2 vols. London: Buckland and Brown, 1995.

von Kortzfleisch, Gustav, *Geschichte des Herzoglich Braunschweigischen Infanterie–Regiments und seiner Stammtruppen 1809–1867*. Vol. I. Braunschweig: Albert Limbach, 1896.

Warre, William, *Letters from the Peninsula: 1808 – 1812*. Staplehurst: Spellmount, 1999.

Waterloo Medal Roll. Dallington: Naval and Military Press, 1992.

Wellington, Duke of, *The Dispatches of Field Marshal the Duke of Wellington, During his Various Campaigns in India Denmark, Portugal, Spain, the Low Countries, and France, from 1799 to 1818*. Edited by Lt.-Col. John Gurwood. London: John Murray; 1834–9. [Referenced as *'WD'*]

———, *Despatches, Correspondence, and Memoranda of Field Marshal Arthur, Duke of Wellington, K. G.* Edited by his son, the Duke of Wellington. 'in continuation of the former series', London: J. Murray 1857–80. [Referenced as *WND* or *Wellington's New Despatches*]

———, *Dispatches of Field Marshal the Duke of Wellington, During his Various Campaigns in India Denmark, Portugal, Spain, the Low Countries, and France*. Edited by Lt.-Col. John Gurwood. London: Parker, Furnivall and Parker, 1844–7. [Referenced as *'WD (enlarged ed.)'*]

———, *Supplementary Dispatches, Correspondence, and Memoranda of Field Marshal Arthur Duke of Wellington, K.G.* Edited by the 2nd Duke of Wellington. London: John Murray; 1860–71. [Referenced as *'WSD'*.]

Name Index

The following is an index of the individuals who appear in the narrative. There are two notable exceptions: Wellington and General Craufurd. Between them they are mentioned over 700 times and thus having their names appear in the index is unnecessary.

Place Index